"Alison Lewis exposes aspects of Stasi infiltration into cultural circles with revelatory nuance. Her genius lies not only in groundbreaking archival research but also in putting those discoveries to stunning and complex effect. Reads like a thriller. A dazzling achievement."
—Susan Signe Morrison, professor of English at Texas State University

"*A State of Secrecy* is a compelling work that anyone interested in the GDR must read. With a balance of patient, in-depth research, ruthlessly clear-sighted analysis, and psychological intuition, Alison Lewis lays bare the dynamics of secrecy in the GDR, but more important, the mechanisms that sustain totalitarianism in the modern world. An intellectual tour de force and a read as gripping as the extraordinary stories contained within it."
—Karen Leeder, professor of modern German literature at New College, Oxford

"Carefully fording the gaps inherent in secret police files, Alison Lewis tells fascinating Cold War stories about Stasi informers who were instrumental in influencing literary production and policing culture in East Germany. Extensively researched, *A State of Secrecy* is an important book that shines a light on the shadowy double lives of agents who were saddled with secrets. It exposes the extent of their collaboration and surveillance activities, as well as their habitus, motivation, and recompenses."
—Valentina Glajar, professor of German at Texas State University

"*A State of Secrecy* presents an inside look into the East German Ministry for State Security and its employment of writers as unofficial collaborators. Alison Lewis traces the intersecting biographies of five Stasi collaborators across the spectrum of informers deployed in the area of literature and culture. By presenting in-depth portraits of these personalities and the different kinds of surveillance they were involved in, *A State of Secrecy* paints a fabulous picture of a collective biography of Stasi informers within the cultural sphere, their motivations, and their justifications, clearly explicating how the Stasi used humane forms of surveillance to control and curtail cultural expression for nearly forty years."

—Carol Anne Costabile-Heming, professor of German at the University of North Texas

"Lewis takes a frank look at the Stasi apparatus and the literary writers who became its willing informants out of ideological persuasion, literary envy, or both, and who so often have been simultaneously demonized and glamorized. The study exposes the cruel banality of the socialist surveillance regime."

—Cathy Gelbin, professor of film and German studies at the University of Manchester

A STATE OF SECRECY

A STATE OF SECRECY

Stasi Informers and the
Culture of Surveillance

ALISON LEWIS

POTOMAC BOOKS   An imprint of the University of Nebraska Press

© 2021 by Alison Lewis

All rights reserved. Potomac Books is an imprint of the University of Nebraska Press.

Library of Congress Cataloging-in-Publication Data
Names: Lewis, Alison, 1958– author.
Title: A state of secrecy: Stasi informers and the culture of surveillance / Alison Lewis.
Description: Lincoln: Potomac Books, an imprint of the University of Nebraska Press, 2021. | Includes bibliographical references and index.
Identifiers: LCCN 2021008006
ISBN 9781640123793 (hardback)
ISBN 9781640124844 (epub)
ISBN 9781640124851 (pdf)
Subjects: LCSH: Germany (East). Ministerium für Staatssicherheit—History. | Intelligence service—Germany (East)—History. | Authors as spies—Germany (East) | Informers—Germany (East)
Classification: LCC JN3971.5.A56 I615 2021 | DDC 327.1243/100922—dc23
LC record available at
https://lccn.loc.gov/2021008006

Set in Lyon by Laura Buis.
Designed by N. Putens.

CONTENTS

List of Illustrations   vii

Acknowledgments   ix

Introduction   xiii

List of Abbreviations   xxxix

1. Recruiting Writers for the Stasi, 1949–1962   1
2. Handling Informants and Sustaining Motivation, 1962–1972   33
3. Policing the "Line on Writers" and Living the Secret Life, 1971–1976   65
4. The Secret War on Political-Ideological Diversion, 1976–1978   99
5. Simulation and Secret Policing the Underground, 1979–1982   133
6. The Culture Wars, 1983–1989   165

   Conclusion   201

   Notes   213

   Selected Bibliography   255

   Index   267

ILLUSTRATIONS

Following page 164

1. Paul Gratzik in the film *Vaterlandsverräter*, by Annekatrin Hendel, 2011
2. The cover of the IM-*Vorgang* file opened on Paul Gratzik in 1962
3. MfS position paper on IMV "Peter," Paul Gratzik, in 1972
4. Report on a meeting with IMV "Peter" in 1972
5. Farewell telegram from Paul Gratzik to his officer, Wenzel
6. A report by IM "Peter" on Heiner Müller
7. A portrait of Paul Wiens with his third wife, Irmtraud Morgner
8. A portrait of Paul Wiens smoking his pipe in 1977
9. One of Maja Wiens's reports on Rudolf Kunze
10 & 11. Meeting report with IMS "David Menzer," alias Sascha Anderson, 1977
12. Portrait of Sascha Anderson in 1990
13. One of the last meeting reports filed by Paul Wiens's case officer, 1982
14. The final meeting report filed by Paul Wiens's case officer, 1982
15. Maja Wiens at a reading on May 10, 1984
16. Maja Wiens chides her case officer
17. Maja Wiens castigates the regime for its failings

18. The OV file opened on Maja Wiens in 1988

19. Sascha Anderson in the documentary *Anderson*, by Annekatrin Hendel, 2014

20. Letter from Sascha Anderson to the MfS

21. Portrait of Sascha Anderson in 1986 after his emigration to the West

22. Helga M. Novak in 1971

ACKNOWLEDGMENTS

The impetus for this project goes back over thirty years to 1986, when I was an overseas student granted a short-term study visa to travel to the German Democratic Republic (GDR). I was working on my dissertation on the feminist writer Irmtraud Morgner and had been accepted by a study scheme designed to allow research stays for international doctoral students from Western countries. Coming from Australia, which had been among the first countries to officially recognize the GDR, I was accepted into the program and permitted to move freely around the libraries in East Berlin and German literature classes in the fall of 1986. Like many of the schemes the politburo introduced in the last decade of the regime, this one aimed to capitalize on the expanding interest among international scholars in East Germany. In reality it was a scheme to earn hard currency and was driven by economic necessity. I paid three hundred U.S. dollars for a four-week stay, during which I had access to the premises of the Humboldt University and to mentoring from experts in my field, such as the Germanist scholar Professor Eva Kaufmann.

During this time I became more aware of the grassroots cultural scene that was spreading below the threshold of official culture throughout the 1980s. Through contacts I was given I was alerted to a vibrant underground nurtured by the Protestant churches and increasing numbers of discontented citizens who were throwing caution to the wind and mobilizing in novel ways. At that time I also gained a brief glimpse of a potentially vast secret police apparatus that underpinned this new openness and semblance of tolerance toward the West. As I was later to learn, the rich seam of underground culture I found myself in the midst of was secretly being mined and undermined by the Stasi in ways that few were aware of at the time. Fortunately, none of my daily contacts proved to be Stasi informants, but one of their much-admired associates was: Sascha Anderson. In many of my conversations with East Germans the name of Sascha Anderson was invoked repeatedly as a beacon of hope and a less orthodox form of culture. For many Anderson was the spokesman of his generation, a literary voice whose star was in the ascendancy—that is, until the fall of the Berlin Wall when it was revealed that he was not a rising star but one in the process of imploding.

This project sets out to explore the secret surveillance society that enabled, controlled, and subverted cultural life in the GDR. It arose out of earlier studies that I conducted on the impact of Stasi informers on the art and politics of the Prenzlauer Berg underground. The focus of this book emerged out of a need to know more about the dynamic and conflicted nature of writers' collaboration with the Stasi and their complex motivations. My principal starting point was the records of the Ministry for State Security, which provided a revealing canvas upon which to trace the narratives of Stasi informers' lives.

The research for this book was facilitated by a 2012–14 Discovery Project grant (DP120101152) from the Australian Research Council. It was made possible by the generous support of the Federal Commissioner for the Records of the State Security Service of the Former German Democratic Republic (Der Bundesbeauftragte für die Unterlagen des Staatssicherheitsdienstes der ehemaligen Deutschen Demokratischen Republik) and its various employees, who always provided me with timely access to the reading room and to archives during my summer visits to Berlin over the life of the project.

Findings from early stages of the project were presented at annual conferences of the German Studies Association (U.S.), the German Studies Association of Australia, the Modern Languages Association, and the American Comparative Literature Association. Many of the approaches to reading the Stasi files adopted here are the collective result of a number of key international research collaborations with German Studies and Eastern European scholars in the United Kingdom and the United States.

In particular, I am indebted to a felicitous meeting of minds that occurred when I was invited to participate in a conference panel in 2013 in Denver. The panel, organized by Valentina Glajar and Corina L. Petrescu, addressed the affinities between life writing and secret-police files. I presented early findings from my research on the habitus of Stasi informers in this forum and published them with Camden House in *Secret Police Files from the Eastern Bloc: Between Surveillance and Life Writing* (with Valentina Glajar and Corina L. Petrescu) in 2016. I am sincerely grateful to my coeditors for their comments on my chapter and to Jim Walker for his meticulous editing and stewardship of the project. A further collaboration with Glajar and Petrescu cemented some of the ideas in this book, particularly in relation to the informer Paul Gratzik. Some of the findings on him were published in a special issue of *Monatshefte* in 2018, and I owe thanks to Hans Adler for his work on that project. I wish to extend a special thanks to Valentina Glajar for her unwavering belief in the importance of this research, her infectious passion, her friendship, and her generosity over the duration of these collaborations.

I am also indebted to Sara Jones for initiating contact with me over ten years ago and kickstarting what has become an enduring and rewarding exchange. The interest we both share in broad questions of memory, complicity, and collaboration with the Stasi has helped in various ways to shape the direction of this book. To Stephen Parker and Cathy Gelbin I also owe a special debt for being willing to share with me their passion for biography and the GDR, and for commenting extensively on various phases of this research in the framework of a Melbourne-Manchester collaborative grant scheme. I would also like to thank Karen Leeder for her generous support of this project and for her comments on early chapters.

The writing of this book was assisted in its latter stages by two fellowships at the Morphomata Center for Advanced Studies at the University of Cologne in 2018 and 2020. I am particularly grateful to Günter Blamberger, one of the center's directors, for his generous mentorship more broadly and for his encouragement to continue to explore more fully the notion of secret-police files as life writing. I would like to thank the many staff and fellows at Morphomata for their interest in my project on the Stasi and biography, and for helping me maintain momentum when I was adding the finishing touches to the manuscript.

I would like to acknowledge the supportive environment in the School of Languages and Linguistics at the University of Melbourne. The Faculty of Arts has provided me with periods of Special Study Leave to pursue archival research in Germany and to write up the findings, as well as with liberal travel funds to attend international conferences. Without these schemes, which have played a pivotal role in enabling me to network regularly with scholars abroad in this exciting new field of study, this book would not have been possible.

Special thanks go to Cynthia Troup for her scrupulous copyediting of the prefinal manuscript and her help with formatting and referencing. I would like to thank the anonymous reader and Susan S. Morrison for giving up their time to engage with the manuscript in detail and for their insightful comments. Above all, I am deeply grateful to Tom Swanson for his spark of interest in *Cold War Spy Stories from Eastern Europe* (with Valentina Glajar and Corina L. Petrescu, 2019) and in this project. It has been a pleasure to work with him and his dedicated team.

I wish to express my gratitude to John Hajek and Janet Fletcher for moral support and good company throughout the researching and writing process. I owe Tom Morton a special vote of thanks over the years for lending his ear to my research and for his unerring knack for coming up with good book titles. Last but not least, I wish to thank my partner, Herbert Meier, for his remarkable patience and forbearance, and for giving me the space to forage through the archives and mine the seams of history to find those hidden nuggets of research gold.

INTRODUCTION

The Ministry for State Security and Informers

During the Cold War much of the warfare was invisible, waged along frontlines that no one could see or hear. Its most powerful weapon was secrets, and to harvest them, foreign and domestic security agencies on both sides relied heavily on humans. Some security agencies, like the East German Ministry for State Security (Ministerium für Staatssicherheit, more commonly known as the MfS or the Stasi) relied to a colossal degree on what is called "human intelligence collection."[1] The Stasi not only gathered enormous quantities of secrets about its own citizens, it also required an inordinate amount of human labor to do so. Cultural life in the German Democratic Republic (GDR) was teeming with secrets that the communist regime was desperate to know, and the regime gave its security forces carte blanche to uncover them.

The Stasi is often described as a "state within a state,"[2] although a more accurate description is probably "society within a society," or "secret surveillance society." With a large degree of latitude, and with tentacles reaching into all corners of social life, the Stasi, or "octopus," as it has fittingly been called, grew monster-like under the unchecked influence of its third minister, Erich Mielke.[3] After a less than illustrious start in 1950, the MfS began its spectacular ascent under Mielke once he took over the reins in 1957.[4] In keeping with East Germany's position as a "client regime" of the Soviet Union, the MfS was modeled along the lines of the first Soviet secret police, called the Cheka.[5] It was soon to become a mammoth that far exceeded Adolf Hitler's Gestapo in size and scale.[6]

At the heart of the ministry's empire was a "dizzying labyrinth of human controls."[7] Its number of officers, or "official employees" (*Hauptamtliche Mitarbeiter*) was estimated in 1989 to be around 90,000.[8] In addition, the Stasi dedicated an entire stratum of its workforce to "informants" or "informers," officially called "unofficial collaborators" (*Inoffizielle Mitarbeiter*, or IM). It was a workforce unmatched in history.[9] When the regime collapsed, there were an estimated 189,000 informants registered in the Stasi's archives, which amounted to one informer for every 120 citizens.[10]

Informants were a central piece in the Stasi armory. Ernst Wollweber, the second Minister for State Security, famously called his organization's informants its "respiratory organs."[11] If the Socialist Unity Party (SED) provided the political compass of the body politic, the Stasi, as its faithful servant, was the party's "shield and sword."[12] Informers in turn allowed the regime to breathe more easily. Above all, informers enabled control to permeate society, transporting power to its remotest corners and deepest recesses. Like lungs, which provide fuel for metabolism, informers fueled the machinery of the ministry. Informers effectively helped East Germany become a self-policing surveillance society.[13]

Informants were a low-tech and low-cost form of what David Lyon calls "surveillance power," and a flexible, mobile, and cheap form of modern intelligence labor.[14] They were the intelligence equivalent of today's casualized, outsourced workforce. In Jeremy Bentham's model of the panopticon, which Michel Foucault adopts to describe the diffusion of power in modern societies, surveillance of the many is enacted by the few.[15] The central source of power (in Bentham's model, the prison watchtower with its guards) does not need to be visible, because the subject in the panopticon self-regulates. He assumes that he is being watched, even though he might not be. As Foucault writes of the panoptical subject: "He is seen, but he does not see; he is the object of information, never a subject of communication."[16] As Mike Dennis argues, the MfS "created a system of panopticism par excellence."[17] The communist panopticon was in this sense true to type and possessed all the hallmarks of the classical panopticon and modern disciplinary methods, including the creation of ways of "normalizing judgment" and deviant behaviors.[18] Like Foucault's model, the communist panopticon did not just reveal truth, it also created the truth about the object of surveillance.[19] To do so, it deployed what I call "para-panoptical" means. That is, it relied on other mechanisms to support its systems of surveillance of citizens. The GDR counted heavily on people's fear of being watched to instill compliance, but to make absolutely sure, it mobilized informers as extra human resources.

Informants had several advantages over high-tech paraphernalia such as hidden cameras, telephone wiretaps, and mail intercepts.[20] Not only could they evaluate information in ways that machines at the time could not, they were also able to get close to sources.[21] The Stasi was by no means the only Cold War intelligence agency to realize that humans possess infinite means of camouflage. Yet it was possibly the agency that invested most resources into honing the art of human intelligence collection in the pre-digital era. Humans, as the Stasi discovered, could be deployed in settings where suspects might do most damage, such as informal networks of artists and writers that were seeding grounds for fomenting dissent. Informants were moveable and itinerant, and did not necessarily need to conceal their point of observation. They could see and hear things openly, as long as no one suspected they were spying. They needed little equipment apart from their perception, memory, a pen and paper, and, at most, a small dictation machine to record reports. Above all, an informant needed good acting skills and a plausible cover story (*Legende*).

Especially from 1979 onward, ministerial guidelines in the MfS document the ever-increasing importance of using informers directly for operational or frontline work. A common refrain in these guidelines is the Stasi's growing concern that its number of informers was insufficient, particularly in the era of détente (1967–79).[22] In the mid-1950s, the Stasi had a mere 20,000 to 30,000 informers.[23] By 1968 the number recruited had increased dramatically, to around 100,000. It peaked at 180,000 by 1975, after which it remained constant until 1989.[24] Where previously the Stasi had been "simply" an instrument of repression, from the mid-1950s it became a multi-pronged political apparatus of control and surveillance.[25] Over the ensuing decades it devised increasingly sophisticated ways to nip dissent in the bud before it could evolve into open unrest or rebellion. The deployment of informers was one facet of this larger strategy, and pivotal to the policing of key areas of culture—literature in particular.

Surveillance of Writers Using Informants

From its inception to its dissolution, the Ministry for State Security recruited an alarmingly high proportion of writers as informants. It recruited sources from deep inside official circles, such as the consecrated spheres of the German Writers' Guild (Deutscher Schriftstellerverband), as well as from the fringes of society. The Stasi touched the life of virtually every writer in the country. Writers, whether of poetry, novels, drama, essays, radio, television, or film scripts, belonged to the intelligentsia. Although writers were persecuted in the Soviet Union by Stalin in his cultural revolution of the 1930s, postwar-era Eastern European regimes desperately relied on them to shape Soviet-style revolutions.[26] Writers were members of the political elite; hence, they were needed to support the socialist cause. As Stephen Brockmann argues, they were an intrinsic part of the "large-scale attempt to use culture to shape the German future."[27] In other words, in Brockmann's view, "every work of literature was also a political speech act" in the new GDR.[28] In this way literature and writers "exerted their own kind of power over politicians."[29]

The East German regime realized that, because writers wielded so much public authority, they had to be politically organized and controlled. Dennis has usefully argued that the regime feared the influence of writers, considering them Trojan horses of the counterrevolution.[30] Thus, literature, like theater, film, and television, was designated one of the key areas that needed security policing. The Stasi's penetration into all branches of cultural production remains astonishing, and scarcely anyone involved in literature and theater escaped its watchful eye, although not everyone had a Stasi file and not everyone collaborated.

The Stasi feared all types of cultural exchange with the West, often politicizing Western connections as a form of pernicious "contact politics" used by the capitalist enemy to destabilize the regime. Despite literature's potential for building bridges between the two Germanies, in the GDR writers were increasingly singled out as a particularly weak link in national security that merited special attention and classification as a designated "security area" (*Sicherungsbereich*).[31] The Stasi was quick to realize that the best sources of information about intellectuals, artists, and writers were other intellectuals, artists, and writers. This was effectively analog surveillance of culture of a different kind, that is, surveillance of like by like, whereby citizens were watched by like-minded citizens.

Surveillance of culture was the task of two sub-departments in the largest of the ministry's main departments, Hauptabteilung (HA) XX, responsible for "state apparatuses, church, culture, sport, underground." From 1969 to 1980 most monitoring was conducted by HA XX/7, the Department for Culture and Mass Communications; from 1981 onward HA XX/9, the Department for Political Underground Activity, took over this responsibility. Both HA XX/7 and HA XX/9 oversaw subdivisions in all fourteen districts (*Bezirke*) of the GDR.[32] Most of the files on writers were held with HA XX, which ran around 150 surveillance operations on writers. The mildest form of surveillance was a security check, called an "operational person check" (*Operative Personenkontrolle*, OPK), and the most severe form was an "operational case" (*Operativer Vorgang*, OV). The MfS required informants for both these kinds of security operations. In 1975 there were approximately 379 IMs working for HA XX.[33] Of East Germany's cultural "organs" (*Organe*), the German Writers' Guild was, apart from the censors and the main publishers, possibly the most important from the Stasi's perspective.[34] From its president to its lowest ranks, the Writers' Guild was well covered by the Stasi.[35] In 1989, among the 123 members of the guild, 49 had been or still were IMs, and among 19 members of the executive committee, 12 were former or current informants.[36]

In the spheres of culture, there were six different categories of informers.[37] For policing the literary world the Stasi drew mainly on the standard category of informer, the IMS, or what John C. Schmeidel calls the "workhorse" category of informer.[38] An IMS was defined as an "unofficial collaborator for the political-operative penetration and securing of an area of responsibility." More important for this study is the *Inoffizieller Mitarbeiter der Abwehr mit Feindverbindung bzw. zur unmittelbaren Bearbeitung im Verdacht der*

Feindtätigkeit stehender Personen (IMB), a term applied to all "unofficial collaborators who were directly assigned to observe individuals suspected of enemy activity." These were regarded as the "aristocrats" among informers.[39]

According to some estimates, a total of 1,500 informants were recruited in the cultural sphere.[40] Although there is no one type of informer, as Barbara Miller has discovered, a sizable number of the regime's critical writers and dissidents, including many of those forced into exile in the West, were registered at some point in their lives as Stasi informers.[41] In most instances they collaborated only briefly—sometimes scarcely at all—before becoming the targets of surveillance themselves. Writers belonging to this category include Christa Wolf, Franz Fühmann, Brigitte Reimann, Ulrich Plenzdorf, Erwin Strittmatter, Fred Wander, Benito Wogatzki, and Bruno Apitz, as well as Helga M. Novak, who is discussed in this book.[42] In the documentary film *Vaterlandsverräter* (Traitor to the fatherland, 2011), Gabriele Dietze, editor of the leftist West German publishing house Rotbuch, confesses that virtually all of her East German authors were Stasi informers, with two exceptions: Kurt Bartsch and Adolf Endler.[43] Among her authors were Sascha Anderson and Paul Gratzik, both of whom are discussed in this book.

Informants and Motivations

In the first few years after German reunification, Stasi informers were demonized and typecast as traitors and denunciators.[44] They served as scapegoats for the moral outrage felt by Germans from both the former East and former West when they discovered the extent of the Stasi's reach.[45] With the opening of the Stasi archives under the watch of a federal commissioner (*Bundesbeauftragter*) in 1992, Germany embarked on a form of "working through the past" (*Vergangenheitsbewältigung*) that has since been adopted in many other Eastern European countries. According to Lavinia Stan, opening security police files can have the effect of "democratizing truth-seeking," because it empowers those directly affected by repression without the use of tribunals or courts.[46] Despite the nuances of the legislation opening the archives,[47] a rather simplistic Stasi myth has persisted in public perceptions that often leaves little room for the complexities of how the Stasi registered victims and perpetrators.[48] The files themselves appear to offer a murky picture of the victim-perpetrator distinction, because informers were often first placed under surveillance before being registered as IMs. Even trickier for historians has been the question of how to classify those who were first informers before becoming victims.

As Ilko-Sascha Kowalczuk has argued, studies of informants that rely on the Stasi's formal categories are of little use without taking into account the nature of the missions that informers were tasked with as well as the duration of informers' association with the Stasi.[49] Historians also need to probe informers' motivations in the wider context of the types of behaviors that were possible under a dictatorship. There were five broad categories of reasons for informing: political and ideological motives; coercion, pressure or blackmail; personal, material, or financial advantage; emotional needs (for acknowledgment and recognition); and what Dennis calls "a desire to influence official policy."[50] Although the Stasi believed that around 60 percent of its informants were prompted by "recognition of society's need" for security measures, many informants had secondary motives that superseded "political-ideological conviction."[51] Of the five broad sets of reasons for informing, Jens Gieseke has argued that nonideological motives and "openly pragmatic and utilitarian considerations" also played a role.[52] In addition, blackmail was less effective than the Stasi would have liked.[53]

Joachim Walther has identified further motivations for informers in literary circles: the thrill of secrecy, the pleasure of role-playing, subterfuge, and the will for power.[54] Writers, he argues, could easily fall prey to the temptation to cross the line between reality and fiction and to live out their fantasies in real life.[55] The cases of writers presented in this study underscore the sobering fact that individuals' intellectual justifications for collaborating could be alarmingly convoluted. These writers certainly became masters at fabricating a complex "lifelong lie" (*Lebenslüge*) for themselves. They construed elaborate myths from all manner of intellectual material, from postmodern ideas of power to notions of the modern subject as free of a fixed or stable identity.

In addition to these primary motivations, other factors fostered informers' careers with the Stasi. These included individuals benefiting from incentives ("carrots") or, at the other end of the spectrum, being exposed to punitive measures ("sticks") such as coercion, blackmail, or even open threats. Informers' original motivations could be enhanced or stifled depending on the degree of hard and soft power that the Stasi applied to them. Some individuals required little prompting to offer up their services. Others were pushed constantly and with ever increasing force to carry out their secret police tasks. If the incentives were adequate and appropriate to an individual's needs, aspirations, and sense of self, informers could easily become entangled in powerful forms of dependency on the Stasi and the state; these in turn ensured that she or he continued to work for the Stasi. Entanglements between humans and institutions consist of a system of dependencies, or even codependencies. The aforementioned "carrots" created and reproduced entanglements of different kinds and magnitude, including both enabling and constraining forms of dependence.[56] As a result, once a degree of habituation had occurred, informers often struggled with the material, emotional, or social forms of their dependency on the Stasi. It took courage for informers to end their association with the Stasi, and they needed a good deal of strength to deal with the dependencies that had been fostered, especially the enabling ones.

Any neat typologies of motives fail, however, to take into account the fact that informers' dependencies and motivations were not static. Such typologies do not capture ways in which motivations became anchored in informers' lives. Nor do they factor in questions of selfhood and identity, and how these were influenced by gender, generation, class, ethnicity, and power—all of which determined how informers' motivations translated into their experiences. The GDR self was the result of a dynamic process comprising forms of self-fashioning in dialogue with pre-given, prescriptive communist norms.[57] Informers were probably no different from ordinary citizens in the GDR. To use a term coined by Sheila Fitzpatrick with reference to Soviet citizens, Stasi informants invented "usable selves" for themselves by cobbling together makeshift identities simply in order to survive. As Fitzpatrick argues, Soviet citizens almost always led double lives, and each had a "non- or anti-Soviet self that [was] being denied."[58] She calls these doubles "shadowy doppelgänger" selves.[59] It is also possible to think of informers as forging shadowy doppelgänger selves—say, as ideal loyal or patriotic selves, or even negative and shameful alter egos. In the Ministry for State Security these shadowy identities were far more varied and individual than Fitzpatrick suggests Soviet selves were. We could even think of these secret police selves as panoptic identities encompassing discrete secret and parallel personas that individuals crafted for themselves through their work in espionage.

Like all citizens, the informers who appear in this book led public and private lives. In their public lives they were students, aspiring writers, or already accredited or unionized writers. Some regarded themselves less as poets than as professionals, and thus as cultural functionaries performing political and administrative roles in the service of the SED, either as members of the Freie Deutsche Jugend (FDJ), the official East German youth organization, or as executives of the German Writers' Guild. Other informers associated with the production of literature worked professionally as editors, publishers, or reviewers. Of course, in addition to these public identities, informers identified as fathers and mothers, daughters and sons, husbands, wives, and lovers. Even as many aspects of citizens' lives in the GDR were concealed from public view (such as the habits of watching Western television or receiving parcels from relatives in the West), informers arguably lived a larger portion of their lives in secret than did their compatriots. Thus they faced greater challenges than most in keeping public and private selves in step with each other.

Officially, the socialist public sphere permitted dialogue and debate. As Joshua Feinstein argues, in reality, the GDR "offered no general communicative space for freely exchanging autonomous opinions."[60] Its public sphere was subject to tight central controls and to manipulation. Toward the end of the regime, public and private lives appeared to drift further apart, as citizens withdrew into what David Bathrick calls "unofficial public enclaves,"[61] or what Steven Pfaff terms "pockets of private life,"[62] where they were freer than usual to voice critical opinions and deviate from expected norms. From the moment informers swore themselves to secrecy and signed an oath to work undercover they committed to sustaining a secret self. Like keeping other secrets, this was the price for doing the work demanded by the ministry, and for some it even became a dubious badge of honor.

Secrecy and the Stasi

The question of secrecy at all levels was of utmost importance to the operations of the MfS. Indeed, the ministry's role in guarding state, economic, and military secrets was written into its statutes.[63] The importance of secrecy was impressed on informers during the recruitment process and reiterated at every meeting, becoming a mantra repeatedly invoked over the course of an informer's association with the Stasi. Secrecy was a central pillar of the training program for informants, and from 1979 it was explicitly mentioned in the guidelines for working with undercover agents.[64] Stasi files were marked confidential and access was restricted to employees with the appropriate clearance; even the ministerial guidelines for "case officers" (*Führungsoffiziere*) responsible for managing, handling, or running informants were top secret.[65] Little is known about how Stasi informers managed to lead the double lives demanded of them—that is, how they dealt with the imposition of secrecy, navigated the constant burden of being saddled with secrets, or coped emotionally, psychologically, and pragmatically. Scant information is available regarding how they negotiated split or multiple identities and balanced their contradictory public and private identities. Did they perceive their allegiance to the Stasi as the cause of a rift in their lives, or did they consider it an enhancement or even an extension of their existing public or private selves? Did some even regard their association with the Stasi as a means of fashioning a new, better self that would attract more esteem? To what extent did informants' self-fashioning lead to a life of deception? Were there ways of managing the presence of shadowy doppelgänger selves and panoptic identities such that they did not disrupt daily life?

The exercise of power in the GDR was late-totalitarian, that is, authoritarian with "limited pluralism."[66] Nevertheless, individuals under such a dictatorship still exercise agency, even if the agency is curtailed or limited by state power. Moreover, they still act in accordance with processes of socialization and learned patterns of behavior that are influenced by myriad external factors. Stasi informers undoubtedly possessed a particular habitus[67]—defined as a "system of durable and transposable dispositions which . . . functions . . . as a matrix of perceptions, appreciations, and actions."⁶⁸ The Stasi was a crucial component in this matrix governing an informer's behavior at any one time. It is unclear, however, to what extent the Stasi was able to structure informers' lives. Further, the Stasi was hardly the only force in an informer's matrix of perceptions, given that other, more durable dispositions, such as class background, artistic ambitions, social milieu, and peer-group pressure, determined his or her behavior. Generational and gender factors also played a role in influencing how susceptible an individual was to antifascist ideologies or socialist promises of a better future. The demands of the Stasi and secrecy could also clash with other desires or aspirations. When involvement with the Stasi placed a person on a collision course with his or her chosen milieu or circle of friends without offering any benefits or trade-offs, the power of the Stasi was severely diminished.

In *The Origins of Totalitarianism* Hannah Arendt argues that "political secrecy hardly ever ends in anything nobler than the vulgar duplicity of a spy."⁶⁹ Secretive behavior such as denunciation is an intrinsic part of totalitarian culture, although it is by no means confined to undemocratic regimes. In totalitarian and authoritarian regimes citizens can be motivated to denounce others for various reasons, and because denunciation is encouraged, all forms of it, whether interested or disinterested, can be an aid to totalitarian power.⁷⁰ In East Germany the willingness on the part of ordinary citizens to denounce others to the secret police was, as research by Gieseke shows, rather limited.⁷¹ Despite the prevalence of denunciation in Soviet culture in the 1930s (as under National Socialist rule) little of this rampant culture of spontaneous denunciation was passed on to East Germany.⁷² Nonetheless, as Christian Booß and Helmut Müller-Enbergs point out, in the GDR there was an unusually high "latent preparedness" to denounce others in more structured ways.⁷³ In the 1950s in particular, many arrests occurred because of tip-offs from the population, and recent research into East Germany's police force, the German People's Police (Deutsche Volkspolizei), suggests that a culture flourished in which ordinary citizens voluntarily reported to the police.⁷⁴ Yet overall in the GDR denunciation was far less often the result of individual initiative, because society was so thoroughly organized and institutionalized.⁷⁵

Along with its organs, such as the MfS, the ruling party developed more systematic, formal means of procuring information from citizens than the National Socialists did, including grooming informers.[76] The ministry's response to the party's fragile claim to power and doubts about its legitimate claims to rule focused on cultivating a secret but quasi-official workforce of citizens dedicated to vigilance.[77] The use of the term *Mitarbeiter*, meaning both employee and collaborator (rather than denunciator or spy), indicates the changed nature of the activity. Viewing the network of informants as a type of workforce was one part of the strategy of extending the party's eyes and ears into all corners of the regime. Not all IMs were, however, involved in denunciation or prepared to denounce. Also, the traditional concept of denunciation, which implies free will or spontaneous reporting, does not adequately capture the reality of the Stasi's network of IMs.[78] A more useful concept is the "denunciation complex" suggested by Booß and Müller-Enbergs. This concept acknowledges that the passing on of discrete information to the authorities was indeed a hallmark of the indiscrete society that East Germany became and possibly also a symptom of that society's "authoritarian character."[79]

A State of Secrecy explores the underpinnings of this indiscrete society: undue surveillance, the violation of citizens' right to privacy, the harvesting of secrets, and the power of secrecy—both as an idea and as a way of life. When coupled with an ideological superstructure, secrets can be extraordinarily compelling. Sociologist Georg Simmel argues that, regardless of their content, secrets acquire their special value because others are excluded from their possession.[80] What is denied to others must be worth possessing. Yet the attractions of secrecy are closely related to "the possibility and temptation of betrayal."[81] The power of a secret culminates in the moment when it is revealed, a moment that is both desired and dreaded. The external danger of the secret being discovered is always accompanied by an internalized sense of the danger of giving oneself away or inadvertently confessing, which beckons like "an abyss."[82]

Covert Operations and the Secret Surveillance Society

Secrets, Simmel argues, bind those initiated into them in inexplicable ways. Secrets create reciprocal knowledge within a secret society and the confidence that the society's members are protected. Yet the secrets kept by secret societies are susceptible to being revealed, and so the protection they offer is never absolute.[83] The moral value that societies attribute to the imposition of secrecy in the organization of secret societies depends on whether they consider a secret society a progressive or regressive social force. If secrecy is the weapon of the subaltern or the persecuted (as it was with the early Christians), it can easily be sold as a noble ideal.[84] When it is used to hold its members hostage or is overly despotic, secrecy can be deeply destructive.[85] For this reason, Simmel compares many secret societies to military organizations and religious communities, which impose rigid rules on their members.[86]

Secrecy for the benefit of national security is a well-accepted principle of all intelligence organizations. Like the East German military and police force, the MfS mandated secrecy for a complex set of interlocked reasons. What Andreas Glaeser writes about the German People's Police applies equally to the MfS. He argues that all communication was subject to secrecy, reinforcing the inextricable "connection between providing security for the country, the need to maintain strict internal security and thus hierarchical levels of secrecy, and military discipline."[87] But when a state's security apparatus is allowed to grow rampantly without the oversight of parliaments and courts and when its access to private data is unfettered and carried out in the service of one-party rule, the result is the unchecked proliferation of illicit secrecy—and often the unchecked proliferation of secrecy for secrecy's sake.[88]

In foreign policy, clandestine activities, or covert operations, are widely regarded as an "indispensable instrument."[89] In domestic intelligence, however, covert operations are far less easy to defend. The morality of applying covert action to one's own citizenry is dubious, to say the least, although moral concerns are generally overridden by the counterintelligence argument that the domestic population is under threat from internal enemies. On both sides of the Cold War nation states conducted covert operations against their own citizens, targeting suspected communists in the West and suspected anticommunists in the East.[90] Writers and intellectuals who were presumed to have sympathies with the enemy were subject to invasive surveillance that was predicated on starkly nonreciprocal relations of concealment. The state in each case demanded to know everything about its particular targets while in return revealing very little about its own covert modus operandi. From the 1920s to the 1950s, for instance, Australian security agencies targeted wide sections of the Australian community, from Russian émigrés to writers' leagues viewed as fronts for the communist cause.[91]

In the GDR surveillance of the population was rampant and "comprehensive" (*flächendeckend*). Communist panopticism, by which the party attempted to control and know all aspects of society, demanded that individuals not be apprised of the workings of its organs of surveillance. This is what Simmel would call a deeply aggressive and destructive kind of secrecy.[92] It produces a one-sided indiscrete society, in which individuals' rights to privacy are eroded by power, whereas the state's secrets are protected at all costs. Positive forms of secret societies, with their particular codes of sharing and togetherness, are typified by a high degree of "reciprocal confidence," argues Simmel.[93] Such confidence and trust was sorely lacking in East German society.[94]

Both Stasi officers and their informers belonged to an elevated stratum of society that in many respects resembled a secret society. The Stasi regarded itself as the extended arm of the party that was spearheading the revolution, and hence it saw itself as the "avant-garde of the avant-garde."[95] Full-time officers of the ministry prided themselves on being members of an elite that enjoyed the party's trust.[96] Even for informers, working for the ministry—with its strict code of silence, its seclusion from the outside world, and its privileges—was like being a member of a secret order or society.[97] Arendt once wrote that for T. E. Lawrence, spying for the imperial British secret police entailed "a mysterious alliance with forces necessarily bigger than himself."[98] Working for the Ministry for State Security offered something similar. The MfS bestowed on its officers and informants a sense of ineffable belonging. As in many historical secret societies, this sense of belonging was based on the beliefs shared by those initiated into an exclusive secret knowledge.[99]

The Stasi fostered a sense of exclusivity along with a degree of moral certainty that its members were on the right side of power and history. As the following chapters demonstrate, the arcane world of secret espionage business and insider knowledge certainly provided informants with an additional justification for doing secret service work.[100] The secret belief that espionage was necessary, even on the invisible front of domestic espionage, was shared by officers and informers. Some also experienced a common feeling of evangelism and acknowledgment that the historical circumstances of the Cold War had created exceptional conditions.

Walther compares the attractions of informing for the Stasi to those of secrecy for early Christians who found themselves surrounded by enemies.[101] Lutz Niethammer writes of officers and informants for the Stasi satisfying their need for "adventure in an administered world" and for truths that could not be articulated in public, only "in an asceticist order of those who [took] on the burden of secrecy, subjugation, and self-instrumentalization."[102] In addition to possessing a common secret, informers shared similar experiences with occult-like practices or rituals of espionage, which bound them together in a "community of destiny" (*Schicksalsgemeinschaft*). This practical experience—generated by secret trysts in safe houses (*konspirative Wohnungen*), special code names (*Decknamen*), and highly conspiratorial exchanges of classified information—produced a knowledge about power that was seductive. Moreover, in addition to arcane espionage knowledge, informants also acquired commonplace, often banal everyday information about suspects' habits and movements. It's possible that the ordinariness of the tasks that informers were asked to perform made the work more palatable, as Arendt recognized in her famous insight that the crimes of Nazism were not the result of monsters masquerading as men or of "demonic profundity," but the work of ordinary men and the sheer "banality of evil."[103]

Some of the arcane secret knowledge that informers accumulated was the sort of informal information about others often classified and dismissed as gossip. In many respects the Stasi was a terrible gossip, and informers were among the worst kinds of gossips, being given virtually unlimited license to indulge their urges to speculate about everything from others' sex lives to their medications. As Fiona Capp writes of Australian Security Intelligence Organisation files compiled on writers and members of the Australian Communist Party during the 1940s and 1950s, "gossip, hearsay and factual errors are integral to the kind of story" that a secret police file tells.[104] Of course, Stasi officers would strenuously deny that they were eager to collect material as trivial as malicious gossip. The Stasi insisted that it needed facts and evidence—at least enough hard evidence that could stand up in a socialist court.[105] However, the climate of distrust and the sorts of communicative settings created by the Stasi in its interactions with its informants encouraged the exchange of gossip. If gossip is defined as "informal evaluative talk," including such talk in formal contexts, then much of the discourse produced between handling officers and their informants was gossip.[106] Although the Stasi did not recruit from bars and restaurants because this kind of informal talk could be exaggerated, it did collect inordinate amounts of information that by most standards would be classified as gossip or hearsay.[107] This intelligence was harvested on the principle that everything, even idle speculation, might one day be useful.

The secret knowledge that informers accrued and could bank for themselves laid the foundations for the formation of secret reserves of economic, political, social, cultural, and symbolic capital. This curious concoction was different for each informer. For instance, secret knowledge provided economic capital in the extra income that informers earned. This income was not large, but for some it represented an incentive. The same knowledge was connected to political capital through the informer's association with an arm or instrument of the party. This political capital could in turn be converted into the "capital of social connections"[108] and cultural capital via the networks of contacts, acquaintances, and friends in the arts that informers cultivated—often on instructions from the Stasi. This secret social and cultural capital was also a type of symbolic capital. Its benefits to its owners, such as prestige and esteem, were nonmaterial.[109] But symbolic capital could sometimes be accumulated and even exchanged for material capital or financial rewards.[110] In some contexts, it could even serve as a type of credit advance or faith placed in society with the long-term expectations of rewards. In the case of informers recruited from the arts, the opportunity to accrue various forms of capital proved to be a persuasive incentive.

The Stasi did not openly flaunt itself as a secret order. It enlisted informers through a patriotic call to duty, which, in essence, could be extended to anyone. Members were by no means equal in their rights and duties, and like many secret societies, the Stasi was organized in a hierarchical manner.[111] Informers were only let into a fraction of the society's secrets—and only as needed. "Under no circumstances," one ministerial guideline stipulated, was an informant "to know and experience more than was necessary for the operation."[112] Many informers mistakenly believed that the Stasi would let them into its secrets. But although the Stasi demanded that its informers make full disclosures, it never reciprocated the favor.

The Stasi Files and Memory

Since the opening of the Stasi archives in 1992, former informers have been extremely reluctant to publicly share their accounts of their experience. In view of the scarcity of informer-witness testimony, historians of the GDR are heavily reliant on source material from the archives, especially the Stasi files. In cases where the informants are deceased or are unwilling to talk about the past, the files are all historians have. No one today seriously doubts the value of the files for truth and justice, given that they offer an unprecedented resource of significant size that has, on the whole, been well preserved.

For historians the Stasi archives are invaluable for their documentation of the workings of the ministry and for clarifying individuals' experience of repression and collusion. Of course, the archive contains instances of fabricated files and falsehoods in files, and there have been cases in which the files have been unable to prove with absolute certainty whether an individual collaborated or not. Like all sources, files should not be read in isolation and need to be augmented with other resources.[113] This acknowledged, the files constitute a detailed source of high quality that can offer unprecedented insights into the secret world of informers' lives.[114] Developing a narrative on the basis of careful interpretation can fashion these archival traces into a life story or a "file story."[115] Before the Stasi archives were opened this secret world was rather shadowy and faceless. It existed only as figments of people's imaginations and featured in their worst nightmares. And yet this secret world had real social, economic, and psychological effects for those who entered its gates, effects that sometimes endured for a lifetime. Some of those effects were partially enabling, taking the form of incentives and entitlements, whereas others were punitive, vengeful, or simply spiteful.

Secret police files reveal much about lives of GDR citizens, but the stories they tell are written from a position of power and a particularly insidious institutional perspective.[116] The Stasi was the guardian of party ideology, and its records reproduce this ideology at all levels. Despite this, the files are able to prize open a window onto the lives and minds of informers as well as victims that we would not otherwise have. With their painful attention to details such as dates, places, addresses, and names, the files are rich sources of motivations, habitus, actions, and behaviors. They make it possible to track the changing motivations of informers and the personal impact of coercion on informants' dispositions. More generally, the files can provide glimpses, sometimes extraordinarily honest ones, of what it felt like to work undercover as an informant and how informants juggled their double lives. They afford insights—for instance, into how informers rationalized secret policing both to themselves and to the Stasi. They are also excellent sources of information about how collaborations were sustained over the long term and why the relationship with the secret police broke down. Sometimes these reasons for severing ties to the Stasi are recorded verbatim, uncensored, as reported by a frustrated officer whose informant refused to cooperate. At other times informants' motives are recorded in simplified ministerial code that requires interpretation.[117]

The regular "meeting reports" (*Treffberichte*) penned by an informer's officer after each covert appointment, or *Treff*, are an especially powerful kind of document within the Stasi files. The files provide a rich metasource of information on the combination of elements that motivated informers and that came together to structure their overall habitus and identity. Above all, they document what the act of spying or informing meant for the informers' sense of self—public and private—and their forms of self-fashioning as individuals. On first glance the IM files do not appear to offer a particularly differentiated picture of motives. At the start of each individual informant's file or dossier the recruitment records summarize briefly the official motives for collaborating, which are invariably connected with a candidate's ideological or political persuasion. Reading beyond the opening pages of the recruitment documents, however, allows a researcher to infer a host of other reasons that belie the official ones. In addition to psychological reasons, the files testify to multiple other social and personal reasons for collaborating that have to do with identity, habitus, and forms of capital.[118] Informers' primary, initial reasons for agreeing to work for the Stasi should be distinguished from secondary reasons that evolved over time. Descriptions of motives should also distinguish between emotions such as dissatisfaction and fear, as well as among interests, values, and attitudes.[119] Moreover, like circumstances, motivations can change, and it is important to develop a dynamic account of why informants collaborated.

The files contain myriad intersecting biographies of the lives the Stasi touched, some brief and sketchy, others rich and detailed in texture, and most disjointed.[120] The files are thin in places and thick in others, inconclusive on some events and instructive on others. Notwithstanding the many challenges in interpreting them, the files can provide the basis for the sort of nuanced analyses and attentive close readings—the "piled-up structures of inference and implication"—that Clifford Geertz envisions when he calls for a modern anthropology that can perform a "thick description" of meaning-making in society.[121] The files are much like Geertz's elusive "raw data" in ethnographical analysis. They are already the result of "thick description"; that is, they are "constructions of other people's constructions."[122] The historian aims to produce a thick description of life under communism with the help of the Stasi files and to unpick those politically and ideologically charged constructions of the Stasi, the often small but richly significant "flecks of culture" embedded in the files.[123] To do so, she or he must also unpick the files' specific structures of signification and how they know what they know. This involves seeing things as the Stasi did and recognizing how and why the Stasi's bureaucratic apparatus turned a specific passing event in a suspect's life into a noteworthy bureaucratic event with security implications. The files inscribe events in particular instrumental ways, often for opaque reasons. It has been my task to attempt to write a thick description of the meaning of these records and thereby to reinscribe their bureaucratic events into alternative narratives.

Secrecy, Trust, and Totalitarianism

The Stasi files are my main source of data about the secret surveillance society of the MfS and the place of literature within it. They contain portraits of Stasi collaborators that paint a grim picture of GDR society as founded on chronic mistrust and born from a misplaced desire for total control. They expose a covert stratum of the social fabric that wielded frightening power over people while devising insidious methods of co-opting collaborators to the regime's cause. The Stasi was the hidden underbelly of the communist dream. Thus, this book is concerned with the secret "anatomy of a dictatorship" (Mary Fulbrook's phrase) and its impact on cultural life.[124]

Most broadly, *A State of Secrecy* seeks answers to questions about how totalitarian rule in the GDR was sustained over a long period of time—whether through fear and terror, like that which occurred during the Third Reich, or through mechanisms of soft power like enticements and incentives. My study proceeds from the hypothesis that it was possible to lead a "perfectly normal life" in the GDR, as Fulbrook has argued.[125] That said, the culture of secrecy that the Stasi cultivated and nurtured and the level of secret surveillance that it maintained was anything but normal. A culture of surveillance was endemic to political and social organizations in the GDR; it permeated education institutions, youth clubs, writers' unions, and virtually the entire world of publishing.[126] Secrecy and betrayal, even when they occurred in the service of the nation and in the GDR's declared Cold War goal—to protect the socialist German republic, which many victims of World War II considered the better and more moral Germany—were not openly condoned. And yet they were rife. In the modern era we have become more comfortable with not knowing everything about the people we deal with on a daily basis. As Simmel has argued, modern society must depend on the supposition that "we have not been deceived,"[127] and there is no need for "complete reciprocal transparency."[128] In short, we trust others despite their secrets. In dictatorships such as the GDR this trust in others was severely undermined. As Jürgen Kocka has stated, the GDR was a "special" kind of modern dictatorship, not merely a "welfare" dictatorship or a "participatory" dictatorship, but one predicated on secrecy.[129] The regime did not value trust, and it filled this gap with modes of control.

Because total control was in practice impossible to achieve, the regime was obliged to content itself with knowing everything about those citizens it could not trust. To be sure, it had an interest in private secrets, objects of shame or embarrassment which it could use to blackmail victims, but it was far more interested in political dirt, such as suspects' putative secret desires to undermine the regime.

What happens when normal social identifications become disrupted by the call to duty issued by an official entity like a secret police outfit? Did an affiliation with the Stasi foster belonging with the secret police as a form of "imagined community"—something like Benedict Anderson's newspaper-reading community, in which individual newspaper readers in a nation feel an affinity with other newspaper readers unknown to them?[130] The community of spies and secret police officers was undoubtedly elite and clandestine, with almost cult-like associations for some. If working for the "Firm" (as the Stasi was often called by those both inside and outside the organization),[131] bestowed a dubious belonging on secret agents, how was the belonging performed by the informant? Unlike the officer, the informer worked only sporadically, and his or her ties to the Stasi were far more tenuous than those of the officer. Yet the archival sources suggest that the informer was expected to show the same loyalty and selfless devotion to the cause as the officer.

*

This book is structured around five extended and in-depth case studies taken from across the spectrum of informers deployed in the area of literature and culture. Each case study is a partial individual biography that focuses on the writer's association with the Stasi. Each represents a different point along the spectrum of personalities involved in collaboration with the Stasi. Each illustrates different kinds of surveillance work carried out, different pressures imposed on, and different courses of action taken by the individual in question. Together the selected cases compose a collective biography of Stasi informers in the cultural sphere. Four of the five cases, taken together, constitute a group biography because these individuals' lives were interconnected in various ways. The selection of cases has been limited to five illustrative instances in order to provide depth of analysis. These extended biographies follow the informers from the moment of recruitment through to the time when their cases files closed, and in some cases beyond. The advantage of extended case studies is that I am able to explore the shifts in motivations over time, the changes in the Stasi's informer-handling strategies, and the impact of both. Above all, the small sample size allows me to offer observations about the long-term impact of recruitment and handling practices that would not otherwise be possible.

The cases have been chosen to offer a mix of genders, although the Stasi was a "veritable bastion of male chauvinism"; only 23 percent of all MfS employees were women.[132] Within the 23 percent, they were well represented in traditional female professions as secretaries, administrative assistants, and in postal control.[133] Estimates of the percentage of MfS informants who were women vary from 10 to 17 percent; the higher number is more likely.[134] In one study of female informants in the city of Gera, 35 percent of those informants worked for the Stasi from five to ten years, and over half were married.[135]

When selecting the particular case studies that feature in this book, I also considered the life story of the individuals discussed. I have chosen cases from a range of backgrounds, including those working in official, state-approved organizations such as the Writers' Guild (on one end of the spectrum) and those working in the underground, outside state structures (on the other end). Background becomes important for my analysis of habitus, and here my focus is twofold. What was it about individuals' backgrounds that made them of interest to the Stasi? Likewise, what was it about their life experiences that made them susceptible to the Stasi? I have tried to incorporate a range of individual circumstances in terms of family backgrounds and careers. My selection of informants encompasses Jewish communists who returned from exile; state orphans and foster children; the offspring of existing secret service agents; and young literary stars. I have included informers from two different generations of writers. Further, I have chosen a mix of loyalist agents and agents who quit. Among those who ceased serving as informers there is also great variety, ranging from those who stopped informing after just a few weeks (Helga M. Novak), those who worked for five to ten years (Sascha Anderson), to those who quit after almost twenty years of service (Paul Gratzik). I have tried to do justice to the many different circumstances around the termination of a person's association with the secret police. In each chapter I analyze a different aspect of the informers' affiliations with the Stasi, which I illustrate through biographical snapshots from their files and other source material. The chapters are structured in more or less chronological order (with slight overlap), allowing me to build a longitudinal (albeit by no means comprehensive) picture of each informant as the book unfolds.

Chapter 1 focuses on the Stasi's early years, before the erection of the Berlin Wall in 1961, during which it recruited writers from diverse backgrounds to its cause. I examine the ministry's reasons for approaching writers while also teasing out each informer's initial motives for agreeing or refusing to collaborate. The years from 1955 to 1961 were pivotal for the party's project of fostering a new socialist intelligentsia.[136] I explore the Stasi's early recruitment tactics in relation to the regime's new political elites and to cosmopolitan writers and the working classes, arguing that the Stasi's secret surveillance society functioned as a pull factor to bind informants to the Stasi.

Chapter 2 deals with the period after the building of the Berlin Wall, when the Stasi began to expand its departments overseeing the surveillance of cultural organizations. The Stasi sought to build long-term relationships with informants from these groups. This chapter concerns the phase following recruitment, when the Stasi endeavored to create solid working relationships with its informers that were conducive to loyalty. This chapter also considers the varied response of writers from different backgrounds to entitlements and incentives and the creation of codependencies. Some informers reaped rewards during this time, whereas for others, political developments such as the crushing of the Prague Spring in Czechoslovakia in 1968 proved to be turning points.

Chapter 3 covers the early period of détente in the 1970s. With a change of party leadership in May 1971 came a brief thaw in cultural politics, which the MfS interpreted as a signal for greater vigilance. This chapter deals with the period of greatest growth in the ministry, focusing on the middle phase of collaboration for some informers and the Stasi's efforts to reactivate other, lapsed key informants. In this context I explore individuals' complex sets of motivations for resuming contact with the Stasi and analyze how informing became habituated, as some informers settled into their role and began to live the secret life as the good life.

Chapter 4 explores an intense and brief period for the policing of literature in the wake of the expulsion from the country of singer-songwriter Wolf Biermann in November 1976. It focuses on what I call "sticky surveillance" in the policing of political-ideological diversion. Informers were required to stick close to suspects, becoming infiltrators of groups. They openly flaunted themselves as like-minded friends on one level, while on another level covertly keeping watch. Sara Ahmed has coined the term "stickiness" to explain how things—"bodies, objects, and signs"—accumulate emotional value through coming into contact with other things.[137] According to Ahmed, stickiness is the result of past "histories of contact" and of what has "rubbed off" onto things in past encounters with other things.[138] In this chapter, I examine how informers were expected to produce ideological stickiness, or positive political impacts on their targets.

In chapter 5 I extend the discussion to an analysis of a radical experiment with simulation in the nascent underground subcultures that exploded in the GDR in the early 1980s. The strategy of simulation went far beyond observation and collection of information through sticking close to targets. A new type of IM was instructed to form attachments to suspicious groups of writers and to actively engage in, even promote, the hostile activities that the Stasi was intent on controlling. This required simulating the habitus of a member of the underground and leading an enemy lifestyle. For the Stasi, this entailed greater risks than with other types of informers.

Chapter 6 is dedicated to the final phase of the regime and follows the life histories of the informants who remained active as well as those the Stasi continued to victimize through to the regime's collapse in late 1989. Also explored in this final chapter are the aporias of the state of secrecy and the Stasi's strategies of collecting human intelligence. In East Germany's final decade the secret surveillance society appeared to crumble from within, as the prestige of collaborating with the secret police was debunked and the system of incentives seemed to fail. By this stage, the secret society of surveillance that many had signed up to had proved that it was far from benign. For many East German citizens it seemed as if, as in Hans Christian Andersen's fairytale, the emperor had no clothes. Eventually, the secret surveillance society began to generate more and more "moments of refusal and resistance" to the Stasi's panoptical practices, which ultimately helped to accelerate its demise.[139]

ABBREVIATIONS

Abt.	*Abteilung*, department
AIM	*Archivierter IM-Vorgang*, archived IM case
AKG	*Auswertungs- und Kontrollgruppe*, assessment and control group
ANS	Amt für Nationale Sicherheit, Office for National Security
AOP	*Archivierter Operativer Vorgang*, archived operational case
AOPK	*Archivierte Operative Personenkontrolle*, archived person check
AP	*Personenablage*, personnel file
BStU	Der Bundesbeauftragte für die Unterlagen des Staatssicherheitsdienstes der ehemaligen Deutschen Demokratischen Republik, the Federal Commissioner for the Records of the State Security Service of the Former German Democratic Republic
BV	*Bezirksverwaltung*, regional administration
BVfS	*Bezirksverwaltung für Staatssicherheit*, regional administration for state security
FDJ	Freie Deutsche Jugend, Free German Youth
GDR	German Democratic Republic, Deutsche Demokratische Republik (DDR)
GI	*Geheimer Informator*, secret informer (used from 1950 to 1968)
GM	*Geheimer Mitarbeiter*, secret collaborator (used from 1950 to 1968)

HA   *Hauptabteilung*, main department
HV A   Hauptverwaltung Aufklärung, Main Directorate for Reconnaissance
IM   *Inoffizieller Mitarbeiter*, unofficial collaborator
IMB   *Inoffizieller Mitarbeiter der Abwehr mit Feindverbindung bzw. zur unmittelbaren Bearbeitung im Verdacht der Feindtätigkeit stehender Personen*, unofficial collaborator in counterintelligence with enemy contacts, for investigating persons under suspicion of hostile activity (used from 1980 to 1989)
IME   *Inoffizieller Mitarbeiter im besonderen Einsatz*, unofficial collaborator for a special task (used from 1968 to 1989)
IMK   *Inoffizieller Mitarbeiter zur Sicherung der Konspiration und des Verbindungswesens*, unofficial collaborator for aiding conspiracy and securing communications (used from 1968 to 1989)
IMS   *Inoffizieller Mitarbeiter zur politisch-operativen Durchdringung und Sicherung des Verantwortungsbereiches*, unofficial collaborator for the political-operative penetration and securing of an area of responsibility (used from 1968 to 1989)
IMV   *Inoffizieller Mitarbeiter mit vertraulichen Beziehungen zur bearbeiteten Person*, unofficial collaborator with close contact to the person under investigation (used from 1968 to 1979)
IM-*Vorgang*   IM case
IM-*Vorlauf*   IM candidate case
IM-*Vorgang-Akte* IM case file
IM-*Vorlauf-Akte* IM candidate case file
KGB   Komitet Gossudarstwennoi Besopasnosti, Soviet Committee for State Security
MfS   Ministerium für Staatssicherheit, the Ministry for State Security
OPK   *Operative Personenkontrolle*, operational person check
OV   *Operativer Vorgang*, operational case (victim file)
PUT   *politische Untergrundtätigkeit*, political underground activity
SED   Sozialistische Einheitspartei, Socialist Unity Party
ZA   Zentralarchiv, Central Archive
ZK   Zentralkomitee, Central Committee

A STATE OF SECRECY

1
Recruiting Writers for the Stasi, 1949–1962

Many roads led to being recruited by the Ministry for State Security. Some were windy and rocky; they followed personal hardship and involved coercion or blackmail. Other routes to the Stasi were remarkably straight and smooth; informants offered up their services "consciously, freely, and willingly."[1] Working for the Stasi presented these recruits with ostensible opportunities or openings. Even after a bumpy start and the occasional detour, these paths could pave the way for a successful secret-police career littered with accolades, medals, business trips, and stylish apartments. For those who joined the Stasi, this was at least the expectation.

Stasi officers and their families enjoyed a swath of material privileges, from better housing to access to travel and rare consumer goods. Even without these material sweeteners, working for one of the state's official organs carried with it a certain nimbus of elitism. In some cases these advantages were extended to the Stasi's undercover agents. From the Stasi's establishment in 1950 through the first decade of its existence, it looked to recruit individuals with an affirmative attitude toward the state and a Marxist-Leninist political orientation.[2] In this period almost all officers in the ministry were members of the ruling party (SED),³ as were around half of informers.⁴ The Stasi liked to think that 90 percent of its informants concerned with literary operations were recruited on "the basis of political-ideological conviction."⁵ But in reality, only just over half of the informants in Hauptabteilung (HA) XX were members of the SED.⁶ In particular, informers who worked on cases involving "contact with the enemy" (*Feindberührung/Feindbekämpfung*), categorized as IMV/B, were almost never members of the SED.⁷

Strictly speaking, all shades of communists and antifascists were welcome—idealists, hardliners, visionaries, dreamers, utopianists, and, especially later, pragmatists; the Stasi was a broad church.⁸ Over time the Stasi came to accept a wide spectrum of motivations. In 1967 the Juristische Hochschule des MfS (MfS Law School) in Potsdam commissioned a doctoral study, carried out by Manfred Hempel, who found that 60.5 percent of informers were motivated by "recognition of society's need" (*Erkennen des gesellschaftlichen Erfordernisses*), whereas 23.4 percent were motivated by "experiences of coercion and force" (*Druck- und Zwangserlebnisse*).⁹ Almost half of informants stated that they were driven by "a sense of moral obligation and duty to one's conscience" (*sittliches Pflichterleben und Gewissenszwang*), and 27.4 percent admitted to joining for "personal gain" (*Vorteilserwägungen*).¹⁰ The Stasi knew by 1967 at the latest that the term "political-ideological conviction" was bureaucratic newspeak. Collaborating because of one's political-ideological conviction could mean many things.

The Stasi's insurance policy for obtaining reliable intelligence was an informer who had been profiled as a baseline loyalist. In an ideal world the Stasi would have recruited only this type of informer. It clearly preferred working with individuals with intrinsic rather than extrinsic motivations—that is, with those who were motivated to serve their country for patriotic or idealistic reasons. Yet such ideal informers were few and far between, and the MfS was often forced to look beyond 100 percent politically loyalist circles.¹¹ To lure noncommittal or indifferent groups into cooperating, the Stasi sanctioned the use of blackmail in recruitment, despite an awareness that this was not always ideal.¹²

Hempel readily acknowledges in his study that fear and anxiety were paramount motivators, and 22.1 percent of recruits mentioned them as secondary factors.[13] The Stasi regularly used fear as a means of recruitment. When hard power proved ineffective, the Stasi resorted to soft power—that is, to inducements and incentives, or crude carrots, rather than sticks. Over the decades, the Stasi came to realize that positive emotions were far better than negative emotions for motivating informers to stay on track. In terms of motivational psychology this meant that informers with a positive attitude, or what E. Tory Higgins calls a "promotion focus orientation,"[14] toward achieving their goals as hopes or aspirations were more likely to succeed than those with a "prevention focus orientation."[15] Informers who were motivated to avoid failure, whether because of fear or coercion, were less likely to succeed.[16] The Stasi naturally preferred to work with the former category of self-motivating and self-regulating informants, although, as my research shows, informers rarely performed their work with the eagerness characteristic of a positive or "promotion" orientation.

Given that few informers were intrinsically motivated and that 40 percent in Hempel's 1967 study reported wanting to achieve "life-practical objectives" (*lebenspraktische Zielsetzungen*), the Stasi was realistic about the need to offer favors, benefits, and advantages.[17] Such positive inducements could vary, depending on the sorts of circles that the informer moved in and on her or his overall effectiveness as a recruit. Although the remuneration for informers was never overly generous in financial terms, the added, illegal income was certainly an incentive for some.

For others, incentives needed to be a combination of intangible rewards and financial or other material perks. The intangibles were forms of capital—symbolic, social, and cultural—that had the added frisson of being a secret privilege. Such rewards, however ephemeral, also needed to be forthcoming in a timely fashion and needed to be adequate for the informers' aspirations. If delivered too late, rewards could foster resentment and frustration, and if they weren't offered at all, informers became angry, disillusioned, and sometimes bitter. The lack of meaningful or adequate rewards could mean that informers altered their goals and practiced self-regulation toward the Stasi. It could lead to them altering their positive orientation—what motivational psychologists call an "eager strategy" or "approach orientation"—and adopting a negative or avoidance orientation.[18]

Repeated negative experiences could severely diminish informers' willingness to use extra effort in performing the tasks assigned. Thus an error signal would arise in the feedback loop, indicating that the informer was not making progress toward his or her goal as hoped. This in turn could result in the informer adjusting his or her goals so as to avoid further disappointment and frustration, an eventuality known as a "discrepancy reducing feedback loop."[19] If the goal shifted from a positive one (wishing to meet the Stasi's demands) to an avoidance goal, or antigoal, (namely, not wishing to work for the Stasi), informants could become caught in a double bind, or more precisely in a double motivational loop.[20]

Among the largest problems faced by the Stasi were negative perceptions of it in the population at large. Recruiting for the secret service meant overcoming candidates' instinctive aversion to spying on or denouncing others. Virtually all informers, when confronted with the choice of cooperating, grappled at first with the question of whether it was "morally defensible" (*moralisch sauber*) to work for the secret police.[21] As Hempel's internal Stasi research reveals, it was crucial to overcome candidates' moral reservations about working for the secret service, and over time at least around half of recruits learned to live with the moral ambiguity of their actions. In other words, converting avoidance behavior into an approach orientation or positive attitudes was essential. Most candidates' fears stemmed from the need for secrecy, and individuals responded differently to this imposition. In many ways the Stasi managed to turn on its head Simmel's account of how a modern, open society copes with high degrees of secrecy. The SED state insisted on its right to know things about its citizens. And it implicated those citizens in its right to know by asking them to participate in secret activities.

Simmel wrote his defense of secrecy in the modern age before the advent of global fascism. He contends that the secret "has no immediate connection with evil," although he also admits the opposite, that "evil has an immediate connection with secrecy."[22] In the Cold War, secrecy was part and parcel of political life on both sides of the Iron Curtain. Ordinary people were prepared to accept a higher degree of secrecy than usual. Indeed, lying and untruthfulness were not only permissible, they were imperative.

Concealment, like surveillance, was a necessary evil. As Simmel argues, we base our lives on a "thousand presuppositions" which we cannot check or verify and must take on faith—and most of the time this does not present a problem.[23] Nevertheless, we act under the assumption that we have not been deceived, and for this reason, the lie becomes, as Simmel remarks, "something much more devastating than it was earlier."[24] Lying in modern societies is no longer a sin, but concealment of the truth needs to be justified by a higher purpose.

The MfS regarded the requirement of secrecy as a fundamental principle, for which it devised several different terms: "not-public" (*nichtöffentlich*), "unofficial" (*inoffiziell*), and "secret" or "confidential" (*geheim*). Rather than use the term "contact person" (*Vertrauensmann*), which is commonly used by many intelligence agencies,[25] the Stasi deliberately avoided associations with spying and sanitized the terms for informing in a language-hygiene program.[26] The expressions "informant" (*Informant*), "secret employee" (*Geheimer Mitarbeiter*, GM) and "secret informant" (*Geheimer Informator*, GI) were used from 1950 to 1968; in the latter year they were replaced by terms for different subcategories of "unofficial collaborator" (*Inoffizieller Mitarbeiter*, IM).[27]

The ministry issued five sets of administrative guidelines for working with informants: three in the 1950s, another in 1968, and a final one in 1979.[28] These guidelines covered topics including recruiting, registering, documenting, filing, and closing files. So important was secrecy that in 1968 the new Guideline 1/68 introduced a section on "conspiring and secrecy" (*Konspiration und Geheimhaltung*). Secrecy was crucial to protect the MfS from its enemies. It was also needed to protect informers themselves and was, moreover, essential for developing a "close relationship of trust" (*enges Vertrauensverhältnis*) between officer and informer.[29] In this chapter, three cases of informers recruited for working in cultural spheres are examined for the years 1949 to 1962. These cases shed light on a number of the ministry's early practices for enlisting new informers and dealing with secrecy as well as on informers' initial personal and professional motivations. Here particular attention is paid to those aspects of the informers' life stories that made them most vulnerable to an approach from the Stasi.

Paul Wiens: The Jewish Communist

From the moment the GDR was proclaimed on October 7, 1949, Paul Wiens was at the forefront of public life. As a young man of twenty-five, in the prime of his life and with his health intact despite the deprivations of war, he needed little prompting to join in the postwar rebuilding effort. Like so many others whose lives had been on hold throughout the twelve nightmarish years of National Socialism and the Second World War, Wiens wanted to make up for lost time. He soon developed leadership aspirations, capitalizing on opportunities that came his way to contribute to cultural life as it was reformed under Soviet occupation. As expressed by one East German biographer, "Wiens had deliberately chosen a path of direct social intervention. Working at his desk did not fulfil him."[30]

However, Wiens's romanticized notions of the life of a poet were forged in very different times from those in which he found himself at the start of the Cold War. It soon became clear to him that the Germany of the GDR was a far cry from either the free-thinking Weimar Republic—where Wiens was first schooled—or the cosmopolitan world of interwar Switzerland, where he spent his adolescence. By the time Wiens turned thirty he had experienced at close quarters the strengths and weaknesses of capitalism, fascism, and communism. During his rapid climb up the social ladder Wiens came to a fork in the road where he was forced to make choices. At the time those choices did not strike him as amoral or reprehensible paths to take, although later generations would take a particularly dim view of writers who chose a lifetime of dedicated service to the secret police over, say, a career in public life. Because he died in 1982, Wiens was spared the public opprobrium that other Stasi functionaries like him were subjected to after German reunification.[31] Had he survived the end of the GDR, no doubt Wiens would have argued in his defense that ideological warfare of a global scale had its price and that integrity was one of the first casualties of such a war. He might have claimed that compromises like secrecy, deception, betrayal, and duplicity, paled into insignificance when national security was at stake.

The Stasi first enlisted Paul Wiens as a GI in 1962, one year after the construction of the Berlin Wall. Wiens was recruited on the basis of his positive ideological stance—code, in his case, for his impeccable antifascist credentials. In the eastern occupied sector of Germany the view took hold that there was only one type of resistance to Adolf Hitler, and that was not Jewish, but communist. Once the GDR was proclaimed, the new sovereign state wanted to show the world that it was serious about antifascism and—far more than the capitalist West—drew its legitimacy from its antifascist lineage. After the war antifascist communists and other victims of Hitler's Germany rose quickly to positions of power and came to dominate public life. As a Jew, Paul Wiens was a victim of fascism; he was also a recent convert to Marxism, having been won over toward the end of World War II.[32]

Assimilated Jews like Wiens were not more predisposed than other demographics to collaborating with the Stasi, but their traumatic histories of persecution by the Nazis made them easy targets. Like many of the Jewish communists who chose to make the GDR their home—such as exiled writers Stephan Hermlin, Stefan Heym, and Anna Seghers—Wiens saw himself first and foremost as a communist, abandoning his Jewish identity in favor of "red assimilation."[33] He and his Jewish compatriots all shared the belief that Jewish emancipation could only be achieved through the communist movement. As Mike Dennis and Norman LaPorte argue, Jewish assimilation in the GDR required a "high level of political and cultural conformity."[34]

Wiens was born in 1922 in the city of Kaliningrad, then Königsberg in East Prussia. His parents moved to Berlin, and there Wiens spent most of his childhood happily settled in the capital city's wealthier western suburbs. After his parents' divorce Wiens remained in the care of his artistic but restless mother. Wiens and his mother were among the city's many assimilated, middle-class Jews. Growing up, however, Wiens did not know that he was Jewish, and his birth certificate records that both parents were Lutheran.[35] According to the story of his youth that Wiens told much later, he celebrated the Nazis' rise to power as a ten- or eleven-year-old. It was only then that his mother let him into her family's secret.[36] She barred him from joining the Hitler Youth organization, revealing that his grandfather was Jewish, like "our Heine" (Henrich Heine), her favorite poet.[37]

The revelation that he was Jewish must have come as a shock to Wiens, and promptly put an end to his childish fantasies of coming of age in the safety of Berlin. No doubt the information caused an irrevocable change in his self-perception at a crucial stage in his development. (The change may have had far-reaching repercussions, setting the scene for his later overinvestment in figures of authority.) The revelation about his secret Jewish identity may have toppled his adolescent role models, and he was catapulted out of his affluent, non-Jewish group of friends. He had effectively been rejected by the very society to which he had thought he belonged and had been robbed of his entitlements. In all likelihood he experienced a deep sense of shame, which his mother tried to quell by replacing it with feelings of familial pride—pride at being like the Romantic German-Jewish poet Heine.

Soon after the National Socialists came to power, Wiens's mother had the prescience to take her eleven-year-old son into exile. They left Berlin before the first deportations and arrests occurred in 1934, and Wiens completed his schooling in neutral Switzerland, far from the harsh realities of the war, while his mother was in Vienna. While other, less privileged European Jews were deported to concentration camps, Wiens was safely ensconced in expensive boarding schools. During the holidays he joined his mother, traipsing with her around Italy, France, and England. In a short biographical portrait commissioned in the GDR shortly before Wiens died, Mathilde Dau describes those years in rather more dramatic terms: "Already as an eleven-year-old he began to flee from the Nazis across many European countries."[38] In interviews Wiens gave during adulthood, he spoke about having attended a boarding school in Villars, which was in the French-speaking part of Switzerland renowned for its upper-class boarding schools. Evidence points to his having been a pupil at one of the less glamorous schools in the neighboring village of Lutry.[39] Needless to say, the school in Wiens's memories was elite and the languages of instruction were French and English.[40]

Irmtraud Morgner was the third of Wiens's four wives. According to her, his childhood was privileged but emotionally impoverished. Morgner's fantastical novel *Amanda* (1983) includes a character with the name Konrad Tenner who bears an uncanny resemblance to Paul Wiens. The novel was written after Morgner divorced Wiens, and the portrait of her ex-husband is brutally honest—possibly a trifle bitter. She writes of Tenner: "His mother lived out of hotel rooms. Not always in the countries in which her son was going to school. In the holidays his mother mostly sent him, much to his disappointment, to camps in the countryside."[41]

By 1943 Wiens was living in Vienna, where his mother was in hiding in a friend's cellar.[42] On August 20, 1943, two years before the war's end, Wiens was arrested for listening to enemy radio broadcasts.[43] Wiens was first sent to the police prison Sankt Pölten, then to the labor camp Oberlanzendorf in Austria. Although he spoke repeatedly about the deep and lasting impact of his incarceration in interviews, there are no extant records of his having passed through either Sankt Pölten or Oberlanzendorf.[44] His account is certainly plausible, given that there were large numbers of people passing through Oberlanzendorf, and it was also used as a transitional camp for transports to the death camp of Mauthausen.[45]

His experience in the camps was deeply formative for the young Wiens, or at least this is the affirmative myth he was keen to propagate about himself. It was in the camps that he learned "courage and solidarity."[46] Wiens's recollections of his wartime experiences repeatedly refer to the camps in terms of a quasi-religious awakening. There he met Russian, Ukrainian, Czech, and French communists, who served as role models for him.[47] In their unerring visions, their energy, and their "revolutionary humanity" they upheld the values of "spiritual freedom," which moved him deeply. Wiens recollects a second experience of freedom when the Red Army liberated him and his fellow prisoners on April 5, 1945. In a public lecture he gave in the Soviet Union in 1953 he spoke about how the Soviet troops gave him "his life" back.[48]

Wiens was one of the few members of his family to survive the war. His father presumably went missing in action, and his mother died of cancer as the war was ending. In a public eulogy to mark Wiens's passing almost forty years later, Günther Rücker, a colleague, friend, and fellow Stasi informant, calls him a survivor. Having evaded death by the Nazis, his adult life was a triumph, Rücker writes, a "double triumph" over Nazi barbarism and "this first death that was planned for him in his youth."[49] After liberation Wiens first moved to Vienna, and in 1947 he decided to emigrate to the Soviet

Occupation Zone in eastern Germany. Moving to the heartland and crucible of classical German culture, Weimar, Wiens secured work as an editor and translator with the GDR's premier publishing house, Aufbau, in 1948–50, and work as a journalist with the newspapers *Sonntag* and *Die Wochenpost*.

Wiens became a card-carrying member of the official German Writers' Guild (Deutscher Schriftstellerverband) at its inception in 1950. From 1951 he had enough work to go freelance, supporting himself writing poetry, radio plays, and film scripts. With his guild membership in hand, opportunities opened to him in radio, film, and, later, television. His career was off to a promising start. He was a professional writer with a permit to write, so to speak, something denied later generations of writers and other new Stasi recruits in the 1950s like the student Helga M. Novak.

Helga M. Novak: The Orphaned Student

In October 1991, just over a year after Germany was reunified, a writer from the former East made a startling confession that went almost unnoticed in the frenetic media scrum that had just erupted over the East German secret police. After the fall of the Berlin Wall the Stasi quickly became a hotly debated topic, particularly, in 1990–91, the alleged complicity of writers of literature with the Stasi.[50] Shortly before the new legislation was passed in November 1991 to open the Stasi archives, allegations began to circulate in earnest about unprecedented levels of collaboration with the secret police. Victims who had had early access to their files leaked some of their more shocking findings, one of which related to the young poet Sascha Anderson. On October 25, 1991, the protest-singer and poet Wolf Biermann was awarded the Büchner Prize, Germany's most prestigious award for literature. During his acceptance speech Biermann unleashed his first hand grenade against his former torturers.

Like Biermann, the nineteenth-century writer Georg Büchner had been branded an enemy of the state, and he narrowly escaped arrest, torture, and certain death. Büchner had also, like so many of Biermann's contemporaries, been denounced by an informer. In his speech of 1991 Biermann spoke about what his intellectual forebear Büchner once called the "dreadful fatalism of history," and the "unavoidable violence" of social conditions.[51] There were few "bright stars" in the East,[52] Biermann contended, few "upright citizens," and too many self-pitying "well-nourished subjects."[53] In the GDR there had been too many writers in cahoots with the SED, and worse still, all opposition groups had been "eaten away by Stasi metastases."[54] Of the five known spies at the time—these five were only the tip of the iceberg—Biermann singled out one for particular attention: the "untalented blatherer Sascha Arsehole" (*der unbegabte Schwätzer Sascha Arschloch*), alias Sascha Anderson, who denied ever having contacts with the Stasi. Biermann called on all Stasi informers to confess to the truth.[55]

Anderson stuck coolly to his story that he had not been a Stasi agent.[56] Other writers were not so unflappable. In an open letter published in *Der Spiegel* only three days later, on October 28, 1991, one writer unexpectedly took up the singer's exhortation to confess to the truth. This admission did not make media headlines and barely rated a mention. In her brief public letter Helga M. Novak admits to also having been a Stasi agent. She writes: "In for a penny, in for a pound—I too was once a spy."[57] At the time confessions, especially voluntary ones, were few and far between. As it transpired, Novak's courage in exposing herself could do little to stem the rising tide of invective directed at Anderson, and her intervention in the debates was largely forgotten. Novak had always been an outsider in literary circles, and in 1991 she was not even a resident of Germany, but living in exile in the Polish countryside. In fact, the revelations did little to damage her career. The media had far bigger fish to fry when, a year later, the icon of East German integrity, Christa Wolf, revealed that she too had been enlisted and run as an agent by the Stasi in the 1950s.[58]

Novak's public statement did, however, establish her as one of a small group of writers brave enough to publicly expose themselves as erstwhile Stasi informants.[59] As a young student Novak was blackmailed, she writes, and in 1957 she agreed to work as an informant for the Stasi. She makes the points that people's decisions were often based on fear and that some were especially vulnerable to threats of punishment or reprisals: "I did not want to spend seven years in Bautzen like Erich Loest, where no one, since I had no family, no blood ties at all, would even have brought me a packet of cigarettes."[60] Equally, she was fearful of being judged for past mistakes, reminding her readers that she had been her own harshest critic: "Shame gnaws away at you for your whole life but it is also a rigorous teacher."[61] As she reveals, she was plagued by feelings of shame for having collaborated, feelings which were only exacerbated during the very public revelations about who was complicit with the Stasi. Most of all she feared being publicly humiliated, and made into a scapegoat. She was defiant that she would prefer anything to being judged and tried by Germans: "I would rather bleed to death in a Polish forest than be tried in a German court of law."[62]

In fact, Novak's brush with the Stasi was extremely minor, and her collaboration was short-lived. She was young, vulnerable, and impressionable when the Stasi made its initial approach to enlist her, but her encounter with power was to have far-reaching consequences. Helga M. Novak was born Maria Karlsdottir on September 8, 1935, in Köpenick in Berlin. She was abandoned by her birth mother when she was two weeks old, spending the first three years of her life in an orphanage.[63] The second volume of her autobiography, *Vogel federlos* (Bird featherless, 1982), tells of how she never knew her birth father, who shot himself in 1937.[64] She was adopted out to Charlotte and Karl Novak, with whom she never bonded. (In an interview in 2006, she said that she "learned early what it was to be abandoned."[65]) She describes her adoptive parents as harsh, especially her adoptive mother, whom she calls "Cold Sophie." At age 16 she fled to a boarding school, which promised "a protected life."[66] Yet life at school brought its own set of challenges, one of which was the fact that she quickly earned the reputation of being an ideological "fanatic" (*Hundertfünfzigprozentige*).[67]

Novak's coming of age coincided with the early years of the GDR. As she remarked in the 2006 interview, she was naïve and took the party at its word: "I thought that the appropriation by the state meant that everything belonged to us [laughs], everything that we were in the process of rebuilding.... I was seduced by the term 'the people's property,' by the community. I thought that we had access to whatever it was that was being made in the factories—whether cannons or sewing machines."[68] Over the next few years the party was to become a surrogate family for her. In the end she came to loathe its actions almost as much as she had hated her adoptive parents. In March 1953, however, her faith in the party was unbroken, and at the age of eighteen she stood as a candidate for the SED and was accepted as a member.[69]

Novak attributed her early political fanaticism to her lack of a family. She recalled: "I had no family or relatives. There were no children's birthdays and no Christmas parties, I was not distracted from daily politics by parents, grandparents, uncles or aunts who knew the old life better than the new one in the GDR."[70] When Novak first applied to study journalism at the University of Leipzig, she had no home address to give. She had no family with whom she spent her weekends and no friends with whom to spend summer holidays. Eventually, so as to fit in, she resorted to fabricating stories of exotic destinations and summer vacations.

Novak spent seven semesters studying journalism from 1954 to 1957. These years coincided with the political freeze that followed the failed workers' uprising of June 17, 1953, against the political and economic situation in the GDR. Universities were central to the Sovietization of Eastern Europe because they trained the new elites of countries in that region.[71] Students were required to support the regime's crackdown, but Novak struggled to find her political feet: "I had no friends, found no one whom I could talk to about our life, about politics and other things, someone I could show my poems to."[72] In the third volume of her autobiography, *Im Schwanenhals* (In the iron trap, 2013), she recalls that she accepted much of the ideological lip-service expected of her.[73]

As Novak was settling into university life, she soon came to the attention of the Stasi. Secret police surveillance at the Institute for Journalism was intense and comprehensive. The Central Committee of the party had not yet secured organizational control over the institute's operations, and the work of the security forces had the full and open support of members of staff, as fellow student Brigitte Klump remembers in her memoir *Das rote Kloster* (The red monastery, 1978). Thus, the Stasi initially contacted Novak via Klaus Höpcke, who was employed as an assistant for theory and practice of the media.[74] Höpcke was later to become deputy minister for culture from 1973 to 1989, with responsibility for the Main Administration for Publishers and Book Trade (Hauptverwaltung Verlage und Buchhandel), earning him the nickname "the book minister." Novak's and Klump's accounts of the

Stasi's almost brazen methods of recruiting reflect much of the climate of paranoia of the time. The MfS was focused on exposing enemy agents, and the minister for state security called for the "increased vigilance of all workers."[75] It transpired that both Klump and Novak had contacts with Westerners, who were immediately suspected of being enemy agents.

The Stasi's cavalier attempt to enlist Novak at the first meeting reflects early practices in the MfS. Officers did not always make contact with a candidate prior to having the first recruitment conversation. The first ministerial guideline for recruiting informants—Guideline 21, issued in 1952—made no explicit mention of separating out these steps when approaching agents. Later guidelines were to stipulate that all approaches to an informant required prior written approval in the form of a "recruitment proposal" (*Werbungsvorschlag*).[76] In this instance, it appears the Stasi had prepared no formal plans to recruit Novak, and upon hearing that she had committed a minor infraction it decided to enlist her on the basis of "compromising material." Guideline 21 lists blackmail as the second main strategy for recruitment after "conviction," although such blackmail was supposed to be only used in connection with the threat of criminal action.[77] In reality, it appears that officers used this method all too frequently, to the extent that in 1954 officers were urged to *not only* use this method.[78] In Guideline 1/58, the revised set of procedures for dealing with informants issued in 1958, the ministry was forced to explicitly acknowledge that enlisting on the basis of compromising material was "not always properly understood"; it often backfired, and should only be deployed with "hostile or negatively disposed persons."[79] Moreover, incriminating material relating to a criminal offense was rarely suitable, the guidelines stated.[80]

According to Klump, Höpcke openly announced that comrades from the security forces were there to speak to her, while reassuring her: "You don't have to be alarmed, it happens to everyone here sooner or later. We are going to become the leading cadres of the nation, it is only natural that we are being controlled."[81] Klump expressed surprise on hearing that the Stasi was working "hand in hand" with the personnel department at the Institute for Journalism. She was told that normally the Stasi was only interested in students in their last year. In her case the matter was more urgent, they claimed, because she had a West German boyfriend: "The class enemy is breathing down our neck. People that we have trusted for years turn out to be enemies. We have to be careful that we are not being tricked. That is why we are here."[82]

Although the tone of these meetings with students was convivial and slightly paternalistic, in the 1950s this did not mean that the Stasi adopted a softer touch when recruiting. Despite the openness of the approach in broad daylight, secrecy and subterfuge were at the heart of the Stasi's operations at the time. With respect to dealing with Novak, the Stasi never lost its punitive habitus, even if this was largely hidden from view. Its purpose for recruiting her was outright cruel.

Helga M. Novak: Recruiting Juliets

Like many of her fellow students in Leipzig, Novak belonged to an ideal ideological pool of potential recruits for the Stasi, both because of her background as an orphan and because she had already undergone strict political vetting upon enrollment. In addition, as Novak writes in *Im Schwanenhals*, the party had no real cause for disgruntlement with her during her years as a student: "The comrades could trust me."[83] However, the shocking revelations of Stalin's crimes at the Twentieth Party Congress of 1956 had left many students confused, unsure whether to expect a loosening of restrictions. Novak remembers her often angry or indignant responses in party, FDJ, and class meetings around this time—and yet Secret Informant (GI) "Diver" (Taucher) from 1955 had a rather different impression of her behavior. According to "Diver," Novak was "an intellectual type," an impression that possibly stemmed from her all-black French existentialist garb and Western ponytail. She behaved "rather reticently,"[84] did not draw attention to herself in public, and had "a flighty nature."[85]

As with Klump, the Stasi had been keeping a close eye on Novak. Immediately after she had begun to invent exotic holiday destinations for herself to save face, rumors that some students were in danger of succumbing to cosmopolitanism started circulating in her party group.[86] Probably these were instigated by the Stasi. Italy, where Novak claimed to have spent her holidays, was a capitalist country. It was not yet unreachable for citizens from Eastern Bloc communist countries, but it was still deemed an odd, if not dubious, destination for a student of journalism. In her desperation to compensate for her lack of family ties, and in her naivety, Novak had failed to realize that her story would work against her.

Around this time, the Stasi started observing Novak as she befriended Boris Djačenko, a communist Latvian writer, and opened their letters. Novak suspected she might already be under surveillance, but Djačenko dismissed the idea: "How are they supposed to find the time to do all that?! Impossible."[87] The Stasi was also a silent witness to Novak's subsequent romantic escapades, watching as she made friends with a group of Icelandic students and spent several late nights partying with them before they traveled to the World Games in Moscow. When the Stasi had found enough incriminating evidence to blackmail her, it pounced and pulled her in for questioning.

The occasion for her first encounter with officers from the security forces was trivial, and yet the events of this single evening were to have repercussions that reverberated far into her future. Novak and her friend Wolfgang had offered three Icelandic students a bed in their college rooms for two nights. They were reprimanded in the middle of the night for breaking the house rules, which forbade them to receive guests late in the evening. The administration of the residential college lodged a formal complaint. On her return from a sports camp Novak found she had been expelled from her dormitory "on grounds of immorality."[88] Although Novak was convinced of a mistake, she had little choice but to seek a room elsewhere. She was too unsettled by her expulsion to wonder why she easily found a private room for lease. Later she discovered that the Stasi had had a hand in this; indeed, this whole tumultuous chapter of her life, from the expulsion to her procurement of private accommodation, was revealed to have been masterminded by the Stasi. It was preparing to blackmail her into collaborating and to groom her for certain delicate tasks.

Shortly after Novak's expulsion from her accommodation in the college in her fourth year (1957), a party secretary summoned her to a meeting in an "almost empty, cold, grey, unused room."[89] The two strangers present addressed her as "comrade" and spoke "dispassionately, in a friendly manner, decisively," commencing with a reprimand for having infringed the college house rules a few months earlier.[90] The officers brought up the topic of her newfound Icelandic friends, who were cause for concern as "guests from an unknown country that [was] a member of NATO and accommodate[d] American bases."[91] By the time Novak realized what was being asked of her—to spy on her Icelandic friends—she knew she "was trapped."[92] In the course of the conversation the officers made veiled threats of withdrawing their assistance in securing her new, private accommodation. The officers then laid out the promise of a good post with a Berlin newspaper after graduation—this promise was to serve as the carrot that would soften the blows of the sticks they would use concurrently. If she refused to cooperate, Novak ran the risk of losing her place at the university and her accommodation. If she complied, she had hopes of finding an exciting post of her dreams in a prime location.

The following piece of contextual information is missing from Novak's autobiography: the Stasi had hatched a plan to deploy the twenty-two-year-old student as a Juliet agent. Juliets were romantic plants assigned the task of seducing suspects, either to elicit intelligence or to create incriminating evidence for laying charges. The MfS often tried to recruit women on the basis of their friendships or intimate relations with men.[93] There are a number of documented instances of the Stasi's use of "operative beds," namely, deploying prostitutes in operative work.[94] Novak must have suspected that the Stasi wished to use her romantic attachment to her Icelandic friend Stenar, guessing the hidden meaning of the Stasi's supposedly innocent comment: "You have the ability to make friendships very quickly?!"[95] In her Stasi file Novak would later find unequivocal evidence of the Stasi's plans for her: "The aim of the recruitment was to win her over to collaborating so that she could be put to work on male persons."[96]

The Stasi officers' approach was straight from the secret-service rule book. They first laid her personal aspirations on the table, then used her "trust" as "bait . . . to hook the fish onto the line."[97] The practice Novak describes here was later associated with infamous spymaster Markus Wolf, the ministry's head of foreign espionage, the Main Directorate for Reconnaissance (Hauptverwaltung Aufklärung, HV A).[98] Novak's case illustrates that domestic espionage departments were experimenting quite early with

Juliets. In all likelihood Novak's reputation for sexual promiscuity fell under the category of blackmailable offenses that the Stasi liked to exploit. Novak was trapped with few options, all of which were unpalatable to her.

Novak recalls of that fateful first meeting that she was unclear whom she was dealing with and thought it was a "cadre discussion," the kind of discussion about leadership typical of a party group.[99] Novak writes in her memoir that she "really did sign" the declaration that was dictated to her.[100] It was not to be the last time she was forced to endure encounters with officers from the Stasi "in some backroom," she writes, because from now on the Stasi "had a search warrant out to get her."[101] Over the following years she was to develop strategies for coping with such encounters: "Sit down comfortably, I told myself on such occasions, don't hang off the front edge of the chair, sit up straight, but lean back, look for support, don't fidget and then pay attention, smile, listen, smile, keep your wits about you, smile, and if necessary even contradict, but do it with restraint."[102]

She would soon realize the enormity of signing an oath to work for the Stasi. As she writes, "Afterward nothing was the same anymore."[103] Of her first meeting with the Stasi officers, she stated, "I have never been able to erase that from my memory."[104] She had, she recalls, massively misjudged the value of a signature, which the Stasi was subsequently to use as a "carte blanche" to lock her into lifelong "servitude."[105]

No sooner did Novak sign the Stasi's declaration than she promptly attempted, largely unsuccessfully, to undo its effects. She first divulged to Steinar, her Icelandic friend, the whole sorry tale of her expulsion from college and the visit from the Stasi. She told him about the Stasi's plans to use her as a honey trap to spy on the Icelandic students. Steinar was "shocked, deeply affected, as if paralyzed," she writes.[106] The Icelandic group was let into the secret, and Novak was emboldened to inform her new Stasi officer that she was not planning to come to their next meeting, thinking, as she writes: "That seemed settled."[107]

Roughly a month later, Novak, Steinar, and fellow student Klump attended a general meeting of all journalism students at which Novak and Klump were singled out for criticism. Their scholarships were to be withdrawn; they were to be banished for one year from the university and sent to work in a factory "because of a lack of political maturity."[108] When some students called for them to be banished "indefinitely," Novak refused to comply with the familiar ritual of offering "self-criticism," saying instead, "No thanks!"[109] She left the lecture theater along with Klump and Steinar. As a youth newspaper reported, this sealed their fate. According to the newspaper, "[Novak and Klump] have exposed themselves. They have become traitors to our socialist cause."[110]

Novak handed in her resignation from the party immediately and was promptly expelled from the university along with Klump. Persuaded by her Icelandic friend's staunch loyalty to her, Novak decided to accompany him back to Iceland. Steinar was so scarred by the event and the "mass hysteria" of his fellow students that he had decided to interrupt his studies in East Germany and return home to Iceland. "An attack like this lasts a lifetime,"[111] Novak writes. The lecture-hall ambush left an enduring and bitter impression on her, particularly the eagerness of her four hundred fellow students to join in the public pillorying: "I had lived three years with some of these students, eaten, discussed together, attended lectures, sat in meetings, hung out in pubs, overcome exam nerves, talked about intimate problems. I listened to their life stories, difficulties, troubles, I laughed with them, danced, trembled, shared in their anticipation, celebrated their successes. Within seconds I found myself condemned and abandoned to my fate."[112] She muses over fifty years later, "How could it happen, I thought, that even the fellow students with whom I was friends, raised their hands against me."[113]

Novak's officer was forced to write a report on the events, in which he described how Novak and Steinar left the general meeting "demonstratively" and resigned from the party. The Stasi consequently formulated a "resolution" on the plan to sever ties to "Renate, alias for Helga Novak, registration number: 817/57."[114] Klump went into exile in West Germany. Novak did well to escape the regime's vengeance by going into exile in Iceland, a country she knew precious little about and whose language she did not speak. She married the loyal Steinar, but she struggled to overcome her homesickness for East Germany. She felt she had left in haste and for the wrong motives: "After all I only left out of lack of courage—I did not have the heart to tell Steinar about my internal conflict."[115]

Despite her treatment by the regime, Novak soon began to hatch plans to return to the life she had abandoned in the GDR. To return would be to make amends for what had gone terribly wrong. She wanted "to finish what she had not even really begun." According to her, "I was already torn out, cut off, chased away, condemned, publicly branded a 'traitor,' without any prospect of correcting and defending this view. Condemned forever to work in the factories."[116] She continued to write desperately homesick letters to old friends, none of which ever reached their destination. The Stasi intercepted them all.[117] In 1958 she managed to return and found work in a fluorescent-tube laboratory connected to a television plant. Although the plans to enlist Novak as a Juliet agent had failed, the MfS hatched further plans for involving her. Possibly it could not believe its luck when Novak decided to return of her own volition to the GDR.

Paul Wiens: Recruiting Cosmopolitan Poets

In May 1961, only months before the construction of the Berlin Wall, Paul Wiens was elected president of the Berlin branch of the German Writers' Guild. Since the early 1950s Wiens had displayed appropriate enthusiasm for the industrial construction boom of the period, writing "factory reportages" that sang the praises of the achievements of "our young republic."[118] Published in 1953, Wiens's first volume of poetry, entitled *Beredte Welt* (Eloquent world), is bursting with revolutionary optimism, evidenced in a preponderance of spring metaphors in poems such as "Frühlingswein" (Spring wine) and "Stadtfrühling" (Spring in the city).[119] Wiens's unashamed panegyric poems in honor of Stalin placed him squarely in the camp of party poetry hacks.[120] Not all of Wiens's works were so openly conceived as party propaganda, however; for example, his "Ballad of Hans Kohlhaas" (1952) tackles a major figure in German literature (a late medieval merchant) and his embittered feud with authority.[121]

Wiens gradually moved away from his early propagandistic style in his next book of poems, *Nachrichten aus der dritten Welt* (News from the Third World, 1957). Written in the aftermath of the suppression of the uprisings in Hungary and Poland, a number of his poems, such as "Zeit für Träume" (Time for dreams), testify to a new sense of disillusionment. "When is the time for dreams? / Never. / And always," concludes "Zeit für Träume," with characteristic ambivalence.[122] Throughout the 1950s Wiens collaborated on a number of East German film projects. In 1957-58 a collaboration with Konrad Wolf, *Sonnensucher* (*Sun Seekers*), was initially banned during a crackdown on film production. Wiens was working with director Frank Vogel on a screenplay involving border crossings, ... *und deine Liebe auch* (... *And Your Love Too*), when the Berlin Wall went up on August 13, 1961. They hastily rewrote the script, producing one of the few films to deal with the theme of the Berlin Wall. It was applauded by the regime as "subtle, tender, and very human."[123]

Throughout the 1950s Wiens had not joined the SED, considering himself more a bourgeois writer rather than a Marxist or working-class one.[124] But he was a member of the key national organizations: the FDJ, the Society for German-Soviet Friendship, and the Free German Trade Union Federation (FDGB).[125] In 1959 he was awarded the National Prize of the GDR. By the ministry Wiens was seen as loyal and ideologically dependable, and, more importantly, his new position at the helm of the Berlin Writers' Guild gave him a key position of influence. Wiens would be a valuable recruit, particularly if he extended his sphere of influence abroad. Indeed, in this respect Wiens lived up to his promise; he went on to become a prized international asset on the literary scene and from 1964 he was a member of the East German chapter of PEN, the worldwide association of writers.[126] His role in the East German PEN Club, particularly as a member of its executive during 1980-82, was a key factor in his success as a secret agent. Along with Hermann Kant, Peter Edel, Fritz Rudolf Fries, and a few others, Wiens was among the PEN members who worked undercover as Stasi agents.[127]

It is easy to see why Wiens was such an attractive prospect for the ministry. He was charismatic, sophisticated, and extremely well connected. He also spoke three foreign languages: Russian, French, and Italian. With his trademark cigarette dangling from the left side of his mouth, he had a certain cachet that most of the communists from poorer, working-class backgrounds lacked.[128] In the files he is described as "proper and resolute" (*korrekt und konsequent*).[129] Unlike the working-class communist émigrés who had installed themselves in power, Wiens had finished secondary schooling and was a true cosmopolitan. That he also harbored serious cultural pretensions is apparent from his undercover name. Of all the writers who collaborated with the Stasi, Wiens chose for himself the most flattering cover name: he was registered as agent "Writer" (Dichter).

Initially Wiens came to the attention of Abteilung (department) 1 of Hauptabteilung V (HA V/1)—the department responsible for the state apparatus, churches, and culture, renamed HA XX in 1964—in connection with a secret operation named "Subverter" (Zersetzer) early in 1962.[130] At the time Wiens was still married to Erika Lautenschlager, and his daughter by this marriage, Maja, was ten years old. By 1961 the marriage had fallen into difficulties and Wiens was involved with a new woman, Erika Lange.[131] On Monday, March 5, 1962, a file was opened on Wiens. The file was commissioned by Johannes Schindler and two other officers from HA V/1, Hans Schiller and Helmut Troike. A promising start had been made, but none of the men involved in the case were under any illusions that Wiens would be "an easy catch." The Stasi files paint a curiously contradictory portrait of Wiens in the 1950s. On the one hand, one entry notes some concern "that in his attitude he objectively partially supported the enemy's attacks [*Angriffe des Gegners*] and negative and hostile elements inside the GDR."[132] On the other hand, the same file entry goes on to state that in the past Wiens had experienced a credibility problem among his peers, who had ridiculed him because he continued to sing the praises of Stalin long after Nikita Khrushchev's denunciation of the deceased Soviet leader in 1956. Although the Stasi was pleased that Wiens was toeing the party line in the Writers' Guild, he had raised eyebrows with "a series of peculiar views" (*eine Reihe eigenwilliger Auffassungen*).[133] Wiens's outspoken interventions at the Fifth Writers' Congress of May 1961 represented an important turning point that possibly cemented the Stasi's interest in him. In a spontaneous speech Wiens launched a stinging attack on West German writer Günter Grass and Grass's views on censorship.[134] Wiens's public partisanship for the regime at a time when its actions had sparked such widespread international opprobrium would not go unnoticed. He was duly acknowledged in 1962 and awarded the Heinrich Heine Prize for his "creative" articulation of support for the regime.[135]

Despite the wealth of detail about Wiens's political views, it is not immediately apparent from his file why Wiens gave in to the Stasi's pressure to enlist him. As a Holocaust survivor and a victim of fascism, perhaps he thought he had a right to be spared such indignities as snooping for the political police. There is no evidence that there were any grounds for blackmail, although Wiens's roving eye and unstable love life could easily have given the Stasi perfect material for constructing a blackmail case around his sexual infidelities. Furthermore, Wiens was not indebted to the Stasi, and he was well established by this stage in his career. The simplest answer to the question of what motivated Wiens at this point to acquiesce to the Stasi's demands is, as banal as it seems, money. His new wife brought two children into the marriage, and the family was soon to expand with the addition of two further children. He may have hoped that the material rewards for informing were greater than they actually proved. It is possible that Wiens believed that he could make a difference to cultural life with a little additional help from the Stasi while at the same time guaranteeing himself a degree of protection from persecution. He was prepared to live with an unsavory secret if it paid some material dividends and provided a buffer between him and the regime.

At the time of Wiens's recruitment the GDR was a little over fifteen years old. With the closing of its borders the crippling bloodletting of the months and years leading to the raising of the Berlin Wall—in official language, the "antifascist protective wall" (*Antifaschistischer Schutzwall*)—was over. For the next few years Wiens saw his role as a type of critical but sympathetic mirror that he held up to his officers in the hope of improving conditions.[136] Furthermore, Wiens may have thought that he could inoculate himself against censorship. In this he proved right; *Sonnensucher* was released soon after Wiens came to an agreement with the Stasi.

Wiens possessed a similarity with others like Novak in this chapter whom the Stasi approached; he was effectively an orphan, after having spent most of his childhood virtually without the company or supervision of parents. In this respect Wiens closely resembled Morgner's fictional character Konrad Tenner, who was scarred by the lack of a stable home environment. Morgner's *Amanda* states: "[Tenner] longed for motherly love and a home. He sought this from all the women he moved in with, without giving fatherly love in return. He had roamed around the country devastated by war, screaming out silently: love me, love me."[137] Tenner's partner, Laura, is used to excusing Tenner's "tyrannical outbursts" with reference to his traumatic wartime experiences.[138] Tenner could not tolerate insecurity, Laura writes, and tried to compensate for his deficient childhood by seeking the company of certain types of women. "Only women with children feel safe," he used to tell her.[139]

Wiens may have compensated for his difficult childhood by looking for father substitutes. He found them in either cultural mentors and superiors or fatherly secret-police officers. Certainly he was not alone in his hankering for strong authoritarian figures. Recent psychological research into the motivations of former informers suggests that informing fulfilled a deep need to belong to a family unit or to replace an absent father or mother.[140] If the inability to mourn the dead was widespread in both Germanies, so was a related inability to love, as Alexander and Margarete Mitscherlich famously argued in Die Unfähigkeit zu trauern (The inability to mourn, 1967). It is not improbable that Wiens's Jewish émigré background seriously predisposed him to all offers of love and support, whether from women with whom he was romantically involved, ideological mothers and fathers from the party and the Writers' Guild, or avuncular officers from the Ministry for State Security.

Wiens was recruited under Guideline 1/58, a more bureaucratic set of instructions than the previous two. Many of the earlier stipulations were tightened. Officers were now instructed to hold conspiratorial meetings in safe houses and to maintain "constant" contact with agents.[141] A written report detailing the reasons for each recruitment was to be filed with the officer's superior prior to making an approach. All of these procedures appear to have been adhered to in the case of Wiens.[142] The report recommending that Wiens be enlisted warns that he is no ordinary recruit. According to the report, he will require special handling: "When issuing assignments, one has to be careful in choosing a form that does not offend his self-esteem [Persönlichkeitsgefühl]."[143] Wiens demanded to be treated with respect and wished to be spared the more demeaning side of undercover work. He clearly viewed joining the Stasi as akin to becoming a member of an elite and prestigious secret society.

Moreover, Wiens apparently refused to commit himself in writing by signing the usual oath that the Stasi demanded of its new recruits. In many respects this was his own peculiar way of agreeing to join the initiated few of Stasi informants as long as it did not impinge on his sense of exceptionality. His files state: "In working for the Stasi the candidate most certainly does not want to enter into a dependent relationship [*Abhängigkeitsverhältnis*] with the Stasi."[144] The Stasi acquiesced on this point, as it often did[145] (and as it had done with other rising literary stars, such as Christa Wolf, whom it tried to recruit in the 1950s).[146] It agreed to use Wiens for information-gathering purposes only, recruiting him "on the basis of harvesting." This meant that the Stasi settled for a less formal association. Despite this waiver, the Stasi insisted on regular meetings (*Treffs*), and on arranging them in an orderly manner, either at prior meetings or by telephone.[147] Although the Stasi appears to have granted Wiens's wish to retain a modicum of independence, this was most likely because of his status. Certain practices could not be deviated from, even if Wiens was to be made to feel special in his relationship to the Stasi. Because of his status, Wiens was to enjoy certain privileges that lesser-known writers and Stasi recruits did not. Paul Gratzik was one such writer.

Paul Gratzik: Recruiting Expellees and Working-Class Writers

Citizens from disadvantaged social backgrounds were a favorite target of the Ministry for State Security. Contrary to common perceptions, East Germany was not an entirely classless society, and its founding led to large-scale social mobility within its borders in the 1940s and 1950s.[148] Specifically, the defeat of the Nazi regime precipitated downward social mobility for old elites and upward movement for the new members of East Germany's socialist intelligentsia.[149] For select groups the party created opportunities to rise up the social ladder, but to benefit from these chances an individual needed to belong to one of the so-called "progressive classes" among laborers or farmers. To this end, and in the spirit of encouraging inclusiveness, the regime tried to ensure that children of working-class parents were the preferred beneficiaries of affirmative-action initiatives. It was also eager to increase participation in education of those from low socio-economic classes.[150]

Members of the "progressive classes" could be receptive to a tap on the shoulder from the Stasi if a request for help was sweetened by the promise of a place at university. With such attention being paid to youth from the progressive classes, young communists with leadership potential—such as those already in the FDJ—presented an obvious loyalist pool from which to draw informers.[151] If the MfS could enlist the support of those who felt indebted to the state, then it was more likely to establish sustainable forms of collaboration. In addition, other developments toward the end of the 1950s contributed to the Stasi's interest in recruiting young writers from the working classes. The first of these was the introduction of the Bitterfeld Way in 1959, a type of socialist cultural revolution that involved a forward-looking scheme of partnerships between state industry and cultural bodies.[152] The program envisaged writers undertaking apprenticeships in the fields and factories and workers becoming writers. Cultural policymakers began to construct a new hero in the working-class writer, or the laborer (*Kumpel*) who writes. The catchcry directed at workers—"Grab a quill, comrade, the socialist German national culture needs you!"—encapsulated this push to manufacture a new class of patriotic writers.[153]

The second development was the advent of Western European- and U.S.-dominated youth culture; the era of rock and roll, blues, jazz, and blue jeans. Young people on both sides of the Iron Curtain were drawn to Western popular music, fashion, and dance crazes,[154] which caught cultural conservatives in both Germanies off guard.[155] In the East young people had been quick to join the insurgents in the uprising of June 17, 1953, and were well represented among those arrested.[156] The regime seemed determined to politicize popular youth culture and to demonize it as an exemplar of U.S. imperialism.[157] The Stasi urgently needed young recruits and reliable persons who could keep an eye on the universities, which by the mid-1950s were threatening to morph into hotbeds of subversion and counterrevolution.

As a twenty-seven-year-old son of a farm laborer who was expelled from East Prussia after the war, Paul Gratzik was the perfect candidate for both these tasks (see fig. 1). Gratzik was born November 30, 1935, in the village of Lindenhof in East Prussia, and he fled with his mother and five siblings at the end of the Second World War. He trained in the GDR as a carpenter, moving quickly into various leadership roles in the FDJ from 1954 onward. A note on his Stasi file states that he was recruited on the basis of his "impartial" (*unvoreingenommen*) ideological outlook.[158] More precisely, his working-class background, his age, and his political affiliations attracted the Stasi's attention. Gratzik's expellee background, in particular, meant that he could be offered irresistible nonfinancial rewards in the form of educational opportunities and career openings. The prospect of a politico-literary career that opened up through the Stasi possibly constituted the single most compelling reason for him to collaborate. Gratzik's father had died during the war, before the family fled westward. Like many expellees, Gratzik arrived in Germany at the end of the war with little more than the clothes on his back. If he was to get ahead, he would need father substitutes, connections, and mentors.

Gratzik epitomizes the type of informer recruited from a position of relative social disadvantage with the promise of greater things: a career, status, and social recognition. If presented as a duty, an honor, or a secret privilege replete with advantages, then the offer of working as an informant for the new regime could seem attractive to someone desperate to belong. Gratzik's refugee background, combined with his staunch anticapitalist beliefs, made him particularly susceptible to manipulation by the Stasi. Simmel argues that secret societies create ineffable bonds for their initiates, and the Stasi forged bonds, often in inexplicable ways, no matter how elusive they may have appeared to new recruits. It spoke to their multiple needs.

Gratzik was only ten years old when the communists installed themselves in the Soviet-occupied zone after the war. He was young enough to benefit from the stability of peace and the offer of schooling and training in the new socialist republic. Nevertheless, in June 1955 he fled to the West—the borders were still open—where he worked in the Ruhr area (Ruhrgebiet), becoming active in the Communist Party of Germany (West). He soon regretted his decision, and in 1956 he returned to East Berlin, inspired by the powerful Cold War ideologies of antifascism and anticapitalism.[159] When he came to the attention of the Stasi he was working in brown-coal mines and running a party clubhouse in Weimar.[160] He was not a party member as such, but as previously mentioned, he was deemed sufficiently impartial in his political views to be able to assist with Stasi enquiries.[161]

During the first year after August 13, 1961, when the borders between East and West Germany had been sealed, the Stasi contemplated initiating recruitment procedures for Gratzik. On February 3, 1962, the Stasi resolved to open an "IM candidate case" (IM-*Vorlauf*) in his name (see fig. 2).[162] The operation was the initiative of the Weimar local unit in the district of Erfurt. In Weimar the Stasi was concerned about the ongoing problems of teenagers (*Halbstarke*) and of "hooliganism." The so-called problem of Western youth culture, fashions, and music was compounded by a chronic lack of leisure options in the cities of the GDR. Young people were disaffected with the older generation and with authority in general—they were East Germany's own generation of "angry young men" and "rebels without a cause." This disaffection would soon culminate in full-scale rebellion in the Leipzig "beat riots" of 1965.[163] East German rebels found that they had an excellent cause in the state's draconian repression of youth culture.

In the Weimar office's IM candidate case file Gratzik is described as having the necessary ability to work with young people and as knowing "how to win their trust."[164] Initially the Stasi approached Gratzik in his office in relation to some worrisome incidents with youths.[165] Yet a handwritten note on file from May 11, 1962, states that he failed to appear at the next four arranged meetings.[166] Eventually, the first real meeting took place on May 17, 1962, when Gratzik (now informant "Peter") was given the task of providing a list of names of youths whom he knew.[167]

Gratzik was recruited after a surprisingly short probationary period.[168] Despite being prone to overindulging in alcohol, Gratzik was deemed an important source. After the next secret meeting (scheduled to take place in a restaurant) Gratzik appears to have cooperated, playing his part, initially at least, in keeping law and order. Around this time he also made observations about his visits to dance bars, often relaying verbatim banal conversations he had with various people. By the end of his first year of cooperation Gratzik was providing the Stasi with relatively useful, albeit low-grade, information on potentially undesirable behaviors—so-called "hooliganism," such as graffiti and defacement of monuments—and on group formations or concentrations of youths, such as biker clubs or "mobs" (*Meuten*).[169] In January 1963 he reported that he was no longer working in the FDJ district office and that he was hoping to train to be a teacher at the Institute for Teacher Education (Institut für Lehrerausbildung) in Weimar. In the meantime he was going to work in the Gas Combine Schwarze Pumpe.[170]

On the occasion of his next meeting with the Stasi, Gratzik was pleased to report that he had passed his entrance exams for the Institute for Teacher Education. He handed over reports on three persons who "had stepped out of line" and made abusive and defamatory comments about the GDR, albeit under the influence of alcohol.[171] According to Gratzik, these individuals had called the GDR "a big heap of shit," uttered profanities about Walter Ulbricht, the head of state, and dared to criticize the poor treatment of workers in the country.[172]

At this stage of his involvement with the Stasi, Gratzik gave the appearance of wanting to please his handlers and perform a useful service for his country. The secrets that he and the Stasi shared appear to have sustained him much in the manner proposed by Simmel, contributing to reciprocal, elite knowledge that only he and the Stasi were privy to. Moreover, this was progressive secret knowledge—secrets premised on what seemed to him to be a fundamentally good cause. As he confessed much later to Annekatrin Hendel, the director of the 2011 documentary film *Vaterlandsverräter* (Traitor to the fatherland), Gratzik was initially a passionate supporter of the regime: "I did not just affirm the GDR with my intellect but with my emotions as well." His patriotism was propelled by a fervent belief in socialism as the only viable alternative to capitalism. Years after the collapse of the regime his hatred of the capitalist bosses—"this pack of bastards" whom he held responsible for fascism—is still almost visceral in the film. There is most surely a grain of truth in Gratzik's truculent remark that "[he] had good reasons to do this work," meaning that he had had sound ideological reasons to work for the Stasi.

*

This chapter presents three cases of recruitment that took place in the period prior to and immediately following the building of the Berlin Wall, and these cases show the diversity of individuals in the cultural sphere whom the Stasis identified as candidates for recruitment. All three individuals were ostensibly chosen because of their political-ideological conviction, but the actuality of such conviction was open to interpretation. As the case of Paul Wiens suggests, the Stasi selected not only members of the SED but also successful non-party members of the new ruling cultural elite—patriots such as Jewish cosmopolitans, who had shown mixed allegiances to the regime. Paul Gratzik, a refugee and an orphan, was chosen because he was identified with the new political and cultural elites that the regime needed to win over. Despite his dubious departure for the West and return to the GDR, Gratzik had redeemed himself sufficiently to be considered trustworthy, and hence worthy of the Stasi's investment. As a university student Helga M. Novak also belonged to the new elites that the Stasi was desperate to enlist. All three were effectively fatherless when they were enlisted, and their varied backgrounds predisposed them, in different ways, to an approach from the Stasi.

Contact with the secret police seemed natural to Wiens and Gratzik when they were first approached. As a successful poet and scriptwriter for films—one who had shown his patriotic colors even at times of national crisis—Wiens possibly saw his recruitment as a logical extension of his affirmative stance and his professional roles. Further, he may have seen it as an appropriate complement to his growing seniority in cultural circles. It was a sign that the regime placed its trust in him and that he was among the chosen few. Perhaps he rationalized being approached by the Stasi in terms of taking on another official, albeit secret, function. The secrecy of his extra duties for the Stasi may have only contributed to their prestige in his eyes. Secrecy was something he tolerated only if his informing work was not seen as spying or snooping, but as leadership.

We can surmise from Gratzik's early activities that he, too, saw informing as a patriotic, antifascist call to duty and as an additional service that someone in leadership could be expected to carry out. Ideological reasons for cooperating were at the forefront for Wiens and Gratzik: commitment to the republic, to antifascism in Wiens's case, and to anticapitalism and the working classes in Gratzik's case. These ideological motivations made them vulnerable to an approach from the Stasi and the imposition of secrecy. Novak's case shows that blackmail was common but problematic, whereas Wiens and Gratzik demonstrate that the Stasi could appeal to a sense of duty and to law and order as added reasons for a person's cooperation.

Recruitment worked best for the Stasi when it did not resort to blackmail, and the secret police found other ways of interpellating subjects, such as flattery or appealing to a sense of duty or feelings of importance and prestige. Almost by way of an insurance policy, the Stasi often mobilized these emotions while exploiting human vulnerability in recruiting orphans, expellees, and victims—(like Wiens, a victim of fascism). Yet exploiting weaknesses was not enough to sustain collaboration, and thus the Stasi came to resort to other means, such as coercion, emotional blackmail, psychological manipulation, incentives, and economic, social, and emotional dependencies. In many instances, especially for writers who had already established themselves, the Stasi helped to create social, cultural, and political capital that informers came to identify with and view as their own achievements. This was a potent secret mix, and once brewed, Stasi informers found it devilishly hard to renounce. Although the temptation to reveal their secrets may have been strong, so too was the fear of consequences if they were dropped by the Stasi or caught out.

The writers discussed in this chapter were approached at two different historical junctures: Novak during the political crackdown in 1956 and Wiens and Gratzik immediately following the building of the Berlin Wall, in 1962. They were enlisted specifically in their capacities as members of the new ruling elites. As seen in chapter 3, this security emphasis changed when writers became a new focal point. But even before then, as discussed in chapter 2, for Wiens, Novak, and Gratzik, recruitment was far from the end of their Stasi file story.

2

Handling Informants and Sustaining Motivation, 1962–1972

Issued by the Ministry for State Security in 1950, 1952, and 1958, the first three ministerial guidelines for working with informants devoted little space to the subtleties of how, exactly, the desired relationship of trust between officer and informant was supposed to eventuate. Only Guideline 1/68 began to put into policy some of the lessons learned from the ministry's past experience with running agents. Apart from stressing the value of secrecy, the section in 1/68 dedicated to "conspiring and secrecy" (*Konspiration und Geheimhaltung*) spelled out in more detail the central pillars on which a sustainable cooperation should be built.[1] As the MfS discovered, many problems with recruits set in after the initial successful enlisting, irrespective of an individual's original motive for joining. Blackmail (as in the case of Helga M. Novak) was a common method of recruitment, despite its obvious drawbacks. It proved even less effective as a long-term means of sustaining a good working relationship and of motivating informers. Where blackmail failed, this failure would prove to be a sore point that the MfS could ill afford to ignore. Moreover, the ministry was often reluctant to admit to having failed to properly recruit a strategically useful informant—and for such an informant, a refusal to participate in the secret surveillance society could have devastating impacts. As explored in this chapter, Novak's case well demonstrates such impacts.

Successful recruitments also continued to pose challenges for the ministry in its second decade. Whether they were writers with existing reputations or aspiring novices, literary recruits in particular belonged to a special breed of recruit that often required kid-glove treatment. In the other two case studies presented in this chapter, those of Paul Wiens and Paul Gratzik, and in the representative anecdotes chosen from their file stories, I focus on several of the operational problems that arose after an apparently smooth and unproblematic recruitment, even one founded on ideological conviction. For writers performing espionage work there were both perceivable benefits and noticeable drawbacks.

The benefits often came in the form of professional advantages. In performing clandestine political tasks assigned to them by the Stasi, writers no doubt gained crucial insight into power and its impact on cultural politics. The practice of espionage work effectively allowed them privileged access to secret knowledge about decisions that affected their livelihood. For informers like Wiens these clandestine connections to power had, in some respects, the desired effect of creating a concealed social and cultural capital. This capital comprised networks and channels to ministers and functionaries high up in the Ministry for Culture, for instance, which Wiens could draw on when needed. Covert social capital was, however, rather limited in its efficacy, given that it could never be mobilized in visible ways that would draw attention to itself. Secret ties to cultural power could nevertheless be a powerful motivator for informers, as long as such ties could be harnessed inconspicuously and put to work behind the scenes. And even when illicit contacts inside the MfS proved to have less clout than informers imagined, at the very least these contacts helped informers to wrangle a better deal for themselves. These rewards, if available (and there was no way of knowing if they would be), could be formative in a writer's career and come at a crucial time when the iciest of freezes otherwise made writing and publishing virtually impossible. Hence these protective forms of capital that shielded informants from repression and censorship proved extraordinarily hard to resist.

By the same token, there were perceptible drawbacks for informants that ranged from a loss of autonomy and independence to a debilitating form of dependency. Trust also loomed large in the lives of some informants, either once they faced some of the side effects of their actions for the Stasi or when they realized that, in their role as informants, trust was a one-way street. Two of the cases discussed in this chapter show how disaffection with the rituals of undercover work came to impede informers' commitment to the ministry. Writers, particularly those with established careers, often became disillusioned with undercover work. What Gary Bruce has observed in relation to some Stasi officers also holds true for informants; they grew disenchanted "with the constant search for regime opponents."[2]

Many writers enlisted as informers felt incapable of reconciling the disparate parts of their double lives (and their double habitus) as professional poets and dramatists by day and Stasi-controlled informants by night. For these writers working for the Stasi did not result in the sorts of internalized behaviors the secret police would have liked. For the Stasi this resistance to having one's life structured by the Stasi was an unwanted side effect of recruiting intellectuals to the ministry. All divisions, district offices, and employees of the Stasi were pressured to meet strict targets for recruiting agents, though there were tough internal controls to ensure that officers did not invent informers or fake their reports.[3] The intense atmosphere of competition within departments and among employees guaranteed that case officers were sufficiently motivated to keep their informers on track to meet targets and to produce high quantities of quality intelligence from their sources so as to further their own careers. Ironically, the institutional demands to improve productivity resulted in the Stasi running agents who were far from satisfactory and, in some cases, openly recalcitrant. The cannier of these informers spotted this pattern as a weakness and used it to their own advantage.

Officers' skills in handling agents were seriously challenged when they were running writers as informants. In many cases the Stasi was unable to keep informants. There were two common scenarios for breaking off relations with the secret police. In one scenario the separation was at the Stasi's behest and was pursued when the informant was inefficient or unreliable.

According to the official line, these files were closed because of the recruit's so-called "lack of perspective" (*Perspektivlosigkeit*).[4] The Stasi could also close a file, sometimes on a productive source, in response to an unforeseen, random event. The most widespread of such events was when an informant's cover was blown, either by accident or deliberately, and the source "deconspired" (*dekonspirierte*).[5] Far less frequently, a source would become a "quitter" (*Aussteiger*), actively endeavoring, either abruptly or over a period of time, to sever his or her connections to the Stasi. The figure of the dropout or quitter, as Joachim Walther points out, contradicts the popular myth that it was impossible to refuse to collaborate with the Stasi. Although the Stasi liked to issue the threat "once a spy always a spy," the reality was rather different.[6]

Two common ways of quitting that informers found were parading their lack of enthusiasm for surveillance work and underwhelming performance in the field.[7] In reality many disaffected informants tried a wide range of different strategies, sometimes over an extended period, to discourage the security forces from pursuing them. Some of these measures were enacted through passive-aggressive behavior, such as missing appointments or turning up late and unprepared to meetings. Informers had a greater chance of success when they coupled such strategies with other, more proactive, forms of resistance or acts of blatant insubordination (disclosing one's Stasi contacts to family members or colleagues, for example, or committing criminal deeds). Such breaches of the sacrosanct code of silence could, however, result in nasty repercussions, and many were not prepared to risk going down this route. Fear and ignorance constrained most novice informants, as well as many seasoned informants, from making full use of their legal right to refuse.

In rare cases, blowing one's cover deliberately, or even engaging in subversive activities, was not enough to put the Stasi off. If the Stasi was particularly keen on running an agent, it could sometimes find ways of circumventing such indiscretions. A common method in cases of "deconspiring" was to force the person who had been inadvertently let into the secret of the informer's Stasi connections to sign a statuary declaration, whereby he or she swore to remain silent. Each case of blown cover, however, was handled differently; the Stasi's response depended on how critical the source was to an operation. Paul Gratzik's case shows that some serially frustrated and intentionally unreliable informants tried to quit over a period of ten to fifteen years.

Paul Gratzik: Questions of Trust and Procrastination

In 1964 three years after the building of the Berlin Wall, and barely two years after Gratzik's recruitment by the Stasi, he first showed impatience with his undercover routine. Although Gratzik at first had been ideologically motivated to cooperate with the Stasi, he had also hoped to further his own cultural ambitions. Yet by 1964 he was experiencing difficulties with sustaining motivation and becoming increasingly aware of the disconnection between his efforts for the Stasi and the outcomes of his actions. Psychologists would say he was caught in an "approach loop," in which he sought opportunities to realize his personal goals—here his desire for career opportunities as a cultural functionary—but was frustrated because he could not see enough opportunities to realize them.[8]

Early in 1964 Gratzik was instructed to observe church groups in Weimar. In a rather lame attempt to vent his disquiet he inserted into one of his reports a juvenile, argumentative postscript that sums up his mounting irritation with the tedium of carrying out undercover operations: "I find it stupid to have to write a report about everything. You must trust my intelligence enough to let me report on things on my own, when I know some precise facts."[9] As though his annoyance were not obvious enough, Gratzik underlined part of this sentence in red pen. He then reiterated his opinion that it was a waste of time to report on each meeting of the church groups individually.

On average Gratzik was earning from thirty to fifty East German marks for each of these reports, and although the extra income was welcome, the money was not a sufficiently powerful incentive for him to continue. He saw little sense in report writing when there was no issue worth reporting on, and he wanted to be given more license to decide for himself when he reported on events. The short leash that the Stasi had secured around him was starting to chafe. Moreover, Gratzik now began to question the

Stasi's motive for wanting to gather intelligence on youth activities in the first place. Perhaps rather perversely, he now decided to pass on less rather than more detailed information. Whereas previously he had had no qualms about relaying derogatory remarks made in public houses, he now appeared to develop scruples about denouncing his teachers and fellow students at Weimar's Institute for Teacher Education.

The Stasi was quick to suppress Gratzik's petulant outburst, hoping to address these teething troubles with the appointment of a new officer, code-named "Anton," on March 18, 1965.[10] Nonetheless, even this more experienced officer was unable to exert greater control over Gratzik. In April 1965 "Anton" assigned Gratzik a new task of far greater complexity that was daunting to the novice informer, who had far more interesting projects underway as a student at the teacher's college. Gratzik's new brief was to assess whether teachers were doing their jobs as socialist educators.[11]

Gratzik drew up a one-page list of his teachers, annotated with their areas of scholarly interest, but the Stasi pushed him further, insisting on more detail and more active participation from him. In fact the one-page list contained little useful information; he was instructed to return with more facts about his teachers. A brief of this kind would be a challenge for any student, given that it required that he assess areas of the institution typically difficult for a student to access. For a student working for the Stasi the task was doubly tricky. Gratzik was supposed to incriminate teachers he may have liked and was dependent on, at the very least for good grades.

From the files, it appears that Gratzik, to his credit, rose to the challenge by not even attempting to undertake the job. Instead, he slyly inserted into his reports some constructive criticism of the education system that fellow students had voiced to him. For instance, he stated that students wanted more freedom to choose their class assignment topics.[12] This was hardly the sort of report the Stasi was hoping for, and again Gratzik incurred a reprimand. He was instructed to provide more evidence of the differences between the party and the management of the institute.[13]

Reading material in Gratzik's file from this time, it is not hard to see that the rookie informer was becoming more adept at refusing or at least sabotaging the Stasi's assignments. He began to procrastinate, presumably reasoning that if he bungled tasks or was too slow to produce results, there was a greater chance that the Stasi would drop him. Indeed, Gratzik's reporting back was found to be deficient, and he was told that his reports "ought to be better formulated" and less "theatrical."[14] In June 1965 Gratzik was instructed to gather opinions about certain teachers. He did so, but collected patently irrelevant views—for instance, teachers calling student cabarets "stupid"[15] and student opinions about the director's attire, such as, "Does he have a suit? As a director he really ought to dress differently."[16]

If Gratzik's intelligence on his teachers was not entirely harmless, it was not incriminating. His comments about a student's view of the director's dress sense, for instance, were too personal to be of operative use. Another remark he passed on may have captured the student's dislike of the director, but it contained little incriminating material: "I know I cannot stand the guy I only need to see his false grin and I feel sick [*mir wird anders*]."[17] Lastly on the subject of the director Gratzik reported that he was more feared than liked by the students.[18] The Stasi would have had trouble distilling any actionable information from this selection of apparently rather uncensored pubescent opinions and unedited reports.

Instead, the file offers persuasive evidence of Gratzik's growing ambivalence toward the Stasi during one of the ideological flashpoints in the history of the GDR, at the end of 1965. As further detailed below, students and teachers in Leipzig came under intense scrutiny, and a number were denounced and expelled on ideological grounds. Reflecting his political conformism, Gratzik does not appear to have been especially outraged by the harsh treatment of his fellow students in Leipzig or in Weimar, remarking simply that the "opinions of students were not taken into account."[19] He mentions students being expelled in Weimar and singles out one case in particular, concluding his report by recommending self-importantly "that this case be investigated once more."[20]

When asked to report on an official event, a writers' congress in May 1965 that he was privileged to attend, Gratzik's reporting style was perfunctory, and his report surprisingly flat. Around 220 people attended, including writers from the United States and the Soviet Union along with East Germany's literary intelligentsia, such as Anna Seghers, Bruno Apitz, and Christa Wolf. But the cocky young Stasi employee reported categorically that the meeting was "not a success."[21] His reason, which would surely have irritated his officers, was that all three speakers—whom he fails to mention by name—"spoke about the same theme and were repetitive."[22] This would hardly have been news to the Stasi; in fact such consistency among the speakers showed that the literary meeting was conducted as it should have been. But stated by someone who should have been counting himself lucky to be at university at all, Gratzik's impression is notably disrespectful. Gratzik goes on to point out that the speakers repeated themselves because all of the talks were "coordinated [*abgesprochen*] in advance."[23] The net effect of these boring talks was that "all creative discussion" was stifled. As refreshing as this verdict is—capturing in a nutshell the lack of spontaneity and freedom of speech in the German Writers' Guild—it was definitely not what the Stasi, the party, or those in the Writers' Guild would have wanted to hear.

Looking back on this episode in an interview given for the film documentary *Vaterlandsverräter*, Gratzik seems almost disgusted by the chutzpah of the Stasi Young Turk who made these cheeky remarks. "Pah! Look at the small fry, the little asshole, Paul Gratzik," he tells the director Annekatrin Hendel. By July 1965 Gratzik's academic successes at the teacher's college had patently made him more gallivant in his manner of reporting. He seemed decidedly more upbeat in his meetings—his officer remarked at one point that his demeanor "border[ed] on the arrogant"[24]—and his increasing professional confidence had perhaps buoyed him in his hopes of shaking off the Stasi altogether. He may even have imagined that one day he would graduate from the Stasi's stifling tutelage, much as he was about to graduate from university. Despite his nonchalance, for the rest of 1965 the Stasi granted Gratzik some latitude to prepare for his exams. In the interim his officers papered over the cracks in the relationship with this informant by using stock phrases, such as "[discussions with him were] objective and reasonable."[25] After all, because Gratzik hoped to go on to further study at university and gain admission to the reputable Institute for Literature Johannes R. Becher, the Stasi was willing to turn a blind eye if it gained a valuable source at the center of the East German literary world.

From Gratzik's perspective, this would bring him a step closer to realizing his goal of becoming a writer.[26]

Meanwhile, in his professional life, Gratzik was busy adding to his academic achievements. He passed his teacher exams and was soon able to list further creative triumphs as well. In 1966 his first play, titled *Der andere Weg* (The other road), was produced in a student theater production. Gratzik's timing was impeccable. His play aligned with the latest political climate shift ushered in by the draconian Eleventh Plenary of the SED's Central Committee of 1965, which made scapegoats of three outspoken figures—author Stefan Heym, chemist and writer Robert Havemann, and poet and ballad singer Wolf Biermann. The Eleventh Plenary represented a particularly severe setback for a new batch of innovative films that were in the pipeline from Deutsche Film-Aktiengesellschaft (DEFA), the GDR's state-run group of film studios. These films were promptly banned and relegated to the East German film industry's bottom draw.[27] By contrast, the party welcomed Gratzik's play because of the exemplary way it tackled the highly topical theme of aimless youths by showing that they could find their way back into society.[28]

More by dint of political circumstance than by virtue of his talents, Gratzik's career as a dramatist was about to take off, and he was granted (albeit not entirely intentionally) a short-lived reprieve by the Stasi. The reprieve occurred as he was making plans to study literature in Leipzig. The move to a new city required that he be handed over to a new department. In July 1966 a final meeting to organize this was held with Gratzik's Weimar handlers.[29] Reading between the lines of the documentation, it appears that the Weimar office may well have been relieved to be rid of their troublesome agent "Peter." It appears that Gratzik made the most of being in a Stasi-induced limbo between departments—he exploited the bureaucratic confusion over who ought to be controlling him.

Although formally handed over to Leipzig in April 1967, Gratzik failed to report for duty. In May he had given assurances that he "was interested in collaborating while he was studying in Leipzig."[30] Yet when Lieutenant Tinneberg from the Leipzig district office (*Kreisdienststelle*) finally managed to establish contact in December 1967, he found to his dismay that he had to engage in "arduous discussions about problems with cultural policy."[31] Pep talks notwithstanding, Gratzik continued to miss appointments for a whole year after the first contact with Tinneberg. The Leipzig office also seems to have been glad to hand Gratzik on to someone else. Tinneberg declared pessimistically: "There is no future for him within our area of responsibility."[32] Such a view was hardly surprising, given that by this time Gratzik and others had been expelled from university. Apart from his "lack of clarity in ideological matters," Gratzik had displayed a cavalier attitude to socialist discipline, and during a potato harvest (part of a compulsory labor program for students) he had absented himself to go drinking.[33] Only once he had been handed over to the district office of Dippoldiswalde in Dresden and assigned a new officer, First Lieutenant Günter Wenzel, in February 1969, was Gratzik finally brought back on track.[34]

The department that first proposed enlisting Gratzik as an informant was convinced that the ideological stars had aligned with its choice of candidate, but Gratzik was far from an ideal recruit. But although he had tried to evade his handlers and been less than diligent in his reporting, his first attempt at quitting had failed. At this point the Stasi managed to salvage its informant by assigning him a new officer, and this proved to be a turning point in Gratzik's relationship with the Stasi.

For the new officer, Wenzel, Gratzik became a major accomplishment. Over the course of the collaboration the interpersonal relationship that Gratzik formed with Wenzel became pivotal in overcoming the initial troubles that the Stasi experienced running Gratzik as an informer. From Gratzik's perspective—that of a budding young dramatist—the relationship was key to converting the prestige he was earning in literary and dramatic circles for his acclaimed plays into a new kind of symbolic and cultural capital that was eminently bankable. Certainly the primary source of this windfall, the Stasi, remained a secret, but the capital his relationship with the Stasi generated was visible and tangible, both for Gratzik and for his peers. Hence Gratzik's membership in the secret surveillance society must be considered an integral part of his public persona and of his sense of self-esteem and entitlement, which was healthy by 1969. If Gratzik was indebted to the Stasi for feathering his career when he most needed support, this was his and the

Stasi's secret. The Stasi had effectively given him a symbolic advance in allowing him to study in Weimar and then in Leipzig and by permitting the limelight to fall on the unknown Gratzik in the aftermath of the Eleventh Plenary, a time when most playwrights' careers were faltering.[35] From the Stasi's perspective, there would soon be time for that "cash advance" to be paid back.

Helga M. Novak: Rehabilitating a Defected Agent

Helga M. Novak belongs to the category of informers who voluntarily quit, namely in a separation that was initiated by the Stasi while having been prompted by inactivity and inappropriate behavior on the part of the agent. As Novak's case shows, even once the Stasi had closed an informant's file, it could still exact revenge for disloyalty. The archive shows that the Stasi had an uncannily good memory with respect to ideological recalcitrance. Once committed to file, the black mark against Novak's name, which stemmed from her run-in with the Stasi in the 1950s, proved almost impossible to remove. The Stasi, it seems, was not prepared to forget her transgression. It is no exaggeration to assert that for the Stasi revenge was sometimes a dish best served cold.

Novak represents a special case of an informer who experienced no benefits and only protracted hardship from her brief encounter with the Stasi. She was an orphan with keen literary aspirations, and the Stasi systematically sought out and identified weaknesses in her behavior and exploited them. When she refused to cooperate it wilfully destroyed her career prospects in her home country. As one reviewer remarked regretfully on the occasion of her death, Novak belongs "unjustly" among the "least known authors in Germany."[36] Moreover, despite crossing the Stasi, in the following years Novak refused to temper her forthright behavior and her staunch criticism of Stalinist practices.

Novak's case challenges strict distinctions between victim and perpetrator. The mere existence of a perpetrator file in the Stasi archives is certainly insufficient grounds for judging her a collaborator. As with all cases of informers, any benefits an informer gained from aligning his or her fortunes with the Stasi need to be weighed against the hardship he or she subsequently suffered at the hands of the security forces or the regime. Novak's period of collaborating was too fleeting and trifling for any benefits to accrue. Instead, Novak suffered an almost epic series of setbacks and disadvantages, all stemming from one fateful encounter that seemed to dog her throughout her adult life.

Early in 1958, upon her hasty and ill-advised first return from exile in Iceland to East Berlin, Novak worked shifts on an assembly line in the Berlin Radio and Television Technology Works with six hundred other women while pregnant with her first child by Steinar. Her delight at seeing old friends was soon tempered when she was reminded that she was supposed to serve a six-month jail sentence for the serious offense of "fleeing the republic" (*Republikflucht*). Her sentence was converted and she was allowed to work instead, provided she did not leave the boundaries of Berlin. The SED was the first to become interested in her. It demanded that she return her party membership book, fearful that she had sold it while in the West. Next to make contact was the Stasi, which had duly registered her reappearance and noted her exact whereabouts: "The assessment of the head of department Sandner states: N. is reliable, punctual, obliging, collegial, performs satisfactorily, she is willing and displays a great interest in her work."[37]

The Stasi continued to keep Novak under observation after the birth of her son. Once she had been moved from shift work to another department in the same factory, under a supervisor she got along well with, two officers decided the time was ripe to pay her a visit. This occurred in "a relatively empty room, an office without the usual mess of papers, coffee cups, typewriter clatter, without these eternally half withered indoor plants and overflowing wastepaper baskets."[38] As she writes in her autobiography, Novak realized that at this point she had nothing to fear from the Stasi: "[I] could not sink any lower in their eyes than becoming an unskilled worker. What could they still do to me, how could they force me? Force me to do what? They could do nothing to me, I thought and recovered my self-confidence."[39]

This visit had the appearance of being more of a social call. The Stasi was no doubt curious about what had motivated an illegal refugee to return to the country she had once fled. In the "report on making contact" (*Bericht zur Kontaktaufnahme*) filed on November 14, 1959, Master Sergeant (*Oberfeldwebel*) Pahl states that the ministry wished to see if "secret informant Renate" could be put back into the field. Novak is reported to have admitted that her behavior in 1957 was wrong.[40] In a report filed a month later, Pahl claims, furthermore, that her regrets were genuine, and that she wished to "make amends for her mistakes."[41] In fact, Novak was keen to resume her studies and to continue her career as a journalist, which is also noted in these reports.[42]

The same meeting was also designed to ascertain whether Novak would inform on her new supervisor. The two reports of late 1959 express this in the general terms of a request to inform on "difficulties in the production of the new television tube plant."[43] According to her file, Novak agreed to this request.[44] However, Novak's recollection is different. When she retorted that she was not willing to sign any documents, the two men laughed at her, replying that they "only wanted to enquire about her working conditions, if [she] wanted to make any complaints. Since [she] wasn't here entirely of [her] own volition."[45] When Novak told them that she was "there entirely voluntarily,"[46] the two men disappeared as quickly as they had appeared. Probably they retained suspicions that Novak was acting on behalf of a hostile espionage agency. Yet their visit still served the purpose of intimidating her. Around the same time, Novak's supervisor, keen to assist her new friend, commenced enquiries about whether Novak could return to Leipzig to complete her journalism studies. By the time Novak could be readmitted to the Institute for Journalism, however, her private life had taken another unpredictable turn, and she had decided to marry Örn, Steinar's Icelandic friend, and return with him to Iceland.

Novak stayed in Iceland after the birth of her daughter, despite quickly becoming estranged from Örn and suffering a bout of depression. Throughout the tumultuous days of the summer of 1961 when the Berlin Wall was built, Novak was working in the north of Iceland, salting fish during the herring season. In the winter of 1961–62 she became homesick for Germany again and returned for a short, legal visit via a trawler on the North Sea. Yet her visit aroused suspicion, her bags were searched, and seventeen of her first poems were confiscated. Soon afterward Novak returned home to Iceland, and thus began a new phase of her life living in a *ménage à trois* with her second husband, Örn, and her new partner, Dagur. A year later she left Iceland and traveled to Palermo in Sicily, where she lived until 1964 with Dagur, writing poetry, until finally she managed to interest the West German publisher Luchterhand in publishing her work.

Back in Iceland and still living with Örn after the trip to Palermo, Novak stumbled across the writings of Robert Havemann. To her, at least, Havemann was an unknown professor at the Humboldt University in East Berlin. After reading his series of lectures *Dialektik ohne Dogma* (Dialectic without dogma), which had been published in the West in 1964, she felt compelled to return to Leipzig University's Institute for Journalism. She wanted to see if socialism had changed. As she writes, Havemann was someone who rebelled against rigid norms under socialism, servility, and hypocrisy, and who did not regard socialism as a goal but as a path and communism as a desirable utopia that would never be attained. He envisioned a society in which all men were equal and free, in which the exploitation of some by others had been abolished.[47] And if enlightened works such as Havemann's could be published—albeit only in the West—Novak thought she could see signs of the winds of change. "Perhaps cultural politics is undergoing a shift," she surmised, only partly correctly. She further explains what motivated her to return to the GDR: "If it was possible to give lectures like these in the GDR then something was afoot that I wanted to be part of. And apart from this I wanted to lay claim to the part of the people's property that I had created. And I was still a citizen of the GDR."[48]

Novak returned to Leipzig in the autumn of 1965 with a volume of poetry in hand that had been published in Iceland, and doors to the Institute for Literature Johannes R. Becher seemed, miraculously, to open to her. Assured by friends that "you [could] speak more openly about things of late,"[49] she arrived at a time when the Russians were more favorably disposed to Icelanders and "Iceland did not seem politically suspect."[50] Impressed by the caliber of her poems, Georg Maurer, professor of poetry at the Institute for Literature, recommended she be accepted back. As Novak had suspected, she arrived in Leipzig at a time when a thorough thaw in cultural politics was underway. "All systems have holes,"[51] she writes in her autobiography—but though Novak had chanced upon a fortuitous opening in what had been a tightly closed system, holes such as these were short-lived. They also proved to be a seductive trap for the hopelessly homesick and idealistic Novak. Just a small window of opportunity was open before December 1965, when one of the frostiest ice ages in East German cultural history struck and Novak found herself trapped at its epicenter.

As she had hoped, Novak was introduced to Havemann; she visited him in his domicile in the village of Grünheide, where he spent most of his time after his dismissal from his professorship and expulsion from the party for those lectures that had so fascinated Novak in Iceland. On one visit Havemann gave Novak a copy of a controversial essay he had written campaigning for the removal of the ten-year ban on the communist party in West Germany. As Novak later discovered, the Stasi's interpretation of this gesture was that she was providing a "courier service"[52] to Havemann.

Havemann and Novak quickly became lovers; she was one of his many, which Novak freely admits in her memoir. Of course this fact did not escape the Stasi, sensitized as it was to the most intimate details of Novak's private life. The second of her Stasi files, which was opened in 1965 by HA XX/1/3, reports that Novak had an "intimate relationship with Professor Havemann and acquired her intellectual instruments from him [*sich dort ihr geistiges Rüstzeug holte*]. She behaved like a ringleader and was inciting others to create riotous scenes."[53] In some respects, the first part of this statement was true. Many of Novak and Havemann's meetings revolved around Havemann's views on Eurocommunism. The Stasi also collected gossip about other affairs that Novak might be having, remarking: "She is also supposed to have an intimate relationship with the writer CZECHOWSKI, Karl-Heinz."[54]

Novak found herself reinvigorated and confirmed in her belief that socialism could be reformed, as she wrote enthusiastically to her husband in Iceland: "The conversations with him [Havemann] got me back on my feet. He could listen, showed interest whenever he asked about Iceland, my work in the fishery industry or my opinions."[55] On her second visit to Havemann, Novak divulged her secret about her brush with the Stasi in 1957 and was astonished to hear that her story was not so very different from his own: "Robert was not only understanding of my behavior eight years ago but hinted at the fact that he too had served this firm. If I understood him correctly it was more than what I did."⁵⁶ Havemann was considered a major security threat to the regime—"enemy of the people no. 1" (*Volksfeind Nr. Eins*).⁵⁷ He was the victim of massive surveillance operations including house arrest in 1976; it has now been confirmed he also had contacts to the Stasi from 1949 to 1963. After he was registered in 1956 as "Secret Informant Leitz,"⁵⁸ Havemann met around sixty times with officers from the Stasi, with the most intense period of informing from 1956 to 1959.⁵⁹

The Stasi promptly planted several spies who were instructed to report on Novak's movements. Novak seems to have suspected one of them, "Natascha."⁶⁰ Another informant was "Anne," who reported on Novak's ostentatious and flirtatious behavior during a cocktail party. "Anne" also passed on a "decadent" poem that Novak had written about her time in Palermo, the contents of which her Stasi officers found difficult to believe, adding a scathing note to this effect on her file: "She claims to have been in Palermo."⁶¹

Apart from her affair with Havemann, Novak considered herself exemplary in her behavior, which had even occasioned the director of the Institute for Literature, Max Walter Schulz, to describe her as "very disciplined."⁶² None of this was to matter, however, when, on the eve of the Eleventh Plenary of the Central Committee, on December 14, 1965, "all tolerance was lost,"⁶³ and Novak received notice that she had been expelled from the university. The party had singled out for public censure another writer, Dieter Mucke, whose "antisocialist" short story Novak had publicly defended.⁶⁴ Both the management of Leipzig University and the party hoped that Novak would leave to protest against the treatment of Mucke, and that, as a result, two unwanted birds would be dispatched with one stone. As her Stasi file records, "it was hoped to solve the problem VIGFUSSEN, Helga this way."⁶⁵ The original plan might have been to deny Novak a re-entry permit when she returned home to the GDR from Iceland after Christmas. But when she refused to leave the university of her own accord—"at the end of the talks and the consultations, however, she declared that she had changed her mind and would stay at the Institute"⁶⁶—she was promptly expelled.

Novak was alleged to have been couriering illegal writings for Havemann. Moreover, one of her poems had touched on the topic of an autumn manoeuver of Warsaw Pact troops, and the regime considered this "a terrible offense."[67] According to one section of her Stasi file, Novak "advocated an anarchic ideal of the writer" because she combined "demands for freedom of criticism and a Havemann-style of freedom of the press" with discussions about writers' "dissolute lifestyle" (*Lotterleben*).[68] The day after Novak was suspended from university, a parcel containing author copies of her Luchterhand volume of poetry arrived for her; the Stasi confiscated one copy for the record. Later, her book was also confiscated at the Leipzig book fair. Her scholarship payments were stopped, and her plans to publish her poems in the East were shelved. By March 1966 she had been issued with an exit visa to emigrate permanently to Iceland, and her East German passport was revoked. As her Stasi file makes perfectly clear, this meant she was effectively banned from ever returning to the country of her birth: "With the revoking of her citizenship an automatic entry and transit ban comes into force."[69] Although she had hitherto been unable to obtain Icelandic citizenship, Novak was nonetheless instructed to apply for it. In the words of her autobiography, "And so I was blacklisted in the GDR until 1989."[70]

Refusing to take no for an answer, in July 1967 Novak applied to return to the GDR but was promptly refused an entry visa. Virtually unknown in the West, she had no means of redress at her disposal. As argued in later chapters, the way she was treated after her refusal to collaborate with the secret service was in many respects typical of the regime's handling of reform socialists such as Havemann and Biermann in the 1960s and 1970s; in many other ways, it was far more vengeful than the usual treatment doled out to those writers whom the Stasi tried but failed to recruit.[71]

Paul Wiens: Giving Up on Agent "Writer"

By the winter of 1967–68, Paul Wiens had been informing for the Stasi sporadically for almost seven years. Still, the preliminary file, the "IM candidate case" (IM-*Vorlauf*) opened in 1962, had not led to a more permanent arrangement or even a proper formal process of registration, namely the creation of an "IM case file" (IM-*Vorgang-Akte*).[72] On January 8, 1968, Lieutenant

Schiller took time out to take stock of his informants. In a written report he admits that Secret Informant "Writer" had veered so far off track as to make further work with him pointless: "The GI [secret informant] adopts a critical [*ablehnende*] viewpoint with regard to the cultural politics of our party and government and advances in part a hostile position. In consequence his information has increasingly assumed a confusing [*desorientierenden*] character which prohibits further cooperation with us on security grounds."[73] Here Schiller explains the sticking point that Wiens was not prepared to sign an oath with the ministry; the writer had stipulated that the Stasi respect his "above average individualism."[74] By now Wiens had strayed too far from current dogma for comfort, and his attitudes on various issues bordered on being downright "antisocialist."

In the course of the 1960s Wiens's opinions on culture and politics had vacillated. Already in 1961 he had taken a stance critical of party politics on the polarizing issue of the dramatist Heiner Müller; he spoke out in support of Müller, who had been expelled from the Writers' Guild because of unpaid dues (Müller himself recounts this rather flippantly).[75] He fell into line soon after and managed to redeem himself by expressing his public approval of the regime's construction of the Berlin Wall, as already discussed. In April 1963 Wiens raised eyebrows again when he defended another recalcitrant writer based in the GDR. This time it was the Jewish satirist Günter Kunert, who had come under fire for lambasting the regime. One informant who was spying on Wiens forcefully concluded that Wiens himself was a problem: "Wiens may be a decent fellow but is by and large a dreamer, who needs to be told when to shut up."[76]

Around the time of the Eleventh Plenary, Wiens's attitudes toward the party's treatment of writers changed again.[77] In 1969 it was noted in his Stasi file that Wiens was said to pose provocative questions about wanting greater freedom of information.[78] In his dual capacity as president of the Berlin section of the German Writers' Guild and undercover provocateur for the Stasi, Wiens was asked to keep the poet Reiner Kunze under surveillance in the mid-1960s. Kunze had well-established contacts to Czech writers, having translated their works. Early in 1961 he was refused a travel visa to go to Czechoslovakia and meet with authors whose works he was translating. Wiens relayed Kunze's frustration to his Stasi officer, and this communique included a personal endorsement that was recorded in Wiens's file as follows: "The informant was of the opinion that these measures were annoying writers and alienating them."[79]

In Wiens's poetry, too, there was a discernible shift in the mid-1960s. Wiens began to embrace more personal and sometimes idiosyncratic themes of identity, masquerade, and transformation. The emotional effects of the double life that he was now leading as a member of the literary establishment and an undercover agent sought an outlet—and found one in his poems. Already in the 1957 collection *Nachrichten aus der Dritten Welt* Wiens had begun to develop aesthetic techniques to translate his autobiographical experiences and his ambivalence into art. In the second part of this volume he included a cycle of new poems titled "Die neuen Harfenlieder von Oswald von Wolkenstein" (The new harp songs of Oswald von Wolkenstein).

In his prefatory remarks in the first edition Wiens writes about the medieval minnesinger Wolkenstein as a "second face" or a mask by which the author dons a period "costume" and assumes a masquerade. As Annegret von Wietersheim argues, Wiens takes refuge in a historical alter ego or "congenial second self."[80] This second self provides a safe speaking position where he can distance himself from the troubled times in which he lives and from the subject making his own poetic statements. It seems that Wolkenstein has a license to speak freely on behalf of Wiens, while Wiens becomes akin to a ventriloquist who projects words into his literary characters. His characters in turn act as a buffer to shield the author from the impact of negative criticism.

The choice of Wolkenstein, a feudal adventurer who became embroiled in conflicts on behalf of the emperor, was not uncontroversial.[81] As depicted by Wiens, and like him, Wolkenstein is a polyglot, a restless wayfarer, and someone who has experienced imprisonment. Wiens was so fond of this persona that he reproduced this cycle of poems, among others, in *Vier Linien aus meiner Hand* (Four lines from my hand), his last collection, which was published in 1972. Here, in a new twist to his persona of Wolkenstein, Wiens introduces a further distance between himself and his aesthetic device, calling himself merely the editor of his friend's songs (rather than the author). Wolkenstein effectively becomes doubled up, serving both as a historical mouthpiece and as a contemporary sounding board.[82]

In 1968 Wiens published a third volume of poetry with the title *Dienstgeheimnis: Ein Nächtebuch* (Professional secret: A night book). Here he republished a selection of earlier poems, as he was accustomed to, but added an entirely new section titled "Professional Secret." This collection marks the beginning of Wiens's abandonment of capitalized nouns, a characteristic feature of his poetry thenceforward. This was adopted by the next generation of poets, in particular other Stasi-supported underground poets such as Sascha Anderson. In his foreword Wiens indicates a much more pronounced attitude of playfulness and irony. The foreword to *Dienstgeheimnis* also contains the first of several cryptic references to always being on duty: "I am and remain my whole small life-long on duty and on song, I have my instructions" (*Ich bin und bleibe mein kleines leblang und liedlang im dienst, ich habe meine vorschriften*).[83] No doubt Wiens's remarks were intended at the time as a commentary on the partisan nature of the East German writer, who, in contrast to his West German counterpart, was "always on duty," working "in the service of a good cause" (*im Dienst einer guten Sache*)—as fellow poet Uwe Berger wrote upon Wiens's death in 1982.[84] The expression "poets on duty" (or "poets in service") (*Dichter im Dienst*) had become a stock phrase to denote East German intellectuals' commitment to socialist politics and an engaged aesthetics of socialist realism.[85] (Berger affirmed that Wiens had dedicated his life to serving "the working people and the modest in our country and around the world."[86])

The title of Wiens's 1968 collection is deliberately conceived as a paradox. Of course any secret that brandishes itself publicly on a book cover is no secret anymore or is at least an open secret. Wiens's decision to couple the stock designation for socialist writers as "writers in service" with the epithet "secret" is perhaps less curious that it appears. On one level the reference could be an allusion to the concept of a "professional secret" in the pledge writers signed when they joined the Writers' Guild—a pledge to adhere to the organization's professional codes of secrecy.⁸⁷ On another level Wiens clearly intends the term "professional secret" to be primarily associated with the idea of the East German writer being "in the service of poetry,"⁸⁸ which was, as he was fond of remarking, "an open secret."⁸⁹

In the 1968 collection Wiens's play on the various meanings of being on duty and having secrets was perhaps a means of testing the waters to see how far he could use his poetry as a vehicle for channeling his frustration. It is also possible to excavate from his poetry an additional semantic field that connects the signifier "secret" to Wiens's illicit undercover work for the Stasi, especially given that he was working undercover when the *Dienstgeheimnis* volume was published. According to this reading, Wiens was on duty in two senses of the word, working tirelessly for the benefit of international socialism and, increasingly, for the benefit of state security. It is certainly plausible that he was growing more and more disillusioned with being on duty for the Stasi and with being obliged to bear the brunt of the state's restrictive cultural politics, as well as being annoyed by constantly having to be "on song," or on message, in his poetry.

There is no evidence that the Stasi perceived the title of Wiens's third volume of poetry as evidence of his blowing his cover, of deliberate insubordination, or of recklessness. In this sense Wiens might have enjoyed the last laugh, given that apparently he was able to get away with encrypting his personal secrets in his poetry and thereby developing an outlet for his growing ambivalence. At the time other veiled allusions to his secret undercover duties began to creep into his poetry. The third section of his 1968 volume is titled "Line" (*Linie*), which was also the exact terminology used by the ministry for the section charged with the surveillance of writers, the Line on Writers. Further, his use of the neologism "night book" (*Nächtebuch*) in the subtitle to *Dienstgeheimnis* is a play on *Tagebuch* (diary), and is also instructive. Wiens is on public record as having preferred to write in the evenings or nights, but the reference to keeping a diary at night could be read in the context of fulfilling his Stasi obligations. Another poem in the collection, "Warum spricht mein Mund" (Why does my mouth speak), refers explicitly to the lyrical "I" as a shadow:

> a shadow am I,
> a shadow alone,
> that of a tree, that of a man,
> that of a child, that of a woman.[90]

Like other members of the Writers' Guild, Wiens believed that the party meddled far too much in cultural affairs and in matters it was incompetent to judge.[91] Schiller believed that such views verged on heresy and that in 1968 Wiens had "exposed" his "true partially hostile ideological position, whose reality he never allowed himself to be convinced of in conversations."[92] In other words, Wiens's insistence on a lighter political touch in cultural affairs was in danger of affecting his presumed partisanship altogether. There were personal reasons, too, for Wiens's dissatisfaction toward the end of the 1960s. His second marriage, which had resulted in two further children, was starting to fail. His financial situation was tight, and the Stasi was not forthcoming with offers of lush or lucrative rewards for his labors during this period of collaborating, at least not yet.[93] By Christmas 1967 the relationship between Wiens and Schiller had broken down completely. At his last meeting for the year Schiller seems to have begun to contemplate dropping "Writer" altogether. As a consequence of the draconian measures of the Eleventh Plenary in 1965, a number of the informants in his department were refusing to cooperate entirely, among them some of his own sources.[94] Wiens was not an isolated case, but he was an annoyance that Schiller was probably having second thoughts about.

By the end of 1967 Schiller was most likely already resigned to the possibility that he might have to give up on Wiens, close his case, and archive his file. His informant's contacts inside the Writers' Guild had been indispensable, but Wiens was needing too much attention and cajoling for far too few gains. If Schiller had any doubts before his last meeting with Wiens, his mind was certainly made up after their final, memorable encounter. On that day in January 1968 Wiens was, according to Schiller's record of the meeting, in fine form. He was argumentative to an extreme, making no attempt to keep his legendary temper under control. Moreover, the sarcasm for which he was known was on full display. If Schiller was at a loss as to how to control Wiens's temper, the record shows he was certainly determined to document it for posterity in Wiens's file. Here Schiller managed to demonstrate to everyone who was privy to the file that Wiens was a lost cause and hopeless case. No doubt he also desperately needed to document his own failure for the benefit of his superiors.

The meeting appeared to begin well, but quickly took a turn for the worse when Schiller asked Wiens to provide him with two more passport photographs. We cannot know the real reason behind Schiller's request—whether Schiller was simply being pernickety and bureaucratic, or whether he was already planning to hand Wiens over to a colleague and did not know how to relay this news. At any rate he told Wiens that new photos were required, in case Schiller was taken ill and needed to hand "Writer" to another officer. This does seem rather unlikely, given that allocating a new officer to an existing informant did not entail opening a new file and so ought not to have required new photographs (unless the new officer needed to identify the new informant). Schiller told Wiens that he should also devise a secret code word for the eventuality that he was given a new officer.

Wiens's indignation at this request is captured exquisitely on file. It is likely that he did not suspect he was being handed over to someone else or that he was being dropped. Instead he focused on the senselessness of the specific request to provide two passport photos. For the seasoned intelligence agent, this was undoubtedly an absurd and preposterous imposition. As an individual who regarded himself as having attained a certain elite standing in the republic, not to mention within the espionage fraternity, he patently considered he was above such petty tasks. So his retort was quick: "He could understand that the MfS was looking for a firm commitment, but he would like to question whether we would also have required Johannes R. Becher provide two passport photos and a mutually agreeable code word."[95] Schiller then noted that Wiens "reiterated once more his preparedness to support the MfS in its work, after all he was a committed citizen of the GDR, but he ruled out all institutional ties to the MfS."[96]

Schiller's record of Wiens's outburst speaks volumes about Wiens's sensitivities at being classed an informant, his strong sense of entitlement, and his healthy ego. It is no accident that he compared himself to the senior statesman of German letters, Johannes R. Becher (who had died in 1958). Schiller had only completed primary school but did not need to be told who Becher was. Wiens knew, of course, that Becher's communist credentials easily trumped his own, and to Schiller it must have smacked of hubris that Wiens dared to compare himself to a canonized figure such as Becher. Yet Schiller was not deterred by such a histrionic and ridiculous comparison. After all, the Stasi could never contemplate recruiting as an informant someone of Becher's stature because, as a high-ranking politician, he was off limits for the secret police. Perhaps it was awareness of this fact that mortified Wiens most.

Schiller decided to close Wiens's file. Apart from the divisional head Karl Brosche, all of Schiller's colleagues were of a similar age—born in the 1930s—and most had come from similar working-class backgrounds. Schiller had only completed an apprenticeship in electrical engineering.[97] He had been recruited from the ranks of the police force. If these men used psychological warfare at all, they did so intuitively rather than according to an intelligence textbook, at least until operative psychology became a recognized area of expertise within the MfS.[98] Schiller no doubt felt ill-equipped to deal with the likes of Paul Wiens. He possibly felt bruised by Wiens's contemptuousness. Wiens had reminded him not only of his inferior education but also of his working-class background, and closing his file was a way to save face.

From 1968 to 1970 the Stasi was sufficiently alarmed by Wiens's political views to place a tap on his telephone, open his mail, and assign informers to keep an eye on his movements.[99] (The telephone surveillance was so extensive that the relevant transcripts fill 531 pages of the first two volumes of the file on Wiens that was newly opened in 1972.[100]) He was suffering a crisis of faith with regard to the Ministry for State Security, but from 1968 his disillusionment ran deeper, fueled by political events on the world stage. Wiens watched with bated breath the reform movement unfolding in Czechoslovakia, hopeful that its vision of socialism with a human face might spill over into East Germany. He hoped to see a loosening of state control in the arts; specifically, less censorship and petty-minded vetting of film scripts and manuscripts. But the manner in which the uprising of the Prague Spring was crushed left him with little hope. Fellow members of the Writers' Guild composed a declaration in support of the Warsaw Pact troops' invasion of Prague, but Wiens refused to sign. In effect this refusal placed him on a collision course with most of the guild's members. Moreover, in 1968 Wiens's term as president of the Berlin section of the Writers' Guild was coming to an end, and the party was preparing to drop him as its candidate. In 1969 SED member Günter Görlich was elected as Wiens's successor.[101]

If Schiller had tired of trying to cajole and corale Wiens into collaborating on the Stasi's terms, feeling it was beyond his capabilities to turn around the wily poet, this did not preclude another from his department from eventually trying his luck with Wiens. By 1970 Wiens was considered a lost cause careering out of control, rather like a comet plummeting out of orbit to earth. But as Schiller and his colleagues knew, things could change; some stars fall to earth and burn out, while others rise. Wiens's star would later enter into another orbit and start to rise, meteorically, rather like the first Russians in outer space he had so admired in poems like "Weltraum und Weltzeit" (Outer space and time) and "Kosmonautenlied" (Cosmonaut song).[102] Another officer would become the launch pad for Wiens's comeback as an informant, although this happened far sooner than Schiller could have expected.

Paul Gratzik: A Crisis of Faith

To the Stasi unreliability and sloppy work in carrying out missions were telltale signs that sources were at risk of not honoring their pact with the MfS. Depending on the circumstances, however, poor performance might be regarded as a forgivable lapse that could be rectified by assigning to the IM another officer with a different skill set. This was a common strategy applied to recalcitrant informants who were still deemed to have potential. In the mid-1960s Paul Gratzik was one such case. On February 11, 1969, First Lieutenant Wenzel became Gratzik's new officer. This change proved pivotal in resurrecting GI "Peter," and reinvigorating the Stasi's maverick source with fresh purpose.

Gratzik had continued to capitalize on his good political fortunes as an authentic working-class dramatist in the Brechtian tradition, adding another feather to his cap with a successful production of his play *Malwa* at the Hans-Otto-Theater in Potsdam in 1968. By this time, with two top-drawer literary mentors in Anna Seghers and the older actress Steffie Spira, who had become his lover, Gratzik had been initiated into the East German literati. Given that he had no need to continue to sell his soul to the Stasi, it remains a mystery why he continued to do so. In *Vaterlandsverräter* Gratzik can be seen confessing to Hendel, the director, that *Malwa* was a personal turning point. He experienced critical success and fame as a form of personal vindication that reinforced his feeling that he was something special. The feeling has stayed with him, he tells the camera, and he has "paid for it bitterly."

Gratzik admits in the film documentary that at first he was 100 percent behind the communist cause and willing to give his all to serving his country: "I was prepared to sacrifice my life for the GDR," he tells Hendel. He also tells her that he saw no harm in working for the Stasi at the start. Perhaps the first few years of unsatisfying stop-and-start policing work were due more to inexpert handling than to any fundamental ideological or, indeed, moral reservations that Gratzik harbored about the secret police. In its guidelines for working with informants, the ministry placed increasing importance on finessing the handling of agents from 1958 onward. For instance, Guideline 1/58 mentions explicitly that "the relationship between officer and agent is a rather weak spot in operative work."[103] By assigning Gratzik a new case officer the Stasi acknowledged the growing importance of the intersubjective side of informing work, and in this instance the strategy seems to have paid dividends. Presented with a new officer who was better versed in handling agents, or simply better suited to him, Gratzik appears to have thrived, at least for a couple of years.

It seems the collaboration with Wenzel enjoyed an auspicious start in 1969. In a scene in *Vaterlandsverräter* where Hendel appears to catch Gratzik off guard in the car after an eye operation, he tells her that Wenzel was good at the start of their relationship. This is contradicted by another statement, however, in which he says that Wenzel had "no talent" for handling agents and that Wenzel always kept him at arm's length. Of course Wenzel would have disapproved of Gratzik's attempts to turn the professional relationship into something more personal and to have Wenzel reciprocate the sharing of information. According to Gratzik, when quizzed about this dynamic Wenzel retorted that using the informal you, the German "Du," did not count for much, saying: "The 'Du' is followed by 'the asshole.'"

The year 1969 was eventful for "Peter" and his officer, Wenzel. Gratzik's informant file is brimming with reports from this time about various persons. These consist mainly of informer accounts, dictated to Wenzel and transcribed later by a secretary. At the commencement of the collaboration Gratzik was instructed to prepare a "list of all of his connections to close friends."[104] Despite the occasional discussion of "problems," for a while Gratzik obliged, even confessing that he had "of late missed the contact."[105] The professional playwright and refugee from a working-class background was soon to become something of a jewel in Wenzel's crown.

Gratzik was of intense interest to the Stasi because of his access to multiple hubs in the creative arts. After the Prague Spring of 1968 in Czechoslovakia, the Johannes R. Becher Institute for Literature and the theaters and universities of Dresden, Leipzig, and Berlin were all marked on the regime's radar as potential hotbeds of insurrection. Surprisingly, however, Gratzik was reluctant to produce the list of his contacts requested by the Stasi. Wenzel noted: "He did not have the drive needed to do so."[106] In documented discussions, the reasons that emerge concern Gratzik's lack of ideological clarity—or rather, as his file says, "his ideological fluctuations."[107]

Around this time Gratzik made a couple of fairly innocuous reports about Heiner Müller, one in February 1970[108] and another in February 1972. In *Vaterlandsverräter* Gratzik confesses to holding Müller in particularly high regard, seeing in him something of a big brother who looked out for his little brother (Gratzik). Gratzik insists in this film that he wrote only one report about someone he was close to. This fact is belied in Gratzik's file by a collection of reports he wrote about individuals who would have considered him a friend, including his mentor Müller. The numerous reports he wrote about Sabine Poppe constitute another example, as does the assignment Gratzik carried out concerning the priest Hans Jörg Dost. It is perhaps more accurate to affirm that he never wrote *malicious* reports about people he regarded as his friends or about his wives or lovers. The opera singer Renate

Biskup, Gratzik's former lover, is shocked in *Vaterlandsverräter* to learn that he was an informant, but there appear to be no reports about her in his file. Steffie Spira appears in his file, but only in connection with other people.

Still, Gratzik did carry out occasional assignments focused on his friends and associates in the theater. For instance, he wrote several reports about Ernst-Georg Hering, a theater director in Potsdam, and his wife, Brigitte Hering. He did so despite being, as Hering himself recalls, a close friend of the family and popular with Hering's young son Matthias. Gratzik passed on incriminating evidence in 1970 that the Herings read literature written by reform Marxists and that they received books illegally from a niece who had left for the West.[109]

The pattern of regular meetings between "Peter" and Wenzel continued throughout 1970 and into 1971, taking place about once a month. The content of Gratzik's reports on theater circles in Dresden, Potsdam, and Berlin from this time is generally focused on artistic activities, and his reporting is not spiteful or malicious with respect to his colleagues' political views or intentions.[110] In one report, for instance, he is at pains to stress that new groups "only want to make theater."[111] When he reports on Benno Besson, the director of the Berlin Volksbühne, and his tirades against the lack of quality in dramatic plays and the decline in the craft of acting, Gratzik seems nonjudgmental and open to Besson's criticisms.[112] Only in connection with political events in the Eastern Bloc does the ever faithful "Peter" seem prepared to denounce one or two people who were suspected of spearheading a counterrevolutionary movement in East Germany akin to the movements that were shaking up Poland and Czechoslovakia.

There were telltale signs in 1971 that Gratzik wanted more than ever to be relieved of his duties undertaken for the Stasi. A major turning point in his attitude to informing occurred in October 1971. One of his targets suspected that he might be working for the Stasi. To the labile "Peter" this was an unwanted stress factor. At the same time his prospects as a writer with impeccable class credentials had never looked rosier. In 1972 he mentioned to his officer that his idol Heiner Müller had offered to produce one of Gratzik's plays for the stage.[113] In the same year Gratzik underwent the first of a series of fundamental crises of faith in the regime. During the following years he repeatedly attempted to disassociate himself from his handlers; the Stasi responded with a string of inducements and a bundle of psychological forms of coercion and persuasion before resorting eventually to threats.

Perhaps unsurprisingly, in 1972 Gratzik's handlers lodged with their superiors a proposal to upgrade GI "Peter's" status to IMV, which was a category of informer with greater responsibility in operational matters. The rank of IMV, which after 1979 was converted into the similarly elite category of IMB,[114] represented the aristocratic elite amongst informants. According to Joachim Walther, being designated an IMB was rather like holding an honorary doctorate, only a secret one.[115] Yet, this recategorization meant that the Stasi needed to be assured that Gratzik was reliable. During the operation on Dost in 1972 the Stasi thought it judicious to place some security controls on Gratzik by deploying another informer of the same type, IMV "Regina Beyer."[116]

Gratzik made no secret of the fact that he wished to see more tolerance of experimentation in the theater. This attitude was interpreted as evidence of certain "negative tendencies." Nevertheless, Lieutenant Colonel Bormann, Wenzel's superior, still considered Gratzik a useful source.[117] The reports of IMV "Regina Beyer" failed to produce any information that the Stasi did not already know. Accounts of Gratzik's "instability, moodiness, and drinking" were nothing new.[118] The department was nonetheless optimistic that contradictions in Gratzik's political views could be ironed out through more systematic training by his handler. Problems with Gratzik continued throughout 1972, however, and proved difficult to address through educational measures—that is, by subjecting him to ideological rhetoric and emotional blackmail. As one file entry reveals, "In conversations with the informant about these [problems] it became partially obvious that he was choosing certain negative occurrences in various areas of our society, seeing them in absolute terms and letting them get the upper hand."[119]

In December 1972 the head of department reported problems with "Peter," who had expressed reservations about continuing to work for the Stasi. It was noted that Gratzik's political views were subject to "fluctuations," especially with respect to cultural policy. His behavior was frequently contradictory; though on the one hand he held "progressive" political views, he was often seen as a "complainer and whinger" and he held "false ideas" about the role of the writer.[120] Wenzel's superior suggests a two-pronged approach to the matter. The first prong consisted of continuing to "work intensively on his [Gratzik's] ideological stance."[121] The method to be deployed was that of reasoning with Gratzik and pointing out what the "ideological opponent" was capable of doing with "ideological diversion" in the arena of cultural politics.[122] In short, Wenzel was to use his proven powers of persuasion and ramp up his training program. The second prong of the Stasi's approach was to increase its surveillance of Gratzik.

Although the Stasi expected unconditional trust from its informants, it had few qualms about withholding trust from them and using other informants to spy on them. To this end, an informant from the State Theater in Dresden, IMV "Stein," was engaged (see fig. 3). As Wenzel comments in *Vaterlandsverräter*, it was common practice to place informants under surveillance as a security precaution when trust was an issue.[123] This often led to an odd looping effect, whereby a less trustworthy informer was spied on by another, slightly more trustworthy informer, and, occasionally, vice versa. Paradoxically, this strategy was supposed to lead to greater trustworthiness for all concerned, even in the event that neither informant was especially trustworthy.

Gratzik's file from December 1972 reveals that IMV "Stein" wrote reports about IMV "Peter" and that "Peter" also penned the occasional report about "Stein." This practice, which Renate Biskup aptly describes as a form of "intellectual incest" (*geistiger Inzest*), may well have been the Stasi's instinctive response to the erosion of trust, but it patently exacerbated "Peter's" already fragile state of mind. In *Vaterlandsverräter* he recalls imagining that there were Stasi spies outside his apartment, and Wenzel confirms in the film that he had in fact placed Gratzik under observation. According to a report from "Stein," two days after a positive review of Gratzik's play *Umwege* (Detours) had been published in the West, he received a telegram from the East German Ministry for Culture announcing that he had won a prize of 3,000 marks. This was, Gratzik tells "Stein," engineered to win back his loyalty.[124]

If Gratzik now understood the workings of the system of kickbacks in the East, incentives such as these were no panacea for his growing cynicism and pessimism. He was acutely aware of the fact that younger writers and dramatists were not being appropriately supported by the regime. As recorded in his file, the lack of consistency in cultural policy was a perennial theme in his discussions with Wenzel, and one that troubled Gratzik deeply. Moreover, he was unsettled by the actions of some of his bolder colleagues, both impressed by their courage in making contacts with Western publishers and journalists, for instance, and at the same time worried that such actions might have negative repercussions. As Gratzik came to feel increasingly at home in the group of writers gathering around fellow writer Martin Stade in Dresden, his disorientation only grew, and he looked increasingly to his officer for political guidance.

*

This chapter examines several of the challenges faced by the Stasi after having recruited particular poets and dramatists during the decade of so-called stability and consolidation of national culture that followed the construction of the Berlin Wall. External factors such as the Eleventh Plenary of the SED's Central Committee in 1965 and the Prague Spring in Czechoslovakia in 1968 represented watersheds for many intellectuals, whether they were more established cultural functionaries such as Wiens or aspiring writers such as Gratzik and Novak.

For Novak the small window of liberalization prior to the Eleventh Plenary was cause for renewed hope that socialism could reform itself. This prompted her to return to the GDR and to come into the purview of the communist panopticon once again. In her case we can see how the Stasi took revenge on its former lapsed informers and attempted to rob them of East German citizenship. Whereas for Paul Wiens cultural restrictions precipitated a severe motivational crisis, for Gratzik the crackdown on cultural expression prompted the opposite response. The Stasi was able to further the latter's career at a crucial time and foster dependencies that became powerful motivating factors. Working for the Stasi went hand in hand, so it seemed for a while, with being welcomed into the hallowed halls of the country's feted writers, and so it led Gratzik to accrue substantial amounts of cultural and symbol capital. During this period the Stasi managed to lock Gratzik into a positive approach loop whereby he was offered benefits and incentives to continue to collaborate. For a time these carrots had the desired effect, although Gratzik, like many informants, began to express concern for his safety.

With Wiens, the Stasi was less successful in creating dependencies; he had acquired his cultural capital prior to being recruited. Likewise, the Stasi proved inexpert in handling Wiens with the finesse that the returned émigré and Holocaust survivor had come to expect. If membership in the elite secret surveillance society and tireless service in its name meant little in terms of career benefits, then during the decade 1962–72 Wiens saw little purpose in continuing to inform. With the advent of détente and the intensified focus on the "security area" of literature in the MfS, his attitude to the Stasi would continue to shift as he discovered new ways of rationalizing spying for the Stasi.

3

Policing the "Line on Writers" and Living the Secret Life, 1971–1976

In March 1970 groundbreaking negotiations began between the newly elected chancellor of the Federal Republic of Germany, Willy Brandt, and Willi Stoph, the head of the GDR Council of Ministers, in the East German city of Erfurt, ushering in the era of détente and *Ostpolitik*. This era was significant for the easing of geopolitical tensions not only between the United States and the Soviet Union but also between the two Germanies. Relations between the Soviet Union and the Federal Republic had improved in the preceding years, and no doubt Soviet pressure played a role in bringing about the historic meeting in Erfurt. For the GDR regime, however, the event was "part triumph and part nightmare."[1] Although the negotiations between the two German leaders signaled recognition for the communist regime, it was unclear if and how détente would lead to reforms.[2] The Stasi was shocked by the jubilant welcome that Brandt received in Erfurt, and this shock prompted some internal rethinking in the MfS.[3]

Given that the West Germans were seeking to redefine their relationship to Moscow, in August 1970 they signed the Soviet–West German Renunciation of Force Treaty, which "symbolized the waning of the cold war" and an acceptance of Europe's postwar borders.[4] Such a rapprochement was perceived as a nightmare by the Ministry for State Security. To address this challenge, the Stasi began to devise new strategies (while honing certain old ones). The present chapter discusses several such strategies in relation to writers who were members of official organs such as the German Writers' Guild, with a focus on the Stasi's informants inside the guild. In this context I demonstrate how the Stasi tried to overcome the practical difficulties of seeking to control cultural expression by improving human forms of surveillance, namely through better recruiting methods and better ways of sustaining relations with its army of informers.

On June 18, 1969, Minister for State Security Erich Mielke issued a directive to establish Abteilung (Department) 7 (HA XX/7) of HA XX, staffed by more or less the same personnel. The new department would police more intensively the area of culture and mass communication. HA XX/7 was the responsibility of Deputy Minister Rudi Mittig and had its counterparts in all fourteen district offices. Writers, publishers, the offices of censorship and copyright, and writers' guilds were looked after by Referat (Section) II, which was headed by Peter Reinhardt. One of the section's "security objects"—as Stasi liked to call strategic areas of concern and responsibility— was the new "Line on Writers." The new officer in charge of the central Writers' Guild was thirty-one-year-old Rolf Pönig, who had come across from the old Referat II. Hans Schiller, who had joined him, had particular responsibility for so-called travel cadres, becoming the officer in charge of issuing travel permits among unionized writers.

Schiller's long-standing colleague Pönig was responsible for reopening Paul Wiens's informant file. In this chapter I investigate how the Stasi managed to lure back some of its disgruntled quitters like Wiens and (with rather less success) to keep in line other serial quitters, such as Paul Gratzik. The files reveal that the Stasi gained more experience in using incentives, or carrots, rather than sticks alone and increasingly desisted from deploying more punitive measures against the GDR's more established writers. As Wiens's case shows, the Stasi managed to win back disaffected writers who had become disillusioned after the Prague Spring and the regime's refusal to go down the path of reform. The case of Paul Wiens and Uwe Berger, who spied on each other, shows that during 1971–76 the Stasi became more pragmatic and less ideologically driven in its recruitment when it turned to more heterogenous types of writers, some of whom were critical but still loyal to the regime. Tailor-made plans were devised to keep informants on track, and the Stasi became willing to make certain concessions with respect to informants' wishes and career aspirations.

In May 1971 Walter Ulbricht was forced to resign as first secretary of the SED; as a result of a leadership putsch, Ulbricht was replaced in that position by the eagerly awaited Erich Honecker.[5] One of Honecker's first actions was to proclaim during the Eighth Party Congress the dawning of a new era of "consumer socialism," thereby addressing deficiencies in both economic and social policy.[6] In the arts, too, Honecker promised a more liberal approach, and his "no taboos" speech at the Fourth Central Committee Conference in December 1971 fueled hopes of a less restrictive cultural politics, albeit with the caveat that artists and writers must not deviate from the "firm position of socialism."[7] Yet, as Roger Wood has argued, Honecker's statements certainly "did not translate into an intellectual free-for-all,"[8] especially given that writers were reminded that they were still expected to remain partisan.

Expectations ran high following Honecker's landmark speech. Some publishers were emboldened to print one or two works by controversial writers such as Reiner Kunze and Stefan Heym, who were both *persona non grata* to the regime.[9] Under the watch of risk-taking editors,[10] the literary journal *Sinn und Form* showed that it could serve as a key site for "intellectual exchange"[11] by tackling provocative texts about youth culture.[12] In addition, theaters displayed a greater willingness to stage dramas on topics previously thought too sensitive or too adventurous.[13] Literary works that had been shelved or delayed in publication, such as Hermann Kant's novel *Das Impressum* (The imprint, 1972),[14] and Christa Wolf's novel *Kindheitsmuster* (*Patterns of Childhood*, 1976) were permitted to be published.[15] Nevertheless, writers were by no means sure how far they could veer from an overtly partisan ethos or whether there would be reprisals if they went too far.

Ironically, under the "no taboos" phase of this ideological thaw, the work of undercover secret service informers, even those who were seasoned, did not become any easier. Fearful that the pendulum would swing too far in the opposite direction, the Ministry for State Security remained ever vigilant, continuing to rely heavily on its pool of informants for crucial intelligence on developments in the cultural field. It continued to pursue a strategy of running key informants at all levels of cultural life—among publishers and their editors, at literary journals, and, above all, deep inside the Writers' Guild, even in the highest echelons of its executive; in 1972 the Stasi ran as informants the president and the vice president of the guild.[16]

The case of Paul Wiens serves to illustrate that there were considerable challenges involved in running agents deep inside powerful organizations such as the Writers' Guild. Wiens's file, moreover, shows that the performance of espionage took its toll on him personally. The Stasi was well aware that a recruit's motivations for collaborating could change in the course of his or her association with the secret service; this was noted in the Stasi-commissioned study undertaken by Manfred Hempel in 1967.[17] Inevitably, Hempel concluded, the experience of undercover work, particularly the "attraction" of the "extraordinary," could influence an informant's emotional attitudes to espionage work.[18] The Stasi, unsurprisingly, admitted only to the positive effects of informing that could accrue over time, yet Wiens's case reveals that negative impacts also ensued from being "on duty" for multiple masters at a time. The necessity of maintaining secrecy and of performing multiple personas did not become easier over time. Rather, individuals were obliged to develop a deft juggling act so as to cultivate discrete sets of dispositions in both their professional and personal lives. Frequently, informers were unable to assimilate separate parts of their habitus with a clear conscience.

Paul Wiens: Lost in Space

After reading that the Stasi had closed its informant file on Wiens, it comes as a shock to the reader of his file to discover that his IM case was made active again only a few years later. As in the instance of Wiens's daughter, discussed below, the Stasi often opened a second file on its informants, but usually this second dossier was a victim file that saw the informant become the target of surveillance. In 1972 Wiens's informant file was reopened by the new head of Section II of HA XX/7, Senior Lieutenant Rolf Pönig. In that year Wiens's handler, Schiller, was reassigned to work on the Line on Writers, which received an injection of funds and resources. It was not uncommon for Schiller and Pönig to swap informants, and Schiller may have been only too happy for Pönig to try his luck with Wiens, given that he had failed to handle the mercurial "Writer."

Pönig, who went by the aliases "Rolf," "König," and "Martin,"[19] was recruited in 1958 after completing an apprenticeship as a metal worker.[20] The nineteen-year-old who had wished to study aeronautics dreamed of one day being able to attend university. His first superiors promised him professional development, which was only forthcoming toward the end of his career in 1978, when he was allowed to undertake study at the Stasi's Law School (Juristische Hochschule) in Potsdam.[21] Pönig graduated with a thesis on how to handle agents in such a way as to neutralize the hostile-negative impact of counterrevolutionary groups.[22] This was fitting for the work he would later do. But in 1972, Pönig was still relatively inexperienced in handling informants and had much to learn.

Early in his career, Pönig's superiors often admonished him for his lack of theoretical understanding of espionage.[23] With Wiens, he proved particularly adept at bending the textbook theory to suit the practical realities of the mission at hand. For the Stasi, Pönig was a rather good shepherd of informants who redeemed a lost but loyal servant for the security forces at a critical juncture in the latter's career; his wager on Wiens would pay off handsomely for him. For Wiens, his secret Faustian pact with the devil would prove profitable in the short term but disastrous in the long run.

Among the most noticeable changes that occurred with the formation of a new division dedicated to policing cultural security objects was that the numbers of informants run by the department rose dramatically. In 1972 HA XX/7 listed 221 informants; by 1989 the number had grown to 350. This recruitment drive may have been behind the reopening of Wiens's file. Otherwise, the circumstances around his resurrection as an agent are a mystery. It appears from the file that Wiens approached the Stasi with a view to resuming work for the ministry. No material on file suggests that the resumption of contact with its lapsed agent was the Stasi's initiative. There is no evidence of an agreed plan to resume meetings; there is no indication of coordinated measures to win Wiens back. We can only surmise that the contact was renewed on Wiens's initiative and that he had pressing reasons for appealing to the Stasi again.

Wiens's poems from the late 1960s provide a number of clues to the existential crisis that he was experiencing. After his more celebratory poems that sing the praises of Yuri Gagarin and the Soviet space program (which had launched the first man into outer space), Wiens's references to the cosmos and space become more abstract and hermetic in meaning.[24] Questions of subjectivity and identity ("who am I?") are coupled with reflections on the precarity of humanity caught between "nothingness and everything / outer space" (*dem nichts und dem all*).[25] Images of the lyrical "I" standing on the "windy" Warsaw Bridge in Berlin crossing over "helpful" (*hilfsbereit*) train tracks can be read autobiographically, as symptomatic of Wiens's dilemma at the time, when he found himself at a crossroads in his relationship to the regime and its security forces. The spatial metaphors are juxtaposed with a mixture of past and present tenses, whereby the I's past biography no longer offers answers to its current problems of identity ("I know the answers / none is enough"). Answers are instead being "gonged," ominously, by the "bell of the signal tower" from the approaching train.[26]

The files offer a few clues as to what these "helpful" train tracks might have been, and what was behind Wiens's decision to approach the Stasi in 1972. Among the many materials filed in his dossier is a list compiled by the Stasi of the overseas trips he made from 1953 onward. The number of countries he visited on a regular basis was impressive by anyone's standards, but for an East German it was extraordinary. His file details trips to capitalist and communist countries—to Bulgaria, China, Finland, France, Italy, the Soviet Union, Yugoslavia, even India.[27] During some periods he traveled as many as six times a year. From 1968 onward, however, his ability to travel had been severely curtailed and his trips reduced to one per year.[28] Used to living out of hotel rooms since childhood, Wiens possibly came to the realization that informing for the Stasi was not too high a price to pay for the freedom to go abroad again. This is the movement alluded to in the image of the "helpful" train tracks: the prospect of ending the stasis of his awkward position, caught in the no-man's land of the "windy" bridge between his past and his future. Most likely, then, the promise of international travel was the hidden motivation behind a pragmatic and purely self-interested decision to reactivate his contact with the Stasi.

After Wiens's relations with the Stasi had soured, the Stasi punished him by making it harder for him to obtain travel visas. International travel was the one casualty of his fall from favor, and the one that Wiens was least able to tolerate. Presumably Wiens struck a deal with the Stasi that he would deliver better quality intelligence on his writer colleagues and report on them abroad, provided that he was able to travel again. Pönig, it seems, was happy with this gentlemen's agreement. From 1972 until his death in 1982 Wiens traveled again, even if it was courtesy of the Stasi, and thus he was always on duty. He was assured of being able to travel in style as a top-level cultural functionary—and as a trusted secret informant. In 1972 the Stasi was more than satisfied with his change of heart, and over the next few years Wiens was to reap the rewards.

The gentlemen's agreement that Pönig and Wiens struck was never explicitly put in writing. Again Wiens refused to sign any declaration or oath; on this occasion, Pönig knew it was futile to insist. Wiens's informant file does, however, record the formal prompt for Wiens's resumption of contact. It occurred just after his marriage on October 9, 1971, to Irmtraud Morgner.[29] Barely a month later, on November 4, Wiens requested an urgent meeting with the Stasi, most likely with Schiller, who passed the request to his colleague Pönig. Pönig, in turn, started up an IM candidate case with the new undercover name "Germain."[30]

Wiens maintained that he had an urgent matter to discuss. He wanted to raise his concerns about the visit of a Western journalist, Conrad Franke, who he thought was an "enemy of the GDR."[31] Somewhat provocatively, Franke had asked Morgner, Wiens's wife, if she could imagine living in West Germany.[32] Fortunately for Morgner, Wiens was pleased to report that she had given a loyal reply, stating she could not imagine living in a capitalist society. "Her home is the GDR,"[33] Wiens told Pönig. This snippet of information may have been designed to tell the Stasi that Wiens had turned the corner.

It is unclear whether Wiens was being paranoid about Franke or simply especially canny in instrumentalizing the visit of a Western journalist. On the part of Wiens the meeting with Pönig on November 4, 1971, could have been an elaborate and calculated performance of loyalty, a cleverly disguised act designed to flaunt his rediscovered faith. Franke's appearance out of the blue at his house might well have seemed suspicious to Wiens. Nevertheless, the occasion of the journalist's visit provided him with the perfect alibi to curry favor with the Stasi and show the ministry that he had changed. Even though Wiens expanded at great length on the suspicious aspects of Franke's visit, we can conclude, as did the Stasi, that the story of Franke's visit was merely an excuse to exhibit to the Stasi that Wiens had undergone a miraculous and total ideological *volte-face*.

Wiens's strategy paid off, and in January 1972 Pönig formally lodged an application to reopen his file. As mentioned, Pönig rather cleverly did not insist that Wiens sign the usual declaration, and the two men agreed to shake hands on the deal.[34] From this point on, the ministry resolved to strike a good balance between the use of carrots and sticks in its dealings with Wiens: copious overseas trips in exchange for top-quality information and regular clandestine meetings, as well as extra income for the added peace of mind that came with hidden connections to power. As long as Wiens's desire for extra special handling was respected (handling he considered appropriate to a well-traveled cosmopolitan and a victim of fascism), it seems he was happy to continue acting as an informant.

To contextualize Wiens's surprising transformation, we need to take a closer look at his personal circumstances. In 1970 and 1971 his situation was remarkably similar to that of a decade earlier, when the Stasi had first approached him. His second marriage had failed, and he had become involved with Irmtraud Morgner. Eventually he had been forced to move out of the house in Grünau where his second family lived; for a brief moment he was homeless.[35] Again, Wiens was in some financial difficulty. His family had grown and, according to sources inside the ministry, he was feeling the financial strain of having multiple families.[36]

Possibly other events contributed to Wiens's decision to try to make his association with the Stasi work. He was no longer editor in chief of the literary journal *Neue Deutsche Literatur* and was feeling the loss of his editor's salary,[37] being obliged to live on a stipend paid by the Writers' Guild.[38] Renewed difficulties with the censors may also have played a role. In 1970 he was experiencing difficulty having poems accepted and published. Throughout 1970 and 1971 the Stasi had continued to keep an eye on Wiens. Apart from tapping his telephone, it placed him under a more benevolent type of surveillance, an "operational person check" (*Operative Personenkontrolle*, OPK), the low-grade kind of observation that sometimes preceded a full-scale investigation. Apparently, while Wiens was having second thoughts about having distanced himself from the Stasi, the Stasi was having second thoughts of its own. One officer in Section II of HA XX/7 was reconsidering the ministry's classification of its former agent. Unbeknownst to Wiens, the Stasi had commissioned a review of one of his poems by one of its newest undercover literary experts, informant "Uwe." "Uwe" was the cover name for Uwe Berger, a freelance poet and reviewer who was Wiens's friend and associate. Berger also worked for the Stasi from 1969 to 1985.[39] The lieutenant handling "Uwe" was Wiens's second case officer, Senior Lieutenant Rolf Pönig.

Paul Wiens and Uwe Berger: Spy versus Spy 1

Perhaps in the spirit of the unexpected climate of rapprochement between the two German states, Pönig may have secretly readied himself to welcome back Paul Wiens. Meeting in April 1970 with Pönig, "Uwe" presented his officer with a copy of Wiens's poems that he had procured. After analyzing them, Berger had quickly reached the conclusion that "in his opinion [Wiens's poems] did not conform to our political views."[40] Rather to Berger's surprise, Pönig was not pleased about Berger's disparaging assessment of Wiens. Pönig had wanted his expert opinion, and he had given it, and yet the filed report of this meeting conveys the distinct sense that Berger gave the wrong answer. Pönig may have been hoping to receive an encouraging sign that Wiens was back on track in all senses, personally and ideologically. Not only was Pönig dissatisfied with Berger's findings but he also seemed irritated about the manner in which Berger delivered his verdict. As if reprimanding a recalcitrant pupil, Pönig told Berger that his "homework" report for the meeting was not of an acceptable standard and asked him to repeat the entire reviewing exercise. He issued explicit instructions: Berger was to prepare a reader's report in relation to the poems "in which he justifie[d] his opinion in precise terms."[41]

Berger's blithe misreading of the situation highlighted to Pönig the broader problem with "Uwe"'s intelligence, which came to a head in 1983. On December 7 of that year Pönig wrote: "With IM the topic of reporting must be dealt with thoroughly at the next meeting. Facts must be compiled in more extensive and concrete fashion. Value judgments should be avoided!"[42] Even in 1970 Berger's views were in danger of becoming too dogmatic to be of use to the MfS. By 1970 hard-liners (or "progressives," as Berger liked to see himself) were starting to become more of a hindrance than a help, even to the security forces.[43]

When compared to Berger's politically overcorrect angle, Wiens's critical-conformist political stance suddenly seems much less orthodox. To the party faithful like Berger (i.e., to disgruntled fanatics with an ax to grind) Wiens was a troublemaker. In his typewritten expert assessment of Wiens's poetry cycle, dated May 1970, Berger could take a savage swipe at Wiens. Wiens's poems advocated Western "'pluralism' of world views."[44] More than displaying anarchic tendencies, the poems actively cultivated such tendencies.[45] Anarchism, like Berger's other favorite terms of abuse—nihilism, decadence, and subjective idealism—was, as Pönig knew only too well, among the most damning epithets that could be applied to socialist literature. In a hyperbolic turn of phrase that underscores Berger's malicious intent, he declared the poems so bad that they were scarcely fit to be published in a student newspaper.[46]

Berger's slightly hysterical assessment of Wiens as a major security risk to the nation was hardly the new objectivity Pönig was hoping for. Pönig, it would appear, had a far less dogmatic view of Wiens. Needless to say, he instructed Berger to keep a close eye on Wiens and to use whatever means he could to befriend him.[47] Berger could not know that Wiens was soon to become one of Pönig's secret agents. Reading between the lines, one could conjecture that Berger was somewhat jealous of Wiens, especially given that Wiens was able to travel to capitalist countries and Berger only to socialist ones.[48] Most likely Berger came to the realization that Wiens was Pönig's main man in the front line of defense, whereas Berger was in the second line. In mid-1970, however, Berger was happy to try to become close to Wiens. As a token of his dedication to the ministry, he proceeded to deepen his friendship with the poet, using the next opportunity to telephone him and arrange a meeting.

The next opportunity, it transpired, was no less than a personal tragedy. In August 1970 Berger broke the news to Pönig at their meeting that his wife was "terminally ill with cancer."[49] His wife had been given only three months to live. Pönig reported: "This matter is troubling the IM immensely at the moment. Nevertheless, he declared to this staff member that we can approach him with tasks because the work must go on."[50] Berger wished to underscore that whatever personal misfortune befell him, he remained fully committed to the aims and objectives of the "Firm." Pönig, it turned out, was never in any doubt about Berger's total loyalty to the cause; in fact, such loyalty was part of the problem.

At the same August meeting Pönig handed over a payment of 400 marks for a review.[51] To show Pönig that he was deeply committed to serving the Stasi, Berger handed over another handwritten report on Wiens. During his wife's brief illness Berger had found time to make contact with his poet colleague several times over the telephone. In one conversation Berger had urged Wiens to write "something for us."[52] Wiens, suspecting Berger wanted him to write the usual dreary panegyric singing the praises of the party, had politely declined. "The world has changed today, and I have too," he told Berger pointedly.[53] At this stage in the recorded conversation Berger blurted out a confession that his wife had a terminal illness. Berger had effectively used the occasion of his wife's illness as a pretext to make contact with Wiens. Berger's ulterior motive was to curry favor with his officer, and if he had to use his personal misfortune to make this happen, he would. In Berger's file we find an account of this conversation that he wrote up in the form of a curious mini-drama, or dialogue. Berger had devised a new method of writing his reports that would seem more objective. Using a thick lead pencil, he now wrote them in direct speech, in the form of short, self-contained dramatic dialogues.

Berger believed that his reports achieved the appearance of far greater neutrality when presented as dialogues. The reports were indeed highly minimalist plays in which Wiens and Berger were the only protagonists with speaking parts. These parts were equally banal. There were no pregnant silences, meaningful omissions, or sinister pauses as in a modernist or absurdist drama by Samuel Beckett or Harold Pinter. Today the "plays" seem staggeringly boring and contrived. And in all likelihood this was Pönig's experience of them, too.

During one mini-drama that allegedly took place on August 8, 1970, Berger managed to bring the conversation with Wiens to the topic of his wife's illness. "You know my wife from before. She is now so sick that I sometimes feel lonely. That is also why I have called," Berger claimed. Wiens replied, rather predictably: "What is the matter with her?" Berger's reply was non-specific and evasive. "What do you get when it is really bad," he offered by clumsy way of explanation. Despite this cryptic reply, Wiens had no trouble understanding the mystifying allusion to cancer. Susan Sontag once described cancer as the disease "that doesn't knock before it enters," the illness that is experienced as a "ruthless, secret invasion"[54]—rather like Berger's invasion of Wiens's privacy. In Berger's worldview cancer was also the illness that literally had no name, rather like his secret connection to the Stasi. Because his response is not recorded, we can only presume that Wiens drew breath; he had understood Berger's predicament, and was alleged to have replied: "I see! Is she at home?" "Yes," said Berger.[55]

On August 11, 1970, Berger took time out from caring for his dying wife to telephone Wiens again. Wiens may have thought his friend merely needed consoling, but, according to Berger's mini-drama, he did not wish to talk about his wife or her pain. Instead he wanted to follow up on their earlier conversation about Wiens writing something in support of the regime. Berger almost begged him: "Don't just say yes to the communists in France and Italy, instead say yes to us communists in the GDR. Say it loud and clear, it doesn't matter how. . . . For once just say yes to us, and no one will hold anything against you. . . . We need you, Paul. Change in our direction," he finally declared.[56] Wiens's response is not recorded. Thus the dramatic play ended in a most undramatic and anticlimactic fashion; the two protagonists bade one another farewell and hung up.

On October 4, 1970, Pönig filed a report about his latest visit to Berger's apartment, made when he learned that Berger's wife was dying.[57] Berger had called the meeting, and Pönig arrived with flowers for his informant's wife, although she was now so poorly that she was barely able to receive them.[58] Berger informed him that he was expecting her death daily. This meeting was kept brief, and Pönig departed soon after, telling Berger he should telephone at any time if he needed him and to report "immediately afterward."[59] Pönig noted for the benefit of his superior that Berger was pleased he had visited.[60]

Two days later, on October 6, 1970, Pönig filed another report. Berger had made contact and arranged a meeting, which promptly occurred.[61] Strangely, the report filed by Pönig includes no further mention of Berger's personal tragedy. Instead, there is much polite chatter about the Romanians who had taken part in maneuvers in East Germany.[62] But Berger had called a meeting so soon after his wife's death because he had secured a face-to-face meeting with Wiens, using the pretext of his recent bereavement. Rather triumphantly Berger recounted to Pönig how Wiens had paid him a personal visit on hearing about his wife's death. Judging from his verbal report, Berger no doubt thought he had incriminating evidence of Wiens's dangerous views. "We should let people write what they want to," Wiens told Berger.[63] "But we claim that everyone can write what he likes and then we carry out secret censorship," he continued.[64] Wiens then outlined his latest position on the unwieldy red tape in the world of publishing and censorship. "I write what I want to, I live in the GDR but that is all, I intend to write about the world," he added provocatively.[65] "If it isn't published then I will get it published in other socialist countries," he concluded.[66] To prove that there was no one better equipped to neutralize Wiens than himself, Berger went on to report: "The atmosphere of the conversation was personal. Upon arrival Wiens embraced me in an expression of sympathy. Our relationship is—at least according to Wiens—characterized by reciprocal respect and tolerance (a tolerance which is based on opposing views). Wiens invited me to pay him a visit."[67]

Berger hastened to reciprocate Wiens's hospitality at the next available opportunity. On October 13, 1970, he visited Wiens at home to find him watching television. Moreover, he had the television tuned into an "enemy" Western station.[68] To be sure, Wiens would not have been the first East German citizen to tune illegally into West German television and radio, but most likely he was among the few encountered by Berger who made no effort to hide this habit. Wiens seemed oblivious to Berger's surprise. Berger offered his portentous opinion of Wiens to Pönig. "There are fairly clear signs of subjective idealism," he declared.[69] Wiens had told him: "I write so that people can actively experience things. If someone is in love then his truth is the feeling of being in love. I want to expose biology, drives. Not social, political phenomena."[70] Art should not be one-sided, Wiens had declared—the conclusion he had come to over the years. For a while he had had trouble getting published, but he was now more blasé about his prospects.[71]

We do not know whether Wiens ever suspected that Berger was a Stasi plant with an ulterior motive for such a visit. He may, however, have thought it suspicious that Berger seemed so determined to elicit some commitment to the socialist cause from an acquaintance while his wife lay dying. If Wiens flattered himself long enough to think that Berger might be trying to convey that his career with the Stasi was salvageable, he may have concluded that the Stasi had changed its mind about him. If this was the case, it appears that the Stasi was sizing up Wiens while Wiens was sizing up his old employer. When the Stasi did not make a direct approach, Wiens took the initiative and seized on the next good opportunity that presented itself. He decided he would ask to be redeemed. When the call came, the Stasi was waiting for him.

There is no evidence of coercion or even of emotional blackmail in Wiens's resurrection: the final phase of Wiens's collaboration was entirely voluntary. Soon a stabilizing routine set in, and Wiens began to meet with his new officer Pönig at least twice a month and sometimes even weekly. Whatever the deep psychological reason for Wiens's consent may have been, judging from his lifestyle—that of the gentleman secret agent and international jetsetter—the Stasi had discovered a recipe for success in running him. If we want to read more into the uneventful last volumes of his file we could be tempted to conclude that a friendship of sorts developed between officer and informant, or at least the illusion of a friendship. The Stasi liked to create the impression that the officer-informant relationship was on occasion more than a professional relationship and could become something more than an instrumental bond. In reality, of course, this was a carefully orchestrated illusion, and Stasi officers had no qualms about withdrawing support if they became suspicious about their sources' loyalty. From Wiens's perspective, at least, these regular meetings with his officer appear to have filled a gap and met some fundamental need. We can only conjecture about the nature of that need, although his poetry and the writings of his wife offer a number of intimations for fruitful analysis.

Paul Wiens: Playing Devil's Advocate

On close analysis Wiens's poetry appears to confirm Stephen Brockmann's claim that East German culture "was more conflicted and ambiguous than is frequently imagined."[72] The ambivalence occasioned by Wiens's secret life is best captured in one of his most acclaimed and successful poems, "Stoffwechsel" ("Metabolism," published in translation), from his 1968 collection *Dienstgeheimnis: Ein Nächtebuch*. The poem presents subjectivity shattering into a series of simultaneous identities that are constantly engaged in direct dispute. The poem features the word "I" some twenty-one times, and each incarnation of the self is in association with a different activity:

> I open the book. I enter a house.
> Someone is being born there: me. But
> I open a window and climb out.

Although the repetition of "me" at the end of each sequence suggests that this subject is still identical with itself—despite its movements in and out of spaces both fictional and real—at several points in the poem one self confronts another: "In a rye field one naked person / teases another: me."[73] The poem's personas are far from unified and identical; they either tease, argue with, or try to harm one another:

> They eat
> one another—supper. But I already
> stand at the crossroads. There two
> were arguing. Now the one has a red hole
> in his stomach and screams: me. The other, in the middle
> of the cathedral atop a column, castrates himself: me.⁷⁴

The lyrical subject is emasculated not by external forces but by his own actions and decisions. That this subjective struggle may initially have begun as a game is indicated by the lines in which one self plays chess with the other: "We roll through nights and play / chess: I versus me." The poem suggests that the stakes of playing such a game are fame and power, although these prove to be the subject's downfall:

> Out there among the sparks,
> someone is aglow: me. Fall, without aiming,
> find the white sheet of paper: me. Burn out.
> Jump fresh out of the fire, anointed and chosen:
> a book is opened, a house entered.⁷⁵

At the end of *Amanda* (1983), Irmtraud Morgner's phantasmagorical novel about witches, angels, and devils, we find another representation of Wiens as deeply conflicted. As discussed in chapter 1, the character Konrad Tenner bears a strong resemblance to Wiens, and Tenner comes to make a startling confession. The main character, Laura, has taken refuge in a secret women's hideaway in the Hörselberg mountains. Here she stumbles across her ex-husband, Tenner, who is disguised in a suit of feathers. Irritated to find a man in a sacred place of secret women's business, Laura asks him why he is looking so nervous. Tenner admits to feeling persecuted, although his superiors, he says, prefer to use the euphemism of control rather than surveillance. Tenner confesses to having been a double agent—working simultaneously for Head Angel Zacharias and Head Devil Kolbuk.

Tenner's motivation, he says, was simply the thrill of the game. The only way to take his revenge on his mythical spymasters was to join in the game that they were playing with him and turn them into objects of play.

With two masters rather than one, Tenner could play each off against the other. He could double the stakes and thus raise his chances of winning. "The greater the risk and fear, the greater the pleasure," Tenner tells Laura, who is speechless and can only mumble nonsensical, witch-like curses. Moreover, the attraction of being a double agent came from the pleasure of betting at two gambling tables at once, he tells her. He placed his bets in such a way that each owner of a gambling table thought he was their only client. At the table of Head Angel Zacharias he played devil's advocate, and at the table of Head Devil Kolbuk he played God's advocate.

Morgner's fantastical depiction of Tenner as double agent offers a perceptive and plausible explanation for Wiens's renewed pact with the Stasi. Wiens most likely thought that he could justify his disloyalty toward his colleagues by playing at being their advocate with the Stasi's devil. By the same token, he may have believed himself justified in playing devil's advocate (or the Stasi's) inside the Writers' Guild. Indeed, there is much evidence that in debates about aesthetics he saw his role in the guild as that of devil's advocate. Like Tenner, Wiens may have thought he had outwitted the Stasi by being a kind of double agent. Possibly this was a form of personal insurance that guaranteed he was not being played for a fool. Moreover, Wiens's double life as a writer with secret connections to power brought benefits, which he obviously thought were his due.

It is not implausible that Wiens rationalized his secret rewards as some covert form of compensation for what had happened to his family in the war. When he first started to gamble with the Stasi, he was confident that he had some control over the game. He set limits on the amounts he wagered and restrictions on the people he exposed to the secret police. At the start some people, like his wife, were even off limits, but as the stakes increased and the Cold War intensified, Wiens was forced to up his hand with each new game. He felt compelled to offer up more information and better intelligence and to feed the insatiable secret-police monster with tastier morsels and tidbits.

Like all gamblers with a serious habit, Wiens lived in denial that his addiction to espionage was harmful. He was oblivious to the fact that each new mission with the Stasi was anything but an abstract game of probability with calculable or definable odds. His bets all had repercussions for those implicated in his tasks; that is, for his targets and others who found their way into his regular reports. The sheer volume of reports he penned and their level of detail suggest that Wiens had few qualms about reporting on anyone and everyone and that he took pride in carrying out his secret missions. By the same token, the satisfaction his officers felt about running their agent—with his productivity, his deep penetration into enemy territory, and the quality of his reporting—leaps out from the pages of the bursting binders that hold the fragments of his file together.

Wiens's file is stark and grim testimony to the sheer range of his activities both at home and abroad. Today his dossier, which contains his *Treffberichte* and volumes I/3, II/2, II/3, II/4, and II/5 (his last volume), reads like a cross between an appointments diary, a photograph album, a travel scrapbook, and an annotated address book. Volume I/3 contains an index that is almost encyclopedic, listing 99 names of German and international persons. Volume II/2 lists in the index 122 names of persons who are mentioned in his reports from 1974 to 1976.[76] Volume II/3 contains more than twice that number of persons, mentioning 245 different individuals from 1976 to 1979.[77] Volumes II/4 and II/5 list 181 and 151 persons, respectively.[78] Volume II/4 and others contain photographs of some of the people he met—for instance, images of the Russian émigré translator and dissident Efim Etkind, whom he spied on in Paris[79]—glued in, two per page, much like holiday snaps in a private photo album.

These sections bear potent witness to Wiens's dogged determination to repeatedly prove himself useful. The photographs underscore how alarmingly fluid the boundaries were for Wiens between his personal life—in which he traveled abroad and stayed with friends—and his assignations for the secret police. Perhaps more than any other Stasi file in this study, that of Wiens exemplifies the fact that Stasi files can be instances of "life writing," indeed of "secret life" writing. Wiens's file is an astonishingly comprehensive record of the activities that characterized his different lives, including his secret life: whom he saw when, where he traveled and with whom, and the general content of the conversations he had with colleagues, associates, and friends. Although there are gaps in the Stasi's methodical record-keeping, his file provides a persistent trace of a life that we can follow. Above all, Wiens's file is a revealing record of the unholy alliance between official echelons of society and the secret police, between the personal and the political, and between the private realm and the secret surveillance society that Wiens became a member of.

Wiens's dossier is thick, amounting to eight volumes. Rather like Clifford Geertz's "thick description," a thick file can tell us about either the intensity or the duration of an individual's collaboration; both factors are crucial to evaluating the impact of an informant's period of working for the Stasi, as Joachim Walther has argued.[80] Indeed, a long-term, stable relationship with the Stasi can often be read into a particularly voluminous file. The thickest parts are symptomatic of a close, even symbiotic relationship or of moments of intense activity, when an agent was catapulted into the foreground of political events or a major espionage operation.

Wiens's file is thick with respect to the specific targets that he worked on. There are too many to list here, but they include domestic cases of writers under surveillance that Wiens played a part in, such as the OV on "Reptile," Frank-Wolf Matthies, which led to his arrest in 1973;[81] and a collaboration with the KGB, the Soviet Union's main security agency, concerning the dissident Russian writer Lew Kopelew.[82] The writers on whom Wiens reported included individuals from East and West Germany, France, Hungary, Yugoslavia, and the Soviet Union.[83] Wiens's file is "thin" rather than "thick" in Geertz's terms where it is inconclusive, especially in relation to those writers who fell outside its purview.

When a file is circumstantially thin, this is usually because an informant was not instructed to report on something, was unable to, or was not even present at a particular event from which a report might have been anticipated. Where a file is intentionally thin this may mean that the informer suppressed information or withheld it from the Stasi (for instance, an informant may have been trying to protect a particular individual who is mentioned only sketchily). We need to be alert to those suspiciously "thin" sections of the files—to brief passages, absences, glosses, and deliberate omissions. It is possible to detect telltale signs of information withheld or even concealed. "Seeing" these invisible sections of files reveals what may be evidence of a desire to protect and *not* incriminate specific persons. This chapter includes my interpretations of certain thick sections of Wiens's file, in search of the impact of his informing and of the thinner, telling silences.

There seems little doubt that Wiens knowingly and consciously penned many incriminating reports about others. Overall, his reporting style is expansive and, in parts, long-winded; his reports usually span several pages. The range of topics he covers is vast, from politics and opinions, to Western visitors, to receptions held at the Permanent Representative of the Federal Republic of Germany in East Berlin, which was effectively West Germany's embassy in the East, to reports on actions and events as they affected his professional circles. In 1972 the instructions he received from the Stasi were at times strikingly concrete. For instance, he was charged with investigating whether a published article was likely to be in violation of Articles 99, 100, and 106 of the GDR Criminal Code.[84] In both cases, Wiens's task was far more complex than merely judging aesthetic merit and content; it also involved making semi-legal judgments.

Wiens achieved an early success in relation to a plan within the Writers' Guild to launch a new literary magazine. At his meeting with Pönig on December 14, 1972, Wiens was pleased to hand Pönig a conception for the magazine. Pönig, we can assume, was less surprised than usual because he already knew of the group's potentially counterrevolutionary plan from two other informants he had planted.[85] This appears to be among the first examples of successful infiltration of oppositional groups and their subsequent neutralization by the MfS. The Stasi was so pleased with Wiens that, as mentioned above, he was duly rewarded on three occasions. His first medal in 1972 was awarded in response to his contribution to the successful operation concerning "Reptile" (alias Matthies). At the time Wiens also worked on another high-priority operation, OV "Saboteur" (Diversant) on the returned emigrant writer Stefan Heym.[86]

The first medal, the Medal of Merit of the National People's Army in Bronze (Verdienstmedaille der Nationalen Volksarmee in Bronze), was tangible proof that the ministry valued Wiens's efforts. With the medal, he was able to bank symbolic capital for himself. In 1974 he was still seen as reliable, discrete, and honest by his officers, and Pönig continued to invest in the relationship with Wiens. In the same year Wiens was again rewarded, this time with the Medal of Merit of the National People's Army in Silver. By this stage he was earning 500 marks per month, and other perks began to come his way. He and Morgner moved into a spacious, modernist, highrise apartment on Leipziger Strasse in Berlin. The building was one of four new apartment blocks built in a radical transformation of the streetscape.[87] Later, Morgner must have asked how her husband paid for the extravagance of such a glamorous, large apartment. At some point she started to openly express to friends that she had no idea how Wiens could afford such a lifestyle, which friends saw as a sign that he was working for the Stasi.[88]

Wiens saw no reason to change his arrangement with the Stasi, not even once his marriage to Morgner was failing. By April 1976, he had been promoted to the rank of IME, the elite category of informant that was deployed because of special expertise. He was now earning the impressive sum of 2,000 marks per month.[89] At this point in his career he was working on cases relating to an assortment of the nation's most prominent writers: Ulrich Plenzdorf, Klaus Schlesinger, Volker Braun, Sarah Kirsch, Günter Kunert, Bernd Jentsch, Reiner Kunze, and Rolf Schneider. Wiens's file reveals that he was also under instructions to follow a number of his colleagues, such as Günter Kunert, on their travels abroad.[90] Wiens traveled extensively on PEN Club business, so much so that his nickname in literary circles was "Interpaule," a play on "Interpol," the common name of the international criminal investigation unit.[91] On all of these trips he was always on duty, observing other delegates from the East, but not only them; he also reported on Günter Grass, whom he called in one entry a "political scatterbrain" (*politischen Wirrkopf*).[92]

The files document extensively Wiens's sometimes bungling attempts to shadow his fellow writers in the PEN Club on overseas trips. For instance, at the Forty-Third International PEN Congress, held in Stockholm on May 21–26, 1978, apart from working on Kunert, he assisted with other surveillance operations, such as "Forked Tongue" (Doppelzüngler), focused on Christa and Gerhard Wolf.[93] When Stephan Hermlin, who barely missed a PEN Congress,[94] announced he was traveling to Yugoslavia at the invitation of the Serbian chapter of PEN, Wiens promptly organized a trip for himself, faking an official invitation so as not to blow his cover. As proof to his officers that this was necessary, he suggested that Hermlin might be intending to spark a confrontation with the party.⁹⁵

Toward the end of the 1970s, Wiens wrote many *Treffberichte* that were deeply incriminating of his writer colleagues. There is even evidence of his involvement in practical operative matters involving manipulation and high levels of deception.⁹⁶ This flies in the face of earlier statements on file that Wiens was not willing to be a full-fledged operative for the Stasi. There is little evidence that Wiens was coerced or blackmailed into taking a loyalist line with his colleagues or that he was forced into surveilling them. On the contrary, the historical record speaks volumes about the fact that Wiens continued to be an extremely important and reliable source inside the Writers' Guild for the Stasi. The number of military and other state accolades Wiens received over the course of his career is second to none for an individual associated with the cultural sphere and a telling indication that the Stasi considered his work invaluable.⁹⁷

The agreement that the Stasi appears to have struck with Wiens permitted him a greater degree of latitude in relation to overseas travel as long as he reciprocated with an informative report from his sojourns abroad, an arrangement that proved highly effective. Travel was clearly the key to the longevity of the relationship cemented between Wiens and the Stasi, and, having found this key, the Stasi continued to use it. Travel provided the essential element of exclusivity to his relationship with the secret service that Wiens patently needed.⁹⁸ Moreover, international travel offset the humdrum nature of much informing work, which perhaps assumed the status of a tedious but necessary exercise in bureaucratic red tape that accompanied luxuries such as overseas travel. The secret surveillance society that Wiens was willing to contribute to was a cosmopolitan one replete with rare travel privileges that were only forthcoming to the political and cultural elite. If informing was the price Wiens was repeatedly obliged to pay for being a member of this secret elite, then from 1972 he dutifully paid his dues year after year.

Paul Gratzik: A Bridge over Troubled Waters

By contrast, for the working-class playwright Paul Gratzik, the fresh winds blowing from the politburo after 1972 were unsettling. By this time he was a prize-winning freelance writer, but he seems to have been rudderless and unsure how to read the political climate. Despite his promotion by the Stasi to the status of IMV and his prize of 3,000 marks from the East German Ministry for Culture, in 1972 he tried to avoid seeing or meeting with his officer, Wenzel, altogether. Then, at a meeting on October 26, 1972, in his apartment, Gratzik reported on an incident that was to become a critical juncture in the development of his relationship with the Stasi.[99] Gratzik's wife had found out that he had "contacts" to the Stasi, and he had confessed that "he did carry out certain tasks for the state authorities [*Staatsorgane*]."[100] Gratzik conveyed to Wenzel his "reservations" (*Bedenken*) about continuing to work for the MfS; Wenzel managed to clear up (*ausgeräumt*) these reservations by forcing Gratzik to sign a declaration dated November 1, 1972, stating that he would continue to serve as an informant. A report from the head of HA XX, Major Tzscheutschler, on December 7, 1972, confirmed this.[101]

In the same report Tzscheutschler noted that Gratzik was plagued by "fluctuations" (*Schwankungen*) over ideological questions but that Wenzel would continue to work "intensively" on these to "firm up his socialist position."[102] Because of his "fluctuations" it would also be necessary to assign an informant to Gratzik, IMV "Stein."[103] A few days after Gratzik's missed meeting on October 30, 1972, Wenzel filed a "proposal to reaffirm an IMV," in which he also confirmed the need to "check on the IM more systematically, in particular his political-ideological behavior in the cultural arena."[104]

It is not clear why Gratzik let himself be talked into renewing his oath to continue to work for the Stasi, but, as indicated, at the next meeting on November 1, 1972, in the safe house "Pilz," he signed a half-page pledge to resume his work (see fig. 4).[105] After much deliberating, he promised to carry out his tasks "with maximum success." A sure sign that the Stasi's motivational pep talk had hit the mark was Gratzik's reversal, in which he renounced his previous negative behavior and blamed himself entirely: "The reasons for it are to be found in my attitude to my tasks."[106]

Of course the specific reasons that Gratzik brought forth for continuing read as if they were dictated by Wenzel. If Gratzik failed to do his part, this would only be of benefit to the class enemy: "Our activity should be directed at thwarting the activities of the opposition. If I withdraw, it will leave a gap, which has to be filled one way or the other, which would mean a victory for the enemy. Since I do not want imperialism to achieve victory or a partial victory, I have to make my contribution to ensuring our people are well informed."[107]

Further, Gratzik finished his dictated statement with a confession that reveals the extraordinary level of psychological manipulation and ideological blackmail that "Peter" was now subject to. Curiously, his declaration does not attempt to efface the validity of his personal misgivings but ultimately subordinates them rather fatalistically to historical necessity. His personal conflicts were a symptom of the broader, objective contradictions of the historical times in which he lived. Gratzik's language of extreme self-denial for the greater good reveals the extent of his martyrdom for the communist cause: "My personal concerns and contradictions are the contradictions of our age. I want to try and resolve these contradictions in such a way that our work and I can move forward."[108] The statement closes with a desperate, almost chastened plea for forgiveness: "I beg you therefore not to hold it against me too much [*nachtragen*]."[109]

Elicited under extreme duress, Gratzik's professed willingness to sacrifice himself on the high altar of the Cold War came at a price. Above all his submission required the suppression or disavowal of his subjective emotions and his deepening ambivalence to informing work. His motivational circuitry necessitated, in effect, a rewiring, whereby all personal desires and motives were rerouted to reflect the wishes of the greater communist good. By his own admission Gratzik was a heavy drinker; in the film documentary *Vaterlandsverräter* he leaves no doubt about his love of a good home brew of schnapps. The same documentary reveals in compelling detail the lasting emotional and psychological damage caused by Gratzik's enduring love-hate relationship to spying for his fatherland. His Stasi file does not document this damage to the same degree. Betrayal, as Crystal Parikh remarks, "costs everyone dearly,"[110] and it cost no one more dearly than Gratzik. His possibly calculated strategy of blowing his cover to his wife, or allowing his cover to be blown, had patently failed to work. He would have known that this tactic was commonly used by informers who wanted to quit. On this occasion the Stasi decided not to end the relationship (as it would have done with others).

Instead, Wenzel merely intensified his "ideological work" on Gratzik at their subsequent meetings. The contents of these one-to-one discussions fill page after page of Gratzik's substantial informer's file. Perhaps Wenzel's superiors had also lost patience with "Peter." On paper, at least, Wenzel needed to reassure them that he could turn Gratzik around. He thought he could do so by working on the ideological position of his headstrong charge. This was code for emotional blackmail. Having expended so much time and effort on modifying Gratzik's recalcitrant behavior, Wenzel was not prepared to stop now.

In 1973 and 1974 Gratzik was experiencing difficulties having dramatic works accepted for staging. It is conceivable that this situation arose because Gratzik wanted to write a play about the Berlin Wall, normally a taboo topic. Before Gratzik put pen to paper the party gained wind of the idea through informant "Stein."[111] Wenzel was only too familiar with Gratzik's unorthodox views on the Berlin Wall, long before "Stein" felt it necessary to remind him of them.[112] Gratzik must have told Wenzel himself at their first meeting that he was planning to write a play about the Berlin Wall; this play would expose the "social effects" of family separation as they were experienced by individuals.[113] No doubt Wenzel sought to talk him out of such a project, while being forced to conclude that "it was hard to change his mind when it was made up."[114] In April 1974 "Stein" told the Stasi that Gratzik claimed that the Dresden State Theater was sabotaging his work.[115] Gratzik's disaffection was so great that he crankily declared that he wished to return to factory work, which he did.

If Gratzik thought that his return to paid employment would let him off the hook with the Stasi, then he was severely mistaken. Having once been brought back into the fold, Gratzik was reeled in yet again to provide more illustrious and onerous services for the organization. Over the following years Gratzik's relationship to the ministry gradually deteriorated, but this seems merely to have spurred Wenzel on in his determination to lure his agent back. Wenzel apparently harbored no illusions about Gratzik's habit of prevaricating on ideological questions. Throughout 1974 Wenzel had plenty of opportunity to hone his skills of manipulation in his meetings with Gratzik. The files document protracted discussions, typically narrated in indirect speech and sometimes recorded word-for-word.

More generally, these detailed records provide insights about the manner in which the Stasi sought to bring disaffected informants back on track. They reveal how officers experimented with what they thought were the latest techniques of psychological manipulation and well as with softer forms of brainwashing. A report filed on March 6, 1974, documents how Gratzik was subjected to a comprehensive reprimand.[116] Gratzik had not been keeping appointments.[117] He was severely rebuked for his "unreliability"[118] and reminded of the need for more positive thinking.[119] By November 1974 Wenzel had seen little improvement in Gratzik's attitude, which necessitated adding to "Peter's" file an extensive three-page report about the informant's lack of engagement. At the November meeting Gratzik mentioned a compelling reason for wanting to quit; he feared for his safety because he now believed people were becoming suspicious of him and were trying "to test him to see whether he was working for the security forces."[120] Wenzel was quick to dismiss his informant's justified fears about his safety, elaborating in painstaking detail on the content of the fraught discussion that ensued. Detail of this kind is rare in the Stasi files, and the extraordinary pains that Wenzel took to document his conversation are especially so. Whether he did so to protect himself in the event that things went awry with Gratzik or to impress his superiors with his efforts at brainwashing we cannot be sure.

Certainly, the use of the first person in his report serves to reinforce Wenzel's agency at the meeting. In this report Wenzel is not a depersonalized filter of intelligence like Paul Wiens's handlers. He is an active participant in this key discussion about real versus apparent reasons and personal versus social contradictions. Espionage is revealed here to be much more than a one-way exchange of information; it is a scene of multiple flows of both information and power.

At this grueling meeting Wenzel summoned all his powers of persuasion and mobilized all the espionage tools in his officer's handbook. Wenzel applied a disarming mixture of sympathy and cold, hard logic. He first allowed Gratzik to voice his concerns before attempting to rationalize and explain them to him. Wenzel argued, for instance, that Gratzik's personal problems stemmed from doubts about the current direction of cultural politics. His emotional "fluctuations" (*Schwankungen*) were motivated by the "deeply pessimistic attitude which he display[ed]."[121] According to Wenzel's argument, for some time this attitude had created "a conflict situation" with Gratzik, which he had found hard to cope with.[122]

After Wenzel's pseudopsychoanalytical diagnosis, there followed an admission of gratitude of sorts—presumably elicited as a result of Wenzel's emotional blackmail—that Gratzik had achieved much as a writer under the tutelage of the Stasi "on the basis of the tuition we carried out with him."[123] Reading between Wenzel's lines, we can see that Gratzik had much to thank the Stasi for, and because of the time invested in "instructing" him he had now achieved a "position among writers and in the Writers' Guild which made it possible for him to undertake greater assignments on our behalf."[124]

Wenzel's filed report on the protracted "ideological therapy" session required in November 1974 highlights the double bind in which Gratzik found himself. On the one hand, he constantly reiterated his reservations about informing work, adding that he did not wish to report on writers he knew well. He was also concerned about turning his back on controversial, "isolated" writers such as Wolf Biermann, who might have fallen from favor but who might later be rehabilitated.[125] On the other hand, Gratzik eventually agreed "to report extensively, comprehensively and irrespective of the individual on the fundamental position and attitude of the various writers that he [knew]," and more specifically on his friend and fellow writer Martin Stade.[126]

Over the following years a pattern emerged in which Gratzik often turned up to meetings with Wenzel disgruntled, aggressive, and full of resolve to end the relationship, only to leave chastened and contrite, with a new set of instructions in hand and a lengthy list of tasks to fulfill. Almost a full year after the difficult conversation of November 1974, Gratzik met with Wenzel in the usual safe house, "Pilz," on November 27, 1975, and announced at the start that he wished to terminate his undercover work for the Stasi.[127] After considerable pressure from Wenzel, Gratzik agreed to give his decision further consideration. A few weeks later at the next meeting, held on December 11, 1975, Wenzel recorded that Gratzik appeared compliant and subdued, and gave his consent to continue under one condition: "continuing to work with me," that is, sticking with Wenzel.[128] Wenzel responded to their rather unexpected reconciliation in a roundabout way by first praising Gratzik, saying that "he had not expected any different decision from him regarding his cooperation,"[129] then by reapplying the sort of psychological pressure he had become so adept at wielding. If Gratzik stopped working for the Stasi, he would only be "deciding against himself," that is, he would not be acting in his best interests, Wenzel told him.[130] Gratzik's contribution to security was for the greater good of "socialist society," and he was doing himself a service (*seiner eigenen Person dient*) by staying on.[131] Of course, this was only true if Gratzik put the state's interests before his own.

The next six years would prove to the Stasi how crucial it was to have informants inside all cultural spheres to warn it of potential risks and to neutralize undesirable political actions. But the same years also demonstrated that there were major drawbacks to running an inside source, particularly when the source could not square his own interests with those of national security. Gratzik had been working for the Stasi since 1962, and the relationship had fluctuated wildly over the years. Nevertheless, the Stasi could not have foreseen that the source it had once found so versatile and productive in monitoring liberal tendencies in cultural circles would stumble because the climate was not liberal enough.

The incongruity of the Stasi's expectations for informants like "Peter" ought to have become blindingly clear in 1975 when a group of writers in the Writers' Guild had the idea to publish an anthology of short stories about Berlin. Such clarity did not occur. For the next fifteen years the Stasi grew increasingly enamored of the idea of using plants or moles that could infiltrate the heart of enemy circles. Wenzel was keen to deploy plants to work on dissenting groups of writers, and he planned to use his agent "Peter" in one such operation. Doubtless he hoped to secure a coup for himself if "Peter" could manage to prevent or at least stymie the plans of the group in question.

Paul Gratzik: Among the Trojan Horses

Possibly the most serious security threat to emerge from literary circles before the Biermann affair of late 1976 came, astonishingly, from the "Berlin

Stories" project mentioned above, which involved around eighteen authors. Initiated by Martin Stade, Klaus Schlesinger, and Ulrich Plenzdorf, the anthology first came to the Stasi's attention late in 1975 after it heard of a gathering of the authors that took place in the autumn of that year. By this stage a 240-page manuscript of contributions had been compiled, but the group had not yet secured a publisher. According to "Peter," who was among the contributors, the group had decided it wanted to retain full control over the editing and selection process. In some official Stasi documents the project was even referred to ominously as a "self-publishing" (*Selbstverlag*) initiative. Curiously, the project's dangers are also implied in "Peter's" rather garbled account to Wenzel given on December 10, 1975, in which he lamely tries to minimize the political nature of the project by arguing that the authors simply wished to have control over their own works.[132]

Gratzik might not have been apprised of the real intentions of the group.[133] If the anthology seemed harmless enough to him, it was considered to represent such a colossal security risk to the regime that HA XX promptly launched a massive surveillance operation to thwart it. The Stasi spared no expense and used every feasible means—postal control, customs control, even bugging devices—on a number of different fronts to prevent the anthology from proceeding. It harassed the organizers of the volume as well as other contributors, reserving its harshest treatment for Heide Härtl and Gert Neumann, who were subjected to a vicious campaign of demoralization and intimidation.[134] Alerted to the matter on November 13, 1975,[135] the head of the HA's Leipzig regional office (*Bezirksverwaltung*) allocated seven staff members to its part of the operation. Paul Gratzik was involved in the case as an informant and was instructed to keep an eye on Martin Stade. At the meeting on December 10, 1975, Wenzel asked Gratzik if he could "briefly" borrow Gratzik's copy of the manuscript.[136] Gratzik agreed, and on December 16 at 12:45pm, in broad daylight, the manuscript was collected from Gratzik's apartment.

Thus in December 1975 Gratzik came to the aid of the district office (*Kreisdienststelle*) of Dippoldiswalde, which belonged to the Dresden regional office, but the Leipzig team had already procured a copy of the offending manuscript from one of its reliable collaborators.[137] Under instructions from

Minister for State Security Mielke, the Berlin head office issued a warning to its outlying offices that the anthology represented a threat of proportions comparable to the counterrevolution in Czechoslovakia in 1968.

In Stasi management circles there seems to have been little disagreement that the plan to publish an anthology on the sensitive topic of a divided city surrounded by a wall without the usual controls of publishers constituted a serious breach of cultural protocol. A challenge of this scale demanded a well-coordinated approach across the GDR, and to this end the Berlin head office summoned representatives from its regional offices for an urgent briefing.[138] They were told that a solution to the problem was crucial in the lead-up to the Ninth Party Congress of May 1976. The ministry was instructed to throw "*all* its forces" and deploy "*all* its ministerial resources, methods and possibilities" to contain the plan and "to ensure the operative processing and comprehensive operative control of *all* persons in connection with this proposal."[139]

A third meeting organized by the Berlin head office in December 1975 outlined a coordinated plan for the operative handling of the case; this included the proposal to allocate progressive, loyal writers to the group, in an attempt to bring about a "process of decomposition" (*Zersetzungsprozeß*) and the eventual neutralization of the project.[140] The cold and clinical vocabulary of decomposition and destruction, which the Stasi reserved for battles with its most entrenched foes, shows the extent of the regime's alarm.

Apart from having supplied the Stasi with a copy of the manuscript, Gratzik does not appear to have been a key player in the quashing of the "Berlin Stories" initiative. Much to the Stasi's annoyance, he was, after all, a contributor to the anthology, and he was eager to see it published. His small contribution to the project's eventual demise was to support the idea of broadening the pool of stories about Berlin and deemphasizing the theme of the Berlin Wall: "In particular he had to ensure that the over-emphasis on border problems in Berlin is removed from the stories."[141] His other contribution was to try to prevent the anthology from being published in West Germany and to suggest that it should be offered to an eastern publisher, which, of course, would compromise its independence.[142] To his officer he was careful to stress that the project was not providing a platform for mounting opposition to the regime.[143] In other words, he tried to neutralize the political impact of the volume so that it could proceed, if at all, in a manner acceptable to the Stasi and the Ministry for Culture.

The coordinated security approach proved successful, as was the proposal to destabilize the group of contributors from inside. The various departments at work on the case managed to defuse the presumed threat and remove the political sting from the anthology's tail. In the end this was achieved mainly through the technique of placing Trojan horses among the key writers who were driving the initiative; these undermining presences could actively destabilize the group, for instance by pulling their stories from the anthology. By all accounts Gratzik was not one of the main Trojan horses. This work of creating breakaway groups of dissenters was carried out by two other contributors: Uwe Kant (informant "Paul") and Jürgen Leskien, who, under pressure from other informants, such as IMS "Martin," declared that they were withdrawing from the project.[144]

Ultimately, in the confusion that resulted from the pressure applied to all those involved, it is hard to delineate clear roles and responsibilities for the participants. For instance, those writers who were bullied by the Stasi's moles and withdrew from the project were not the only individuals to disassociate themselves from the anthology.[145] Gratzik reported to Wenzel in May 1976 that Martin Stade had distanced himself from the project. Stade had apprised Gratzik of disputes between the three editors and key members of the Writers' Guild, at least one of whom was under Stasi instructions to subvert the project. One of those present at these project meetings was Hermann Kant, who had promised his Stasi handling officers that he would block the initiative.[146] Stade confessed to Gratzik that the anthology had become "relatively uninteresting" for him, mainly because an editor from the Mitteldeutscher Publishing House, based in the East German town of Halle, had taken it on.[147]

As it transpired, the radically modified anthology was eventually published in 1976 by Aufbau, the largest publishing house in the GDR. With the title *Berliner Schriftsteller erzählen* (Berlin authors tell stories) and Werner Neubert as the new editor, the volume had the blessing of the Writers' Guild, and, inevitably, of the Stasi. We now know that Neubert was the active Stasi IM "Wolfgang Köhler."[148] Of the forty authors included in the final anthology, most were closely affiliated with the SED, and eighteen had Stasi connections.[149] Notwithstanding the project's reinvention by the secret police, some of the original authors, such as Gert Neumann, managed to retaliate. They initiated another independent anthology project; the Stasi would pursue this just as vigorously, but less successfully, under a new operation, OV "Anthology II."[150]

*

The period of détente under First Secretary Honecker necessitated particular vigilance on the part of the East German security forces, especially in the sphere of literature—mainly because East German writers were deemed "gateways" for enemy influence; they were closely networked with writers based in West Germany and in other Eastern Bloc countries.[151] As presaged in the 1969 Line on Writers, according to the Stasi mindset the risk that writers could act as conduit points (*Stützpunkte*) for enemy contact and influence was real. This increased vigilance is borne out by the growth in numbers of informants recruited during the years 1971–76, by the importance accorded to these IMs as sources of information, and by invasive operations to attempt to control writers' activities. During this period the Stasi learned that it could rely on informants with critical, non-orthodox views, especially in cultural politics, as long as their fundamental loyalty was not in question, as the cases of Gratzik and Wiens both show.

Although the Stasi lost a certain ideological purity in the profile of some informants, it gained new skills and techniques in handling such agents. Through special handling regimes, which could involve turning a blind eye to certain behaviors, even including breaches of secrecy, officers could keep key informers in the field. Where trust was an issue, officers attempted to place their own informants under surveillance by other informants, thereby creating a self-referential, circular, and hence almost incestuous system of informing. By tailoring individual plans for bringing informants back on track or for cajoling them into continuing when they vacillated, and by applying various kinds of emotional blackmail, the Stasi found that it could put to work even ambivalent informants.

Both Wiens and Gratzik proved to have deeply conflicted attitudes to working for the Stasi; these attitudes posed ongoing challenges for their case officers. In handling Wiens the Stasi counteracted his ambivalence by keeping in play substantial incentives, most notably that of travel. The incentives fostered a positive motivational approach loop, whereby Wiens met his professional and personal objectives while largely satisfying the Stasi's demands. By contrast, the Stasi was far less successful in convincing Gratzik that his collaboration was personally and professionally worthwhile. During this phase his positive orientation toward achieving his goals slipped into a predominant avoidance orientation, whereby the main obstacle preventing him from ceasing to inform for the Stasi was his fear for his personal safety and wellbeing. Thus, during the earlier years of détente, Wiens appears to have settled into living the secret life as the good life, but Gratzik balked more and more often at the nature of his tasks and at the level of risk that the job involved. The Stasi had created codependencies. It had assisted Gratzik's career and provided welcome cultural capital, while Gratzik had supplied crucial intelligence, namely, the manuscript of the "Berlin Stories" project, in the Stasi's new Line on Writers. But concrete incentives were insufficient for him to enjoy enough benefits from participating in the secret surveillance society. As argued in the following chapter, these issues remained unresolved—just as the Stasi's greatest challenges were yet to unfold in certain official and unofficial cultural spheres that were not yet on the radar of the MfS.

4
The Secret War on Political-Ideological Diversion, 1976–1978

By the middle of the 1970s, détente at the level of the two superpowers, the United States and the Soviet Union, had effectively collapsed.[1] Erich Honecker began to roll back the tide of liberalization that he had initiated as first secretary of the Central Committee of the SED during the optimistic days of the thaw of 1972.[2] An ominous sign that Honecker never fully trusted his new liberal course is the sobering fact that during the liberalization experiment he began to expand the Ministry for State Security.[3] In the 1970s, particularly after the diplomatic recognition of the GDR by the Federal Republic of Germany, the regime's efforts focused increasingly on the problem of "enemy contact and influence." Literature was understood to be especially at risk of enemy attack, despite the fact that the causes of domestic unrest were homegrown.[4]

In the aftermath of détente Minister for State Security Erich Mielke devoted extra resources to the special branches, or "lines," that were overseeing control of culture.[5] In the middle phase from 1963 to 1974 writers were not a major area of priority for HA XX;[6] along with publishers and other cultural institutions, writers were handled by HA XX's Referat (Section)

II.[7] This was all to change. In an extraordinarily short space of time, from 1974 to 1976, the number of surveillance operations undertaken against writers rose by a staggering 288 percent.[8] By 1976-77 HA XX was running thirty-one full-scale OV investigations, when only two years previously it had run a total of eight.[9] Those sections of the MfS that dealt with writers and publishing, the "line" on writers, received a boost in resources. Priority was given to a new section, called HA XX/OG (Operativgruppe), which was formed from Referat IV.

HA XX/OG focussed on four cases of "political-ideological diversion" of national significance. These were centrally run OVs that targeted, respectively, poet and singer Wolf Biermann, chemist Robert Havemann, writer Stefan Heym, and reform Marxist Rudolf Bahro.[10] In 1976 HA XX/OG employed 20 full-time officers and ran 76 registered informants.[11] Two years later, in 1978, Section IV was reinstated and allocated responsibility for publishers and the press.[12] By 1980 the number of officers in HA XX/OG had decreased by one—but the number of informants had grown markedly, from 76 to 108.[13] And rather unusually, in 1980 there was a high percentage of women among them, 44 percent of all 108 informers were female.[14] This was the only period in the history of the ministry when women achieved anything like parity.

Despite the East German government's rhetoric of a "peaceful co-existence" between East and West, Mielke dismissed the overtures issuing from the West German government as "Trojan horses carrying new espionage menaces."[15] The minister hoped that the new threats could be contained through expanded networks of informants creating "a seamless web of observation and control of everyday life."[16] Mielke attempted to tackle the problem of cultural dissent by recruiting better qualified IMs and recruiting them more carefully.[17] This entailed selecting from the pool of school leavers and university graduates.[18] The recruitment of Maja Wiens during this period serves to illustrate how such selection was put into practice.

Yet by the mid-1970s the rapidly growing army of IMs brought with it a new set of problems. The next few years of the regime would severely test the limits of the Stasi's push to recruit more informants who were better qualified.[19] The MfS's strategy of increasingly relying on human labor to harvest and evaluate critical intelligence would also be tested. As already seen in the cases of the IMs Paul Wiens and Paul Gratzik, over the course of the 1960s and 1970s informers who were recruited mainly on the basis of their gratitude to the socialist state and their broad commitment to socialist ideals could easily become disaffected. If the Stasi was going to increase its reliance on such precarious sources of intelligence, it needed to find other means of ensuring their long-term loyalty. This chapter explores a number of the methods that officers implemented to deal with vacillating informers.

During 1976–78 the ministry continued to adapt its mode of human contact surveillance, especially the technique that I call "sticky surveillance." Détente was for Mielke merely an extension of class warfare by other means, and he feared especially the "politics of human contacts."[20] As he discovered, the advantage of deploying human intelligence collection was that informers were able to approach their targets naturalistically and thereby achieve a relationship far closer than was possible through technological forms of information harvesting. Because the source of surveillance was not geographically fixed in one place (as occurs with a camera or bugging device), surveillers were able to zoom in on their objects. Parasite-like, they could attach themselves to their targets, if not physically, then at least socially and potentially even emotionally. This technique was an insidious type of state tagging service that simultaneously observed the world openly, secretly, and from close-up. When the target moved, so too did the informer, sticking as close as circumstances allowed.

Because sticky human surveillance worked on attachments to humans and on connections of varying intensities and kinds, it had many benefits. The first was that the source could materialize out of nowhere; the informant could pop up when the target's defenses were down and attach himself or herself to the target's circle of friends. The source could join in social and professional activities, entering the target's lifeworld inconspicuously. As we shall see with Paul Wiens, if the source already happened to be part of the target's professional milieu, this was an added bonus. Yet being a habituated member of a target's milieu also presented difficulties, given that an informant could be called on to engage with his or her peer's hostile or dissenting views. An informant had to play on and with the target's attachments—often to friends, ideas, and even the country—but never in such a way as to arouse suspicion. It was crucial that an informant stayed on script, that is, adhered strictly to the agreed fictional explanation, or *Legende* (legend), for becoming friends or for approaching the target. Otherwise, he or she would risk deconspiring and coming unstuck.

The infiltrator of social circles functioned rather like a rhizome that lays down concealed runners, or "lines of flight," as Gilles Deleuze and Félix Guattari call them, often in multiple directions at once. In the GDR these "runners" disguised themselves as "aboveground" (as opposed to underground) connections to other likeminded citizens.[21] Indeed, the image of a rhizome describes especially well the Stasi informers' main modes of operating as they crept surreptitiously from one secret assignation to the next. Rhizomatic IMs on surveillance business could rear their heads on occasions a target least expected an intervention by the state. They could make public appearances at key events in a target's life and then return to the safety and solidity of the rhizome's node, where they would meet their secret-police officers, debrief, and regroup. This was analog, nomadic surveillance. Maja Wiens exemplified this approach; she ventured forth and ducked back, maneuvering just as swiftly into position to make contact as she retreated from the field to assess and receive further instructions. The cases of Paul Wiens, Paul Gratzik, and Maja Wiens serve here to demonstrate the shortcomings of human surveillance and illustrate that infiltrating a target's private world proved far from easy. The challenges when dealing with aboveground communities were different from those that arose when tackling underground groups. This chapter primarily discusses aboveground circles (whereas chapters 5 and 6 are concerned with the sphere of underground culture).

Maja Wiens: Recruiting the Functionary's Daughter

By the 1970s the Stasi had become far more cautious in its approach to recruiting agents. It sometimes tried to prevent things from going awry by conscripting informants' family members; as the saying goes, the Stasi liked to "keep things in the family." Drawing on the sizable pool of informants' relatives was one pragmatic way in which the Stasi could, at the very least, be assured that a recruit was from appropriate ideological stock. If a potential candidate was the son or daughter of an existing agent, this could obviate the need for watertight security checks on his or her background. If both parents happened to be registered as informants, then the Stasi may have thought that a smooth recruitment was a foregone conclusion.

Maja Wiens's Stasi file comprises 2,491 pages in ten volumes.[22] Reading the opening of this file, it comes as a surprise that "Marion" (her code name) was neither an easy nor a straightforward recruit. As mentioned in chapter 1, Maja Wiens was the daughter of writer and informant Paul Wiens from his first marriage, to Erika Lautenschlager, who was also a Stasi agent. Lautenschlager was first recruited in 1974 as an IMK, a designation referring to those who offered their apartments as safe houses.[23]

Thus, Maja Wiens grew up in a family with considerable cultural pretentions and some dark secrets. Born in 1952, she was only ten years old when her father first began working undercover; most likely she did not know about her parents' association with the Stasi until much later.[24] It is possible that, despite her flawless pedigree, Wiens was not regarded as suitable for undercover work. For the forty years of its existence the Stasi was suffused by a chronic misogyny that considered women innately incapable of serving as reliable informers. In all likelihood the Stasi assumed that Maja Wiens could not keep a secret. As it transpired, she was very good at keeping secrets, better than many men, and probably better than her father.

We can safely presume that Wiens was first approached by the Stasi because of her father's long-standing association with the ministry. Moreover, she was recruited in December 1977, when, as mentioned above, the Stasi was urgently seeking informants to deal with the latest crisis. The regime was grappling with the disastrous public-relations fallout from the Wolf Biermann affair; the regime had expelled the protest poet and songwriter in November 1976 by stripping him, without warning, of his citizenship. Over the course of 1977 prominent actors and writers had left East Germany, and the Stasi was intensifying its efforts to stifle the worrying groundswell of dissent in the country.

By 1977 structural changes in the Stasi's cultural departments undertaken in 1974–76 had been integrated, and the new, special branch HA

XX/OG that coordinated security operations in the literary sector was fully operational. As already discussed, one of its main concerns was OV "Poet," focused on Biermann. This represented one of the largest operations the Stasi conducted against a single individual.[25] From 1976 onward the various operations dealing with Biermann's sympathizers were all centralized in this section.[26] Regional and district offices of the MfS often supplied information to HA XX, and in the wake of Biermann's expulsion many, including the office from which Maja Wiens was run as an agent, were eager to make active contributions.

Despite Mielke's emphasis on improving methods of recruitment and the quality of recruits, the Stasi's approach to drafting Maja Wiens seems to have been outright haphazard. As the relevant guidelines prescribed, Stasi officers who wished to make first contact with a potential informant typically did so in the workplace—or, in the case of students, at their university, as discussed in chapter 1. Another common method was to post the target an official letter, requesting that she or he report at the local police station "to clarify a matter" (*zur Klärung eines Sachverhalts*). In Maja Wiens's case the Stasi took neither of these conventional routes. Instead, an officer from the ministry appeared unannounced at her apartment when her husband and son were also at home. This was an inauspicious start to the relationship; proper contact could not be made, and the recruitment encounter had to be postponed.

The plan to enlist Wiens was the rather poorly executed idea of the Pankow district office (*Kreisdienststelle*) of the Stasi. Surprisingly, the home visit out of the blue was the result of careful but inexpert preparation on the part of Comrade Peter Reise. The start of the first volume of Wiens's informer file contains various biographical documents, and in the middle of this personal section of her file is the proposing officer's formal plan for recruiting her. As per ministerial Guidelines 1/58 and 1/68 for working with informants, Reise was obliged to present the plan to his superior for written approval. The first formal step in recruitment was "making the acquaintance" of the informant under some pretext.[27] Reise's idea was to make contact by visiting Wiens's apartment under a plausible pretext.[28] The official line he proposed taking was that the officers were simply following up on a statement she had recently made at the local police station about delinquent behavior.

At the initial meeting Reise explained to Wiens that the Stasi was looking for "capable" citizens to assist it and to "act as intellectual mentors."[29] In a clumsy attempt at flattery Reise pointed out that it was no accident he was making contact with her; she was known to have a large number of contacts. She also possessed the "intellect" and the appropriate positive attitude to the ministry to be of assistance.[30] In a report dated December 6, 1977, the department stated its intention to "win her over" to working for the ministry.[31] To this end, the Pankow officers unleashed what they undoubtedly considered a charm offensive. They told her that they needed the active support of a "select group" of "trustworthy people" to help them. Reading between the lines, it's obvious that they thought she was trustworthy because of her family background.[32] The Pankow district office would have been well aware that Wiens's father and mother were sources for the Stasi, and in 1977 her father was still being run by Berlin's HA XX.

Despite her family background, Wiens was anything but impressed by the Stasi's blunt line of attack. "The candidate objected vociferously and rejected our assertion that she had aforementioned contacts,"[33] Reise wrote. Although Wiens resisted the Stasi's initial approach, she did promise to maintain the security force's strict code of secrecy.[34] Reise set another date for a meeting, but at the second meeting Wiens repeated her reluctance to collaborate. The officer's persistence paid off, however. He reported that she appeared skeptical but begrudgingly agreed to be recruited when the urgency of the Stasi's needs was explained to her. Reise left Wiens's apartment satisfied that his mission had been accomplished. He wrote for the record: "In general she is of good repute and leads a morally irreproachable lifestyle."[35] She would most certainly be a "stellar recruit" (*Senkrechtstarter*), he boasted rather prematurely.[36]

Not surprisingly, given his misreading of the situation, Reise did not get off to a promising start with his new star performer. Wiens's officers soon conceded that the Stasi first needed to win her over "through carefully managed conversations" (*durch geschickte Gesprächsführung*).[37] To be fair, the undue haste of the Pankow district office was born from a sense of urgency; it needed to assign her to a pressing case of "hostile-negative" activity in the case of OV "Aspirant" (Doctoral Candidate). Wiens seemed the perfect candidate for this task. Her officer noted that she read "antisocialist literature" and liked engaging in discussions. As the Stasi came to realize, the only drawback was that Wiens was not "always objective" and was often "too subjective" to see the bigger social picture.[38] Indeed, ultimately this supposed character flaw would be Wiens's undoing as an informer.

Before Wiens could be let loose in the field, however, she was required to undertake a series of tests. She appears to have passed these; her officer expressed optimism that she had a "promising operative aptitude" and demonstrated "the necessary combative spirit and intellectual agility" for operative work.[39] It was noted that she could follow instructions and use them creatively, qualities that could qualify her for more serious operational tasks.[40] A plan was prepared and lodged for approval with the Pankow district office to officially register Wiens. The rather unusual decision was made to desist from asking her to sign a declaration to work for the Stasi. A secret code word and a clandestine mode of making contact were arranged. She was to telephone her officer when information cropped up, and he was to leave messages for her under the name of "Peter."[41]

Wiens appears to have been fast-tracked in the hierarchy of informants. After an extremely short probationary period she was elevated to the rank of IMV, the specialist class of informant "who cooperated directly on the operative processing and exposure of suspected persons."[42] The Stasi had such high hopes for Wiens that she was immediately charged to work on two major operations: OV "Schreiberling" (Scribbler) and OV "Doctoral Candidate." There is no evidence that she played an active role in relation to "Scribbler," which was the code name for the operation focused on Klaus Schlesinger, although her father had been tailing him, and, as discussed in chapter 3, Paul Gratzik had also been keeping Schlesinger under observation during the thwarted "Berlin Stories" project. Still, Wiens quickly had her hands full with OV "Doctoral Candidate."

Paul Gratzik: Psychological Blackmail and Codependency

By the time the Stasi was poised to enlist Maja Wiens to work on OV "Scribbler" and OV "Doctoral Candidate"—one old case and one new case—it was experiencing increasing difficulties running some of its earlier recruits, such as Paul Gratzik. As described in earlier chapters, Gratzik's dependency on the Stasi had grown throughout the 1970s, becoming less financial and material and more bound up with intangible benefits such as status, esteem, and reputation.

The advantages that Gratzik had accumulated over the course of his literary career amounted to important symbolic and educational capital, which he needed to survive in the cutthroat world of communist cultural politics. His good repute in dramatic circles was bolstered by access to professional networks—also a type of social capital—in the form of contacts to all the major theatrical circles in Dresden, Berlin, and Potsdam. In feathering Gratzik's career the Stasi had cleverly engineered a knotted set of entanglements with itself and with other state-sponsored institutions in the arts scene. In addition, because he was an expellee from the East, the same dependencies created conditions for Gratzik's far deeper, existential need to be accepted by his adopted country. In turn, once he had begun informing, such dependencies made it virtually impossible to unstick himself from the Stasi's clutches. The Stasi came to acknowledge such intractability in relationships with informers fairly late. Only in the last of the ministerial guidelines for working with informers, Guideline 1/79, did it explicitly state that "social needs" directed at "acquiring particular prestige and reputation" could be used to retain the loyalty of informants.[43]

By November 1976 a group of established writers—some of whom had been involved in the failed "Berlin Stories" anthology—had openly declared their solidarity with Biermann after he was stripped of his citizenship. Twelve writers wrote a petition asking the government of East Germany to reverse its decision to exile Biermann; they sent the petition to the Western news agency Reuters because the East German press would not print it.[44] Paul Gratzik, the charming carpenter who had shot to fame in the 1960s, was not one of its signatories. During the crisis Gratzik was preoccupied, especially because of delays with the publication of his latest work, the novel he had titled *Transportpaule: Monolog*; the Ministry for Culture had refused to issue a "print authorization" (*Druckgenehmigung*).[45] He had alerted his officer to these difficulties in January 1976 and again in May 1976, but the problem remained unresolved.

When the Biermann story broke, Gratzik had been studiously avoiding Wenzel and not returning his calls. Nonetheless, within two weeks of hearing the news, in what can only be described as a fit of fear-induced preemptive obedience, Gratzik leaped voluntarily to his officer's assistance. On November 27, 1976, Gratzik wrote a one-page, four-point assessment of the Biermann incident. He criticized Biermann for singing his anti-GDR songs "immediately on the first day of his performance tour . . . that is all much too one-sided for me."[46] As Biermann recalls, he had in fact left his most critical songs off the program for fear of reprisals on returning home.[47]

Yet Gratzik was openly critical of the way that the authorities had dealt with Biermann, stating in his second point that "the measure [of canceling Biermann's citizenship] was much too extreme."[48] Moreover, he supported the broad tenor of the protest petition.[49] This was hardly the breakthrough report that would earn Wenzel laurels higher up within the Stasi. Yet on this occasion Wenzel was willing to overlook the overt "political-ideological negative tendencies"[50] in Gratzik's work. Wenzel still held out hopes that he could turn Gratzik around. Gratzik kept his next two scheduled appointments with Wenzel, but each time he admitted to drinking too much.[51]

At a meeting in April 1977 Gratzik announced that he wanted to be discharged from his duties for the Stasi; these had forced him into a "conflict situation" with regard to his friend Martin Stade, who was being branded an enemy of the state.[52] Furthermore, he was worried about what happened to his intelligence once he had passed it on—the Stasi never apprised its informants of the exact purpose that was served by their information.[53] He had been "shocked" by the fact that someone he had spied on had been arrested five days after filing his report.[54] He feared that the small circle of writers involved in the "Berlin Stories" anthology already suspected him through a simple process of elimination. This was not the first time that Gratzik had expressed concerns about his security, and Wenzel duly noted that, along with his pessimism and "certain character traits," these were part of his particular personality "complex."[55]

According to the account on file, Wenzel listened patiently to Gratzik's grumbles. Then, rather like a psychotherapist or social worker, he attempted to diagnose his source's problems. Unlike a psychotherapist, however, who might seek to defuse a patient's anxieties, Wenzel took a decidedly untherapeutic approach. He endeavored to reattach Gratzik to the secret police by turning ideological questions into individual psychological problems, thereby compounding Gratzik's already considerable distress. He insisted that Gratzik could influence matters outside of his personal control if he really wanted to. Above all, Wenzel suggested that by quitting Gratzik would only be running away from his problems, implying that he ought to face them "manfully." In addition to the pseudopsychological pep talk, Wenzel brought forward stock ideological reasons why the Stasi needed Gratzik, naming the "current situation in the class struggle" and "the intensified activities of the enemy."[56]

Faced with Wenzel's glib pseudopsychologizing, Gratzik capitulated again. On this occasion the Stasi offered him concrete incentives in exchange for information. As it turns out, Gratzik had good reason to be grateful to the Stasi, and to Wenzel in particular. Another note on file reveals that Wenzel had tried to intervene in the standoff between Gratzik, his publisher, and the censors in the Ministry for Culture. Gratzik had been waiting now for eighteen months for the authorization to publish *Transportpaule*. Wenzel had been able to procure the permit Gratzik so craved.

If Wenzel was unhappy with Gratzik's attempts to evade the Stasi by missing appointments, he was also less than pleased by Gratzik's next move. At their next meeting, in October 1977, Gratzik announced that he was planning a trip to Italy to explore "the life of vignerons" in collectives. Such a trip would be useful as professional development, and it would help him see certain aspects of socialist life "correctly" in perspective.[57] In reality Gratzik desperately needed to escape Germany for his own sanity. We do not know whether Wenzel fell for this line of attack—most likely not—but from the record of the conversation with Wenzel we know that Gratzik had apparently also requested permission from elsewhere for this trip.

Rather sneakily, Gratzik had appealed directly to the deputy minister for culture, Klaus Höpcke. From Gratzik's perspective, going over Wenzel's head was a bold and smart move—but telling Wenzel would prove unwise. Wenzel was displeased at having been outmaneuvered by his informant and scurried to rectify the damage done. He went behind Gratzik's back and, through HA XVIII, which was processing the application, did his best to ensure that the request to travel was rejected. Interestingly, it was Gratzik who had the last laugh in this power tussle. Gratzik was allowed to travel, despite the combined efforts within the MfS of Horst Böhm and Wenzel, who both tried to mobilize their professional contacts to thwart the trip. This was the last in a series of turning points for Gratzik and a key moment in which relations with his Stasi officer appeared to sour to the point of no return.

Gratzik had acquired a degree of financial independence through the legal sale of the rights of his latest book to Rotbuch publishing house. He was correct to surmise, though, that the Stasi was now seeking revenge for his obtaining the travel permit. Gratzik was probably not being paranoid when he suspected that his latest work, "Staatsgammler" (State hobo) was "withdrawn by the state security authorities," although Wenzel was quick to deny any involvement—rather unconvincingly, judging from the files.[58] At a meeting on February 15, 1978, Gratzik declared that he was no longer willing to work for the Stasi, given that he was now being labeled "ideologically unreliable."[59] This time, he refused to put information in writing or speak it on tape.[60]

Although this was not the first occasion on which Gratzik had threatened to quit, it was the first time he had enough ammunition to do so. When a West German journalist contacted him about making a television program, Gratzik typed up a brief and reckless parting note, which he sent to Wenzel by express courier: "This is my last assignment, have had enough of such things, all the best to you" (*Dies ist mein letzter Dienst, hab von solchen Sachen genug, laß es Dir gut gehen*) (see fig. 5).[61] In the film documentary *Vaterlandsverräter* Wenzel acknowledges, with the barest hint of a grin, that this was typical of Gratzik's unpredictable and hotheaded mode of operating.

According to opera singer Renate Biskup, the charismatic bohemian writer she had fallen in love with was changed after his return from Italy. Suffering from writer's block, Gratzik was irritable and prone to outbursts of anger. In retrospect she surmises that he lost his "communist innocence" in Italy. This astute observation tallies with the serious quarrel with Wenzel just before Gratzik's departure for Italy that is documented in his Stasi file. But the archival documents reveal that Wenzel did not give up easily. In

May 1978 and again in September 1978 he managed to arrange a meeting with Gratzik. In September 1978 Wenzel filed another report without issuing any tasks, and three further reports were filed in February 1979, May 1979, and March 1981. The report of February 1979 mentions Gratzik's alcohol dependency.[62] In connection with this Wenzel refers to another, far more serious problem, namely that he could not guarantee that his agent would keep his Stasi contacts a secret: "He [Gratzik] repeated his line that he was under time pressure and due to his fondness for alcohol he could not give any guarantee that he would keep to the rules of conspiration completely."[63] In his report in March 1981 Wenzel elaborated further on Gratzik's "personal decline," noting that he was shaking: "He can't get off the alcohol."[64] After their last appointment in 1981 Wenzel reported that agent "Peter" reiterated his unwillingness to work for the Stasi. Wenzel now agreed to close Gratzik's file, and reminded Gratzik again of his oath of secrecy.[65]

Gratzik tells his side of the story to filmmaker Annekatrin Hendel in *Vaterlandsverräter*. He explains how he eventually managed to sever his ties to the Stasi. He speaks openly of seeking refuge in alcohol and of how he suffered a nervous breakdown, requiring a period of hospitalization. At his wit's end, he resorted to a trick he had used previously but which had failed. According to his file, he had divulged his ties to the Stasi to his wife sometime in 1974, but the damage had been rectified by forcing his wife to swear to silence.[66] This time he confided in fellow dramatist Heiner Müller and actress Steffie Spira, letting them know that he was inextricably entangled in the Stasi's web (see fig. 6). Spira wisely encouraged him to let the Stasi know that he had broken his pledge of silence. Gratzik was right to expose his confession, because this time it worked.

Years later, in an interview with Hendel captured in *Vaterlandsverräter*, Wenzel appears rather sanguine about how he was eventually outdone by Gratzik. At first Wenzel had always managed to cajole Gratzik into sacrificing his personal interests for the greater socialist good. For a while, Wenzel remarks, Gratzik had correctly "chosen state interests" over his own. In the end, however, as Wenzel confirms in the documentary, the Stasi lost out to Gratzik's circle of "negative" friends in Berlin, which made it impossible for Wenzel to win Gratzik back.

Until that point Wenzel had believed he could rescue his relationship with Gratzik, through persistent and repeated "ideological work." Reflecting on the huge toll that secret policing took on both their lives, Gratzik reveals that both he and Wenzel consumed far too much alcohol and had trouble sleeping. "We were all falling apart. We were suffering too," he tells Hendel. In the documentary he even expresses some sympathy for Wenzel, who was also forced to imbibe large quantities of alcohol, according to Gratzik, "even though he couldn't hold his liquor."

It comes as a surprise that in the film Gratzik expresses some empathy toward Wenzel. Wenzel, too, smiles wryly when Hendel asks him how the collaboration ended. "That was Paule," he smirks in response to an anecdote narrated by Hendel about Gratzik's irascible behavior. Similarly, Gratzik seems keen to avoid demonizing or blaming Wenzel, as if to stress the fact that both had been in the same boat. They were scarred by their Cold War battles, wearied and worn down by the common war of attrition against the capitalist West. In Gratzik's eyes they were, after all, on the same side; both wanted the same outcome—to repel the capitalist fascists.

It could be argued that Gratzik mistook the personal turn that conversations with Wenzel sometimes took for a sign of genuine friendship. There is no evidence in *Vaterlandsverräter* that there was a mutual attachment, although Wenzel's fondness for Gratzik, if he had any, may have evaporated in the ensuing years. Wenzel gives no indication that there was much reciprocal sentiment between the two men or that the relationship was anything but strictly professional. Gratzik, by contrast, expresses a far more sentimental recollection of the relationship. Gratzik labored for a long time under the illusion that he could win over Wenzel to his way of thinking before admitting defeat, remarking: "I knew that I could not pull him over to my side." Wenzel, by contrast, reverted to type and simply began to issue veiled threats. In later years, says Gratzik, Wenzel wore his revolver inside his jacket so that Gratzik could see it. This was, says Gratzik, "so that I would shit my pants."

In the final report that closes Gratzik's informant dossier, filed on October 13, 1981, we find a pithy summary of the reasons why the Stasi abandoned one of its prized sources. Gratzik's attitude to key issues had changed, especially his views on cultural restrictions.[67] An egregious turning point for the Stasi was Gratzik's mishandling of the "Berlin Stories" anthology project in 1975–76, when he did not stick to the agreement to achieve a better balance of stories. According to this last report, Gratzik failed to "understand" the Stasi's position. Gratzik repeatedly pointed out that "the goodwill of the Stasi is one thing," but that things pan out in life differently. The report goes on to state: "After that he systematically withdrew his preparedness, no longer appeared at scheduled meetings and expressed on repeated occasions his opposition."[68]

After Gratzik had severed his ties with the ministry he was fortunate that the Stasi did not pursue active revenge. He was placed under a relatively benevolent type of surveillance, an OPK, until 1989. Gratzik paid a high emotional and psychological price for his collaboration, however. The fact that he eventually managed to unattach himself is testament to his tenacity. It is also evidence of a more general shift that occurred in the early 1980s, which saw more intellectuals throw caution to the wind and express their opposition to the regime. For Gratzik, aligning himself with these "hostile-negative" elements in society meant breaking with established patterns of behavior and state- and Stasi-nurtured dependencies, as well as, more generally, a period of painful readjustment.

Paul Wiens: Limits to Surveilling Others

The Biermann affair was a watershed for all GDR citizens working in the arts and a turning point for many informers as well. It was a test of such severe proportions for writers working undercover because it polarized cultural producers as no event had before. In effect, writers were forced to disclose their position and take sides, to express either their support for Biermann or their approval of his expulsion. Never before had so many intellectuals taken such a public stance and risked so much in doing so. There was enormous pressure exerted on those who signed the declaration of protest initiated by Stephan Hermlin, and the Stasi was heavily invested in the whole gamut of security measures implemented to deal with the crisis. As a key source on the inside, Paul Wiens played a major role in documenting the sentiments expressed within the Writers' Guild, as well as exerting pressure on writers to retract their support for Biermann. Wiens's dossier reveals that he was more than willing to get his hands dirty and assist the Stasi in silencing critical voices at this crucial juncture. In this section I explore some ways in which sticky surveillance played out in professional and private, even intimate, lifeworlds.

Sticky surveillance relied on exploiting private lives. Its aim was to exert pressure on targets and to influence their mindsets in ways that served the interests of the party. A salient example of this type of contact surveillance is the surreptitious operational work performed by Paul Wiens. Wiens was prepared to blur the lines between his professional duties and his private life and, specifically, to inform on poet Sarah Kirsch, a colleague and close friend of his family and of his third wife, Irmtraud Morgner (see fig. 7). Wiens's Stasi file clearly documents this willingness to exploit his friendship. For instance, we read that at one meeting with his handlers, on April 7, 1977, he handed over a sketch of Kirsch's apartment.[69]

To be fair, Wiens may have experienced scruples about the degree of stickiness demanded of him in his surveillance work connected with his closer professional associates, particularly in the early years. Although the overwhelming bulk of his files on his colleagues were what I call "hostile biographies," namely life stories of subjects that were written from an unsympathetic perspective, not all of Wiens's reports for the Stasi were incriminating and accusatory. In a few cases he penned slightly equivocal accounts—offering mitigating circumstances and soft assessments of characters. In early discussions with the Stasi around 1961 Wiens had expressed quite outspoken opinions about writers such as Heiner Müller; as mentioned in chapter 2, he had disapproved of Müller's exclusion from the Writers' Guild.

A few years later, in April 1963, Wiens's tone was unchanged when at a meeting of the Writers' Guild he defended Günter Kunert, saying that his poems were "in his opinion . . . not in need of criticism."[70] This coincided with the time when Wiens was under surveillance himself and his telephone was being tapped. Like many informants, Wiens found himself in a strange twilight zone, neither a full-fledged member of the political machinery nor a marked or stigmatized outsider, informing on others while being informed on himself. The precarity of this in-between status is underscored by snippets of files from other departments. One file, for instance, portrays Wiens as part of the growing problem of dissidence that the Stasi wanted to prevent.[71]

Just as Wiens occasionally showed discomfort at betraying colleagues that he seemed to like or approve of, he sometimes balked at performing acts of sticky surveillance in the intimate realms of his own lifeworld. Unfortunately, he did nonetheless inform on those closest to him. Wiens was relatively circumspect in reporting on his wife, Irmtraud Morgner, a feminist writer of some of German literature's most fascinating works of fantasy. Although listed fourteen times in the index of volume II/3 of Wiens's dossier, Morgner is rarely mentioned in his meeting reports. When she is referenced, Wiens appears to have been at pains to shield her from the Stasi's purview.[72] Apparently Wiens usually drew the line at spying on immediate family members such as his wives and children. If he was pressed to report on Morgner's views, Wiens was careful to write placatory reports. The few reports he did write on her are characterized by what Geoffrey Westgate calls a "tactical loyalty" to Morgner.[73] He appears to deliberately stress her "political reliability" and thereby hides her from the prying eyes of the ministry. For most of her marriage to Wiens Morgner probably did not suspect that he worked for the Stasi.[74]

Wiens does mention Morgner, however, in the reconciliation meeting report that was filed in November 1971 after Wiens was deregistered. As described in chapter 3, Wiens had requested an urgent meeting with the Stasi, presumably through his old officer, to talk about a suspicious approach made by the Western journalist Conrad Franke. As already discussed, Wiens reported the incident, possibly as a pretext for initiating contact with the Stasi again. This shows that Wiens was not averse to using his wife's name instrumentally when it advanced his cause. He was trying, rather unsuccessfully, to compartmentalize his private life and his professional duties. In March 1976 Wiens tried to protect Morgner in a report he wrote about a radio interview Robert Havemann had given to the West: "As is already known, writers Irmtraud Morgner, Rudi Strahl and Paul Wiens likewise condemned the interview of Havemann."[75] As previously mentioned, Wiens was less scrupulous with regard to Morgner's close friend Sarah Kirsch. In the aftermath of the Biermann affair Wiens even sought to obtain from Morgner more information about Kirsch for the Stasi.[76]

Wiens's file contains letters from Morgner to her publisher and vice versa, which Wiens confiscated and passed on to the Stasi.[77] This could easily have had nasty consequences for Morgner. She registered the disappearance of her mail in her last completed work of fiction, *Amanda*. In the chain-smoking (see fig. 8), hot-tempered figure of Konrad Tenner, Morgner may have been tempted to obtain her revenge. Tenner is described as a double agent working for Kolbuk, also known as Head Devil (see the discussion in chapter 3).[78] As Westgate writes, Tenner is "working on the inside to destabilize Kolbuk's regime, but is hoping in the meantime to gain personal advancement and privilege."[79] This is a particularly apt summary of Wiens's role for the Stasi. Morgner captures Wiens's slipperiness in her characterization of Tenner: "His eyes which had seen many countries and deaths, formed small smile lines when he had to offer an opinion. He had firm opinions but he avoided your gaze when expressing them. Laura admired this way of passing judgment which was inimitable. She loved uniqueness in humans. That it came in the form of the male sex was of secondary importance."[80]

We do not know for sure if Morgner's suspicions about Wiens's pact with the security forces played a role in her decision to divorce him. Based on a report made by a Stasi lieutenant in April 1977, the Stasi certainly thought this was the case. According to the report, Morgner had discovered that her husband was a "provocateur" for the Stasi.[81] By the time the couple were divorced in 1977, both were in other relationships. Morgner and Wiens continued to live together in their large apartment in Berlin's Leipziger Strasse; Morgner is said to have observed that she did not know how Wiens financed the apartment.[82]

Maja Wiens: Active Service to Liquidate Enemies

The Biermann affair proved to be a crucial test for the younger generation of recent secret police recruits, such as Maja Wiens, as well as of the older generation of seasoned informants. Indeed, though the period after 1976 was trying for Paul Wiens, it proved even more challenging for his daughter. The parts of her file relating to her first top-secret operation focused on "Doctoral Candidate" are especially instructive in this regard. Within a short time Wiens was delivering enough hard evidence of alleged criminal activity for the security forces to swoop and make three arrests in a meticulously planned and executed cloak-and-dagger operation. As stated in a report summarizing Wiens's achievements, her work proved pivotal to the operation described chillingly as "the liquidation of enemy activity of Dr. KUNZE, Rudolf."[83] Kunze regards his victimization as moderate by comparison with that of others.[84] But by any standards, even those in the GDR in the 1970s, his treatment was draconian and brutal.

The third volume of Wiens's dossier contains regular meeting reports relating to the operation; these date from December 21, 1977, through to May 19, 1980, during which time she met with Reise, her officer, twice a month on average. For June 1978, the month when Rudolf Kunze was arrested, there are some eleven recorded meetings. This part of her file—the section containing her reports on Kunze, or "Rudi" as she calls him, and his friends—is fifty pages long and provides an astoundingly detailed record of Wiens's espionage activities.

The Stasi became interested in biologist Rudolf Kunze when he helped the artist Manfred Kastner organize an exhibition in March 1976. Kastner was a promising surrealist painter who had been refused admission to art school and professional guilds.[85] He painted rather stylized canvases depicting stark landscapes and mysterious, imposing architectural spaces in the manner of the Italian surrealist Giorgio de Chirico.[86] With their lone, almost emaciated human figures dwarfed by monumental, often industrial structures, Kastner's works express an existential pessimism that the regime found confrontational. There were no healthy laborers involved in uplifting collective work, no glorified images of the fine-tuned, muscular socialist body at work. Although the exhibition of 1976 had received the necessary formal approval, the MfS experienced apprehension soon after it opened. In particular, the threat of West German media attention appears to have galvanized the Stasi into action.[87]

Perhaps more than anything, the regime feared negative publicity in the wake of the Biermann affair. Kunze was thought to be spearheading the movement turning Kastner into a martyr for disaffected gruops. According to the Stasi, the exhibition could be viewed as a major coup for Kunze and his friends and as a successful example of "how one can subliminally infiltrate the system."88 Kunze, a report concluded, possessed a "hostile basic attitude to social conditions in the GDR and to the politics of the party and the government of our Republic, in particular to problems of cultural politics."89

A little over two years after the exhibition, Kunze found himself at the epicenter of a full-blown OV investigation. Kunze was a young, liberal-minded, free-thinking intellectual. He possessed a large collection of world literature, which he shared generously with friends and any interested others; he was passionate about modernist art. Like other well-educated citizens at the time, his views on socialism as practiced in the Eastern Bloc were heavily influenced by the groundbreaking publication of Rudolf Bahro's *Die Alternative: Zur Kritik des real existierenden Sozialismus* (1977, published in English in 1978 as *The Alternative in Eastern Europe*), a work involving a harsh critique of the SED. As had Biermann earlier, Kunze became caught between several different political crosscurrents that converged at a particularly repressive and punitive juncture in the regime's history. It remains unclear when the Stasi first suspected him, but by 1977 a new, hard-line cultural politics ensured that Kunze was singled out for especially harsh treatment. It is even possible that, in its hysteria, the regime feared that Kunze could become another Biermann. According to Kunze, his support of surrealist art was "a thorn in the side of the dimwits from the Stasi just like writing literature."90 Perhaps the real cause of the ministry's interest in him lay in his unorthodox Marxist views. The Stasi file for Kunze notes that he was also under surveillance because of his contacts to "Trotskyite and Maoist circles in West Germany who were supplying him with anti-Marxist literature."91

When Wiens was put to work on Kunze's case in 1978, the international community had started to rally around Bahro, who was in detention.92 Further, Kunze had lodged an "application to leave the country" (*Ausreiseantrag*) early in 1978. Thus, among other circumstances, he found himself a victim of a nationwide push to clamp down on citizens who had lodged exit applications. Applicants were regarded as ideological defectors and mostly branded as enemies.[93] New legal clauses, such as the second Criminal Code Amendment Act, passed in 1977, and the third Criminal Code Amendment Act of 1979, were designed to assist the regime with prosecutions.[94] Criminal action was most likely to be taken when the applicant was known to cultivate connections to the West.[95] Kunze had an old school friend in the West; moreover, he was alleged to be writing a defamatory manuscript, possibly inspired by Bahro's *Die Alternative*.

Kunze's manuscript, or "pamphlet," as it is frequently referred to in the files, becomes something of a recurrent theme—possibly even a red herring—running throughout Kunze's dossier. It is often cited by Wiens, and as the OV "Doctoral Candidate" intensified in mid-June 1978, this manuscript became the center of attention for Wiens's case officers. The Stasi suspected that Kunze's old school friend was working as a courier for his inflammatory writings. As Kunze claims, "In reality he was acting as my lawyer helping with my emigration."[96] The subversive tract that Kunze was allegedly working on may simply have been part of his exit application.

Wiens's Stasi file contains rare insights into how the new type of sticky contact surveillance operated in practice. Wiens proved to be a natural at performing the tasks required. Her file contains an extensive report on her first attempt to make contact with Kunze. Under instructions, she approached him at his thirty-first birthday celebration on February 12, 1978. She had been instructed to wait on the same public premises, ostensibly for another purpose, and make contact at an opportune moment. Her legend, for the purposes of making contact, was wanting to wish the stranger a happy birthday. Wiens's report to the Stasi on the evening's events describes how she managed to strike up a naturalistic enough conversation with Kunze after midnight, when the party was dying down. She offered him a spontaneous present, a French novel she happened to have with her.

The transcript of her report on her follow-up visit to Kunze's apartment is voluminous, filling twelve pages (she delivered the report orally). Amid the unrelenting trivial detail that Wiens supplied about Rudi's apartment, his impressive book collection, and his forthright views on Bahro, there are derogatory comments about him that give glimpses of Wiens's disrespect for her target. She claimed that Kunze was convinced that "he was the greatest,"⁹⁷ and she could not refrain from observing that "he possibly tended to overestimate himself, not only on an intellectual level."⁹⁸ For reports such as these Wiens received, on average, 100 marks per month. In May she more than doubled her previous earnings, and in June she earned 100–200 marks at each of her meetings. This was welcome extra income but hardly enough to offset the elaborate subterfuge she was about to embark on.

Her file zooms into the heart of events as they unfolded in the middle of June 1978. In this thick section of the file the Stasi brought OV "Doctoral Candidate" to its desired conclusion: an arrest. Reading Wiens's file is rather like applying a magnifying glass to these days; it documents events in meticulous detail. It is worth reconstructing them from Wiens's file because they reveal how human-to-human surveillance could involve far more than sticking close to targets; it could entail various kinds of "sticky," that is, tricky and compromising, situations. Such surveillance also involved a massive risk that an informant could come "unstuck" in various ways, by being caught dissembling, feigning identity, faking her or his actions, or by spreading disinformation.

Maja Wiens: "She Came In through the Bathroom Window"

Maja Wiens's Stasi dossier records a flurry of activity in the summer of 1978. On June 2, 1978, some ten days before Kunze's arrest, a long report was filed. Information that Wiens provided in this and subsequent reports was crucial to the Stasi; in fact it seems she was the lynchpin for the entire operation. Her evidence was to prove crucial at Kunze's trial, but more importantly, it furnished the Stasi with sufficient information to make an arrest. In this sense Wiens's reports on Kunze are "arresting" in terms of both their alarming nature and their sinister purpose. Thus her writing about Kunze merits being classified as an "arresting biography," a term coined by Cristina Vatulescu for Soviet security files.⁹⁹

Not only a secret political police and a secret service, the Stasi was entrusted by statute—and from 1963 onward by the "prosecutor's act" (*Staatsanwaltschaftsgesetz*)—with powers to conduct criminal investigations and trials in relation to "all kinds of enemy activity" (*alle Feindtätigkeit*).¹⁰⁰

In this regard the MfS was part of the GDR justice system, working alongside the criminal police and customs investigators.[101] Reliable statistics for 1978 reveal that the Stasi dealt with 2 to 3 percent of all criminal investigations, sentencing 1,656 persons for various crimes, which included 627 cases of "illegal escape" (*Republikflucht*), 82 cases of written forms of "incitement" (*Hetze*), and 206 cases of "enemy connections" (*staatsfeindliche Verbindungen*).[102]

A Stasi file does not often culminate so rapidly in the apprehension of a suspect, but in this instance Wiens's extensive accounts led directly to a swift arrest; Kunze's was one of the 1,766 Stasi arrests made in 1978.[103] A complicating aspect in this disturbing operation, and one downplayed in the Stasi files, was the fact that Kunze was suffering from cancer and in the middle of chemotherapy. This was to end when he was intercepted on his way to the hospital for another round of treatment.[104] The callous and brutal circumstances of his arrest, indeed of the whole operation, do not appear to have overly concerned Wiens. There is no indication that she felt any scruples about spying on a man who was gravely ill. There is no evidence of compassion in her reports, although they do allude to other worries—for instance, that Kunze, or Rudi, might not think she was especially intelligent, or that she might misuse foreign words.[105] In other words, she worried about whether her alibis were unassailable. She paid scrupulous attention to giving a seamless performance, taking care not to fluff her lines or confuse details about her assumed identity and background. She had to stay on script, within reasonable limits. She was permitted to improvise if necessary, and improvise she did.

This was Wiens's first mission for the Stasi, and she was preoccupied with carrying off the requisite deception that sticky one-on-one surveillance entailed. In her reports she hastened to reassure the Stasi that in her encounters with Kunze she was "very open" and always behaved normally.[106] For instance, she smoked her usual amount of cigarettes, drank tea, and talked openly, as was her wont, about books and art (see fig. 9).[107] She feigned an interest in him, hid her real intentions,[108] and also masterfully disguised her real motivations for befriending the couple Hedwig ("Luschka") and Bernhardt Simon, Kunze's friends, whom the Stasi believed to be co-conspirators.

When Wiens could not find any explicitly incriminating information she simply passed on gossip about Rudi's various women friends.[109]

Wiens was instructed to elicit information about the pamphlet that Kunze was alleged to be working on, and about his Western friends, as well as to provide exact information on "the precise structure of Dr. K.'s daily routine."[110] Above all, she was to evaluate the state of his health. And, as if she were a medical expert, she was supposed to write "an assessment of his physical and psychic fitness in particular with regard to the consequences of his chemotherapy and the pressure to finish off his manuscript."[111] This request was clearly ominous, and it is hard to imagine that Wiens did not know what the Stasi was planning for Kunze. Possibly the most incriminating section of Wiens's dossier, and the section that was crucial to Kunze's arrest, is the classified report she filed about his medical treatment. She told her officer that he was returning to the hospital on the following Monday to start his next round of chemotherapy and that his treatment would last for thirty days. The meeting in which Wiens imparted this vital piece of the jigsaw took place on Tuesday, June 6, 1978. Kunze was arrested the following week, on Monday, June 12. No sooner had Wiens's intelligence been processed than the Stasi, it seems, promptly gave the green light to apprehend the man on the very day referred to by Wiens.

It appears that all of Wiens's assessments about the state of Kunze's health and his "decadent" lifestyle were indispensable to the Stasi's operation.[112] Moreover, she was able to verify the existence of the incriminating ten-page manuscript—she had found evidence of three copies being made—and given information about its whereabouts.[113] Two days after receiving this pivotal piece of intelligence (and four days prior to Kunze's arrest), Reise convened an urgent meeting. Wiens was told to see if she could find out where Kunze's manuscript was stored and whether copies had been sent to the West.[114] Wiens appeared annoyed, even angry, and complained vociferously to her officer. This was the second meeting that week, and Wiens was probably feeling the pressure of the top-secret operation, which had by now escalated well beyond her control. Her sense of heightened anxiety is palpable from the files. She complained that the operation had caused her considerable grief: "She told us in no uncertain terms that the high additional strain to which she was exposed carrying out the mission pertaining to Dr. K. had had a *noticeable* impact on her marriage. She can no longer make plausible excuses to her husband about her *future* absences."[115]

On Thursday, June 8, and Friday, June 9, 1978, Reise held two urgent meetings with Wiens in a car outside the S-Bahnhof Schönhauser Allee.[116] On Thursday, Wiens filed a detailed report about visiting Luschka and Rudi, noting that "Rudi has now gathered a lot of young people around him," and briefly mentioned his "pamphlet."[117] On the following day, she presented a new report, an update on her last one, which had been filed scarcely twenty-four hours earlier. This meeting lasted almost two hours, and she delivered her report verbally; it was recorded and later transcribed. The upshot of this meeting was that Wiens had managed to pay Rudi a visit on the morning of Friday, June 9. Kunze's poor health notwithstanding, she had managed to elicit from him that he had obtained copies of Bahro's work from a Western source.[118] She added that Rudi had plans for disseminating these copies in the East.[119]

With each fresh piece of intelligence she supplied from inside Kunze's close-knit circle of friends, Wiens willingly and proactively assisted the Stasi in building an incriminating body of evidence against Kunze. In her embellishments about his manuscript and his expanding group of acquaintances, Wiens gladly fueled the Stasi's acute paranoia. Any single piece of information that Wiens passed on could have been sufficient to convict Kunze of several crimes against the state: "incitement against the state" (*staatsfeindliche Hetze*) according to Article 106 of the GDR Criminal Code; "treacherous passing on of information" under Article 99; "making illegal contacts" under Article 219; "hampering state or social activity" under Article 214, or "public vilification" under Article 220.[120]

In her debriefings with Reise, Wiens was unable to resist repeating a throwaway line that Kunze had made to her about the Stasi. In the context of telling her about his copies of Bahro's blacklisted book, he said, "If only the Stasi knew."[121] The Stasi knew far more than he could have dreamed, and far more quickly.[122] And the consequences for Kunze would be drastic. By the time Wiens next met with her handler, Kunze had been arrested. For Kunze, who was well-connected but not prominent, the Stasi reserved its most draconian methods of repression: an ambush in broad daylight under the most callous circumstances imaginable.[123] It is not clear from the files whether Wiens knew Kunze was to be arrested while on his way to the hospital. Nor is it clear whether she knew that his cancer treatment would only occur under prison conditions, behind the high-security walls of the Stasi hospital in Hohenschönhausen. It would be conducted under such dreadful circumstances that Kunze himself can barely remember the details of his first few weeks in incarceration. He was heavily sedated with a cocktail of drugs, becoming so sick that his treatment had to be broken off.[124] Kunze was sentenced to three years' imprisonment, eighteen months of which he spent in Hohenschönhausen. He was released thirteen months later, not into the West as he had requested, but back into the GDR.

After Kunze's disappearance on June 12, his friends were concerned about him, but Wiens did little to enlighten them. Although the part of the operation relating to Kunze had proceeded smoothly, the remainder of the plan quickly unraveled over the next twenty-four hours. In the aftermath of the operation Wiens's Stasi-concocted strategy, her elaborate fake identity and simulated friendship, came unstuck. Luschka and Bernhardt were anticipating a raid on their house.[125] On the afternoon of June 16, the Simons' home was searched by a team of six, and the couple was dragged off for interrogation. During the arrest their young daughter Sabina disappeared. At this point Wiens decided to take matters into her own hands and returned to the Simons' house, breaking in through the bathroom window. While she was still inside the house, the Simons, who had been released from custody, returned home unexpectedly. When caught red-handed, Wiens claimed, rather implausibly, that she had wanted to check on Sabina and had let herself in. The Simons were unnerved to see her and sent her home.[126]

After being caught in the Simons' home, Wiens needed to quickly devise a plan to regain the family's trust. A meeting between Reise and his superior, Major Krüger, was hastily arranged for June 17, 1978, to agree on a "behavior plan" for Wiens. The agreed scenario was that Wiens had "to contribute to the promulgation of uncertainty and to prepare for the possible prevention of activities."[127] In other words, Wiens was to sow disinformation about

Kunze's whereabouts and, if possible, prevent any publicity connected with his disappearance.

The Simons now suspected that they had been betrayed by a mole deep in their midst. The Stasi was anxious to work out a credible counternarrative that Wiens was comfortable with, and above all, that would prevent her cover being completely blown.[128] Bernhardt Simon remained convinced he had heard Wiens's muffled voice on tape during his interrogation.[129] We can assume that, in its haste to arrest the Simons, the Stasi had not been quick enough to process Wiens's oral intelligence and was probably replaying her tape so as to use her key pieces of evidence against the Simons.

In another meeting, conducted on June 20, Wiens mentioned the Simons' indignation about being interrogated while Hedwig was pregnant. According to a newspaper article of 1996, Burkhardt Brennecke, the twenty-eight-year-old Stasi employee who interrogated Kunze, also interrogated Hedwig and Bernhardt. Moreover, Hedwig was questioned by the Stasi despite her husband requesting that she be spared because of her delicate condition.[130] Brennecke had given his "word of honor" that Bernhardt's wife would not be taken in for questioning. She was, however, cross-examined for fourteen hours—and miscarried as a result.[131] The Simons later filed a legal suit against Brennecke, seeking to have his license to practice as a lawyer revoked. Wiens had reason to believe that the Simons were testing her, but she stuck to her plan, maintaining contact with them until Kunze's trial in September. The trial itself did little to allay her friends' suspicions. Her file records ongoing mistrust and her paranoia about being tested by others.[132]

The Stasi was quick to acknowledge Wiens's contribution to this major operation and a proposal dated June 22, 1978, only ten days after Kunze's arrest, suggested rewarding her with a trip to Romania.[133] The report on her informing work is fulsome with praise: "[The informant] distinguished herself in previous collaborations by her 'extremely high levels of commitment' (*äußerst hohe Einsatzbereitschaft*), 'initiative' (*Eigeninitiative*) and 'reliability' (*Zuverlässigkeit*)."[134] It notes that informant "Marion" placed herself entirely at the disposal of the ministry "every hour of the day and night" (*zu jeder Tages- und Nachtstunde*), at considerable risk to herself, and "even at the expense of triggering a marital conflict."[135]

In January 1979 "Marion" was ready to take on a new challenge involving a different target: the well-known poet, singer-songwriter, and political activist Bettina Wegner. A slightly cryptic note in one of Wiens's file entries from this time alludes to the need to train "Marion"; the Stasi is to "prepare to make contact with Bettina Wegner (the IM must acquaint herself with the intellectual outpourings of her future partner in order to have a genuine basis for discussion)."[136] In 1982 it was noted once more that "Marion" had proved herself useful: "The IM has won the trust of several operatively known actively hostile persons, and was producing extensive operatively significant information and evidence in the course of the operation."[137] IM "Marion" was still proving such a useful source that Reise nominated her for the Medal of Merit of the National People's Army in Bronze (Verdienstmedaille der Nationalen Volksarmee in Bronze). By this stage her status had been upgraded to that of an IMB, to reflect her involvement in the political underground.

Paul Wiens: Monitoring the Writers' Guild

Around the time of the Biermann affair Paul Wiens increased the intensity of his surveillance of his professional circles. The brush fire that the Biermann incident had ignited, which was threatening to explode, burned to the heart of literary life in East Germany. The Writers' Guild, the regime's official mouthpiece on literature, was urgently required to take a leadership role. Yet the guild was riven by internal divisions and fractures that could no longer be papered over, split between those who supported Stephan Hermlin, the initiator of the petition that protested Biermann's exile, and those who did not. Once the signatories' names had been published by the Reuters news agency, there was a new faction—those who supported Hermlin but subsequently withdrew their support under pressure. Wiens clearly sided with those who condemned Biermann outright, which was the official line. The problem for Wiens was that most of his colleagues in the guild were deeply shocked at the regime's handling of the affair.

Despite sensing that he was in a minority among his colleagues, Wiens fell in behind the regime on this issue. He intensified his efforts within the guild to neutralize the impact of the Biermann affair. Wiens continued throughout 1977 to provide the Stasi with good-quality information from deep inside the guild. This was the year in which East Germany shed itself of the most outspoken elements of its intelligentsia, losing, in the process, debilitating amounts of intellectual and cultural capital.[138] Wiens proved a key cultural agent in facilitating the departure of many of the nation's most talented writers, actors, and poets. Although he saw his role otherwise, he wittingly contributed to this cultural crisis. Many of the poets who left the GDR proceeded to win prestigious literary prizes in the West, while others became acclaimed television and film actors. The East's losses were the West's gains.

Wiens seems to have been happy to document the crisis from his position close to the action. In one report he related to the Stasi that there was much disunity among writers in the wake of the open protest letter. In December 1976, for instance, Wiens reported that those who withdrew their support for the letter—largely because of political interference, either from the Stasi or directly from the SED's politburo—were isolated from the others. He mentioned the beleaguered Günter Kunert, who was allegedly no longer talking to some of his friends.[139] Moreover, Wiens reported that Sarah Kirsch and Irmtraud Morgner were no longer talking to one another.[140] The strategy of divide and conquer among Biermann's supporters that the Stasi pursued was bearing fruit, and Wiens was playing a key role.

In an entry concerning Morgner, Wiens's file offers a clue as to how he justified his surveillance of those close to him. As previously discussed, the file contains no explicit tasks allocated to him in relation to his wife. However, he was incapable of separating his wife from the messiness of other events he was required to report on, and eventually, as discussed above, he did include references to Morgner in his reports. The Stasi's background security check on Wiens states that Wiens had always been willing to talk about journalists and writers in the East and West.[141] Wiens felt obliged to report on any Western attempts to influence others, even his wife. Therefore, when the Swiss writer Theodor Pinkus paid Morgner a visit early in 1977, Wiens reported the visit. He revealed that Pinkus's wife was planning to write an article for a feminist journal together with Morgner.[142] Thus, though Wiens apparently wished to allay the Stasi's suspicions about

Morgner, he was keen to implicate the Westerners, who, to his mind, were engaging in inflammatory Cold War activities. As a result, he caused the Stasi to consider his wife susceptible to enemy influence, and if she herself was not a security risk then she certainly became *at risk*.

Wiens allowed himself to become a willing accomplice to the Stasi's plans to sow disunity in the Writers' Guild. As such, he played a significant part in destabilizing members who strayed too far from SED orthodoxy. This was especially evident in the case of Hans Joachim Schädlich. At a public reception in 1977 Wiens spoke with fellow Jew and prizewinning writer Jurek Becker.[143] Becker, it appears, was unhappy with Wiens because Wiens had disqualified Schädlich's new book, the collection of short prose texts titled *Versuchte Nähe* (Approximation). Wiens had panned the work as "a bad book" and an "antisocialist read."[144] During the reception, Becker rather brazenly asked Wiens whether this was his real opinion, or whether he was under "a degree of pressure."[145] No doubt Becker suspected that Wiens was working for the Stasi. From Wiens's extremely guarded reaction it seems that he sensed Becker was testing him.

According to Wiens's verbatim self-reporting to the Stasi, he went on the offensive. In his almost snooty response to Becker, Wiens replied that no one had "inspired" or pressurized him into making critical comments about Schädlich's book. It was, he claimed, his true conviction that it was a bad piece of literature. Not content to let the matter of Wiens's lack of support for Schädlich rest, Becker appealed to Wiens's sense of solidarity toward fellow writers: "Even if it is your firm opinion you cannot just say so because in doing so you just push him deeper into the shit which he is already in."[146] Becker called the condemnation of Schädlich's book by the profession a form of Stalinist terror.[147] Wiens, tellingly, was defensive but also slightly smug, retorting that events had shown that most writers were not behind Becker.[148]

In this intense exchange between two old friends, both of Jewish backgrounds, we can see that Wiens was not above engaging in what could be seen as a type of partisan psychological warfare, in which he played the role of proactive ideological neutralizer. With Becker he explicitly defended the official line that the Ministry for Culture and the Stasi were seeking to promote at the time with all of Biermann's supporters. Backed by the Stasi, Wiens seemed to think he was vindicated, or at least soon would be, in his conservative political views. In the 1960s Wiens had been caught out in the brief phase of de-Stalinization and dropped by the Stasi. Conceivably, Wiens did not wish to lose his relationship with the MfS a second time.

Wiens was desperate to be seen as one of the few remaining party faithful, and he actively used his position of influence in the Writers' Guild to harass writers, often in informal, interpersonal interactions in semiprofessional spaces. Wiens played a major role in isolating dissenting writers like Schädlich. As a result of the collective harassment, writers such as Schädlich, Sarah Kirsch, Jurek Becker, Günter Kunert, and Reiner Kunze elected to leave the country. Within two years of the Biermann fiasco, all moved into exile, along with their partners and families—many with small, frightened, and confused children in tow.[149]

Early in December 1977 members of the Writers' Guild executive met to decide on Schädlich's candidacy for membership, and Wiens defended his assessment of *Versuchte Nähe* as antisocialist. His critique of the work can be found in both his Stasi file and that of Schädlich. Schädlich had intended to publish his book in the East, but because of "November events" late in 1976, namely the Biermann affair, the manuscript had been rejected. Schädlich had few alternatives other than to publish in the West, and when the West German publishing house Rowohlt made him an offer, he agreed to proceed.[150]

The December 1977 meeting of the Writers' Guild executive was to become a defining moment in Schädlich's career. Members met beforehand to agree on their "line" that Schädlich's candidature be dropped. Further, Wiens and his colleagues agreed they would first seek to clarify Schädlich's attitude to the GDR, and that if he intended to proceed with his application to go into exile, he would be allowed to leave.[151] Schädlich, however, had by no means decided that he would or should leave, as became clear from his determination to negotiate a better outcome for himself. According to Wiens's report on the meeting found in Schädlich's file, Schädlich threw down the gauntlet and demanded that Wiens withdraw his slanderous remarks about his book. Wiens responded that Schädlich had made his views publicly known and had also applied to leave the GDR, neither of which helped his case.[152] According to Wiens, Schädlich deserved no better treatment: "He had to accept the consequences if authors had rejected his book as a bad book and expressed this publicly."[153] In Wiens's eyes the book's antisocialist content was a betrayal that fully justified the savage bullying that Schädlich received.

Schädlich's protests that he was being treated like an enemy of the GDR, "which in reality he wasn't," fell on deaf ears.[154] Unlike two female colleagues present at the meeting, the hardliner Wiens remained intransigent.[155] The Stasi dossiers of both Wiens and Schädlich illustrate just how little empathy Wiens felt for his colleagues and show how closely he was wedded to the draconian party line of the era. Needless to say, Schädlich was promptly notified that his visa application had been granted, and he was advised on Monday, December 5, 1977, that his family could leave for the West on Saturday.[156] As part of a controlled form of "blood-letting," the head of HA VII and Deputy Minister for State Security Maj. Gen. Rudi Mittig agreed to permit Schädlich and three others to leave.[157]

*

The post-Biermann period from late 1976 to 1978 marked a veritable low point in the GDR regime's internal relations with intellectuals and writers, heralding an ice age in cultural politics. The persecution of writers by the MfS was in blatant breach of human rights, despite the GDR having been a signatory to the Helsinki Accords of 1975 obliging the regime to desist from human rights breaches. The expulsion of Biermann was a victory for the hardliners in the politburo, but a pyrrhic victory, given that it led to an unprecedented erosion of intellectual capital in the GDR. In the years immediately afterward the security forces unleashed a massive rearguard action against all those writers, actors, and public intellectuals who failed to fall into line. For damage control the Stasi relied heavily, albeit rather unfruitfully, on its reliable sources who were inside official organizations, such as Paul Wiens. It was also forced to lean on less reliable informants that it was in danger of losing.

Such shortcomings in the Stasi's workforce of secret agents could not be recouped by a recruitment drive, as we have seen in the case of Maja Wiens. Not only did the Stasi need better qualified recruits, it now required them to engage in sticky forms of surveillance. Sticky surveillance entailed unforeseen risks for both novice informers and seasoned informers like Paul Wiens, who was now required to inform on his wife and friends and to bring fellow Jewish colleagues into line. This technique of surveillance thus expanded to include informers' observation of their professional and private circles, demanding higher levels of commitment and sacrifice. Inevitably, such commitment took its toll on informers, psychologically, emotionally, and healthwise, as explored in the chapters that follow. Gratzik's experiences during 1976–78 of intense pressures—from the regime to conform, from his peers to show solidarity, and possibly from his conscience—proved too great, and, by 1981 he and his case officer proved unable to patch up their irreparable differences.

5
Simulation and Secret Policing the Underground, 1979–1982

In January 1981 the Ministry for State Security's HA XX, charged with oversight of all state apparatuses, the churches, opposition, and culture, underwent a significant restructure. Its operative group, HA XX/OG, which had been dealing with key cases of dissenters since 1976, warranted upgrading to the status of a separate branch, HA XX/9, within HA XX. Unlike other "lines" in the ministry, which were defined by security areas, this one was defined by "lines of enemy attack."[1] The new branch was needed to combat the emerging problem of "political underground activity" (*politische Untergrundtätigkeit*, PUT).[2] It was headed by Wolfgang Reuter, who would later become the Berlin handler of a major new recruit, Sascha Anderson.

The branch continued to increase in size, growing from nineteen full-time officers in 1981 to thirty-six in 1989.[3] It was designed with the single aim of policing underground cultures, subcultures, and alternative cultures.[4] These phenomena had taken root in the mid to late 1970s.[5] They took the form of a spontaneous culture of happenings and a type of salon culture accompanied by exhibitions, live music, parties, and readings from unpublished works. Out of this emerged an East German brand of *samizdat* that included in-house publications of literary journals and limited-edition graphic art books.⁶ The centers of activity were Dresden, Magdeburg, Erfurt, Leipzig, Weimar, and Berlin.

The root cause of the rise of PUT lay in the restrictive cultural policies of the period. The new generation of nonunionized writers and artists responded to their exclusion from state-run guilds by organizing events without formal approval from the authorities. To make matters worse from the MfS's point of view, these events were drawing worrying numbers of followers. The threat that had emanated from "political-ideological diversion" in the 1970s had now transformed into the far larger problem of PUT. A further worrisome trend was the endorsement of this underground by disaffected writers from the older generation, who moved in both official and underground circles⁷ and who were mentoring underground writers. These older disaffected authors were now operating independently of state structures. Moreover, many mentors were, unsurprisingly, also Stasi IMs. What is unusual is that this support from mentors sometimes resulted in the younger writer being recruited by the Stasi. One established writer who fostered the careers of young poets was the IM Paul Wiens, and one of his protégés was Sascha Anderson who also became an IM.

A further reason for the ministry's new focus on underground cultures can be found in the signing of the Helsinki Accords in 1975.⁸ One longer-term effect of the inclusion of human rights clauses in the accords was that state repression became more selective.⁹ The ministry adopted a differentiated strategy in relation to cultural producers. Rather than oscillate between periods of frost and thaw or between phases of "de-escalation"¹⁰ and "intense repression,"¹¹ the MfS developed a more insidious mode of reacting to security threats. Stasi departments, and the new HA XX/9 in particular, began to respond to perceived challenges more flexibly and to differentiate, often for no apparent reason, in their treatment of similar cases. This new approach was a policy of sorts—or, at least an interpretation of a policy shift handed down from above. In a speech given in 1979 by Minister for Culture Hans-Joachim Hoffmann to MfS cadres, explicit mention was made of adopting a policy of differentiation with regard to writers, "to treat them in a differentiated manner, some one way, others another way" (*den einen so den anderen so*).[12] The lack of transparency was designed specifically to add to fear and uncertainty.

As early as 1972 the Stasi had made a discernible shift toward a softer treatment of writers. After 1975 the regime was far more circumspect about holding writers in prisons for any period.[13] With a few notable exceptions, it refrained from deploying against writers those more draconian measures that had been typical of earlier decades. This chapter scrutinizes several of the softer, invisible forms of repression used after 1979. Many of these newer examples resembled kinds of soft power, which emphasized cooperation and incentives rather than force.[14] Even in a late-totalitarian system, however, soft power had a decidedly nasty face.

On January 1, 1980, the last of the ministerial guidelines, Guideline 1/79, for working with secret informants were released. These represented a belated attempt to come to grips with the lasting effects of détente.[15] Although Minister for State Security Erich Mielke had responded by expanding his network of informants, he was still dissatisfied with the quality and efficiency of his "system of informants" (IM-*System*).[16] Moreover, the Transit Agreement signed in December 1971, along with the Basic Treaty of December 1972, which established diplomatic relations between the two Germanies, caused Mielke to panic; he foresaw greater risks of exposure to the class enemy.[17] Guideline 1/79 was by far the most thorough of the guidelines and contained a set of criteria for achieving higher "social and political-operative effectiveness" in working with informants.[18] They included a strong emphasis on the "education" (*Erziehung*) of IMs. Other innovations were improvements in recruiting informants; thenceforward officers had to provide a detailed "plan to conscript" (*Plan zur Verpflichtung*) and better "recruitment suggestions" (*Werbungsvorschlag*),[19] as well as involve higher levels of management in approvals processes.[20] Character assessments were to be more realistic and differentiated. "Instant recruitments" (*Sofortwerbungen*), which sometimes occurred before the paperwork had been completed, were still permitted, but needed to meet minimum standards.[21]

Just how these shifts panned out in the period 1979–82 is well illustrated in two contrasting cases: that of long-serving, experienced informant and cultural functionary Paul Wiens, on the one hand, and, on the other hand, that of new recruit Sascha Anderson. Both represent relatively successful instances of the Stasi's work with IMs, albeit of differing degrees. Both show how perks and kickbacks could succeed, and both reveal the importance of handlers dealing sensitively with agents on the ground. Yet even these so-called success stories expose cracks in the secret police's mode of operating. Recruiting informers from within official apparatuses entailed fewer risks, because such individuals were already closely aligned with the SED. The two further cases discussed in this chapter—those of Maja Wiens and Paul Gratzik—show that for all the rhetoric of improving its work with informants, the Stasi made few tangible gains in this regard. There were substantial flaws in its strategy for recruiting writers that made it difficult for the Stasi to establish and maintain strong ties with them.

In one respect, however, the Stasi's strategy of infiltration of "hostile-negative" groups such as the underground underwent a major overhaul. Joachim Walther writes in this regard of a new type of IM, an "IM-leader" (*Spitzen*-IM).[22] In 1986 the MfS proudly reported that it had managed to build up "several IM-leaders" who had successfully detected "the most significant plans, intentions and activities of the most important of those hostile-negative associations that were under investigation."[23] Moreover, these high-level IMs had developed "long-term individual concepts that had constantly been adapted to the situation and refined."[24] In this instance it was not the quality but the "suitability" (*Paßfähigkeit*) of the candidate that was crucial.[25] These informants were able to penetrate underground circles because of their "real or invented serious conflicts with socialist society."[26] As Walther writes, the demands on such informants were huge, and could even involve engineering a person's "social decline."[27] The original idea was that informants should take on leading positions in enemy groups, be active in "setting the tone" (*tonangebend*), and then paralyze the group's activities from within. Ideally, the end result would be either a "new profile" (*umprofilieren*) for or the "disintegration" (*zersetzen*) of the hostile group.[28] Although Guideline 1/79 makes no mention of this as a strategy, per se, evidence that HA XX/9 experimented with this strategy, with mixed results, can be pieced together from statements made by Sascha Anderson and from his Stasi dossier, as well as from the dossier of his main accomplice, Rainer Schedlinski.[29]

This chapter explores the Stasi's experiment with the strategy that I call "simulation" and define as a more complex and risky variant of infiltration. The logic behind simulation was simply that infiltrators could be more effective if they took a defining role in the circles they penetrated. If the Stasi could position enough informers in key positions, then it could effectively take over a target group, in the process of which the group would become an edifice propped up by the Stasi—that is, a Stasi simulation. Placing "its own people" on the inside had worked with official bodies such as the German Writers' Guild, although less so with the prestigious East German Academy of the Arts (Akademie der Künste der DDR).[30] It also worked, albeit to a far more limited extent, with the independent international journal *Sinn und Form* when Paul Wiens became editor in chief in 1982.[31]

On the face of things, the same method of control could also work with the underground. Simulation, however, proved to be a far more demanding strategy. Simulation was fundamentally a form of sticky surveillance, in that the IMs tried to neutralize a group through sustained interpersonal interaction. Yet simulation implies replacing a particular reality with a simulacrum, an imitation that is indistinguishable from the real. This implies a high degree of similarity between the real and the copy, something that Jean Baudrillard calls the third order of simulacra. In the third order, he claims, the "sovereign difference between the two disappears, and the real is produced by the simulacra."[32] In 1979 the Stasi was about to broach uncharted waters in which socialist reality was to be engineered by simulacra, fakes, or copies. This was a brave new world of human surveillance and it was to take secrecy to a whole new level.

The idea of the East German underground being a mere simulation was first touted by leading journalist Frank Schirrmacher in 1991 in the wake of discoveries about Stasi informants in the Prenzlauer Berg neighborhood of Berlin.[33] The Stasi had made "reality a simulation," he contended. In sentiment this proposition echoed the allegations made by Wolf Biermann around the same time. Biermann traduced the alternative literature of the GDR as a "Stasi cultivation from the hot houses of the main departments HA-XX/9 und HA-XX/7."[34] Biermann proceeded to condemn the entire subcultural scene, calling it scathingly a "luxuriant garden-allotment of the

Stasi" (*blühender Schrebergarten der Stasi*).[35] The charge of simulation, as seductive as it may be, is an understandable overstatement of the reality, which was infinitely more complex.

From around 1976 onward, Sascha Anderson found himself at the heart of this underground in the making. Like others, he was looking for alternative forms of expression and experimenting with new forms of sociability in private spaces. Anderson would prove an ideal catch for the Stasi because he moved in the same circles as bohemian artists, writers, and musicians. He perfectly fit the bill of having "real or invented" connections to the milieu that he was tasked with bringing under control, although it was not quite clear to which category he belonged: real or invented.

Sascha Anderson: Introducing the Underground Poet

Sascha Anderson was born on August 24, 1953, only two months after the failed uprising of June 17, 1953. He was born in Weimar, one of the many towns affected by the unrest.[36] By contrast, the East Germany of Anderson's childhood years was peaceful and uneventful. Sometimes called "generation one,"[37] or the "first FDJ generation,"[38] Anderson's generation had not known any other system than the GDR. Anderson's mother, Monika Krauße-Anderson, worked in Dresden in the DEFA film studios, and his father was a dramaturg and an actor in a theater in Bautzen. In his memoirs Anderson alludes to his father as a man "willing to learn the main part of being a father. My father was not the author who he wanted to be."[39] He mentions his mother by her real name in a quasi-autobiographical poem: "I was born under a star that my father happened to call monika."[40] Anderson's writing also includes other references to his father as a shadowy figure behind the scenes, pulling the strings of a marionette: "He wanted to make the puppets dance, to make them speak."[41]

Anderson loved to cultivate an aura of mystery around himself. Most of all he delighted in fabricating legends about his origins, consisting mainly of wildly imaginative stories about fictive parents, some of which made their way into his files. In one version in his own Stasi file Anderson used to tell people he was the son of a Swedish mother and an American military pilot who died in Vietnam.[42] In another he was the son of the Jewish,

American-born journalist and writer Edith Anderson, who was married to a German communist.[43] According to Walther, it is unclear whether Anderson was born in Weimar, and he speculates that Anderson may have been adopted by his parents.[44]

From 1969 to 1971 Anderson undertook an apprenticeship as a printer in Dresden. There he learned how to do print runs of art works and made his first forays into self-publishing, printing his own poems on used proofs and wrapping paper.[45] Anderson sold his illegal prints at bazars, and they promptly came to the attention of the security police. In his memoir he writes that he was charged with "dissemination of print matter without approval"[46] and "resistance to state power"[47] and given a six-month suspended sentence. His early years in Dresden also brought him into contact with like-minded art students. During the day he worked at the printer, while at night he posed as a nude model for his art friends.[48] Inspired by them, he "wanted to speak in pictures,"[49] and he began experimenting with printing in formats that were influenced by Japanese calligraphy and woodcuts.

Anderson's first recorded contact with the secret police dates from 1973, if we believe his memoirs, or 1974, if we believe the Stasi files.[50] In his memoir he recalls returning from a trip to Moscow and finding a summons issued by the local police station.[51] The meeting he describes as having occurred in 1973 is probably a "transcript of a hearing" (*Befragungsprotokoll*) that took place on October 31, 1974, and lasted five and a half hours.[52] Senior Sergeant Lehmann had singled him out from members of a state-sponsored youth organization "singing club" (*Singeklub*) and questioned him in connection with a questionable blues song about Lenin.[53]

When asked about his future plans, Anderson spoke openly about wanting to study film in Berlin and his aspirations to become "active in this profession in terms of writing and ideologically."[54] At the end of the handwritten transcript Anderson signed that statement: "My words have been reproduced accurately. It corresponds to the truth."[55] Although this document conveys an eagerness to oblige the Stasi, the beginnings of Anderson's collaboration are shrouded in mystery. The interview with Lehmann suggests that he was recruited on the initiative of the Stasi, but elsewhere his file indicates that the contact occurred around this time "at his behest."[56]

On January 28, 1975, the Dresden regional office opened an IM case, apparently without first opening the usual preliminary IM-*Vorlauf*. The original paperwork appears to have gone missing, and Senior Lieutenant Graupner didn't sign off on the original IM file until February 27, 1981, a few days before Anderson was reregistered as an IMB (on March 11, 1981).[57] Anderson chose the code name "David Menzer," which he changed to "Fritz Müller" in 1983, and "Peters" in 1986.[58] His first undercover efforts were less than impressive, and the superior of Lieutenant Wasinski, his first handler, requested in a scribbled note at the bottom of the report that "educational work" (*Erziehungsarbeit*) be carried out with the new recruit, so that he would learn the basics of "objective, comprehensive, current reporting."[59]

Toward the end of 1975 Anderson worked as an "intern" (*Volontariat*) in the DEFA film studios in Babelsberg, Potsdam (in his memoir he claims this occurred in "autumn 1974").[60] It is likely that the internship was the first perk that the Stasi threw his way. Soon after, in May 1976, the Dresden regional office attempted unsuccessfully to hand Anderson over to a colleague closer to Potsdam.[61] From May 1976 to January 1977 Anderson missed arranged meetings with his Dresden handlers. Lieutenant Graupner noted in his report from January 28, 1977 (soon after Biermann's expatriation) that "he still had not managed to contact the informant."[62]

From 1977 to 1980, with few exceptions,[63] Anderson held his Stasi handlers at bay, repeatedly missing meetings. Because there is an inexplicable discrepancy between the file story and Anderson's memory (which I have discussed elsewhere), I will refer here only to the account on file.[64] On one occasion, on March 17, 1977, Graupner and Captain Vetter located him at the residential college of the Writers' Guild; with the help of his mentor Heinz Kahlau, Anderson had secured a residency there (see fig. 10). Kahlau worked for the Stasi as GI "Hochschulz" from 1958 to 1964.[65] At this unscheduled meeting in 1977 Anderson cited a series of personal and financial problems, but reassured the Stasi that he was now leading a respectable existence. His officers were less reassured to learn that Anderson "was no longer taking a Marxist line" in ideological matters, as they recorded.[66] His officers concluded their account with a note stating that Anderson was "fairly bitter" about the fact that his volume of poetry had been rejected for publication.[67] The end of the report states: "In conversations the informant was not explicitly against collaborating with the Stasi, but expressed the view that he wanted to know precisely what exactly the employees expected of him" (see fig. 11).[68]

For the following twenty months, the files indicate Anderson (see fig. 12) continued to evade the Stasi, which periodically tried to follow up on him and bind him tighter to the ministry. At a rare meeting he attended on November 21, 1978, in a safe house, Anderson expressed strong reservations about working for the Stasi: "The informant expressed the view in conversations that he did not want to be an informant for the employees but that he was prepared to talk to the employees with regard to concrete occurrences."[69] In February 1979 he failed to appear at a prearranged meeting, necessitating another unscheduled visit from the Stasi. Anderson repeated his position, that "he did not think much about the idea of collaborating with the Stasi" and "did not want to meet regularly."[70] Anderson failed to keep his next scheduled meeting, on March 13, 1979. This was presumably because he had been arrested (as he had feared) for check fraud; the "file note" lodged a month later indicates as much.[71] A file entry on May 29, 1979, states that Anderson was in the Correctional Institution "Schwarze Pumpe" in Spremberg, near Dresden.[72]

Although Anderson's prison sentence is recorded in his file, there is some doubt about whether Anderson ever served time in Schwarze Pumpe. Walther calls the year 1979 "one of those remarkable blind spots in his vitae"[73] and speculates that Anderson was "at this time being prepared for long-term operational work."[74] In the twenty years since Walther's initial research no firm evidence has been uncovered; the notion that Anderson was whisked away to an intelligence training camp to prepare him for special espionage work may well be the stuff of urban myth. If he was groomed for infiltrating the opposition, certainly his Dresden and Berlin officers knew nothing about it.

After his release from prison, Anderson remained firm, telling his handlers in January 1980 that he "had no interest in conducting further conversations with the officer from the Stasi."[75] By April 1980 the Stasi took a more coercive tack, issuing Anderson with a summons to present himself at the local police station. In light of this it seems surprising that in his memoir Anderson blithely states that his officers did not resort to coercion; they didn't approve of his poetry, "but they did not put me under pressure," he contends.[76] According to his recollections of these months, however, Anderson waited for his officers to appear. "They did not come," he writes.[77] He continues: "I was troubled by the fact, something I found incomprehensible, that my officers were not accessible."[78] This admission that he was secretly longing to hear from them seems surprising, given that they had tried to make contact on numerous occasions. In August 1980 his officers noted that "several attempts at making contact failed because the informant was not present."[79]

In fact, when Anderson's officers did manage to touch base with him in August 1980 he trotted out a slightly softened response. He "had nothing against collaborating with the Stasi but he wanted to make contact when he had something urgent to report."[80] At any rate, the files from this time give no indication that the Stasi had lost interest in Anderson, but rather the reverse. In August 1980 the Stasi had an urgent matter to discuss with him: a literary reading that Anderson had just attended. On October 30, 1980, his officers followed him after another reading.[81] This is the last recorded meeting in which Anderson resists. His personal circumstances had by now changed. He had married and had a family, he maintained, and he swore to "keep his promise from now on and work on a regular basis for the officers."[82] He refused to "write reports" or "to sign these," a commitment that he would not keep for long.[83]

After almost four years the Stasi finally elicited from Anderson a firmer commitment to attending more regular meetings and to writing formal reports. At this meeting on October 30, 1980, around a year after his release from prison, Anderson was promptly given instructions to attend further readings and to determine who was involved.[84] To Anderson's credit it does seem as if he tried to launch his literary career through normal official channels and through his mentors before he came to work regularly for the Stasi. That much said, his choice of literary mentors is telling and reveals at least an unconscious desire to involve the MfS in some way in advancing his career. His mentor Kahlau was a lapsed informant, and Paul Wiens, his other mentor, was an active and experienced one. In 1978 Wiens helped Anderson publish his first poem in *Neue Deutsche Literatur*, the journal published by the Writers' Guild.[85]

Anderson's poem raises the topic of a city brutally divided into two. On the one side "the dreams tried / to build the dream a harbour," while on the other side people tried to find "the endless / sea where the cheap salt swims."[86] Enigmatically titled *Jeder Satellit hat einen Killersatelliten* (Every satellite has a killer satellite, 1982), Anderson's first volume of poetry includes an oblique tribute to Wiens. One untitled poem is written in the form of a crossword puzzle; Wiens was notorious for solving crosswords in public.[87] There are no clues provided, perhaps because the poem itself was intended as a clue or to give us a clue as to Anderson's identity. "The monologues are cruising [*gehen fremd*] / across the train station," he writes.[88] The poem, which was read as a declaration of Anderson's generation's refusal of dialogue with the state, is also about communication and betrayal.[89] Many years later, critics were to see something of a confession in these lines.

Although Paul Wiens did not participate in events in the underground, many of the other older writers did. Readings and exhibitions were organized in various Protestant churches and a handful of private apartments. Without informants, these informal salons were off limits for the Stasi. By the same token, it was no easy feat to use infiltrators in such instances, given that they would easily be recognized as such unless their subcultural credentials were impeccable. By dint of his actual background in such artistic and literary circles, Anderson had faultless credentials for infiltrating the underground, and he needed no elaborate legend to justify his presence at events. He was an eager, independent participant without the backing or prompting of the Stasi. Anderson did not need to dissemble; he was in his element in the underground and also oddly comfortable with the invisible status that his secret connections to the Stasi bestowed on him.

Paul Wiens: Informing until Death Do Us Part

Although the Biermann affair represented a watershed for many of the older generation of writers, some—such as IM "Poet" Paul Wiens—weathered the crisis, it could be said, both with the help of their Stasi connections and despite them. In the years that followed, Wiens settled back down into the routine of undercover work and his other professional work in the PEN Club and the Writers' Guild. Wiens was now more at ease than ever before with juggling the official and clandestine aspects of his professional work. After a shaky start he had gone on to establish strong, durable ties with the Ministry for State Security that by 1982 spanned an entire decade. The repetitive nature of much of Wiens's file offers some indications as to why this collaboration proved ultimately so successful. Part 2 of the file, containing his informant reports, reveals the secret to the success of the relationship.

The manner in which meetings occur and are filed—that is, how the "file story" is told—is a distinctive feature of all secret-police files. The Stasi files use what Gérard Genette has termed a "singulative" mode of narration that rarely resorts to repetition or summarizing in relation to meetings with informants.[90] The effect is slightly numbing and yet somehow soothing; for the reader this effect may mimic the routinized nature of the informing experience. When combined with the long time span of an individual's collaboration and the intensity of espionage activity and reporting (the length of the filed reports), this mode of singulative narration produces a thick dossier and a time-consuming read. Wiens's dossier is therefore thick in a literal sense, given that it spans multiple volumes. It is also thick in Clifford Geertz's sense of providing a "thick," rich account or commentary on many aspects of the secret culture of informing.

However, as a reflection of Wiens's mindset in the final phase of his collaboration, the latter part of his dossier appears thin and inconclusive. Only the regular meeting reports filed by his officer, Rolf Pönig, give some clues as to the value Wiens placed on his links to the Stasi. Wiens's file for the later years appears orderly and well kept, with a separate report being lodged after each meeting. The Stasi's record-keeping requirements stipulated that officers should list each instance of an occurrence, here a meeting, separately. This distinctive narrative feature of secret-police files can yield vital clues for the historian. Seemingly trivial notes or references, such as a change of setting from the usual safe house, can act as prompts to read between the lines. Such prompts may indicate a loss of faith or something more ominous, such as a serious illness or death.

Over time Wiens's reports for the Stasi became more perfunctory, and the meetings more repetitive and routinized. For a bureaucracy such as the Stasi, this was testament to the stabilization of identity that Wiens achieved in the performance of informing. Despite the impost of secrecy, Wiens clearly had learned to accommodate his double life better over time. Possibly the comfortable routine of his file is also evidence of a deep-seated dependency on the Stasi. The Stasi may have become a substitute father-figure or figure of authority, an "attachment figure" or mentor who had been missing from Wiens's childhood.[91] The interpersonal dimension of informing work seems to have been immensely important to him. The rhythm of the files suggests that the professional nature of the relationship receded into the background and the relationship transformed into something more personal.

We can see evidence of this shift in the perfunctory nature of Pönig's reporting. The sparse reports mask an evolving rapport between the two men that cannot be contained within the parameters of the bureaucratic dossier. The mutual understanding between Wiens and his handler is, although invisible, still palpable in the almost respectful tone of the documentation. Each report states that the meeting occurred uneventfully and that the IM reported "openly and frankly."[92] To be sure, these lines were stock phrases straight from a handler's handbook. Yet such lines could hide all kinds of interpersonal situations. In this case they were a type of linguistic cover for a far more personalized bond, fostered and nurtured over ten years between informer and handler. This linguistic cover was rudely disrupted, however, when the chain-smoking Wiens was hospitalized for treatment for pancreatic cancer.

The last reports that Pönig filed were from Wiens's hospital bed when he visited his terminally ill agent. The special box on the meeting report reserved for filing information about the place of the meeting merely states that it occurred "in [the] hospital" (see fig. 13).[93] In fact, Pönig paid Wiens several visits in the hospital, and on one occasion Wiens handed over what would be his last report for the Stasi, which concerned the writer Erwin Strittmatter.[94] Wiens had unfinished business he wished to complete, or his sense of duty was by now so ingrained, so habituated that it did not occur to him *not* to hand over his last report. Reading between the lines, on his deathbed Wiens was unperturbed by visits from the secret police. On the contrary, he seemed pleased to see his officer. And Pönig does not seem to see anything untoward in visiting his loyal source in the hospital, although a hospital room was a far cry from a Stasi-run safe house. There would be, for instance, no coffee served in pretty cups, no whiskey or cognac drunk, no cigars smoked; there would only be flowers, as per usual.[95]

At their last official meeting, on March 30, 1982, seven days before Wiens's death, Wiens thanked his officer for visiting. The remaining short report is devoted to his health. Wiens appeared resigned and composed, and remarked that this meeting would be his last. Wiens asked Pönig to take care of his wife. Still unable to mention Wiens's pending death explicitly, Pönig concluded the formalities of the report with the comment that he was unable to issue any further assignments because it was unlikely that Wiens would be leaving the hospital (see fig. 14).[96] Thus, Wiens's collaboration literally continued until days before his death. After his passing Wiens's Stasi dossier comes to an abrupt and unceremonious end. There is no evidence that the Stasi noted or even registered his passing in any formal way.

Stasi officers lacked a stamp for the death of an agent and used no technical term or acronym to signal that an informer had died on the job. Guidelines did not, for instance, stipulate that a death certificate be filed or entered. Passport photographs were required with a change of handler (much to Wiens's chagrin, as noted in chapter 2), but no proof was needed that an agent had died. Nor did the Stasi's form include a special column to complete or a box to tick for death or illness. In effect, Wiens died in action, and his death is one of the few casualties that occurred on file; that is, that occurred while the dossier was open (i.e., agents rarely died while their dossiers were open). Yet his death is palpable on reading his file. Death does not occur years after the file was closed but only days or weeks before it was closed. Death occurs quietly in the blanks at the end of the file, unexpectedly, and a little poignantly, somewhere in the nether region of the blank space between the last file entry and the file's gray cardboard cover.

The grim ending to Wiens's life as a secret agent is a stark reminder of the deeply symbiotic relationship that developed between Wiens and the Stasi and of his deluded entanglement with the secret police. It was an ideal but fateful marriage of personalities and interests, almost a marriage "until death do us part" in the traditional sense. It was even a marriage in which the partners were rather fond of one another, each in their own way. This unsettling ending to Wiens's file story is possibly even fitting for the sort of agent that Wiens was. His going missing in action speaks volumes about the nexus between Wiens's habitus as an international, jet-setting writer and senior literary statesman from the Eastern Bloc and his darker, secret life as a Stasi agent.

If we read backward from this death scene of relative peace and harmony it is possible to infer Wiens's motivations for remaining loyal to the Stasi for so long. Wiens may have stayed on because the interpersonal dimensions of his secret espionage work made it more palatable. It is also possible that he could reconcile himself to the secrecy and the subterfuge because the connections to the Stasi somehow flattered him and perhaps bolstered his self-image, or shored up his insecurities. Above all, Wiens was able to travel and to live a glamorous, pampered international lifestyle of circumscribed freedom to which he had become accustomed from an early age. Denied to most citizens of the GDR, this was a privilege he would otherwise not have enjoyed. These links to the Stasi were like an insurance policy against political reprisals, a security blanket for him during cold, tough, uncertain times. His justification to himself may have been that it was better to be on the side of power than to find himself trapped once again on the other side. And he could always play one side against the other.

Wiens's second stint of collaborating was far better managed by the Stasi than his first. To his credit, Pönig had learned how to respect Wiens's gentleman sensibilities and well-developed sense of entitlement. By the 1970s Pönig's own career was on a steep upward trajectory. He had amassed a wealth of knowledge on how to run agents of all stripes in the field.[97] By 1980, as discussed in chapter 3, Pönig had also honed his knowledge of espionage psychology by studying at the Stasi's Law School (Juristische Hochschule) in Potsdam.[98] We can assume he tried out some of his acquired expertise when handling Wiens.

The Stasi's investment in Wiens, and indeed in his handler, finally started to bear fruit. The ideological trade-off for Wiens was simply that he should peddle the official party line, and he did so religiously from 1972 on. By contrast with his daughter Maja, Wiens needed no particular legend to do his work for the Stasi. In fact, Wiens needed no false identity or simulated habitus at all; he could simply be himself. He could possibly even be a better, more inflated, and more powerful version of himself. Nor did he need to disavow his loyalty to the SED in his interactions with his peers—he was, after all, an esteemed member of the Writers' Guild. If he expressed orthodox views, this did not automatically suggest that he worked for the Stasi.

The MfS appears to have realized that patriotism, rather than ideological orthodoxy, was a powerful motivator in itself. Heterodoxy in writers could be tolerated, provided there was another basis on which to build a sustainable collaboration. Patriotism provided that basis. The example of Paul Wiens shows that the Stasi was capable of some flexibility in its handling of informants. In such cases it was possible to establish a stable, enduring working relationship with agents. Like Wiens, the Stasi had learned its lessons, and its added care and personalized supervision had paid off. For Wiens the secret links to the Stasi contributed to his self-esteem and added to his stores of symbolic capital, despite the fact that the cause of this extra capital—the Stasi—remained hidden from view. In the end being a long-standing member of an elite secret society with its own rules of engagement became a naturalized part of his life. This was not the case with some other members of this secret surveillance society, such as his daughter.

Maja Wiens: Speaking Truth to Power

The death of Maja Wiens's father on April 6, 1982, is not registered in her informer file. Like most human emotions in the world of espionage, this personal tragedy fell between the cracks of organizational record-keeping. There is no trace of her grief on file, not even a request from Wiens for a little breathing space after her recent bereavement. Instead her file trucks along as if nothing had happened. In the file version of her life, of course, nothing had happened, at least not for the time being. But the death of Paul Wiens did change a good number of things for his eldest daughter. As a consequence, she became more forthright in her dealings with the Stasi. Her approach to fulfilling her goals shifted from a promotion orientation to a negative or avoidance orientation. This changed state of play does rate a mention in her file. Starting at the time of her father's death, we find more and more references to Wiens's growing dissatisfaction with the Stasi's modes of operation. Wiens was despondent about her lack of professional prospects as a writer. She felt constrained more generally by the lack of freedom in the GDR. Already in March 1979, her handler, Lt. Peter Reise, reported: "She needs some comradely emotional morale boosting because at the moment she predominantly sees the countless negative things in society again."[99]

Matters came to a head in late November 1982, about six months after the death of Wiens's father. The occasion was a change of handler. Reise, her trusted case officer, was about to retire from the ministry for health reasons. At her last meeting with him she received 500 marks for the Medal of Merit of the National People's Army in Bronze, along with her monthly rate of 400 marks for her surveillance of Bettina Wegner, bringing her remuneration to a total of 900 marks.[100] From her perspective this monetary recognition was a fitting ending to the first phase of her undercover career, and Wiens must have felt vindicated and appreciated. The payment was also meant to smooth the way for the handover to a new officer, Maj. Eberhard Plaumann.[101] It is not clear what transpired before, during, or after the handover, which was a routine matter, but "Marion" plainly did not take to Plaumann. Plaumann lodged an official search warrant for her in December 1982, a sure sign that the collaboration had not begun smoothly. She had been promoted within the Stasi, but the 1978 OV focused on Kunze had shown her how taxing it could be to maintain the constant, secret charade with her friends. Moreover, the Stasi seemed oblivious to the lingering consequences of arrests and interrogations for informers on the ground.

In April 1981 (a year and a half before the handover to Plaumann), Wiens's file mentions a stipend that she had secured for her novel in progress, *Traumgrenzen* (The verge of dreams). She was to receive the monthly sum of 500 marks over six months until delivery of a finished manuscript to Neues Leben state publishing house.[102] The attraction of the stipend was that it was unconditional; she would not be obliged to repay the sum if the novel could not be published.[103] The stipend, it appears, was the start of radical *volte-face* in Wiens's attitude to the state. This would see her transition in a relatively short space of time from the decorated darling of the Pankow district office to a prickly and poisonous thorn in the side of the same office. The catalyst was Wiens's firsthand experience of censorship, excessive state tutelage, and unauthorized secret-police meddling.

Wiens's story of trying to publish her novel is instructive, because it tells us much about her evolving critical habitus in relation to the East German regime; moreover, it reveals that her aspirations to be a writer were pivotal to her work for the Stasi. Once finished, Wiens's manuscript first had to pass muster with the in-house editors at Neues Leben and then with the Ministry for Culture. At both these stages the Stasi could interfere, either through the publisher's hidden Stasi informants or by commissioning its own secret readers' reports.[104]

Unbeknownst to Wiens, the Stasi's HA XX/7 in Berlin commissioned a damning assessment of her manuscript, which found the novel "unpublishable."[105] The reviewer criticizes the novel's "mindset, its underlying ideological premise," which the reviewer considers responsible for the story's "sense of resignation" with respect to socialism.[106] The reviewer concludes that "all cooperation" with Wiens should be based on "sustained work on her ideological convictions."[107] Above all, the assessor disapproves of the almost exhaustive list of social issues that are criticized in the novel.[108] "There is a lot of tea drunk in this story," the assessment continues, and "a lot of superficial, albeit ambitious waffle about literature and art."[109] Despite this deeply unsympathetic review, Wiens was in luck. Another review of her novel, also commissioned by the Stasi, was carried out by a member of the Writers' Guild who was a friend and colleague of Paul Wiens. Unsurprisingly, this reviewer recommended that the book be published, praising the work for the same reasons that the previous reviewer had condemned it. She liked the personal crisis at the center of the novel, which was a chance for the protagonist "to examine the possibilities and opportunities available to her."[110] In this assessment the "responsible, critical, deeply human and morally uncompromised basic attitude towards our society" was highlighted.[111]

A handwritten note on Wiens's file, dated November 23, 1982, states that "in consultation" with the publishing house the Stasi had managed to prevent the manuscript from being published. The principal reason given was offensive political passages criticizing the SED as a "narrow gauge party."[112] The files do not fill in the many gaps in this particular story, and it is with some surprise that we read in a later section of Wiens's file that the book was eventually published and the Pankow district office overruled.

The meddling behind the scenes in connection with Maja Wiens's novel was to take its toll on her undercover work (see fig. 15). Although she was not privy to the Stasi's machinations in manipulating publishers, she correctly surmised that the Stasi had been deliberately placing hurdles in her way. After the handover to her new officer her file repeatedly registers her growing resentment of the Stasi. The next file entry is dated a year later, on November 14, 1983. At her meeting with Plaumann, Wiens was patently aggrieved and declared that she could see "no common basis" for working for the ministry.[113] Moreover, her annoyance had now found another bugbear. She called the Stasi's interference in activities of the West German Greens in the East and the suppression of the East German peace movement "politically blind."[114] In a further move designed to antagonize her officer, Wiens launched a personal attack on him. She called him blind and narrow and expressed her unhappiness that he had made contact outside of the agreed meeting times and places. Her response to this particular visit at her apartment was to remark sarcastically that it was "useful" because it allowed her son, who was present at the time, to see the ministry's "true face."[115] As incredible as it sounds, Plaumann had gone to no effort to disguise the purpose of his visit and arrived equipped with tape recorder in hand. Her son and husband had had no trouble guessing who the unwelcome intruder was. Incensed, Wiens accused the MfS of only coming to her "when they urgently need a favor" (*wenn es brennt*) and of instrumentalizing her, declaring that "[she] was not a computer for the ministry" (see fig. 16).[116]

This meeting is a rare example of "speaking truth to power" archived in the Stasi files. The snapshot lodged in this section of her file is unusual because she was a seasoned informer with a distinguished track record. Wiens is captured on file hectoring her officer, chastising him as if he were a trainee or schoolboy. This colorful outburst, which would normally have been interpreted as an open act of insubordination, is documented in its full glory. In her file the personal slur on her officer's character is followed, for instance, by an exhaustive list of her political gripes with the regime. She disputed the Stasi's notion that the West German peace movement was being "controlled" (*gesteuert*) by Western intelligence agencies; this was, she said, pure propaganda. The rest of the conversation continued in the same vein, with her complaining to her handler that there was no freedom of opinion or expression in the GDR and that false news items (*Manipulations- und Falschmeldungen*) were common.[117] She finished by listing all the glaring social problems she had identified: the country was bankrupt;[118] discipline and cleanliness were lifestyles; "regimentation" started in kindergarten; the education system in schools was narrow minded; and instruction was poor (see fig. 17).[119]

On the subject of her targets, Wiens revealed to her officer that she did not approve of the surveillance measures against Bettina Wegner.[120] Wiens also insisted on knowing what happened to her information: "After all, the whole existence of an informer depends on this."[121] Plaumann concluded his report with the none-too-astute observation that his informant "did not want to maintain ties," and that she wondered whether collaboration "even had a purpose."[122] Although Wiens was frank to the point of rudeness, Plaumann committed these insults to paper seemingly without flinching, including an unfavorable comparison to his predecessor: "With Peter [Reise is meant here] it was different, he knew a lot and knew how to use his knowledge to find his way around. He gave the impression of being informed about things—you knew what happened to your information."[123]

Wiens had managed to make herself unattractive to the Stasi, in the hope of ending the association altogether. Yet having worked on several major operations, she did not find quitting easy.[124] She had come to admire Wegner and her circle of friends in the peace movement; she started to approve of their activities. Also, she may have been tired of having to invent alibis that were becoming increasingly ludicrous. The demands of leading a double life, as well as the secrecy of her clandestine meetings with her officer, were a burden that she would happily have shed. Despite Wiens's outburst, her case officer kept her informer file open. One more meeting is recorded, which was convened for June 26, 1985, to work through outstanding issues.

Astoundingly, the Stasi appears to still have been determined to win Wiens back. This last-ditch attempt to force Wiens into cooperating is striking for the meticulous planning involved. Not only did the MfS no longer trust Wiens, it had realized that she was beating them at their own game.

Wiens used her insider's knowledge to keep one step ahead of the Stasi. Neither she nor her pursuers were to know that this was the desperate final act in what was to be the regime's endgame. Her defiance of the Stasi is remarkable, given that she could not know that the regime would soon completely implode. The Stasi showed no sign of softening its approach to Wiens. The more information it collected on her, the more obvious it became that it would wage a war of attrition against her. The file contains elaborate contingency plans that rehearse various scenarios for the last encounter in June 1985; Major Plaumann prepared with his superior for the meeting with Wiens, as per Guideline 1/79, even running through potential topics of conversation. This time the handling officer was careful to make clear and acceptable arrangements for their meeting and not to appear unannounced.[125] Still, despite the rehearsals and the collective brainpower of Plaumann and his superior, the meeting proved a disaster.

Wiens was so enraged to see her officer again that she no longer bothered to be polite, retorting, "What was he doing here, we have nothing to say to each other."[126] In the heated exchange that followed, the same bones of contention were restated. Wiens repeated her disapproval of the surveillance of the peace movement, protesting that Bärbel Bohley and Ulrike Poppe were "the real freedom-fighters."[127] This time Wiens's officer was no longer quite so restrained in his reporting, remarking that Wiens dressed like a bohemian and, with her arrogant behavior, behaved like one as well.[128] Plaumann had given the relationship one last try and had failed miserably.

Paul Gratzik: Closing the File

At the time the Stasi finally closed the file on IM "Peter" early in 1981, Gratzik's life had begun to unravel in other respects as well. In 1980 he was living in Dresden and was in the process of obtaining a divorce. After his divorce he resigned from his job and moved to the suburb of Berlin-Weißensee. By this stage Gratzik was firmly ensconced in oppositional and bohemian circles. His officers continued to keep a close eye on him, but as Günter Wenzel remarks in the film *Vaterlandsverräter*, Gratzik now moved in a "circle of influence that was not positive for him." For the first time in almost twenty years Gratzik was free of the Stasi and of the insidious pressure of having to hide his secret police connections. He was at liberty to write what he wanted and to publish where he pleased. His confessions to close friends had cleared the air.

Freedom, however, turned out to be an unfamiliar state of being. In the film documentary, when Hendel asks Gratzik what happened when he finally stopped informing, he replies: "The next crisis! Suddenly I had nothing to do. He [Wenzel] had assured me I would not get a foothold in the GDR, you know, wouldn't find a safe place in the GDR." Moreover, he now had further reason to fear the Stasi's retribution. Gratzik appears to have been haunted by the prospect of the Stasi taking revenge on him. As he tells Hendel, he pictured that one day he would disappear and land at the bottom of a lake. In other words, Gratzik was now suffering from paranoia, and everywhere saw Stasi phantoms who threatened to do Wenzel's dirty work for him.

It is hard to know how serious Wenzel's blustering threats of ruining Gratzik's career were. Had Gratzik's fertile imagination got the better of him? Since the early 1980s Gratzik was no longer reliant on East German publishers and he had secured the support of the small but influential West German publisher, Rotbuch. Moreover, it was not entirely illegal to publish with Rotbuch, provided the author applied for and was granted a legal release from the East German Office for Copyright (Büro für Urheberrechte). Many writers who were denied a permit simply published their works illegally with impunity. In 1977 Gratzik had been lucky with his novel; the East German publisher Hinstorff, based in Rostock, had published *Transportpaule: Monolog* after Wenzel had intervened on Gratzik's behalf. Without Wenzel to pull strings for him anymore it was not clear to Gratzik how he would continue to publish. Indeed, from 1981 onward Gratzik had no insider help: he had no more friends in either the Stasi or in the Ministry for Culture to intervene on his behalf.

When Gratzik tried to have his next novel, *Kohlenkutte* (Coalminer's garb), published in the West, he did not bother going through the usual channels of first applying for a publication permit. An entry in the new surveillance file that the Stasi opened on Gratzik registers this noncompliance. Curiously, the same file entry concludes in a tone of uncharacteristic apathy, stating that it probably was not "worthwhile" (*zweckmäßig*) to try to charge him.[129] This is an astonishing admission of powerlessness on the part of the Stasi officer writing the report. The reason given in the file for not taking action against Gratzik is neatly encapsulated in the comment that there are "political-legal considerations" to take into account.[130] Still not yet willing to be beaten, the Stasi remained on the watch for opportunities to at least prevent Gratzik's works from reaching a wider audience. Over the following few years the Stasi managed to confiscate copies of several of Gratzik's manuscripts, in the hope that some punitive action would result.[131] One work was scrutinized by security experts and found to contain "massive attacks on the Ministry for State Security whose employees are depicted as spineless instruments in the hands of power."[132] The Stasi did manage to prevent this manuscript from being published in the West, as a note on Gratzik's file states: "A publication of the manuscript in the Federal Republic of Germany could be operatively prevented."[133]

By 1984 Gratzik was integrated into the close-knit alternative scene of the literary underground in the Prenzlauer Berg district in East Berlin. He was among the older, more established writers who frequented events. Because Gratzik was not a member of the official Writers' Guild,[134] there were limited public places in which he could share his works. It is ironic that Gratzik became a member of this loose and rather heterogeneous group of writers, artists, and musicians. The irony lies less in the fact that he felt at home with such a bohemian literary set and more in the reality that the Prenzlauer Berg scene was infiltrated by Stasi spies. In a manner of speaking, having only just extricated himself from informing for the Stasi, Gratzik moved out of the frying pan straight into the fire; he found himself shadowed by a couple of Stasi agents. These were not the Stasi's hit men lying in wait to murder him; instead the agents instructed to keep an eye on him were his new-found friends, such as Sascha Anderson. The milieu that had become his new safe haven, far from the reaches of the Firm, was infiltrated by marionettes whose strings were being manipulated from afar by the same ministry he had tried to escape.

Sascha Anderson: The Rosencrantz of His Generation

The Stasi's usual technique of using infiltrators had hitherto required informants simulate the dispositions of their targets, placing undue stresses on informers' ability to lie and dissemble. Some in the ministry came to realize that policing the underground would require a more nuanced approach. Infiltrators were more plausible if they had existing ties to enemy circles or were already embedded in such groups. Yet accepting this fact involved a higher level of risk for the Stasi, which naturally had far less control over "real enemy" informants such as these. Moreover, informers deployed in the underground had little to fear, given that they had no established careers and little that could be jeopardized in the way of social comforts or privileges. As such, the Stasi had limited leverage with these recruits, other than to threaten them, often impotently, with criminal action. As the Stasi knew well, threats might instill docility in citizens in the short term, but they were a poor basis for establishing a long-term working relationship. Instead, as outlined in chapter 1, threats fed straight into an error signal in the motivational feedback loop, indicating to the informant that this was not the best path to goal fulfillment. Fear, too, was ultimately too strong an emotion to be truly useful as a motivation for collaborating in the long term; it fostered a negative or avoidance orientation.

In response to the new threat from political underground activity, the Stasi was forced to extemporize in much of its handling of agents. Anderson was one such experiment in human intelligence gathering. From 1980 through the last decade of the Cold War, surveillance moved into an indeterminate gray zone, in which the watchers were also the watched and the source of surveillance became almost indistinguishable from the target. In the underground the Stasi's simulacra became almost identical to the real. With Anderson, the simulacrum preceded the real thing in many ways. In other words, without the Stasi, Anderson might never have become the charismatic and hyperactive figurehead of an outlawed subculture. Yet he was by no means a pure Stasi invention either before his involvement with this subculture or during it. In his memoir Anderson writes that after his release from prison in 1980 he began "to cultivate a concept of production that in retrospect appeared pathological."[135] With his contacts to Dresden's art scene, in 1979 Anderson experimented with combining poetry with block prints or etchings, producing semi-legal limited-edition art books.[136]

Around the same time Anderson became a frequent visitor to literary readings in private apartments as well as to secular cultural events in churches. He and others thus found a way to bypass the party's ironclad control over public gatherings.[137] By opening up the spacious living rooms of their own apartments and collaborating with the more liberal-minded pastors in the Lutheran churches, Anderson and his friends retreated into semi-private spaces to be impervious to the prying eyes of the state. In these private spaces "contact" with the state was "only a marginal phenomenon." Indeed, this phrase was the title of the first poetry collection by the new generation of writers to be published in the West, *Berührung ist eine Randerscheinung*.[138]

Most of those involved in such events thought the phrase was true. From the perspective of the Stasi, of course, such gatherings were the prelude to establishing an illegal underground movement. Moreover, as claimed by a departmental strategy paper from HA XX/AKG (Auswertungs- und Kontrollgruppe) dated January 4, 1982, most of these alternative events deliberately set out to deceive the authorities about their true (political) nature.[139] The initiators disguised their intentions by calling the events "birthday parties" or "class reunions" and were "deliberately" misusing church premises.[140] They advertised the gatherings with placards, issued personalized invitations, and publicized them by "word-of-mouth propaganda."[141] Over the course of 1981 the Stasi noted that there were some sixty-five readings, thirty-four exhibitions, eight song or musical events, ten discussion forums, and eleven nonspecific gatherings.[142]

By November 1980 the Stasi was so pleased with Anderson—its source at the heart of this exploding underground scene—that his officers offered him a glass of champagne at their meeting. Anderson, surprised, professed to not having "done much."[143] This is entirely plausible, and Anderson may have thought he could combine the Stasi's demands with his own artistic ambitions with no extra effort. He hints at this in his memoirs where he writes: "And so they met their objectives with the information that I gave them and I, by means of the information that they gave me, met mine."[144] He obliged the Stasi, for example, by handing over hard evidence of his activities, such as copies of art catalogs; he even made tape recordings of readings.[145]

At the beginning of 1981 the Stasi began to scale up its deployment of Anderson. His earnings for his reports, which were now handwritten on graph paper, averaged 100 marks per meeting. His officers, however, make constant reference to continuing work on "his motives" for helping "our organization."[146] In this context they note that Anderson was "also willing to carry out unofficial work outside of the GDR."[147] Now Anderson's activities began to take on a dynamism of their own as the Stasi started to lose its grip on its cherished simulacrum. It seems that his hyperactivity was largely the result of his own restless personality and an almost manic desire to be in the limelight. There is scant evidence to suggest that he penetrated deep into subcultural circles just to expose or betray their members. Hence, a pattern emerges early on in his reporting, particularly about events in which he was a prominent participant; he plays down their subversive character. For instance, he writes about an art exchange that "the event proceeded without any incidents and provocations."[148] With a few notable exceptions, this placatory tone is a consistent aspect of his reports.[149]

During 1981 Anderson ceased to be a mere bystander and started to be an initiator of some of the underground happenings. Part of his success lay in his ability to recognize talent.[150] Wilfriede Maaß recalls that after Anderson came on the scene the readings in her and her husband's apartment started to become more regular and more organized.[151] Anderson's officers were pleased with all this activity; no wonder, given that he tape-recorded some of these events for them.[152] "My officers were well disposed towards me," his memoir states.[153] Anderson was not involved in all of the different subcultural circles—for example, he was not a regular at the readings held in the apartment of Ulrike and Gerd Poppe[154]—but the events he set in train took on a life of their own and "the machinery began to kick over."[155]

It is possible that the Stasi viewed Anderson's role as that of a Trojan horse in the underground. What started out as a simulacrum inevitably became real, and Anderson developed into an influential and independent social actor as well as a rather unreliable secret-police agent. This is exemplified by his connection with another poetry anthology, planned by Franz Fühmann with the support of the Academy of the Arts.[156] In his memoir Anderson recalls meeting Fühmann and being entrusted with the task of making a selection of works by younger writers, together with Uwe Kolbe.[157] Kolbe was editor of the underground literary journals *Der Kaiser ist nackt* (The emperor is naked) and *Mikado*—and Anderson was at the avant-garde, experimental end of the spectrum, known for his art books titled *Poesiealbum*. Fühmann, once an ardent supporter of the regime, had become a "tireless advocate" for the younger generation and for greater liberalization.[158]

In November 1981, however, the Academy of the Arts put an end to the anthology because it was feared that those involved, including Anderson, were a "hostile-negative group."[159] Moreover, the threat associated with the project was thought sufficiently serious to warrant the intervention of the Central Committee (Zentralkomitee, ZK) of the SED. As Anderson recalls, and documents from September 1981 prepared by HA XX/9 prove, the MfS decided to "divide up" the "imaginary family" of young writers.[160] The ZK identified three groupings: those who could be "useful for socialism in a positive way"[161] and should be considered for membership in the Writers' Guild; those who should be forced to seek other paid work; and those who behaved in an "asocial and treasonous" manner, who would be dealt with through the justice system.

A month later, the Stasi began gathering intelligence on the writers. In December 1981 martial law was imposed in Poland, and in response to the emerging crisis, the Stasi increased its vigilance.[162] For IMB "David Menzer," alias Sascha Anderson, involvement in the anthology began to have personal repercussions. Around this time, his application to join the Writers' Guild was rejected. His Stasi officers suggested that he should either enroll to study in Leipzig or join the Guild for Entertainment.[163] Anderson recalls being dumbfounded by this suggestion: "Something had gone wrong. What was the internal logic to them trying, almost ten years after our first contact, and I was twenty-seven, to talk me into studying."[164] If he had been hoping that his ten years of service to the Stasi would open up opportunities for him, he was sorely mistaken. Anderson's response was then to flout the law and publish his poetry in the West. When the first book review appeared in the West, the Stasi was alarmed. On file we find a photocopy of the review with a scribbled note across it: "What is wrong with A? I was always told we had him operatively under control?"[165]

The story of the Fühmann anthology project has a postscript. In February 1982 Anderson wrote a forty-three-page strategy paper for his officers, offering advice on how to proceed with the writers involved. His report differs markedly from that penned by IMB "Günther," who claimed in his evaluation for the Stasi that virtually all the writers were "clearly hostile and displayed a hardened hostile political-ideological basic stance towards the GDR."[166] Hopeful that he could influence matters, Anderson maintained that most poets were harmless.[167] In short, as Anderson recalls in his memoir, "they should all be allowed to do what they please"[168]—hardly what the regime wanted to hear.

In a revealing passage in his report Anderson takes on the Stasi's question of "who is willing to play a positive political role." He rejects the premise of the question, then hastens to add: "Please don't think I am schizophrenic."[169] He suggests that the Stasi should instead be asking who is willing to play a role "in the sense of being contradictory and contradicting, [since] ideas also have to be contradicted over the course of time."[170] It is symptomatic of Anderson's subcultural habitus that he believed that writers should be permitted to engage productively with society's contradictions. Whereas the ministry divided the writers into three groups, Anderson invents his own three categories. In his first group are those who have been forced into the "apparent margins" through society's rejection of them.[171] He places himself in the second group of "dropouts" who "were preoccupied neither thematically nor formally with GDR-specific reality."[172] The third group was not "interested in cultural politics," and "not yet integrated."[173]

According to Klaus Michael, Anderson's line was directed at integration rather than provoking an escalation of the conflict; later in his report Anderson argues that the simplest way would be to "neutralize" the whole "mass" of writers by allowing them all into the Writers' Guild.[174] This is the clearest evidence yet that Anderson seems to have perceived his role in terms of subtly channeling social energies rather than forbidding or blocking them.¹⁷⁵ In a report dated October 14, 1981, his officers suggested he should scale back his activities.¹⁷⁶ Given that Anderson's "art combine" was now running at full throttle,¹⁷⁷ clearly he did not wish to scale it back, as he said, "from one day to the next."¹⁷⁸ From this, we can see that Anderson was attempting, with decreasing success, to retain his positive "promotion orientation" toward attaining his goals. Nonetheless, increasingly he was encountering obstacles in squaring his own wishes with those of the Stasi.

Anderson had no intention of reining in his limited-edition works. Although he knew the Stasi was not pleased with his activities, it appears that contributing to the growth of the underground was the price that the Stasi was begrudgingly obliged to pay. Anderson may not have known how many other informers who were doing similar work in other circles, but he did have a fair idea that his position guaranteed him a good degree of license. He was determined to use this influence to further his own interests. A poem Anderson wrote around this time reflects on the paradoxical nature of his situation. Presented as a series of revelations of secrets, the poem suggests that the lyrical I is not who he seems:

i am mary westmacott
...
but that is of course not everything
...
& even that is not everything
... & and even that is not everything¹⁷⁹

Here the poet speaks through a mask, while commenting on the fact that his lyrical persona—Mary Westmacott was a pseudonym used by Agatha Christie—is just a mask, possibly even one of many. The poet describes himself as "chasing words" into the "double heart albums" for the "rosencrantz of his generations" in the "name of s. anderson." By invoking the sycophantic figures of Rosencrantz and Guildenstern from Shakespeare's *Hamlet*, Anderson positions himself first and foremost in the tradition of Heiner Müller's play *Die Hamletmaschine*, written in 1977. Müller's Hamlet stands with the "ruins of European civilization behind him,"¹⁸⁰ and likewise Anderson's lyric subject is caught between the alternatives of the "ruins of ideology, history, truth," on the one hand, and the "void of 'posthistory,'" on the other.[181]

For Anderson there were additional resonances in the figure of Hamlet. Shakespeare's Hamlet is being observed by the king's spies, Rosencrantz and Guildenstern; with Hamlet, they represent the next generation of ruling elites, waiting to assume the reins of power. Like Rosencrantz and Guildenstern, Anderson and his friends felt "born into" a particular political system, and as Karen Leeder has pointed out, they also felt that they had been "born too late"[182]—doomed to remain perpetually waiting in the wings for their cues to come on stage and play their part in national cultural life. On another level Anderson's comparison to Hamlet's shadowy friends aptly describes his own existential dilemma of wanting to serve the Stasi by spying on his friends while also remaining on good terms with them. Anderson would have known that in Shakespeare's play Rosencrantz and Guildenstern eventually receive their just deserts; Hamlet foils the king's plan to have him killed and sends his friends to their deaths instead. Like the two court spies in *Hamlet*, Anderson would eventually pay a high, if justified, price for betraying his friends. In the meantime he was preoccupied with finding a way to keep all the balls he was juggling in the air at the same time.

*

By the end of 1982 the Stasi's solution for containing the ever-expanding phenomenon of the underground under the watchful gaze of a few influential informants was not going entirely to plan. Anderson had seemed an ideal figure in the masterplan to simulate an alternative, less subversive scene, and in many ways, he was driven enough—even to the point of being manic—to achieve the Stasi's goals. Yet by 1982 there were signs that Anderson was becoming too independent for the Stasi's liking and that the Stasi was failing to fully control him. Moreover, as was becoming apparent, Anderson's loyalties lay with his peers and his own career—possibly they always had.

A further challenge was beginning to emerge by 1982. The magnitude of the problem represented by the politico-cultural underground was such that it was unrealistic for the MfS to expect solid results from one or two inside sources. If the underground was to become a Stasi simulation, as the Stasi may have dreamed, the ministry would need far more resources, and better ones at that. For all his complex psychology, Anderson took his poetry and his entrepreneurship of art and literature extremely seriously. His influence was greatest in his close circle of friends—whose style has been called the New Manner of Speaking (Die neue Sagart)—represented by Bert Papenfuß-Gorek, Stefan Döring, Rainer Schedlinski, and Detlef Opitz. These poets displayed a heterogeneity of styles ranging from Dadaism, to the Viennese School of Concrete Poetry, to pop culture, to word plays and philosophical-linguistic games.[183] Their political habitus was remarkably similar; all showed a lack of interest in direct political activism. As the title of *Berührung war eine Randerscheinung* suggests, contact with the state and power was indeed a marginal phenomenon, and all writers in the underground distanced themselves from official culture and from previous generations of poets.

Anderson increasingly came to serve less as a miniaturized mobile panopticon than as an opaque, partial, and often distorting lens of surveillance. This can be seen in his reporting style when he introduced subtle, subjective filters into his observations. His reports on most of his friend's activities are less interested in prying into private lives than in registering and archiving the diversity of culture in his environs. In his autobiography Anderson expresses bemusement about the fact that his officers naively expected him to write about what people thought: "But—apart from in literature—I have never gotten close enough to someone to be able to hear them think."[184] At the height of the underground in 1982 Anderson was starting to withhold information and play down the risks entailed in his friends' activities.[185] In the years that followed, as discussed in chapter 6, the list of salons across the republic grew, as did the number of disaffected writers. In addition, the number of samizdat publications that reproduced their writing was rising, as this list reveals: *Anschlag, Ariadnefabrik, A3, Der Kaiser ist nackt, Entwerter/Oder, Mikado, Und, Und so weiter,* and *Schaden*.

In the years since the heated Stasi debates of the 1990s, research has shown that the Stasi did try to infiltrate the Berlin underground and positioned two key informers, the main one being Anderson, at its head to neutralize[186] and depoliticize it.[187] But the underground was older, larger, and far more diverse than the spheres of the two moles involved.[188] The simulation thesis often presumes that the Stasi informants at the heart of the "fake" writers' circles were shams, phonies, or simulated writers. As the foregoing reveals, this was far from the truth. In this chapter the snapshot of secret policing provided by four of my case histories supports recent research, which has concluded that the Stasi's achievements in influencing literary culture in Berlin in the 1980s were rather modest.[189] The broad strategy used by HA XX of relying on humans to control literary spheres had many unforeseen side effects. The cases of Maja Wiens and Paul Gratzik furnish ample evidence of the limitations of using human contact surveillance. Further, the above examination of Anderson makes apparent that the strategy of deploying IMs as "a type of extended arm of the MfS" was illusory.[190] Finally, all these cases underscore the limits that constrained the Stasi's handling of its agents. Moreover, the same cases indicate that from at least 1979 onward some of these limits lay in the inability of the MfS and the SED party leadership to respond to GDR citizens' calls for reform and change.

Fig. 1. Paul Gratzik in the film *Vaterlandsverräter* (Traitor to the fatherland), 2011. Annekatrin Hendel, dir., *Vaterlandsverräter* (Berlin: IT WORKS! 2011), DVD.

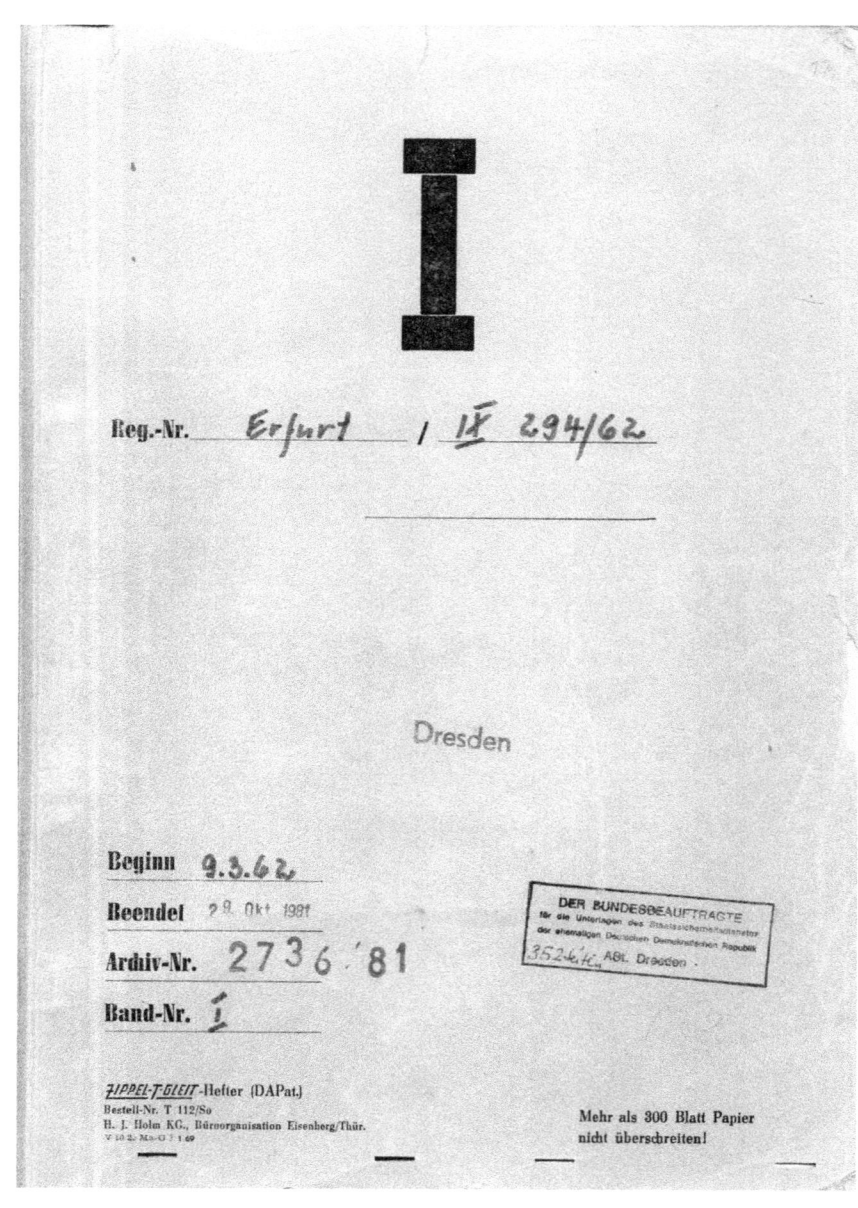

Fig. 2. The cover of the IM-*Vorgang* file opened on Paul Gratzik on March 9, 1962. BStU, MfS, BV Dresden, AIM, file 2736/81, vol. I/I.

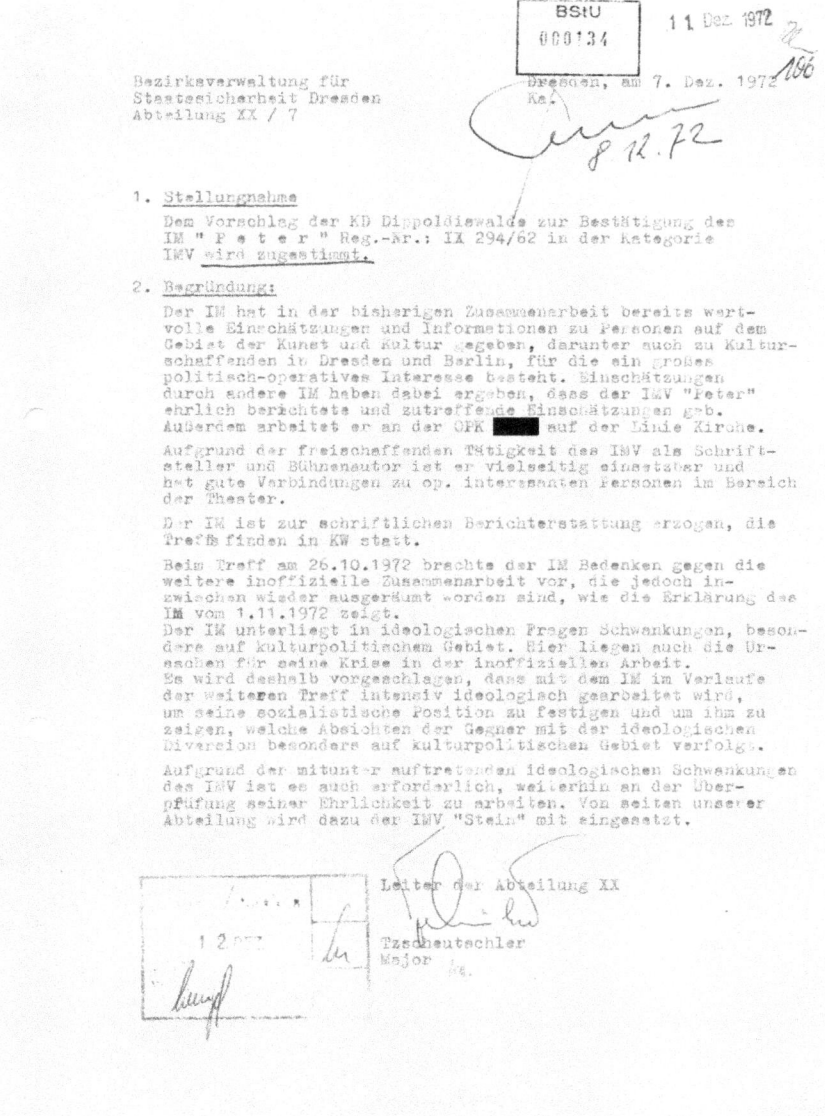

Fig. 3. MfS position paper on IMV "Peter," Paul Gratzik, dated December 7, 1972. Gratzik is to be kept under surveillance by IMV "Stein." BStU, MfS, BV Dresden, AIM, file 2736/81, vol. I/I, fol. 134.

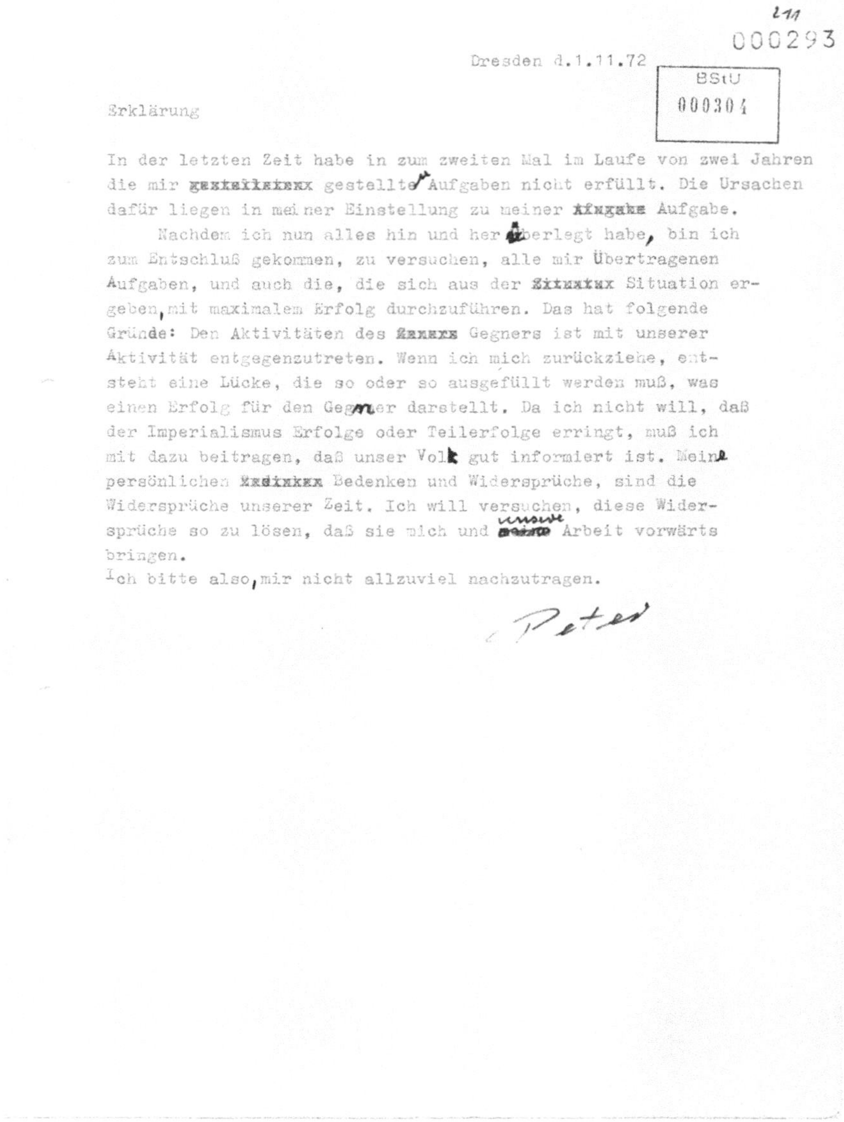

Dresden d.1.11.72

Erklärung

In der letzten Zeit habe in zum zweiten Mal im Laufe von zwei Jahren die mir gestellten Aufgaben nicht erfüllt. Die Ursachen dafür liegen in meiner Einstellung zu meiner Aufgabe.
   Nachdem ich nun alles hin und her überlegt habe, bin ich zum Entschluß gekommen, zu versuchen, alle mir übertragenen Aufgaben, und auch die, die sich aus der Situation ergeben, mit maximalem Erfolg durchzuführen. Das hat folgende Gründe: Den Aktivitäten des Gegners ist mit unserer Aktivität entgegenzutreten. Wenn ich mich zurückziehe, entsteht eine Lücke, die so oder so ausgefüllt werden muß, was einen Erfolg für den Gegner darstellt. Da ich nicht will, daß der Imperialismus Erfolge oder Teilerfolge erringt, muß ich mit dazu beitragen, daß unser Volk gut informiert ist. Meine persönlichen Bedenken und Widersprüche, sind die Widersprüche unserer Zeit. Ich will versuchen, diese Widersprüche so zu lösen, daß sie mich und unsere Arbeit vorwärts bringen.
   Ich bitte also, mir nicht allzuviel nachzutragen.

                                                       Peter

Fig. 4. A declaration signed by IMV "Peter" at a meeting with his handler Wenzel in 1972. BStU, MfS, BV Dresden, AIM, file 2736/81, vol. II/II, fol. 304.

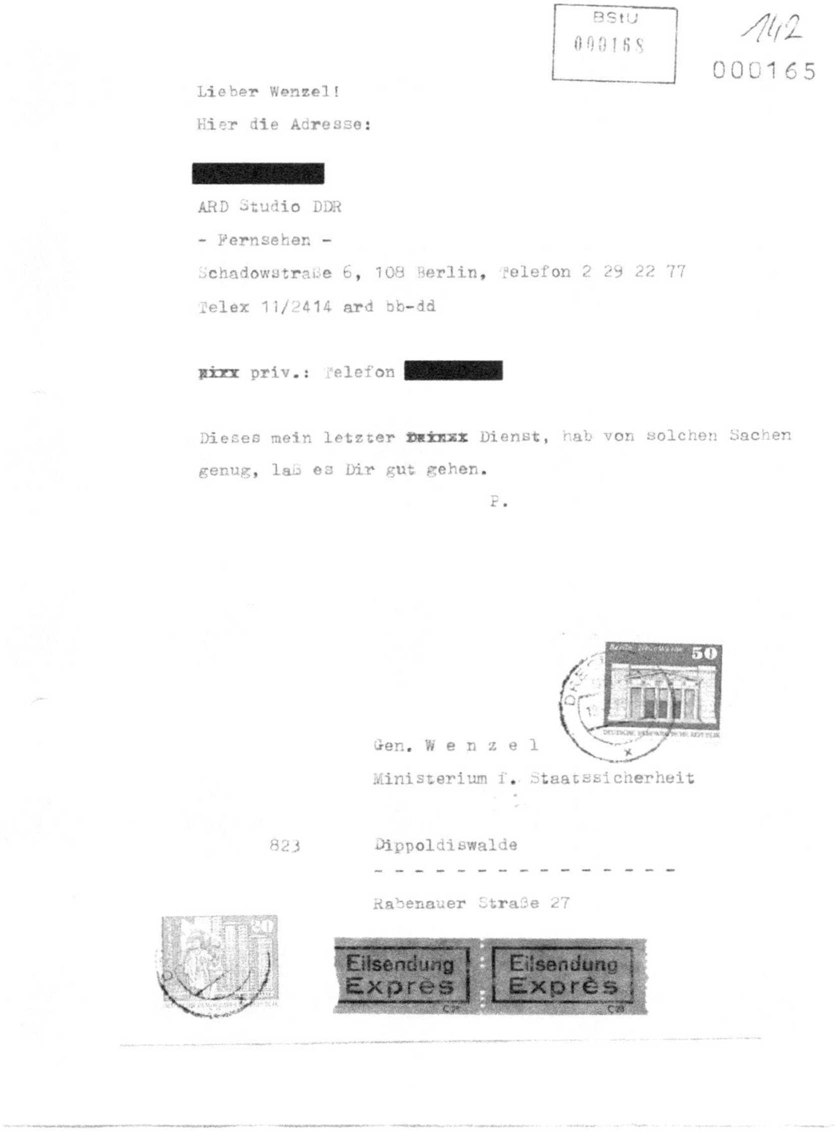

Lieber Wenzel!
Hier die Adresse:

▮▮▮▮▮▮▮

ARD Studio DDR
- Fernsehen -
Schadowstraße 6, 108 Berlin, Telefon 2 29 22 77
Telex 11/2414 ard bb-dd

priv.: Telefon ▮▮▮▮▮

Dieses mein letzter Dienst, hab von solchen Sachen
genug, laß es Dir gut gehen.

P.

Gen. W e n z e l
Ministerium f. Staatssicherheit

823   Dippoldiswalde

Rabenauer Straße 27

Fig. 5. Farewell telegram from Paul Gratzik to his officer, Wenzel. BStU, MfS, BV Dresden, AIM, file 2736/81, vol. II/III, fol. 168.

000227
BStU
000238
159

Abschrift Tonband

Bericht vom

Heiner M ü l l e r , freischaffender Schriftsteller in Berlin

Bei einer Zusammenkunft, die ich arrangiert hatte, wo Frau Steffi
S p i e r a dabei war, fragte ich ihn, warum er nicht wieder
im Schriftstellerverband ist, un d das sagte er zu mir fast würt-
lich, die Sache verhält sich so, daß nicht die zu mir kommen,
sonern ich zu denen hinkommen müßte. Ich weiß bloß nicht, wie
ich das machen soll, ich würde ganz gerne wieder eintreten, wir
werden sehen, wie die Zeit läuft.

Weiter fragte er Steffi Spiera, sag mal, wie ist denn das, wie denker
die Leute über mich so, sieht man mich für einen Aussätzigen an,
verkehrt man mit mir gerne oder hat man Bedenken mit gegenüber.
Dazu sagte die Frau Spiera, wie das im Leben einmal ist, wenn einer
mal auf eine andere Bahn gekommen ist und wieder zurückkehrt, daß
der es dann doppelt schwer hat.

Im Verlauf des weiteren Gespräches fragte er mich, ob ich mich
mit Kinderliteratur beschäftige oder dort was geschrieben hätte,
was ich bejaht, und er bat mich sehr darum und fragte wiederholt,
ob ich ihm nicht etwas schicken könnte, denn er beschäftigt sich
damit und plant etwas, aus der Gegenwart für die Bühne zu machen.

Peter
....

Fig. 6. A report by IMV "Peter" on Heiner Müller. BStU, MfS, BV Dresden, AIM, file 2736/81, vol. II/II, fol. 238.

Fig. 7. A portrait of Paul Wiens with his third wife, Irmtraud Morgner, at home in East Berlin. Photograph by Mehner/ullstein bild. Courtesy of Getty Images.

Fig. 8. A portrait of Paul Wiens smoking his pipe in 1977. Photograph by Andree/ullstein bild. Courtesy of Getty Images.

Diese Frau scheint sich mit Malerei und Ähnlichem zu beschäftigen, zumindest theoretisch, ob sie selber malt, das weiß ich nicht. Sie ist sehr groß, kräftig, stabil - also ein richtiges Pferdeindruck. Sie hat eine ganz sympathische Stimme und scheint nicht dem Drang zu unterliegen, also unbedingt unheimlich intellektuell zu wirken. Das liegt wahrscheinlich daran, daß sie selber sehr intelligent ist. Da hat sie das nicht nötig.

Zu meinem Verhalten beim ▮▮▮
Ich habe mich so verhalten, so wie ich mich ganz normaler Weise zu verhalten pflege, nämlich sehr aufgeschlossen. So verhalte ich mich auch ansonsten immer, habe mir also die Bücher angeguckt. Meine Freunde wissen, daß ich das immer als erstes mache. Habe mir, wenn ich mir Bücher rausgenommen habe - ich kann sagen, was ich rausgenommen habe - z.B. Bosch, der d.h. ein Buch von Bosch, das ich nicht kannte, eigentlich nicht kennen konnte, da es nicht bei uns erschienen ist und etwas über Hypnose...., das bei uns erschienen ist, das ich aber noch nicht gesehen hatte. Ich habe mir also solche Dinge gewählt, die mich also normaler Weise auch interessieren, aber keine politische Literatur vordergründig, die habe ich mir zwar angeguckt und was dazu gesagt, was er da so alles hat, so wie ich das normaler Weise tun würde.
Ich habe mich auch in meinem persönlichen Verhalten ganz so verhalten wie ich mich normaler Weise verhalten würde, also genauso viel Karo geraucht wie ansonsten, habe meinen Tee getrunken. Wir haben uns ganz kurz unterhalten über meine Familie sowohl die engere, was ▮▮▮ betrifft, meine Ehe als auch meine Eltern, die ihm z.T. bekannt sind, zumindest vom Hörensagen und so in dieser Art. Das führte dazu, daß ihn das etwas sicherer machte im Umgang mit mir, so sehe ich das. Desgleichen im Telefongespräch, das ich dort geführt habe mit meiner Mutter, bei dem es eigentlich nur darum ging, sie zu informieren, daß ich gesund meiste., da ich von einer Arztuntersuchung kam. Ansonsten hat aufgrund verschiedener, allerdings von mir unbeabsichtigter Sachen, er sehr schnell mitbekommen, daß ich über logisches Denkvermögen verfüge und Fremdworte nicht falsch gebrauche. Es ging z.B. um das Wort "Alternative", das sehr oft falsch gebraucht wird, nämlich in seinem Plural. Das mache ich instinktiv und logischer Weise nicht, weil es den Plural natürlich nicht gibt. Solche Dinge fallen mir aber nicht auf, die fielen ihm aber auf. Da hat er mir ganz schön, so wie man sagt Honig um's Maul geschmiert, auch in anderer Beziehung.

Wir haben uns unterhalten anhand von Gesprächen über Personen, über die Schwierigkeit, die manche Leute haben, wobei er mir immer zustimmte, er hat mir sehr viel zugestimmt übrigens, für mich unerklärlich warum so viel, von ihrer Schwierigkeit, von ihrer erlebten Praxis auf die Theorie zu übertragen, in dem Sinne, daß sie wirklich abstrahieren und nicht als Individuum sehen und nicht als gesamte Gesellschaft, um es im Klartext zu sagen - wer negative Erfahrungen in irgendeiner Art macht, sei es in einer Liebesbeziehung oder im Leben in einer Gruppe - muß, damit diese negativen Erfahrungen nicht auf das Gesamte beziehen. Hier liegt bei ▮▮▮ auch der ideologische Fehler, daß er nämlich verschiedene negative Erscheinungen im Sozialismus, die wir ohne Zweifel haben, auf das gesamte System abstrahiert. Hier sucht er Ansatzpunkte in Diskussionen, ja, wo ich ihm nicht mehr ganz zustimmen werden.

Fig. 9. One of Maja Wiens's reports on Rudolf Kunze. BStU, MfS, BVfS Berlin, AOP, file 1224/91, vol. 3, fol. 47.

```
Bezirksverwaltung für                    Dresden, den 21.03.1977
Staatssicherheit Dresden
Abteilung XX/2
                                         BStU
                                         000053    0..C27
```

T r e f f b e r i c h t

IMS: "David Menzer"   am: 17.03.77   von: 17.30 bis: 18.15

durchgeführt: Hptm. Vetter   in: Petzow (Schriftstellerheim
              Ltn. Graupner   d. Schriftstellerverb.)

Es wurde bekannt, daß sich der IMS z.Zt. in o.g. Heim aufhält
und an einem Lehrgang teilnimmt.
Da sich der IM nicht mehr gemeldet hatte und dem Mitarbeiter aus-
wich, wurde kurzfristig der Treff durchgeführt.
Die Mitarbeiter fuhren zunächst nach Werder, Adolf-Damaschke-Str. 35
(Wohnheim der DEFA) wo der IM längere Zeit polizeilich gemeldet
war. Dort wurde er nicht angetroffen.
Anschließend fuhren die Mitarbeiter nach Petzow (Bez. Potsdam), um
den IM im dortigen Schriftstellerheim vom Schruftstellerverband
zu erreichen, was auch gelang.
Der IM bat die Mitarbeiter in sein Zimmer, wo ein kurzes Gespräch
stattfand.
Auf die Frage, warum er dem MfS ausweicht, antwortete er, daß er
erst "persönlich mit sich ins reine" kommen mußte. Die Hilfe der
Mitarbeiter des MfS beanspruchte er nicht, da er persönliche Dinge
gern allein klärt.
Um welche persönlichen Probleme es sich hierbei handelt, kam nicht
eindeutig zum Ausdruck, offensichtlich handelt es sich aber um
Dinge seiner jetzigen Tätigkeit und auch um finanzielle Probleme.
Der IM sagte, daß es sich bei dem Lehrgang in besagtem Heim um
eine Zusammenkunft der Liedermacher der DDR handelt um sich über
die weitere Perspektive dieser "Kunstrichtung" zu unterhalten.
Der IM brachte zum Ausdruck, daß er sehr viel "arbeitet" und zwar
von ca. 5.00 - zum Frühstück, er habe dann "viel geschafft"
Er sei in Verbindung mit seinem Mentor "Heinz Calau" und habe
jetzt eine Steuernummer und werde demnächst als Kandidat in den
Schriftstellerverband aufgenommen.
Auf den Vorwurf, warum er sich polizeilich nicht melde, antwortete er, daß er dies nachholen werde. Polizeilich ist er als Neben-
wohnung immer noch in Werder, Adolf Damaschke-Str. 35 gemeldet.
Im Gespräch wurden einige Ideologische Fragen angeschnitten, wo
zum Ausdruck, kam, daß der IM in dieser Richtung nicht auf der
marxistischen Linie liegt.
Durch seinen Umgangskreis, mit dem er verkehrt, ist auch nicht zu
erwarten, daß sich dies in der nächsten Zeit ändert.
Er war einigermaßen verbittert, daß man einen Gedichtband, den er
mit einigen anderen in ähnlicher Richtung liegenden "Künstlern"
verfasst hat und der schon gedruckt werden sollte, abgelehnt hat.
Das habe mit den Ereignissen vom November 1976 (gemeint war die
Ausbürgerung Biermanns) zusammengehangen.

Figs. 10 & 11. Meeting report with IMS "David Menzer," alias Sascha Anderson, 1977. BStU, MfS, ZA, AIM, file 7423/91, 1st addendum, fols. 53–54.

Der IM stellte sich im Gespräch nicht direkt gegen die Zusammenarbeit mit dem MfS, brachte aber zum Ausdruck, daß er genau wissen müsse, was die Mitarbeiter "konkret" von ihm wollen.
Er sei sehr beschäftigt, so daß er sich seine Zeit sehr einteilen müsse.
Weiter berichtete er, daß er in der nächsten Zeit, wahrscheinlich Anfang April, nach Wolgograd fahre, da er mit anderen den Auftrag habe, einen Dokumentarfilm über die Oktoberrevolution zu drehen, man müsse sich dort zu diesem Zweck einiges ansehen. Weiterhin fahre er mit seinem Regisseur und einem ehemaligen Häftling des KZ dorthin, um ebenfalls den Film vorzubereiten.
Zu diesem Zweck müsse er spätestens am Mittwoch, dem 23.03.77 fahren.
In der Zeit vom 19.03. bis zum 22.03.77 halte er sich in Dresden auf.
Er sei in dieser Zeit in der Wohnung eines gewissen W i t t i g , Heinz, wh. 8054 Dresden, ▮▮▮▮▮▮▮▮ zu erreichen, der aber nicht zu Hause sei, da er auswärts arbeitet.
Bei dem W. handele es sich um einen bildenden Künstler.
Dieser habe Telefon, ▮▮▮▮▮
Es wurde vereinbart, am 22.03.77 vormittags dort mit dem IM einen Treff durchzuführen.
Vorherige Absprache mit Gen. Mieder ist erforderlich.

Graupner
Leutnant

Fig. 12. Portrait of Sascha Anderson, 1990. Photograph by Susanne Schleyer/autorenarchiv.de.

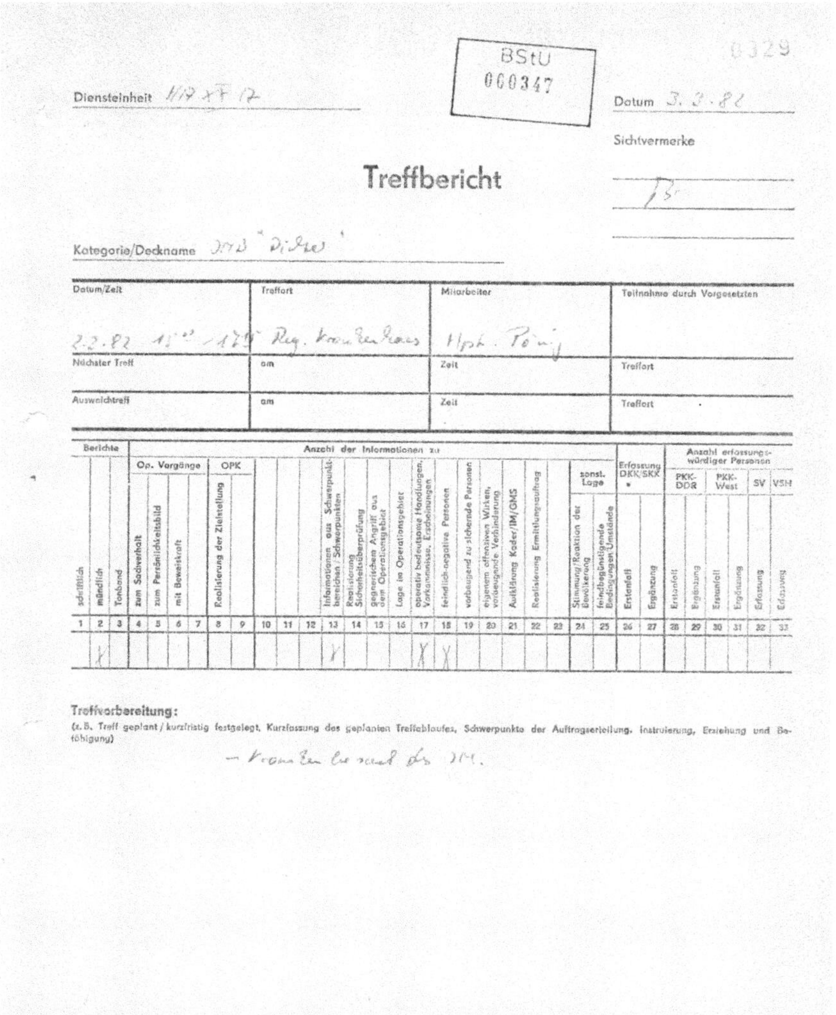

BStU
000347

0329

Diensteinheit II/7 XX 17

Datum 3. 3. 82

Sichtvermerke

Treffbericht

Kategorie/Deckname IMB "Dichter"

Datum/Zeit	Treffort	Mitarbeiter	Teilnahme durch Vorgesetzten
2.2.82 11⁰⁰–12¹⁵	Reg. Krankenhaus	Hptm. Pönig	
Nächster Treff	am	Zeit	Treffort
Ausweichtreff	am	Zeit	Treffort

Berichte: schriftlich (1), mündlich (2) X, Tonband (3)

Anzahl der Informationen zu: Op. Vorgänge: zum Sachverhalt (4), zum Persönlichkeitsbild (5), mit Beweiskraft (6), (7); OPK: Realisierung der Zielstellung (8), (9); (10), (11), (12); Informationen aus Schwerpunktbereichen/Schwerpunkten (13) X; Realisierung Sicherheitsüberprüfung (14); gegnerischem Angriff aus dem Operationsgebiet (15); Lage im Operationsgebiet (16); operativ bedeutsame Handlungen, Vorkommnisse, Erscheinungen (17) X; feindlich-negative Personen (18) X; vorbeugend zu sichernde Personen (19); eigenem offensiven Wirken, vorbeugende Verhinderung (20); Aufklärung Kader/IM/GMS (21); Realisierung Ermittlungsauftrag (22); (23); sonst. Lage: Stimmung/Reaktion der Bevölkerung (24), feindbegünstigende Bedingungen/Umstände (25)

Erfassung DKK/SKK: Erstanlauf (26), Ergänzung (27)

Anzahl erfassungswürdiger Personen: PKK-DDR: Erstanlauf (28), Ergänzung (29); PKK-West: Erstanlauf (30), Ergänzung (31); SV: Erfassung (32); VSH: Ergänzung (33)

Treffvorbereitung:
(z.B. Treff geplant/kurzfristig festgelegt, Kurzfassung des geplanten Treffablaufes, Schwerpunkte der Auftragserteilung, Instruierung, Erziehung und Befähigung)

– Krankenbesuch des IM.

Form 450

Fig. 13. One of the last meeting reports filed by Paul Wiens's case officer, on a meeting at the hospital on March 3, 1982. BStU, MfS, AIM, file 7781/83, vol. II/5, fol. 347.

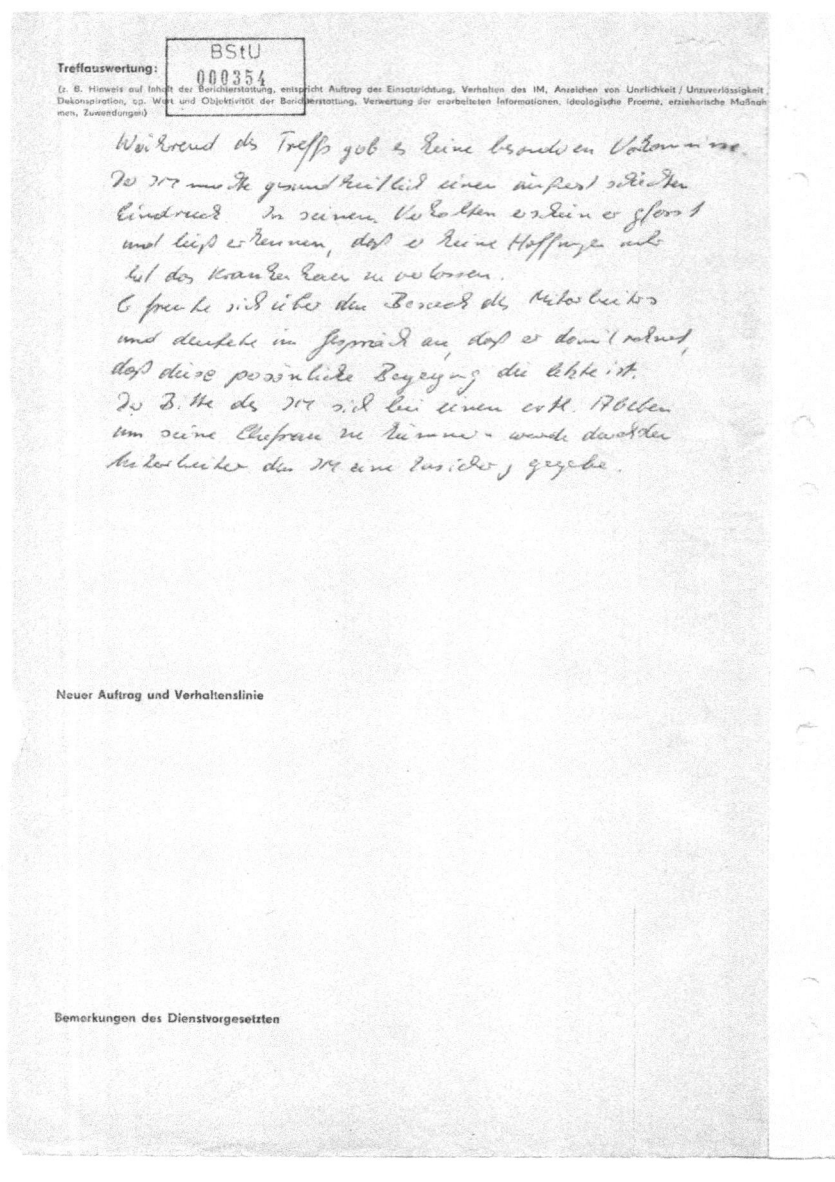

Fig. 14. The final meeting report by Paul Wiens's case officer, filed as Wiens was dying on March 31, 1982. BStU, MfS, AIM, file 7781/83, vol. II/5, fol. 354.

Fig. 15. Maja Wiens at a reading on May 10, 1984. Photograph by Klaus Morgenstern/ddrbildarchiv.de.

Dem Mitarbeiter warf der IM politische Blindheit und Engstirnigkeit vor, der nur Befehle ausführe, ohne tiefgründig darüber nachzudenken.

Dem IM wurde versucht klarzumachen, daß die Machtausübung in bestimmten Situationen auch etwas mit militärischer Disziplin zu tun habe. Die Ausübung der politischen und militärischen Macht wurde differenziert auch am 04.11.83 ausgeübt. Der IM führte zu den Maßnahmen nochmals an:

- das Aufsuchen durch den Mitarbeiter (Gen. Klauer) in der Wohnung des IM sei völlig sinnlos gewesen (nicht nur weil noch Personen anwesend waren, die an den Aktionen beteiligt waren, bzw. sein könnten),
- der IM hätte auch unter anderen Umständen nichts zu den geplanten Aktionen gesagt,
- das Auftreten unserer Gen. am 04.11.1983 sei unmöglich gewesen, der anwesende ▇▇▇▇ hätte so gleich das wahre Gesicht unseres Organs erlebt, daß er bisher nur vom Hörensagen kannte,
- ein Genosse hätte angeblich ein Tonbandgerät unter der Jacke gehabt (der ▇▇▇▇ will dies selbst gesehen haben),
- die Auskunft des ▇▇▇▇ war auch unwahr, denn er ging nicht zur Arbeit, sondern war gerade gekommen (er nutzte die Möglichkeit dazu, die Wohnung zu verlassen und andere Personen zu benachrichtigen)
- ihr wurde untersagt, eine Veranstaltung/Versammlung bei der Volksbildung zu besuchen
  (dort gab sie später an, daß sie durch das MfS daran gehindert wurde).

Die Feststellungen des Mitarbeiters, daß es sich bei den Ausführungen z. T. um Unterstellungen handelt wies der IM energisch zurück.

Auf eine Frage, ob der IM zum Treff erschienen wäre, wenn es telefonisch am 04.11.83 vereinbart worden wäre, antwortete er mit der Bemerkung "das hätte auch nichts geändert". Der IM vertrat wiederum die Auffassung daß das MfS nur auf ihn zukommt, wenn es brennt. Er wäre kein Computer für das MfS. Wir müssen wissen, was um ihn herum geschieht und dementsprechend die Einweisung vornehmen. Dazu sind Detailkenntnisse über Personen und Gruppen Voraussetzung. Selbst dazu wesentlich beizutragen, war auch diesmal dem IM nicht erklärbar.

Zur Zusammenkunft mit dem ▇▇▇▇▇▇▇▇▇▇▇▇ der Grünen ▇▇▇▇ wurde der IM am Vortage durch eine angeblich unbekannte männliche Person eingeladen. An dieser Zusammenkunft nahmen nur ca. 15 Personen teil. Angeblich bestand das Motiv der Teilnahme darin "unsere Haltung" (der Grünen?) die der von Eppelmann entgegenzusetzen.

Fig. 16. Maja Wiens chides her case officer. BStU, MfS, BVfS Berlin, AOP, file 1224/91, vol. 1, fol. 170.

Die Aneinanderreihung negativer Erscheinungen ging weiter. Es gäbe zahllose Arbeitslose in der DDR; in Jena sitzen die Mathematiker herum; die Volksbildung hat ein unmögliches Lehrprogramm, was sich anderen darin ausdrückt:

- keine eigene Meinungsbildung der Jugend erwünscht,
- nur immer Disziplin, Ordnung, Sauberkeit als Lebens- und Verhaltensweise,
- im Kindergarten beginnen die Reglementierungen (aufessen, alles essen, anstellen zur Toilette usw. usf.),
- in der Schule Engstirnigkeit und keine offene Atmosphäre (hier führte der IM ein Beispiel an - zum wiederholten Male - daß die Lehrerin für Staatsbürgerkunde in der Klasse ihres 10/11-jähriges Sohnes Jesus mit Gott verwechselte und den Sohn, der das berichtigte, dazu ermahnt, daß hier keine Kirchenstunde stattfinde),
- auch in naturwissenschaftlichen Fächern gibt es nichts zumDEnken - ob in Chemie oder Physik - überall gibt es vorgelegte Resultate,
- der Deutschunterricht ist ebenfalls nicht besser - nur die Lehrmeinung ist richtig.

Auch zu dieser Aufzählung wurden aus eigner Sicht Erläuterungen gemacht, ohne jedoch die vorgefaßten Meinungen zu beeinflussen. Es zeigte sich, daß der IM offensichtlich nur Mißstände sieht (selbst dort, wo es kaum welche gibt, bzw. wo zu erkennen ist, daß es subjektive Ursachen sind, die dazu führten bzw. führen). In der weiteren Gesprächsführung wurde seitens des IM zum Ausdruck gebracht, daß vor allem die Maßnahmen gegen ▇▇▇▇▇▇

bei ihm auf Unverständnis stießen. Dadurch sind eine Reihe von Auffassungen revidiert, die die Ehrlichkeit unserer Politik betreffen. Dieser Anhänglichkeit an ▇▇▇▇▇▇ wurde auch äußerlich wahrgenommen. Ein Bild von ihr steht im Bücherregal, obwohl sonst kaum Bilder von Personen zu sehen sind. Ein weiteres Bild (Bildmontage, Collage) fiel auf und jeder Besucher muß es sehen.

> Lenin sitz gebeugt über eine schriftlichen Tätigkeit - aus einem Frösikalender zum hochklappen (Überraschung) darunter Zeitungsausschnitt über die Auszeichnung von Dr. hc. Vogel - Rechtsanwalt - auf der rechten Seite die Abrisse der SU und ein Sowjetstern.
>
> (Zu deuten wäre das Bild für Personen des Umgangskreises des IM dahingehend, daß durch RA Vogel, der für Ausreiseangelegenheiten die er vertritt, Geld erhält, auch noch ausgezeichnet wird, während andere Kommunisten wie Lenin gründlich arbeiten)

Fig. 17. Maja Wiens castigates the regime for its failings. BStU, MfS, BVfS Berlin, AOP, file 1224/91, vol. 1, fol. 172.

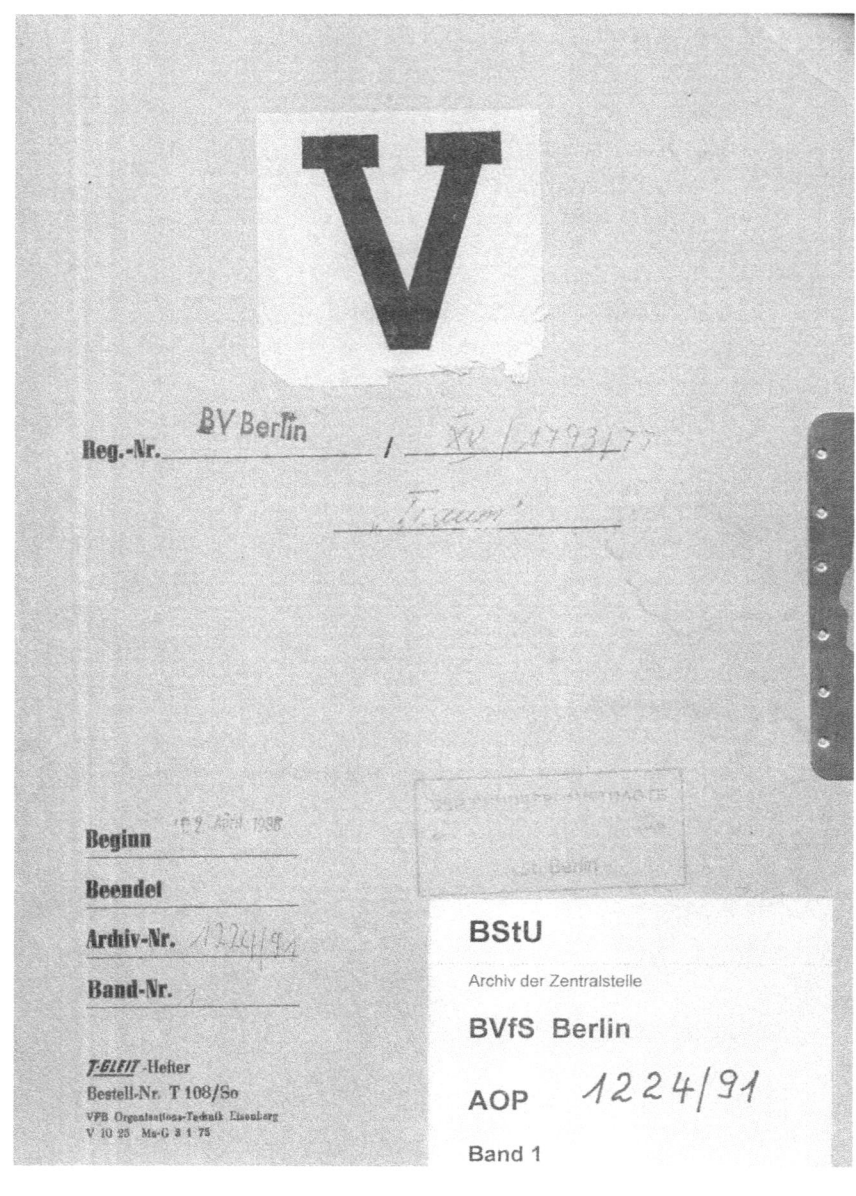

Fig. 18. The OV file opened on Maja Wiens in 1988, code-named "Traum." BStU, MfS, BVfS Berlin, AOP, file 1224/91, vol. 1.

Fig. 19. Sascha Anderson playing chess with himself in the documentary *Anderson*. Annekatrin Hendel, dir., *Anderson* (Berlin: IT WORKS!, 2014), DVD.

ich bin nach dem 2. weltkrieg geboren worden. mein vater ist
ein dogmatiker und hysterisch, meine mutter hat dreissig jahre
lang ihre ansprüche bis zu kleinbürgerlichem geniessen zurück
geschraubt. meine eltern sind in der SED. sie leben seit drei
zehn jahren geschieden. die mich prägenden eindrücke sind
beschreibungen des 2. weltkrieges in büchern, von meinen eltern,
lehrern und grosseltern. erinnerungen aus der kindheit, die
mein (deutsches) menschenbild geform haben. 1970 habe ich ange-
fangen gedichte zu schreiben. zu kontakten mit dem MfS ist es
vor ungefähr zehn jahren auf meine bitte hin gekommen. mein wille
für das MfS zu arbeiten basiert auf meinem grundverständnis,
dass die einzige aufgabe dieses staates mit dieser vergangenheit
und dieser geografischen lage die beseitigung aller wurzeln
und erscheinungen des faschismus ist. meine sicht auf diese
dinge hat sich in den letzten 10 jahren sicher verändert. die
aufgabe aber ist geblieben. und ich überblicke die wirkung und
den nutzen meiner arbeit besser. eine grundlegend andere haltung
als die genossen für die ich arbeite habe ich in fragen der
kulturpolitik und in fragen der lösung akuter probleme. manchmal
hatte ich sogar den eindruck, dass ich dafür bezahlt werde, mich
selbst zu überwachen. hoffe aber, dass meine arbeit trotzdem so
nützlich ist, dass sich der einsatz lohnt. ich arbeite im kultu-
rellen bereich. ich glaube, dass die entscheidenden dinge eher
im ökonomischen, militärischen geschehen. ich habe versucht meine
literarische arbeit und meine arbeit für das MfS konsequent bis
zur schizophrenie zu trennen. das war für mich die einzige möglichkeit beides gut zu machen. aus verschiedenen gründen wohne
ich jetzt in berlin, habe starke persöhnlichkeitsprobleme und
lebe getrennt von ralf kerbach, der in westberlin lebt (vorher
dresden), mit dem mich eine existenzielle arbeitsgemeinschaft
verbindet. ich habe sehr oft darüber gesprochen, dass ich es
für wichtiger halte, im westen für das MfS zu arbeiten. und ich
bitte gerade jetzt darum, mich auf diese aufgabe vorzubereiten,
weil ich merke, dass mein denken, auch im zusammenhang mit meiner
literarischen arbeit an einem wendepunkt angelangt ist, so dass
es mir in der folgezeit immer schwerer wird in der ddr mein
literarisch-gesellschaftliches denken und meine arbeit für das
MfS ohne schaden meiner physis und psyche zu erfüllen.

Fig. 20. Letter from Sascha Anderson to the MfS requesting to be allowed to leave for the West. BStU, MfS, ZA, AIM, file 7423/91, 11th addendum, fol. 3.

Fig. 21. Portrait of Sascha Anderson on August 22, 1986, after his emigration to the West. Photograph by Mehner/ullstein bild. Courtesy of Getty Images.

Fig. 22. Helga M. Novak in 1971. Photograph by Brigitte Friedrich/*Süddeutsche Zeitung*. Courtesy of Alamy Stock Photo.

6

The Culture Wars, 1983–1989

Throughout the 1980s those departments of the Ministry for State Security tasked with policing literature found themselves fighting a multifront war against dissenting and disaffected writers. The Stasi continued to tackle unionized writers through the German Writers' Guild, which remained the responsibility of HA XX/7. At the same time it attempted to keep in check the steadily growing number of cultural producers working outside formal structures through the specialist department in charge of policing the underground, HA XX/9. Although officer staff numbers in both HA XX/7 and HA XX/9 rose markedly over the last decade of the GDR (from twenty-seven to forty in HA XX/7,[1] and from nineteen to thirty-six in HA XX/9), this growth was not matched by an increase in informants, which even declined slightly in HA XX/9.[2] After the exodus of writers from the Writers' Guild in the post-Biermann era, there was little renewal within the guilds, and most of the new talent in the republic was to be found in the underground. Furthermore, *samizdat* and, increasingly, *tamizdat*—the burgeoning illegal literature published in West Germany that returned to the GDR via indirect routes—threatened to career out of control.[3] Over the course of the 1980s the intricate and continual culture wars against writers, waged both underground and aboveground, proved to be wars of attrition, with the ministry and writers locked in intractable battles that neither side seemed to be winning.[4]

In 1983 and for a couple years after, however, it seemed to the MfS that the underground might be kept in check through key agents planted deep inside various circles. In reality the Stasi was losing its grip on these agents. As explored in earlier chapters, it encountered the same issues with sustaining motivation and offering acceptable incentives that had been plaguing it since the 1960s. Moreover, the simulation strategy itself began to unravel.

By the second half of the 1980s a further problem arose in the shortage of informants as more people found the courage to refuse to collaborate. As Gary Bruce has shown, by the mid-1980s it was becoming harder to recruit informants based on their personal convictions regarding state ideology.[5] By 1984, of the five informers at the center of this study, one was deceased; another had refused to fully cooperate; two had definitively chosen to cease informing; and thus only one was still operating, albeit in opaque, unpredictable ways that were causing the Stasi serious concern. A further pressure during the last decade of the GDR regime was the number of aboveground writers who were blurring the boundaries between underground and official cultures; many of these were former Stasi informers. Once privy to the innermost secrets of the secret surveillance society constituted by the MfS, these informers presented a challenge of a different order; they threatened to unveil the very rituals that were holding the secret society of Stasi initiates together.

Informers who severed their ties with the Stasi—the dropouts from the secret service—often tried to hide or fade from the Stasi's purview. Most tried to disappear from the regime's security radar or fly under it. They often chose to refrain from any activity that the Stasi might consider oppositional, subversive, or hostile to the regime. If informants were openly oppositional or joined forces with "hostile-negative" subjects, they could in turn become the target of surveillance.

The Stasi expected greater loyalty from a current recruit. Indeed, although the MfS was largely immune to human emotions, betrayal was one emotion that it had internalized since its beginnings. When informants or officers defected to the other side—even if that simply meant joining forces with critical and reformist intellectuals, as seen with the case of Helga M. Novak—the ministry felt betrayed. If lapsed recruits behaved provocatively, even if they had never been successful recruits, the MfS was quick to retaliate. In those cases where the Stasi had invested much time and effort in managing a difficult informant, it could still show, even in the last decade of the regime, that it had not forgotten its more draconian methods—open threats and intimidation—to force a lapsed informer back into the fold.

As Kevin Haggerty remarks, surveillance regimes are "designed for particular purposes," but they may "evolve" in different directions from those intended.[6] At the "sharp" end of the panopticon, we are likely to find "moments of refusal and resistance that militate against the production of docile bodies," as David Lyon notes; at the soft end of the spectrum we are also likely to find forms of compliance and willing conformity.[7] The Stasi might have hoped that the individuals it recruited as informants participated willingly in its surveillance regime; in reality far too many informants resisted becoming docile subjects. This was especially the case with the informants tasked with controlling the underground.

Informers had many reasons for terminating their work for the Stasi. Disillusionment with the security forces, the party, and its politics, as well as disaffection with their career prospects or with communism more generally could all come into play, as described in previous chapters. Ironically, some of these reasons could be exacerbated by contact with those "hostile" circles that the informant was supposed to keep in check.[8] Inevitably, the mindset of oppositional circles took its toll on informants; in human surveillance regimes the policing subjects were susceptible to ideological contamination. The Stasi was ever vigilant in trying to prevent contamination from enemy circles and viewed quitters who came under enemy influence as a serious affront. Informers with a foot in each camp—that is, who claimed loyalty to the Stasi while being known to dissent—were of particular concern, because this bifurcation could lead to them having an ill-defined habitus, conflicting loyalties, and competing identifications. This chapter considers the fortunes of the Stasi's informers in literary circles over East Germany's last decade, examining what happened to Sascha Anderson, the Stasi's simulacrum who was supposed to remove the sting from the tail of the underground; to Maja Wiens and Paul Gratzik, who quit their association with the Stasi; and to Helga M. Novak, who had the least amount of contact of all.

Maja Wiens: Dropping Out of the Secret Service

Maja Wiens represents a striking example of enemy contamination that was an unwanted side effect of infiltration. Here I examine an important piece missing in the jigsaw puzzle of Wiens's Stasi dossier, which relates to her transition from informant to hostile-negative element. From 1985 onward the Stasi reluctantly relinquished all attempts to sway Wiens into cooperating through the use of sweeteners and other incentives. In February 1986 she became the target of OV "Dream" (see fig. 18). Her second parallel life was about to begin. This life was overshadowed by the Stasi in its incarnation as an Orwellian Big Brother, and in this respect the Stasi's activities lived up to the reputation of fictional espionage outfits. There were no benevolent OVs, but the operation targeting Wiens was especially vicious and invasive, designed to police her contacts to the West German Greens and her involvement in the unofficial peace movement more generally. Unlike other lapsed informants like Gratzik who refused to cooperate and were left in relative peace, Wiens was not spared the Stasi's wrath. The ministry seems to have been determined to stop her dead in her tracks. A number of factors, however, conspired against its efforts to curtail this former IM's hostile activities.

The Stasi was forced to confront the fact that Wiens possessed an impressive insider's knowledge of its workings. The problem of Wiens's firsthand experience of espionage is the subject of several file entries from this time. In the "opening report" from February 20, 1986, special mention is made of her intimate knowledge of "secret modes of behavior" and "working with legends."[9] She knew about the Stasi's use of "safe houses and objects" and was apprised of some of its financial arrangements.[10] Possibly even more damaging to the Stasi was Wiens's ability to spot officers of the ministry immediately: "Above all, she knows a series of previous and still active employees."[11] As a consequence, she could probably detect other agents working undercover among her friends by seeing through their alibis. She would also have been able to identify handlers of other informants if they turned up unannounced at group meetings or public events.[12] The Stasi remained concerned that Wiens's knowledge of the inner workings of espionage was "too much for comfort"; on one occasion the Pankow district office reminded another department that hers was a "very differentiated familiarity" with operative work.[13]

One of the first battles in the Stasi's war of attrition against Wiens occurred during a visit of West German Greens leaders in April 1986. In an especially heavy-handed move the Stasi placed Wiens under house arrest to prevent her from visiting members of the Greens.[14] Wiens was subsequently suspected of having composed a political pamphlet concerning the April 26 Chernobyl nuclear accident, and in May 1986 the MfS sent a copy of the pamphlet for analysis by the Stasi's special branch that compared typescripts and handwriting.[15] Around this time, two informers, "Kati Jakob" and "Caroline Schlegel," were assigned to Wiens. The Stasi was particularly worried because Wiens owned a computer. Her informants noted that she and others had decided to publish in samizdat format, using their own means of reproduction.[16]

The files capture the interesting anecdote that Wiens offered to help Stasi informant Sascha Anderson use a Commodore typewriter. As mentioned previously, Anderson was also in the business of producing his own underground works. In fact, according to his file records, Anderson was instructed to spy on Wiens. He reports that she was a candidate for membership of the Writers' Guild and was called "Wasp Maja . . . because she advocated opposition at any price."[17] It is surely ironic that Wiens had no sooner stopped working for the Stasi than she was spied on by other informants. This was only months before Anderson himself quit informing for the Stasi.

Wiens's old department was unrelenting in its pursuit of revenge. What initially appears to be a strategy to win her back changed into a much harsher, vindictive desire to punish her. In March 1987 the Pankow district office sent a request to HA XX/7/IV to ascertain whether Wiens was standing as a candidate for the Writers' Guild and who was supervising her.[18] The department had already collected intelligence from its Jena district office about readings that Wiens had planned in 1987.[19] HA XX/7/IV wrote back with information about literary evenings held in Wiens's apartment in January 1987.[20] An official character assessment filed at this time underscores how far Wiens had fallen from grace. It states that she was a major security risk to the Stasi; that she had an almost "entrenched negative attitude" toward East Germany; and that she was integrated into the activities of the Independent Peace Movement.[21]

Around this time the Pankow district office filed an application to have Wiens's telephone tapped.[22] By this stage her husband had also been gathered into the Stasi dragnet. The two of them were printing their own political pamphlets that agitated against the regime. Although the Stasi had by the mid-1980s well and truly lost the battle to control the flood of illegal political material being printed, the more overtly political underground newsletters and journals remained vulnerable to Stasi interference. That is, the Stasi's focus had shifted from literary circles to political circles associated with peace and those connected to the Environmental Library (Umwelt-Bibliothek), which opened in 1986 in the parish hall of East Berlin's Zion Church.

Wiens was thus typical of a new type of security threat that emerged in the last few years of the regime. She had good connections to writers; she was in touch with prominent West German figures; and she lived in close proximity to other hostile-negative persons such as Wolfgang Templin.[23] Furthermore, Wiens and her husband were suspected of having a negative influence on young people in their professional capacities as a youth worker and a leader of a writing circle, respectively.[24] A year later, in March 1987, the Stasi was still worried about the damaging impact of Wiens and her husband and busied itself gathering intelligence, still hoping to be able to instigate criminal proceedings. Because such proceedings were dependent on power struggles much higher up in the MfS, the Pankow office endeavored in the meantime to "bring [Wiens] under control."[25] Hard evidence that she was writing political texts was lacking, and the Stasi was determined to prove her authorship.

To these ends it engaged its best technical resource available: the same specialist section in charge of analyzing suspects' handwriting and typewriting that had been deployed in 1986. The Stasi was capable of examining the typeface of typewriters as well as the content and style of scripts. In

Wiens's file we find an "assessment report": a comparative textual analysis of two of Wiens's texts to establish if they had the same author. The texts were scrutinized for their use of vocabulary and foreign words, and, last but not least, for their literary qualities. The tests showed that there were differences between the two texts. Nonetheless, the analysts concluded that both texts were authored by the same person. The Stasi, to be sure, was paranoid—it is in the nature of security agencies to be so—but no one could accuse it of lacking scientific methods to prove there was a "real" basis for its paranoid fantasies.[26]

Until the final days of the regime, Wiens and her husband were subject to extensive and persistent surveillance, which included psychological terror. The Stasi organized a watch on their mail, a car outside their apartment, and a telephone tap (even arranging nuisance calls); the confiscation of Wiens's manuscripts was also engineered.[27] In June 1988, a little over a year before the Berlin Wall was breached, husband and wife retaliated. They filed a complaint against "unknown persons with the public prosecutor" because their mail was being opened.[28] When their son and four others, including the son of peace activist Vera Wollenberger, were expelled from Upper High School Carl von Ossietzky, the Stasi was quick to identify Maja Wiens as "the organizer and intellectual force" behind the pupils' actions. This prompted an almost hysterical response from three MfS departments, HA XX/7, the local branch of XX/7, and the Pankow district office.[29]

One report about a reading in Potsdam in 1987 contains a long list of the GDR's major and minor faults that Wiens publicly announced at the event. The reporting officer mentions all the details of socialism's flaws: the bureaucratic state system of distributing apartments; the long time needed to have something repaired; the high price of children's clothing; the lack of a range of sizes in children's clothing; and the impediments to studying if one had relatives in the West.[30] Thus, unwittingly, in these highly critical passages, the Stasi became a chronicler of its own inadequacies.

Sascha Anderson and Paul Gratzik: Spy versus Spy 2

If Gratzik joined the Berlin underground in the hope of evading the Stasi's scrutiny, his tactic surely failed. Like others who were part of Berlin's subcultures, he effected a retreat from public life and from the visible existence he had led at the height of his fame as a dramatist. By linking up with the artists and writers associated with the Prenzlauer Berg scene, he tried to reinvent himself. At the same time, after years of being in the spotlight of the Stasi's panopticon, he was keen to hide from its prying eyes and to slip under the surveillance radar.

Gratzik was unaware that this choice of refuge, his niche society, was part of the communist panopticon that now extended its reach into those cultural spaces most removed from official culture. In effect he walked into a carefully laid Stasi trap by connecting with those agile human bearers of instruments of state surveillance—those duplicitous informers with a friendly face that targeted likeminded individuals. Among those that Gratzik encountered was Sascha Anderson. Another was Maja Wiens.

In 1982 Wiens was a regular at the readings in the apartment of Ekkehard and Wilfriede Maaß, and she was offered a copy of Gratzik's *Kohlenkutte* manuscript, which was published in that year by the West German publisher Rotbuch.[31] In Gratzik's victim file we find a report from November 1984, written by an unnamed source, about an event in the Maaßes' apartment at which he was billed to read from this new manuscript. Its theme was, according to this report, "an assassination attempt on the Secretary General of the CC [Central Committee] of the SED and the Chairman of the State Council of the GDR, Comrade Erich Honecker."[32] The report singles out a response from Lutz Rathenow, who described the work as "the most scorching criticism he had heard so far because it completely brought the state into contempt, a dream of a revolt."[33] Unsurprisingly, the Stasi was keen to prevent Gratzik disseminating works with such content, and it hatched a plan to have him hand over the manuscript. Failing this, it organized to search his apartment and contemplated launching a criminal investigation. Should this not be possible, the file states defiantly, other avenues would be pursued to stop Gratzik from sending the manuscript to the West.[34] These were bold words, but they proved to be empty threats. They testify to the gradual loosening of the Stasi's grip on the security domain of literature, and ultimately to damaging losses in the Stasi's secret war of attrition against the underground.

One of the Stasi agents who filed a report on this event in the Maaßes' apartment was the omnipresent and irrepressible Anderson, whose history of working for the Stasi, like Gratzik's was checkered. In Anderson's dossier we find a report with a rather different "memory" of the event. Anderson, who was not actually present, "recalls" via other sources that it was all in all "a very amusing reading."[35] Code-named "Fritz Müller" at the time, Anderson makes no mention of the writing's subversive or mocking content, remarking simply that the scene Gratzik read concerned "reflections" of a security officer "who reminisces about himself and the cases he has solved."[36] Anderson played down the inflammatory nature of the scene, which the other informant had thought offensive enough to comment on. Moreover, Anderson explicitly mentioned the fact that there was no tape recording of the evening.

As a curious footnote to this episode, it can be observed that Gratzik and Anderson had an especially close relationship. In the film *Vaterlandsverräter* Gratzik confesses to seeing in Anderson a kind of adoptive son. Anderson makes an appearance in the documentary and seems to have been fond of Gratzik. It is not entirely clear, however, whether Gratzik knew of Anderson's links to the Stasi. It cannot be discounted that Gratzik may have suspected Anderson of having an ulterior motive for many of his creative activities. Actually, Anderson introduced Gratzik to Gabriele Dietze, who was a senior editor at Rotbuch publishing house, and Anderson accompanied Gratzik to his first meeting with Dietze. Somewhat incongruously, as Dietze recalls, this meeting took place in a public swimming pool, because this way they would be safe from Stasi eyes and ears (at least so she was told).

The eleven volumes of Anderson's extensive dossier contain many more references to Gratzik. The earliest is from September–October 1981, when Gratzik appears on a list of five tasks assigned to Anderson. Anderson's file includes a one-page report on Gratzik that concerns Gratzik's challenges in seeking to publish *Kohlenkutte*. These would have been known to the Stasi, given that Gratzik was being surveilled by others.[37] Anderson was instructed to keep Gratzik, among others, under observation. Anderson's other reports on Gratzik are written in a similarly neutral and nonincriminating tone.

In 1984 he told his handlers that Gratzik displayed none of the ambitions of some of the younger members of the group: "Paul Gratzik does not put himself under constant pressure to publish, he is never in a hurry to publish after he has written something."[38] Anderson paints Gratzik as a moderate and considered figure, something of a respected elder, who is measured in his decisions: "He is the type of person who is careful about where he publishes and whether he should and whether it isn't politically too risky."[39]

Reading between the lines of these placatory reports, we could infer that Anderson saw Gratzik as a friend. This is most apparent in his empathetic comment in 1984 that Gratzik "had changed a lot in appearance, he had aged a lot."[40] Anderson's assessments of Gratzik's intentions were most likely designed to cover for his older mentor. Interestingly, Anderson's judiciously formulated remarks about Gratzik's carefully calculated decisions about where to publish do not stack up against other evidence we have from Gratzik's file. Moreover, they do not tally with the impression we have from Annekatrin Hendel's film documentary, which reveals that Gratzik was often hot-tempered and cranky, as well as frequently in disharmony with his collaborators in the theater and with his editors. In fact Anderson's own reports contain more than a hint of the ongoing disputes between Gratzik and his East German publisher Hinstorff.

In November 1981 Gratzik appeared on a list of no fewer than ten contacts whom Anderson, alias "David Menzer," was instructed to work on. In a shortish report written soon after, Anderson commented on Gratzik's conflicted frame of mind, prompted by having to decide whether to stay with Hinstorff or go with Rotbuch, which had just paid him a handsome advance for his book.[41] On this occasion, it could be argued, Anderson showed little mercy, passing on the precise incriminating information that Gratzik had already received hard currency for his manuscript, including the amount. This is clearly an instance of the problem Anderson himself pinpoints in a rare moment of insight in *Vaterlandsverräter* of informers being "hell-bent" (*förmlich erpicht*) on finding something, sometimes anything, that could be of interest to the Stasi. And in those circumstances, they betrayed the trust of those they might want to protect.

Sascha Anderson: A Puppet on a String

Anderson's complex, defiantly countercultural habitus was no secret to the Stasi, and at the height of his collaboration it was even evident in numerous meeting reports. Anderson's relationship to the Stasi remained deeply ambivalent and conflicted. His officers noted in 1982 that they were aware "from extensive discussions of ideological questions" that his views on cultural politics were diametrically opposed to those of the party.[42] At this time, when Anderson and his friends managed to stay one step ahead of the Stasi, continuing to organize readings and negotiate contracts with West German publishers, Anderson no doubt thought he could live with the contradictions of leading a double life. Possibly he believed that he could compartmentalize his disparate activities and keep his contradictory parts of himself separate. In Hendel's biographical film *Anderson* (2014), Anderson offers an irritatingly abstract explanation when he says: "I was acting on the border between theory and practice." His autobiography offers an even more depersonalized but telling explanation, based on the bilateral agreements of the Helsinki Accords: "I mapped . . . the metaphor of bilateralism that was hyped after the Helsinki agreements in European politics of the time onto my body."[43]

One of many carefully choreographed scenes in Hendel's documentary provides a filmic representation of this psychic and physical bilateralism. She stages Anderson playing a game of chess with himself, or perhaps with his double (see fig. 19). Tellingly, Anderson sees no contradiction in playing chess with and against himself, just as he played with and against everyone he encountered in the GDR—his peers, diplomats, journalists, and the Stasi. In the film, when Hendel asks him which part he is playing in the chess game, he looks genuinely puzzled, and says, he is either white or black, depending on whose turn it is.

As the film biography makes plain, Anderson possessed an unnerving ability to adapt to his surroundings, whether in the last decade of the GDR or in literary circles in postunification Frankfurt. In the 1980s in East Berlin he allowed himself to become a Stasi invention and a surveillance puppet. He even fancied himself as a discursive creation, that is, as a mere projection of the surveillance state that was all surface without depth or a real identity. Thus there was a point at which he was an effective simulation, and he appears to have relished the adventure of playing with fire in organizing illegal activities. He did so, moreover, while enjoying the security of being able to report back to his Stasi officer on his own naughty behavior. Anderson's undercover work certainly fulfilled a desire to always be at the center of things that mattered and a desire to belong.[44] This played out in conflicting loyalties, which he perceived instead as parallel loyalties.

Like so many others in the Prenzlauer Berg scene, Anderson saw himself as a postmodern subject par excellence, with no stable identity, no fixed sense of self—as a "decentered subject"[45] and a creation of language and networks of power.[46] Yet, as David Bathrick has argued, this pose was riddled with contradictions. The Prenzlauer Berg poets' "own self-stylizations reveal them asserting nolens volens the viability of a self-conscious, autonomous, subject-centered, indeed Archimedean locus outside of the dominant discourse."[47] Anderson's inflated and confident sense of self is everywhere in evidence in his autobiography *Sascha Anderson*, for instance, shining through in those passages where he appears to speak as an authority on cultural power and justifies his Stasi connections. He defends his Stasi contacts and argues that he maintained them for the greater good of the group; he contends he only tried to help his friends by enlisting the assistance of the Stasi.[48] Anderson's sense of self is also in evidence in his indignant comment that after 1991 he became a scapegoat for everyone's failed "artistic career,"[49] when in reality he saw himself more as an enabler of careers.

The contradictions begin to make sense if we think of Anderson as attempting to be a cultural functionary, but one that operated in the underground, without official legal authorization and without visible signs of status or authority. But doing so was an impossibility, given that culture was only an aboveground activity in the eyes of the state. Hence Anderson might have seen himself not as having a split identity but as having two or more identities. Yet, as his Stasi dossier shows, although Anderson's actions in the underground were partly sanctioned by the Stasi and his career in alternative circles only really began to succeed once he was informing for the Stasi, he remained, for all his efforts, a member of a minority subculture, living on the edge of legality in poor housing and precarious conditions. The secret capital of his Stasi-engineered identity failed to have a sustainable, positive impact on the real conditions of his life in the GDR. Moreover, he identified with the subculture he inhabited, was shaped by its structures, and wrote from a position that was marginal to official discourse and structures.

The truth of this fragile status may have dawned on him when, at the end of 1981, two of his best artist friends, Ralf Kerbach and Cornelia Schleime, applied to emigrate. Anderson was instructed to keep Kerbach under observation and try to make him stay in East Germany.[50] After Kerbach was permitted to leave, Anderson was told to keep an eye on Schleime and check whether she could be persuaded to stay.[51] Although Anderson obviously did not want to jeopardize his friend's application to go into exile, he could not help stressing that she had become more politicized and provocative since Kerbach's departure.[52] He thereby put her at risk of further chicanery. After five unsuccessful applications to leave Schleime was finally only allowed to depart once she threatened to begin a hunger strike.[53]

In his memoir Anderson recalls trying to explain to the Stasi the meaning of his self-identification with the Prenzlauer Berg underground and telling his handlers that it was futile to attempt to influence the decisions of his friends. He argues that he tried to impress upon the Stasi the fact that his friends' decisions needed only its "toleration" and not its "support."[54] But just as Anderson seemed to run into an impasse with his officers from Dresden and the Fühmann anthology, the same officers attempted to hire him out to the Berlin headquarters. In a telling but metaphorically challenging passage of his memoir Anderson writes that they convinced their Berlin colleagues they had "hooked the fat and faithful fish, who would pull the intellectually hot-blooded school after him into the net, and therefore into shallow waters, which would no longer make such waves."[55] In one report sent from Dresden to Berlin, the Dresden officers connected Anderson with nine different assignments, all related to various activities in Berlin.[56] It is indeed plausible that the Stasi regarded him as a type of Pied Piper of Hamlin who would assist them to lead the wayward elements of his generation safely back to conformity.

Despite Anderson's growing misgivings, a new undercover name of "Fritz Müller," and a sense of "claustrophobia,"[57] for a few more years after 1981 he convinced himself that he could continue as before. By his own admission, he was a "herd animal who feared being alone" and yet also "feared contact."[58] Just before Kerbach's application to emigrate was approved, he and Anderson went on a road trip around East Germany in the summer of 1982 with an advance from his West German publisher and Anderson's extra earnings from the Stasi. The Prenzlauer Berg underground communities had by this time come to the attention of art collectors and literary scholars from abroad, Western media, and diplomats, but Anderson was starting to realize that the niche society, in which citizens fled from the state-controlled public spaces into private venues, was "one of the dumbest inventions."[59] He was in danger of becoming a puppet on a string in his own milieu, beholden to the growing activism in the underground. As he writes, he was a "jumping jack of a scene talked up by me who with their performances guaranteed the rent and the alimony of freelance journalists."[60] His self-diagnosis was not far from the truth. Anderson's public persona had increasingly become marionette-like, reacting to demands from all directions—all of which helped him escape the "chaos in his chaos," as he recalls.[61] The multiple threads connecting him to the centers of power grew shorter and tighter, especially through the years 1983 and 1984.

The poetry anthology that had been initiated by Franz Fühmann in 1981 (discussed in chapter 5) had been dear to Anderson's heart, and after its forced failure his officers appear to have issued clear instructions that he desist from any political activities, such as petitions or demonstrations. He interpreted this reaction as obliging him to play the role of a political functionary: "It was not work. It was a function, a political, a cultural-political."[62] In March 1984 he was provided with one last opportunity to demonstrate his goodwill in this regard to his new Berlin officers. On March 5–10, his friends organized a happening that they called "Dis-Assembly" (Zersammlung). In the course of the week various writers discussed the pressing issue that none had any prospects for publishing in the GDR, and some suggested creating an alternative writers' union.[63] At a follow-up meeting held on March 28, at which Anderson was present, most of those attending urged each other to lose their inhibitions about confronting the authorities with respect to publishing in the West.[64] At a further meeting held on April 8 Uwe Kolbe spoke about the need for some "spectacular event" as well as a "social safety net" for those writers in social and financial need. Anderson neutralized the situation by arguing that both ends could be met without forming a formal association.[65] It was only at the next meeting, on June 25, 1984, which was held, rather ominously, in Anderson's apartment, that Anderson managed to talk his friends out of undertaking any radical measures, "since most were against it." By way of a harmless alternative he suggested that they organize a bus outing and hold readings on the bus.[66] Because of his considerable influence in the group, Anderson's plan of sewing disunity and delaying activities worked, and the political initiative was stifled.

Given that the main impact of Anderson's collusion with the Stasi was to prevent political provocations and to encourage less overtly political initiatives, what was his impact on the art produced, if any? Certainly, Anderson set an example for his contemporaries, and by 1986 there were more and more samizdat magazines and self-publishing initiatives across the country. The Stasi was unable to control the emergence of countless new journals with small print runs, such as *Schaden, Entwerter/Oder, Und, A3*, and *Verwendung*. In a top-level eighty-four-page evaluation report from July 1986 about the dire situation with writers in the country, HA XX/AKG was forced to face some harsh truths. The "intensification of the class war" had led to massive problems with younger writers who were excluded from the guild system[67] and had the support of "hostile" media outlets,[68] a dozen West German presses,[69] and accredited Western diplomats.[70] The work of Amnesty International and the International PEN Club was another thorn in the side of the regime,[71] and the report lists writers in thirteen cities of the GDR who were bypassing the laws and organizing readings.[72] In addition to naming the failure of the guilds, the report openly admits to having a "differentiated" assessment of the number and quality of informants, which was overall insufficient and inadequate. Particularly lacking were informants who could police multiple cities at once.[73] Tellingly, the report cites the wholesale dismissal of such work as "spying" (*Spitzeltätigkeit*) as one reason why the Stasi was losing the battle to recruit more effective informants.[74] The other reason noted is the widespread belief that "literature and the writer lives from giving shape to conflicts,"[75] a view Anderson had often articulated to his officers.

Anderson's impact on the literature produced at this time is hard to assess. He was taken seriously as someone who facilitated and promoted the literature of his generation and also regarded as a talented poet. However, his own poetry had limited, if any, influence on the aesthetic direction taken by most of his friends. Despite their individual styles, they all shared similar interests in philosophy and were less interested in making political statements with their poetry than in making existential, subjective statements. We can, however, see the limits of Anderson's influence in the subcultural opposition in the growing influence of the more political members of the underground, such as Lutz Rathenow, Rüdiger Rosenthal, and Ulrike and Gerd Poppe. Although Anderson reported diligently and at length on their activities, he was powerless to suppress them. As Klaus Michael has remarked, only around 10 percent of writers who participated in the underground were also informants.[76]

Hence, Anderson's influence was restricted to ensuring that the samizdat literature of his generation became less overtly political and provocative. Yet Anderson was not named as an initiator of any of the seven literary journals listed in the 1986 report.[77] Although his hyperactivity gives the impression that there was scarcely a corner of subcultural activity that was not exposed to surveillance, this is not borne out by the Stasi's own statistics. Anderson's immediate effect was to contain the political energies of his closest peer group, as seen when he stymied the formation of an alternative guild structure. Overall, Anderson's ability to control the momentum that was gathering around him was extremely limited.[78]

Undoubtedly the Stasi's strategy of infiltration with informants such as Anderson helped to turn the niche of the underground into a highly exposed aspect of the panopticon, revealing his colleagues to the gaze of the security forces and making them vulnerable to fines,[79] Stasi harassment, or arrests.[80] Armed and forewarned with good-quality information, the Stasi successfully worked together with other authorities to prevent this generation of writers from gaining a foothold in the GDR. Anderson thus contributed to the dispersal of his generation and played a part in driving his friends westward into exile, even though this was far from his intention. He contributed to the ministry's overarching plan, which was to divide and conquer and to destroy the underground groups' cohesion and solidarity. Moreover, he fostered an apolitical stance among poets and contributed to the general stagnation in the politics of much of the underground that was in evidence by the mid-1980s. He played a large part in producing what the writer and musician Leonhard Lorek decried as a type of "underground in aspic."[81]

In 1985 the doomed Academy of Arts poetry anthology was resurrected and finally published in the West, with a slightly different constellation of contributors. By the time Elke Erb asked Anderson to join her in publishing the collection *Berührung ist eine Randerscheinung* with the Cologne publisher Kiepenheuer & Witsch, nine of the original twenty-nine authors had already left for the West. There the volume was enthusiastically received.[82] In September 1985 the author of a review in the West German news weekly *Der Spiegel* noted that the writers no longer represented an "underground reading circle" and were no longer a "literary minority" but a development that "was hitherto not acknowledged by the GDR."[83] The position taken by the writers was considered an "existential cry raised against walls and borders" and a "product of walls and borders" that reflected the marginal social existence of the contributors. With the help of this anthology the East German artistic underground was garnering acclaim abroad.

In the first half of 1986, with the knowledge of his Stasi officers, Anderson applied in writing to the ministry for an exit permit (see fig. 20). The official line was that he wanted to be allowed to work for the Stasi in the West:

> i am now requesting that i be able to prepare for this role because i have noticed that my thoughts, also in connection with my literary work, have reached a turning point as a result of which it has become harder and harder for me to reconcile my literary-social way of thinking and my work for the Stasi in the gdr without causing damage to my psychological and my physical wellbeing.[84]

The application is a curious combination of formality and informality. Anderson mixes the public aspect of his collaboration with the Stasi with his personal, existential reasons for wishing to leave:

i have tried to strictly separate my literary work and my work for the Stasi to the point of schizophrenia. That was for me the only possibility to do justice to both. For various reasons i am now living in berlin, have massive personality problems and am living separated from ralf kerbach, who lives in west berlin (previously dresden), with whom i share an existential collaborative relationship.[85]

Anderson's anguish at the constant bloodletting of East Germany's best artistic and literary talents is undoubtedly genuine. By this stage he held out little hope that his generation would be integrated before they had all emigrated. Moreover, he had begun to see the absurdity of his undercover role in the underground. He had begun to realize that his activities were illogical in nature and that he seemed to be policing himself as much as others. His policing had not produced any tangible benefits for his generation or for the state, and clearly he did not see any point to organizing events if they were only to be banned. He writes: "Sometimes i have the impression that i am being paid to keep myself under observation but hope that my work is still useful, that my efforts are worth it."[86]

Perhaps because Anderson feared that the Stasi would not let him emigrate, and possibly also because his officers instructed him to do so, in his petition to leave he made an offer to keep working for the Stasi when in West Germany (see fig. 21). To this end, he was given a new code name, "Peters." There are no files extant from 1986 to the end of the GDR regime, and it can be assumed that Anderson's last file was destroyed. He indicates this much in his memoir, writing: "[My officers] were in the process of destroying their archives and were sure that there would be no government which could do without them—and released me on good terms [*in Ehren*]."[87] Also in his memoir, Anderson mentions further meetings with his officers that he conducted from Prague and Budapest, but not the assignments he was working on. Further, a small file, OV "Satellit," was opened on Anderson after his departure for the West, which indicates that not even the Stasi was entirely sure about Anderson's identity and loyalty.[88] Thus, the final chapter on Anderson remains incomplete, and his testimony in Hendel's postunification film documentary *Anderson* offers no further evidence of his activities after he left the GDR.

Paul Gratzik: Life on the Fringes

The last entry in Gratzik's OPK file is from 1989, the year in which the Berlin Wall fell. Gratzik was working in various theaters and was still of considerable concern to the Stasi, although his file had not been escalated into a full-blown OV. By this time there were far too many threats from other quarters, and, as already discussed, writers were no longer considered the greatest or most immediate security risk. We find a long report from HA XX/7, dated March 3, 1989, that attempts to take stock of the history of the Stasi's interest in Gratzik. We read that Gratzik was living in the small town of Beenz to the north of Berlin, a location especially noteworthy because it made it hard for the Stasi to keep an eye on him.[89]

We also discover that Gratzik was still of interest to the ministry "due to his continuing to produce politically negative to hostile manuscripts whose content is directed principally at the officers of the GDR entrusted with protecting and safeguarding the GDR."[90] It is noted that he had taken part in significant underground political activities but that he was not among the main agitators. Gratzik was nonetheless known for his "entrenched politically negative to hostile attitude."[91]

In her documentary, Annekatrin Hendel is less interested in the outsider figure that Gratzik became in the last decade of the regime than in exploring Gratzik's motivations for collaborating with the Stasi. We see facets of Gratzik's character that are mostly hidden from view in the Stasi files: his vanity and his undisputed rough-hewn charm. There are scenes in which Hendel and Gratzik converse in a rowboat on a lake near his home; in one of these, we glimpse the healthy ego and sense of pride that may also have been a factor in motivating Gratzik's work for the Stasi. As he is landing his boat, he calls out to the young people who are standing on the banks of the lake. Only partly in jest, he asks whether a bystander would help "a German poet." Undoubtedly it was this pride and ambition that made him easy prey for the security forces.

It is instructive that when we first meet Gratzik in Hendel's documentary he announces to her that he has never forgotten his mother's reminder—"the worst enemy in the whole land is and remains the traitor." His fear of losing esteem and status without the Stasi's support was for a long time a strong motivation, but one which competed with his other deep fear, which was of being discovered, exposed, and humiliated. This in turn was exacerbated by a deep-rooted sense of shame at being "the worst enemy in the whole land." To offset his fears the Stasi engineered a complex and hopelessly entwined set of dependencies. The Stasi enabled Gratzik to publish his work and to receive an education; it even created an emotional codependency by giving him his own confidante and life coach in the form of his Stasi handler. Clearly Gratzik was made to feel that he was fundamentally indebted to the Stasi.

Gratzik spent the last decade of the GDR more sporadically than systematically involved in the activities of the literary-artistic underground and of the civic groups that helped to bring down the regime. And yet, in her documentary, Hendel is shocked to encounter an unreconstructed, dyed-in-the-wool communist, who twenty years after the GDR's end still refuses to believe that socialism failed. The film reveals another side to Gratzik in his splenetic temperament, evident in the opening and closing scenes where he literally curses the fascist capitalists still in power in Germany. Here there is a link to the ideological coercion that was at the heart of Gratzik's entanglement with the Stasi. Whenever Gratzik expressed doubts about the rightness of his work for the Stasi, there was one surefire method of winning him back; his officers merely needed to tap into the deeply embedded vein of Gratzik's antifascism, the bedrock upon which his collaboration was founded. By provoking his hatred of the capitalist bosses and invoking a familiar rhetoric of class warfare, his officers successfully managed their difficult conversations with Gratzik.

In *Vaterlandsverräter* we also catch glimpses of remorse and contrition, as well as fleeting signs that Gratzik is on one level greatly ashamed of his past actions. Gratzik displays his shame about having been an informer, and by his mother's definition a traitor, when he weeps on reading his own Stasi files. But this shame and his fear of exposure are only part of the story. In the end Gratzik's ideological beliefs—more articles of blind faith than rational intellectual positions—proved to be his downfall. Thus any expressions of regret uttered while filming with Hendel should be balanced against his outbursts of resentment at being made to feel guilty for his actions after German reunification and against his acerbic statements about the innate "fascism" of the capitalist West and the unbroken power of global capital.

Maja Wiens: Eleventh Hour Efforts to Turn a Lapsed Agent

Whereas the Stasi was content to watch Gratzik from afar at the end of the 1980s, the same cannot be said for its lapsed agent Maja Wiens. Her handling officer in the Pankow district office was frustrated in his efforts to turn her around. Therefore, no stone was to be left unturned, and a new plan was devised. In volume 8 of her 10-volume Stasi dossier, which also contains her victim dossier, we find a record of the Stasi's last-ditch attempt to influence her.[92] In its desperation, the department turned to the ministry's head office with an "appeal for support."[93]

Presented to HA XX/7 for approval, the plan was elaborate and ambitious. The Pankow office wanted HA XX/7 to organize an informant who would contact Wiens under the pretext of editing a collection of her father's works to commemorate his seventieth birthday. The outright rejection received from Lieutenant Colonel Tischendorf of HA XX was disappointing. Simulating a literary project such as this, Tischendorf protested, was not the sort of thing that was within the HA XX/7's capabilities: "In compliance with its [the Pankow district office's] request, finding a suitable partner who could be used to influence Wiens on the basis of a joint, literary project has been initiated through suitable key roles as well as through IM measures. An author collective cannot be created for the purposes of producing a collection of selected works [*Auswahlband*] of Paul Wiens through us, because such a mode of operating [*Arbeitsweise*] is unusual."[94] The dry comment from HA XX/7 that this approach was "unusual" is amusing. HA XX was able to assign individuals to shadow dissidents, fabricate legends, and articulate fictitious reasons for sidling up to suspects, but the harebrained scheme of faking a collective of undercover Paul Wiens devotees was perhaps simply too farfetched, even for the Stasi.

Half a year away from the collapse of the regime, the opposition in East Germany was gathering momentum daily. In May 1989 the Hungarians began to dismantle the Iron Curtain between Hungary and Austria, and by August the first East Germans were fleeing through the resultant chink in the border. Soviet leader Mikhail Gorbachev's politics of *perestroika* and *glasnost* were inspiring East Germans to push for change, leaving the security forces unsure how to respond. Still, the new winds of change blowing from the Soviet Union did not prevent the Pankow office from trying to curb Wiens's activism once and for all. Around this time the Stasi tried a new line of attack in the war of attrition it was waging on Wiens. A new informant, IM "Wittmann," was commissioned to draw up a plan of Wiens's apartment.[95] A raid on her house would produce the much-needed hard evidence of her subversive intent and might help the department secure a warrant for her arrest.

In June 1989 the Stasi decided to abandon its surveillance of Wiens and pursue a more interventionist tack of direct intimidation. In an attempt to unsettle her Wiens was physically prevented from entering the center of Berlin. In her file we read that she was incensed by the Stasi's brazen attempt to block her moving freely around the city. She had been en route to a reading and had discovered that she was being shadowed by a Stasi car. When she returned home to collect her son, so as to have a witness, the pursuit continued until she arrived at her destination. Not to be intimidated, she demanded that the drivers of the secret police car get out and show their identity papers. She was told that she was not permitted to enter the center of Berlin (otherwise she would be taken for questioning). The officers told her they were acting according to Article 12 of the GDR Criminal Code "to ensure public safety and order."[96]

The Stasi, true to its word, took Wiens in for questioning when she defied the ban.[97] Not content to let the matter rest, Wiens lodged a complaint about her treatment with the head office of the Ministry for State Security. This promptly led to her being called in for questioning again. In a barefaced blackmail attempt Wiens was told that if she did not comply the Stasi would make it known to her friends that she had once been a Stasi agent. The Stasi would also expose her mother's past association with the secret police. To this point the Stasi had maintained its pact of silence, and in return it also expected silence—and compliance—from Wiens.

The situation was complicated by the fact that, after her mother's death on May 12, 1989, Wiens had discovered Stasi documents among her mother's papers. They were "of a confidential character, internal to the ministry,"[98] and she threatened to make them public. At the meeting her officers were keen to elicit her agreement to remain silent about these documents, and Wiens agreed, even offering to hand the material back.[99] Again she was asked to work for the Stasi; she was even offered the same handling officers. Unsurprisingly, she rejected the offer, saying she had had enough negative experiences with the ministry.[100]

The Stasi surveillance machinery had by now shifted into top gear, and still Wiens showed no signs of desisting from her provocative activities. In a final desperate effort to contain her the Pankow district office proposed a smear campaign to discredit her in oppositional circles. Presumably this was to be achieved through spreading rumors—which, in her case, were true—that she had been a Stasi agent. Yet by the time the office had resolved to go down this path, it was overtaken by historical events. Wiens and her husband, and others like them, were openly demonstrating on the streets across the GDR, and the Stasi's offices in East Berlin and around the country were soon to be stormed by angry citizens calling for the ministry's closure.

Maja Wiens: From Stellar Recruit to Enemy of the State

Replete with all its contradictions, Wiens's story is instructive on many accounts. On one level it reveals the enduring impact that collaboration with the security forces could have on an individual's family and children. As the daughter of a successful, high-ranking literary informant with a reasonable degree of privilege, Wiens was at greater risk of being recruited. The Stasi clearly exploited the fact that Wiens was an agent's daughter. And when she showed signs of wanting to quit, it took a particularly hard line by insisting on keeping her on the books. It proved more difficult for her to give the Stasi its marching orders than it did for others. By the same token, her parents' associations probably also meant that Wiens could take liberties in her dealings with the Stasi. The best example of this is her sometimes scathing treatment of officers whom she did not like or thought were not her equals. To be sure, her fearlessness was a product of her elitist and privileged habitus and upbringing and points to a strong sense of entitlement that derived from being a member of the intelligentsia.

On another level this case illustrates that informants were enlisted to participate in far more than surveillance work. Informers may have been the Stasi's eyes and ears, but they were also deployed in intricate operations, either to unsettle or liquidate potential internal enemies, or to procure key evidence for apprehending suspects. Wiens's case demonstrates how far some informants were prepared to go to establish their support for the ministry. She was willing to act out an elaborately prepared scenario of deception and subterfuge; she was also willing to play a major role in a real-life espionage drama to arrest a suspect. She risked exposure, which would have damaged her reputation, and she risked losing friends and possibly her marriage as well. Such readiness to cooperate with the Stasi attests to the fact that by the 1970s Cold War surveillance of the domestic population had become normalized, and it shows how willingly certain sections of the population gave their consent to violations of human and civil rights that were happening in plain sight.

It must be acknowledged that Wiens's track record as an informant is also a measure of her opportunism. She was not being coerced, intimidated, or blackmailed at the time when she agreed to join in the operation on Kunze. She played her part entirely voluntarily and, by all accounts, rather convincingly. The files show unequivocally that she was, at least at the time, an eager and extremely useful partner in the operation and that her intelligence was immensely valuable in securing Kunze's arrest. But the files do not offer much insight into Wiens's motivations for collaborating. We can surmise that material and professional considerations played a role in ensuring that Wiens did not renege on her promise. Once the carrots with which the Stasi had enticed Wiens were no longer forthcoming, however, and she could see the damage that her collaboration had done, she became far less docile.

A considerable factor influencing her decision to withdraw her support from the Stasi was the impact that her close contact with oppositional circles was having on her once loyalist attitude to the state. Although in 1979 Wiens was happy to pass on personal comments about Bettina Wegner's drinking and her consumption of sleeping tablets,[101] by the end of 1983 her attitude to Wegner had changed considerably; she berated the Stasi for its "measures" against the singer.[102] There is some irony in this, given that Wiens herself had contributed, albeit less directly than in Kunze's case, to the chicanery that Wegner experienced. Wiens had, for instance, apprised the Stasi of a petition that Wegner and Klaus Schlesinger had initiated to protest the repressive treatment of Stefan Heym when he was charged for bypassing the Office for Copyright.[103] There is an interesting passage in Wiens's dossier in which Wiens tells her officer that she wants to know well in advance if the regime is planning to take criminal actions against Wegner and Schlesinger.[104] It remains unclear whether this was because she had come to care for them or because she was concerned for her own safety.

There is one further piece of evidence in Wiens's dossier that suggests she may have wanted to spare Wegner. By June 1980 Wiens was proactively collecting intelligence on members of the Prenzlauer Berg underground, but she expressed reluctance to continue her surveillance of Wegner "since too little operatively relevant facts can be adduced, or rather the necessary time and effort stands in no real relation to the anticipated operative usefulness."[105] It is likely that her softening attitude to Wegner spread to her views on other members of oppositional circles and their initiatives. Although there does not appear to be any one specific turning point in her file, one entry from September 1982 indicates that some transformation took place when she took part in a protest—a bicycle ride for peace—and was quizzed by the Stasi about it.[106]

The Stasi was well aware of Wiens's vacillating stance toward a host of issues. A March 1981 report noted, "The IM must not become independent" (*darf sich nicht verselbständigen*).[107] If she appeared to disapprove of Kunze in her often spiteful and petty reports on him, she was certainly fully supportive of the underground peace activists, the West German Greens, and the many social-reformist activists she associated with. It does seem that once she found herself in the thick of the burgeoning peace movement, she found her feet ideologically. Eventually she came to share the peace activists' critique of socialism and the values they stood for. Yet, according to Kunze, her oppositional habitus was unconvincing and she "only appeared to become a resistance fighter. Much points to the fact that this was a legend and that she was being prepared for higher things in an overseas posting."[108] To this day, unsurprisingly, both Kunze and Wegner remain unconvinced that Wiens ever really joined the opposition movement.

Despite her active role in Kunze's arrest, Wiens's case is a clear example of how the Stasi's infiltration strategy of oppositional circles could and did go horribly wrong. Wiens belonged to a different generation from her parents. Although she shared a similar sense of entitlement that came from being a member of a socialist elite with special contacts to the Stasi, she inevitably came to identify in part with the enemy she was supposed to keep under surveillance. Ultimately, the tipping point might have been her identification with her generational cohort, which, like Anderson, was afforded few legal opportunities to realize its ambitions.

Curiously, Wiens's establishment background—the way her parents had benefited from the *nomenklatura* system of party privileges—played little affirmative role in her dealings with the Stasi in the long term, except to sharpen her sense of entitlement to civil rights such as freedom of speech, and possibly also to travel privileges. The promise of travel may even have been a factor in her willingness to denounce Kunze and in her scathing assessments of his intentions and character, given that an overseas trip was one of her rewards. It may also have played a role in her two-faced dealings with Bettina Wegner, whom she counted among her close friends, and vice versa. Her elitist background, and her family's habit of speaking truth to power, ironically made her more susceptible to the politics of the peace movement and assisted her transformation from a loyalist to an opponent of the regime.

A further crucial factor in Wiens's political development seems to have been the considerable difficulties in securing an East German publisher for her first novel.[109] Hence, in the absence of sufficient rewards and benefits, and given the close-knit solidarity of her dissident milieu, it is no surprise that Wiens could not square the circle and in good conscience continue to inform on those activists she most admired. Wiens does not appear to have ever identified fully with the Stasi's objectives, and to have only initially identified with the goals of the socialist state. Gradually her habitus shifted to that of a critical and disaffected second-generation, dissident activist. In particular, her negative firsthand experience with the Stasi and possibly her witnessing the fallout from the undercover operation against Kunze eventually shook the scales from her eyes. She came to recognize the desperate need for sweeping social and political reforms in the land and, ironically, went on to become a dogged champion for freedom, democratization, and human rights, joining the throngs of citizens' groups that brought about East Germany's nonviolent revolution of 1989.

Helga M. Novak: A Hostage for Life

Although the dying days of the regime saw a number of the Stasi's most experienced informers in literary circles lapse, going into exile in the West or becoming the subject of surveillance themselves, the situation for many recalcitrant ex-informers, such as Helga M. Novak, was more dire. At the end of her last memoir, *Im Schwanenhals*, in lyrical passages that intercept and disrupt the logic and flow of her prose, Novak takes stock of her life. What she once expressed in the paradoxical formulation of surviving "departure" and "homecoming" and their repetition,[110] she further elaborates, identifying a series of identity crises in which she was "always only visiting... I am visiting this world" (*immer nur zu Besuch ... ich bin zu Besuch auf der Welt*).[111] Her deep restlessness, which saw her constantly on the move, traveling back and forth between East Germany and Iceland, north and south, east and west, masks a lifelong struggle for belonging and identity.

Most of all, Novak writes, she desires a passport or document that can definitively attest to her existence, that she can be defined by ("*dass es mich dingfest macht*"), and that confirms unequivocally not the mere facts of her birth but her existence ("*dass es meine Existenz bestätigt*").[112] Such hankering for something that can confer basic rights and is universally recognized, starting with Novak's name and place of birth, is rooted in a double trauma. The first trauma has its origins in the circumstances surrounding her adoption and is encapsulated in the memory of her adoptive mother threatening to withdraw her adopted name:

> my adopted mother threatened
> to take my name
> which was her name und only belonged to her
> for a name they demanded early on
> from me fees
> yet I received my identity card
> with my name
> which my mother did not take away
> like my poems.[113]

The second trauma she recounts in this passage is the formal loss of citizenship in Leipzig in 1965:

> but then at age twenty-two
> a student in Leipzig
> my identity shattered completely
> overnight we had expired
> my identity card and I
> worthless lapsed invalid
> branded a refugee was I
> without papers without a way out.[114]

Novak describes herself as having many names but no real name and as having many places of residence but no real home. As recorded in the remainder of her memoir, subsequent events exacerbated her fears of losing her identity and her right to belong. The series of repetitions in her life were painful not merely because she experienced the same bad luck twice, but also because she was unable to foresee the fact that bad luck could strike twice. Her second return to her home country in 1965 ended in her flight from East Germany, just as did her first return from exile in 1958. The second time she was stripped of any proof of her "deregistration" (*Exmatrikulation*) from the university—to prevent her from capitalizing on it in the West—and bereft of her identity papers. So that her release from her East German citizenship did not render her stateless, the authorities recommended that she apply for Icelandic citizenship. She would then be placed on a "blacklist" (*Fahndungsliste*), and even as a "future foreigner" she would be refused entry "to the territory of the GDR."[115]

The symmetry in her life story is striking and made more poignant because the second time she returned to the GDR she was optimistic that it had changed. She was convinced that she could make amends and finish what she had set out to achieve. But in the winter of 1965 the GDR had just undergone one of its most repressive periods of cultural history, and Novak was caught up in the fierce struggles for the future direction of the republic. Despite her best intentions, she was unable to escape the stigma attached to her name and her personal records, once she had thwarted the Stasi's plans to deploy her as a "honey trap." On her second sojourn in Leipzig, in 1965, she associated herself with reform socialists who were deemed heretics and subversives; she provoked the wrath of the Stasi for a second time. Thus, the debt she owed the regime for resisting the Stasi's approaches at age twenty-two became a lifelong burden that she was never to fully shake off, a debt that she could never pay off or amortize. Furthermore, this debt attracted compound interest when she began to associate with reform socialists.[116] The GDR, in particular the Stasi, became, to use her own metaphor, a vise or a trap from which she was never to extricate herself and in which she would perpetually be "rubbed raw" (*wund gestoßen*).[117]

In the summer of 1965 the regime hatched a diversionary plan to quell the unrest fomenting in the universities and sent Novak and her fellow journalism students into machine-tractor stations to produce village newspapers. During her stint in one village, she recalls, she had a conversation about a monstrous iron trap an instructor brought in for all to see. The contraption was a "leghold trap" (*Fangeisen/Tellereisen*) that he had found in the forest, designed to catch foxes, weasels, and stray dogs. She was told that these traps were illegal but that the hunters called the traps a "swan's neck" (*Schwanenhals*). Hunters, Novak was informed, "have a code name [*Decknamen*] for everything" to which someone replied, "like a secret service."[118] This type of trap was especially cruel: "Sometimes the caught animals drag the iron around with them until they die. Some bite off their own feet in order to get free."[119] Like the animals who are trapped in such a vise and still manage to escape while forever dragging the vise with them,

Novak managed to extricate herself from the worst culturo-political ice age in the history of the GDR. But she still carried the vise with her as emotional baggage.

Once in the West for the second time, Novak was free from the ironclad fist of the Stasi. Yet her inability to find lasting happiness and a crushing sense of homesickness led her to harbor an irrational urge to return to East Germany. Moreover, she recalls how in 1968, three weeks after arriving in Frankfurt, she tried to take her life "and landed in psychiatric care."[120] Notwithstanding her love of travel, Novak found she could not live in Iceland for longer periods. As a writer, she felt robbed of an essential part of her identity, the German language. Her language was her constant companion when she moved

> into the freedom of the neon city,
> into the freedom of the hot trams,
> into the three-dimensional colorfulness of the shop windows

as she writes in her poem "meine Sprache" (my language).[121] Closely linked to her language is her love of politics: "On no account did I want to languish in Laugarvatn, without discussions in my native tongue and without political activity."[122]

During her time in Frankfurt Novak (see fig. 22) continued to write poetry, which met with critical acclaim. In his foreword to her volume *Grünheide Grünheide* (Green heath, green heath, 1983), dissident Jürgen Fuchs writes of being blown away by her poems when he first encountered them as a young man. To him they appeared like a "poetic suggestive hammer,"[123] seductive in their commitment to telling the truth. They were "radical, direct and beautiful."[124] He was fascinated by the uncompromising way that they confronted "dominant lies" and "half-truths."[125] Never before had he read a poem like her "Tragoballade vom Spitzel Winfried Schütze in platten Reimen" (Tragic ballade of the spy Winfried Schütze in simple rhymes), which dared to broach taboo topics such as the Stasi and the privileges of functionaries. He was shocked to find the Stasi represented "so openly, with so few lyrical means creating meaning in between the lines and in the familiar language of the slave."[126]

After twelve years in Frankfurt Novak moved to West Berlin. Despite the years in exile she still retained "her own unsentimental feminine form of homesickness."[127] In West Berlin she joined the many other dissident artists, intellectuals, and actors who moved there in the wake of Wolf Biermann's expulsion, feeling for a brief period vindicated that she was not the only one to be branded a traitor: "Finally the name-calling as a traitor for all those who left for the West stopped. Many were convinced and honest socialists."[128] Toward the end of the 1970s she risked a return visit to her home country using her Icelandic passport, visiting Robert Havemann on several occasions, although he was under permanent surveillance.

In 1987 Novak moved into "voluntary exile" in Poland, from where she experienced the fall of the Berlin Wall and the first denunciations of Stasi informants. When she tried to obtain German citizenship in 2004—motivated by a need for medical treatment for a serious illness—she discovered to her astonishment that she was refused and that her West German residency permit (originally valid for thirty years) had been declared null and void. She writes bitterly: "Germany can't afford a poet, over seventy, who has no health and old-age insurance."[129] Without the protection of insurance, she was also unable to settle in a country within the European Union, despite her Icelandic passport. Her status was deemed to be "unemployed foreigner with no fixed address."[130] Worn down by her altercations with German bureaucracy, she decided to forego her right to a German passport "because I could muster neither the time nor the strength to write more and more letters begging and pleading [*Bitt- und Bettelbriefe*], applications and copied proof of my existence, which I am starting to doubt."[131]

Novak suffered substantial and sustained hardship from her encounter with the Stasi, as her biography makes plain; for most of her life she remained an outsider in each country where she resided. As she writes, she had never identified with power and never had "contacts in higher places" (*Kontakte zu Oberen*),[132] but rather kept company with "burglars and robbers," and occasionally with "murderers."[133] Yet, as suggested by her 1991 public confession of having once been a Stasi informer, her victimology stems from the fact that her experience of being hounded by the regime was compounded by being erroneously branded a collaborator after reunification and publicly pilloried. Most of all, in 1991 she feared that the Stasi allegations would unleash a massive "witch hunt" (*Jagd, Hatz, Kesseltreiben*),[134] and a wave of harmful denunciations. She foresaw a scramble to side with the victors of history, to whitewash the past and disavow all complicity with the regime. It was illusory to believe that the Stasi had only infiltrated parts of society, such as the Prenzlauer Berg underground circles—"the Stasi controlled the whole of the GDR, and Prenzlauer Berg was no island of the blessed" (*keine Insel der Seligen*).[135] The problem lay with Stalinism itself, she argues, which "was the most brazen slave-owning society [*war die unverschämteste Sklavenhaltergesellschaft*] . . . it subjugated lives and bodies, enlisted minds and stole all, and I mean all of our ideals."[136]

Indeed, it seems as if Novak's earlier wounds sustained while enduring Stasi persecution and state harassment were reopened in 1991. Her confession in 1991 is a plea for compassion and understanding in the face of human weakness and almost universal human debasement by Stalinism. Her memoir ends with three pages of free verse in which she lists the sources of her fears in 1991, revealing an all-encompassing, irreconcilable trauma. Although many of her fears relate to the divisive reckoning with the Stasi past— including fears of ill-wishing journalists disturbing the peace of her isolation in Poland and of her Polish neighbors "excluding" (*ausgrenzen*) her—other fears are more personal and relate to her son in Iceland and her reputation as a writer. Above all, she fears the righteousness of those who think they are beyond reproach, who pass judgment on all fellow East Germans:

> since the righteous ones free from guilt
> since the righteous and guiltless ones
> since the righteous and innocent ones
> the untarnished ones and those beyond all reproach
> that is the superior ones
> since the righteous and courageous
> the innocent ones the unblemished ones and
> those beyond all reproach
> that is those superior ones who strike a triumphant pose
> I am afraid[137]

Mixed in with these poetic outpourings are a series of rather disconnected, at times incoherent attempts at clearing her name. She offers various kinds of justification for her naivety and impulsiveness, which led her to be corralled into signing an oath with the Stasi. She compares herself to her "masochistic" cat, who lost a leg and an eye: "Like Krolowabona [her cat] I am perpetually standing where the next roof landslide comes rushing down."[138] Novak obviously feels compelled to restate for the record her position vis-à-vis the regime and itemize the damage caused to her: "The injury, insult, the harm, the humiliation already begins the moment they address a person, thinking it might be possible to transform the person into a spy."[139] Finally, in the chapter titled "Portrait of a Fear" Novak revisits her fears as a twenty-two-year-old, when the Stasi first approached her. As she had already remarked in her open letter to Biermann of October 1991, she was fearful of throwing away her future at university and of being persecuted, imprisoned, and sentenced to hard labor. She also feared being abandoned by her Icelandic friends and "isolated from the world" with no support.

*

In the 1980s the Stasi faced an uphill battle working with informants from literary spheres that could no longer be addressed through greater attention to the bureaucratic side of espionage—that is, to better handling or greater attention to processes of recruitment. Despite officers' greater finesse in controlling reluctant or recalcitrant agents (seen with Rolf Pönig's running of Paul Wiens), many informants dropped out, some without serious consequences, others suffering harsh reprisals and sustained harassment. Through the last decade of the GDR even older, lapsed agents such as Helga M. Novak continued to suffer disadvantages, demonstrating that the Stasi was very good at harboring a grudge against those it was unable to intimidate.

The reasons why informants dropped out were complex. All involved a loss of illusions about the Stasi's secret surveillance society and the purpose it served. More concretely, the reasons invariably related to informants' resentment of state and Stasi interference in their literary careers and personal lives. Other reasons thrown up by the case studies in this book are more general disaffection with the lived, daily realities of socialism, and the East

German regime's inability to reform itself. Anderson's case—a high-risk, failed experiment with infiltration that tried to simulate the underground in order to stifle it—and the case of Maja Wiens both reveal that "stickiness" in surveillance could work both ways. This approach proved that sustained contact and networking, even on behalf of the Stasi, with likeminded but "enemy" artists and writers could inadvertently have an enduring impact on informants' views of the future of socialism and its cultural politics.

Working for the Stasi involved a splintering of writers' professional and personal habitus in ways that most, with the exception of Paul Wiens, found psychologically and morally impossible to reconcile in the long run. Serving a secret society with no tangible benefits or power advantages was a task that not even Sascha Anderson could withstand, despite his complex psychology. The cases of both Anderson and Maja Wiens highlight in different ways the Stasi's failure to keep loyalist and striving informers on its side. Maja Wiens came from loyalist political stock and, according to the reasoning of the MfS, ought to have been far more committed to the Stasi's aims than she was. Likewise, with his extreme narcissism and blatant ambitions, Anderson ought to have been more effective for the Stasi than he was. Although Anderson did not drop out, in desperation he chose to go into exile, which reduced his ability to operate effectively in the underground. Ultimately, with the exception of Paul Wiens and the few others like him, the Stasi lost the battle to control the hearts and minds of its own eyes and ears, and thus in the dying days of the Cold War relinquished control over its most important weapon: its undercover agents.

The file stories of Gratzik, Maja Wiens, and Anderson indicate that the Stasi was very likely undone by its own excesses and transgressions. These three informants all became disaffected because they realized that something fundamentally flawed was at the heart of the regime's victimization of innocent, partisan citizens, its total control over free speech, and its infringement of writers' liberties. Ironically, Paul Wiens also believed in allowing writers the freedom to write what they wished. Yet because of self-interest and a misguided sense of patriotism, he allowed himself to be instrumentalized by the Stasi and the politburo.

All cases of literary informers highlight that the GDR's regime of blanket surveillance often blurred the boundaries between those performing the surveillance and those under surveillance. Each of my cases experienced a period of being on the receiving end of Stasi observation; each knew what a dictatorship was capable of. By the time of the peaceful demonstrations in the autumn of 1989, literature was less of a direct risk than groups forming in the political opposition. Even as more resources were injected into HA XX/9 and the policing of the underground, the underground continued to generate offshoots such as women's peace initiatives, environmental groups, and groups concerned about voting irregularities. These groups had far fewer qualms about direct action and open provocation of the regime. Although Stasi informants infiltrated these milieus as well, they were unable and often unwilling to stem the tide of support for change. As Uwe Spiekermann writes, the history of the Stasi is an important part of the "history of the GDR's failure."[140] With its almost obsessive focus on internal enemies, it assisted the party in blocking all reform agendas. Toward the end of the regime, MfS officers and ministerial staff became disaffected with their work and resigned.[141] Not only did the Ministry for State Security fail to stifle the creative efforts of younger writers and artists, it also was unable to stop the spread of a broad-based underground and alternative political culture. Hence it could not silence the voices calling for reform and for democratization. The Stasi may well have prolonged the life of the East German regime, but it could not prevent the much larger problem of the permanent erosion of the population's trust.[142]

Conclusion

The case histories of Cold War literary informants interwoven through the foregoing chapters reveal a ferocious secret war fought over ideas, words, and books. Whereas most Western democracies abandoned their suspicion of writers as fifth columns of communism by the late 1950s, Eastern Bloc dictatorships did not give up their distrust of authors of creative works. The East German Ministry for State Security persisted in regarding writers who held dissenting, independent, or simply critical views of certain practices as subversives and security threats. This continued even once the politics of bilateral rapprochement had begun to improve relations between East and West Germany. Until the last few years of the East German regime writers continued to be a sensitive priority area eliciting excessive policing and surveillance.

For the first three decades of its existence the ministry developed responses to perceived threats from the cultural arena, and from writers in particular, that spanned the full panoptic spectrum, from the sharp, repressive end to the softer end.[1] In the 1950s arrests, incarceration, expulsion from university, and deportation were typically harsh responses that the ministry applied to discipline its new elites (among others)—even budding writers such as Helga M. Novak, whom the MfS tried to recruit as an informant in 1956. But with a few notable exceptions, such as Jürgen Fuchs and Wolf Biermann, writers were mostly shielded from the more openly punitive of the Stasi's measures by virtue of their associations with West German counterparts, Western journalists, and international scholars of German literature. The regime feared international pressure and negative publicity. Writers were an important instrument in the regime's cultural diplomacy and pivotal to the culture wars that East Germany fought against West Germany. Hence the panoptic system of creating a network of writers who doubled as informants served as a practical response to two problems: the regime's need for control and its desire for international recognition. Analog, human means of collecting information provided a form of self-regulation, allowing the regime to continually keep writers in check without needing to resort to hard power.

Over the decades, the MfS honed its techniques of recruitment and handling of agents. Better ways were devised for keeping informants on track and reining them in when they showed signs of vacillating, although they could also be placed under the highest forms of surveillance through wiretaps and mail intercepts. Eventually, however, the regime's strategy for disciplining the writing profession proved delusionary, especially its expectation that writers of all stripes would sacrifice time and energy to police and sometimes to harass others like themselves. The Stasi may have improved officers' knowledge of operational psychology through extra training, but it failed in its inability and unwillingness to offer sufficient rewards or incentives for those informants studied here. The most effective carrots were international travel opportunities, career advantages, and chances to publish within the GDR, yet most of these incentives were not forthcoming or only appeared after frustrating delays.

Perhaps the ministry's strategy of using human intelligence that involved large sections of the population in security was naïve at best and came to rely too heavily on the goodwill of a large contingent of laborers over whom MfS officials could exercise only limited control.[2] Unlike officers who were in full-time professional employment, informers had no legally binding work contracts, no regular remuneration, and none of the other benefits associated with continuing employment. Their clandestine work for the ministry was always carried out in addition to other paid work. Informants' ties to the ministry were fairly tenuous, as were their obligations. Even the oaths that they took to maintain the Stasi's strict code of silence—although compelling tools of soft power—had no legal status. Once this fact became something of an open secret, many informants who were tired of the coercion and of their dependence on the Stasi began to rebel and "militate against the production of docile bodies."[3]

The GDR and its ever-expanding secret surveillance police relied less on sheer terror than they did on engendering other motivations among informants, especially those from disadvantaged social, expellee, or Jewish backgrounds. Further, over time the Stasi relied less and less on deterrents and overt, demonstrative display of powers, the latter of which were seen to harm East Germany's international reputation. The Stasi valued long-term collaboration and came to develop several systems of enforcing and sustaining loyalty. Stasi officers learned, for instance, that loyalty was not a given quality and that informants needed to find other reasons for cooperating. In this context the MfS discovered the value of other psychological and social motivators, such as the desire for status or for material and professional advantages, as well as the need to belong. None of the informants studied in this book continued to maintain their working relationship with the Stasi simply because of fear of reprisals; their reasons were more complex. The Stasi became reasonably adept at manipulating the messy life stories and particular vulnerabilities of those individuals whom it recruited.

In four out of the five case studies that are the focus of this book, the promise of the secret life of a Stasi agent was, at least initially, attractive and compelling to the new recruits. The role of informant was understood to bestow favors and privileges, even a special vantage point from which life was, or appeared to be, easier to cope with. Some of the elitism that was typical of officers rubbed off onto informants as well.[4] Arguably, secret knowledge of the workings of the Stasi acted rather like an insurance policy against the real possibility of becoming a victim of the repressive regime—Paul Wiens experienced this benefit firsthand. Further, it is possible that informing offered a subtle and perverse form of distinction, a sense of being different or even better than the rest of the population, imparting a sense of satisfaction that set the informer apart from his or her peers and satisfied a need to feel both useful and important. At base informing might even have met a need to belong and to feel part of the national community of otherwise loyal citizens, thus compensating for feelings of not belonging.

For many, however, maintaining an association with a ministry such as the Stasi proved a burden. Those who informed begrudgingly because of a sense of duty to the state (say, because of blackmail or as a type of penance in compensation for minor misdemeanors) needed constant cajoling to sustain motivation. As four out of my five cases reveal, the allure of the Stasi's secret surveillance society, which might have held appeal for some in the 1960s and even into the 1970s, rapidly lost traction once a writer's publishing career was in jeopardy. Other disadvantages of informing, relating to the need for secrecy, acted as disincentives for many to continue working for the Stasi. These included the dangers of an individual's cover being blown, the risk of losing new friends, and the loss of reputation if a person was discovered to be an informant. For many the business of being a denunciator never lost its negative connotations.

The episodes from the life story of Helga M. Novak analyzed here demonstrate that in the 1950s the Stasi was eager to recruit informants from among the new elites, but frequently failed to develop a productive working relationship because of its clumsy handling of recruits and its overuse of blackmail. Novak is one of three individuals foregrounded in this book who lost their fathers at an early age. As such, and, indeed, as an orphan, Novak was certainly susceptible to threats and coercion. Yet in her case the ministry's system of panopticism did not lead to a docile body, but to open defiance and resistance. In comparison with other cases of orphans whom the Stasi succeeded in recruiting, such as Ibrahim Böhme[5] and Monika Haeger—both of whom suffered difficult childhoods[6]—Novak seems to have been more the exception than the rule.

The Stasi became a master at exploiting the vulnerability of those, such as Paul Wiens, Paul Gratzik, and Sascha Anderson, who lacked a strong father figure in their childhoods. Stasi officers instinctively knew that many potential recruits were susceptible to an offer of a father substitute or an attachment figure. And if the offer was refused—as occurred with failed recruits like Novak—the Stasi proved that its memory of past misdemeanors and transgressions was extraordinarily good. It continued to expend resources policing lapsed recruits and settling old scores. Novak's case history also shows incontrovertibly that many citizens with an IM dossier were victims of harsh repression, and that the Stasi could prove proficient at taking revenge on those who were not intimidated.

Also virtually an orphan, Paul Gratzik harbored high social aspirations. His case serves to show how the Stasi managed to recruit and retain an informant in the 1960s despite his ambivalence. A succession of officers became adept at deploying an insidious combination of incentives and emotional blackmail whenever Gratzik showed signs of slipping from the Stasi's grasp, making it especially hard for him to quit. Gratzik's history as an informant establishes that it was possible to retract a pledge to work for the MfS, but it also provides glimpses of the immense toll that the effort to break off relations with the Stasi could take on informers' health. Once a certain routine had set in and dependencies had become established, it became even harder.

Even once Gratzik had attended university and established himself as an up-and-coming working-class dramatist, he was unable to rid himself of the Stasi's helping hand. For years Gratzik was indebted to the Stasi for feathering his career, and his officers were quick to exploit his gratitude. By the time he was old enough to know better it was too late to unravel the dense web of interdependencies in which he was trapped. The perks he had unthinkingly accepted as a young man had led to a debilitating form of codependency. In addition, Gratzik's original ideological reasons for collaborating never entirely disappeared, although over time these were replaced by other, private rationalizations. These complex entanglements became part of who he was.

Among its informers the Stasi sought to foster the sense of being part of a secret society that was an elite organization with connections to real power. When Gratzik tried to leave, his officer reminded him that someone would only take his place, implying that there were limited places and that he would be missing out on the secrets and the prestige that informing afforded him. For Paul Wiens, the Jewish communist and cosmopolitan man of letters, such elitism, replete with a back channel to power, proved a primary form of motivation—especially once he realized that the rewards for belonging were an open door to publishing and nearly unlimited access to travel. Both of these gains were close to his heart, and if they were covert signs of being a member of the Stasi then this was a public masquerade he was willing to be complicit in.

On occasion it has been argued that the Stasi constituted an alternative forum or public sphere that allowed East Germany's governing Socialist Unity Party and its institutions to obtain feedback on their performance in the absence of free and open elections. To be sure, the Stasi's reports to the party's committees served to provide validation, and the regime was always keen to be validated at all levels, both public and private.[7] As a rule, the evaluations that the Stasi delivered were more honest and uncensored than most other forms of reporting.[8] Nonetheless, if the Stasi was better informed than most other state and party institutions, these insights were rarely passed on to officers' agents in the field. Hence, even if the desire to gain access to secret insider information about the workings of power was a reason for some—such as Paul Wiens and Sascha Anderson—to collaborate, the desire was not fulfilled. Informers were never given access to the bigger picture of cultural strategy, nor were they given tip-offs; all they could glean from their short encounters with their handlers were, at best, insinuations and inferences.

The cases of both Paul Wiens and Gratzik show that the bonds between members of the secret surveillance society were all-important. The key to success in running agents lay in officers developing an attachment to and a pseudopersonal rapport with their informants. The relationship between officer and informant relied on a sham of reciprocity, a pretense that both officer and informer were in the same boat—as the opening scene of Graztik rowing a boat on a lake in *Vaterlandsverräter* suggests—or part of the same family, as the family reference in the film's title (Traitor to the fatherland) indicates. Certainly officer and informer shared common goals and interests—a mantra that was repeatedly invoked. Yet, as Gratzik was to learn, in this context trust was only ever one-sided.

The Stasi archives contain two extensive and elaborate dossiers for Maja Wiens: the first as an informant, the second as a victim of surveillance. Therefore her case raises many questions as to how to evaluate her contradictory association with the MfS. Her history with the Stasi cannot be dismissed as a transgression of youth or a momentary lapse of conscience. When she was enlisted at the age of twenty-five, she gave her full consent and was not duped or blackmailed. Viewed from this perspective, it is hard to believe that she later became a victim, and so her subsequent victim dossier seems incongruous, almost out of character. Indeed, some of her victims dispute that she was ever a genuine dissident. Although Wiens collaborated for longer than she was a dissident, oddly enough there are more archive folders devoted to the four years in which she was an activist. Wiens was deemed a threat, this much is clear from her files. And yet, the various parts of her double dossier fail to fit neatly together, and they do not add up to a coherent whole.

In view of Maja Wiens's contradictory file history, we might be excused for wondering how useful her declassified files are in shedding light on her relationship to the regime, on her habitus, and on her identity more broadly. Which dossier most closely captures her personality—that which documents her railing against the regime, or that in which she was a secret operative who gave 100 percent to the party cause? Does the end of someone's life determine how we see them, or do we need a more holistic approach to historical subjects' often fractured lives?

The simplest explanation for Maja Wiens's two dossiers is that she underwent a transformation from supporter to opponent of the regime. Her two contrasting dossiers indicate a slow change of heart rather than a sudden flash of insight. Yet other interpretations are possible. Her different Stasi dossiers could simply mean that the security forces altered their assessment of her and reclassified her. It is also possible that one of the two file stories is fake—an elaborate and convincing lie propagated to dupe the world. If we believe in conspiracy theories then we could be tempted to conclude that Wiens was only pretending to be a victim of the regime—say, in order to infiltrate dissident circles. This would make her part of the Stasi's strategy of simulation designed to undermine the opposition. To this day some of her victims believe this is the more plausible explanation for her two files. As seductive as such theories may be, to accede to them would be to view Wiens's life less in historical than in fictional terms, as shaped by a narrative straight from a Cold War spy novel. Reality can be stranger than fiction, but in Wiens's case there is, regrettably, no evidence to suggest that she was a double agent. Both her dossiers appear genuine and must be taken at face value.

Maja Wiens's file story might not be stranger than fiction, but it still includes elements of a gripping tale, not least because Wiens had two contradictory lives scripted for her by the Stasi. Thus, within her file story Wiens has a split or double personality. In the story about the protagonist IM "Marion" the Stasi was Wiens's good shepherd, and in the story about the protagonist "Dream" the Stasi was Wiens's tormentor that cast a long, malevolent shadow over her life. Living in the Stasi's shadow meant that Wiens did end up living a double life of sorts, even if not as a double agent. While leading a fairly conventional life as a daughter, wife, mother, and aspiring writer, she also led a parallel life as a so-called "hostile-negative" activist, fabricated for her by the Stasi, and one as a collaborator, partly engineered by the Stasi. Although she was fully complicit in her other life as an informant, it later came to haunt her.

It seems most likely that Wiens's two personas on file were the result of sticky surveillance that failed. It failed not because the informant was unable to stick close to her target, but because close contact meant that something from the enemy target stuck to her—Wiens became infected by the contact with hostile persons she was supposed to surveil. Their ideas and political views affected her and filled the vacuum that was created when the regime refused to reform. Maja Wiens had limited stocks of economic and cultural capital, except those she inherited from her *nomenklatura* parents. To her working for the Stasi did not impart any sense of elitism or belonging that served as a strong incentive to maintain the relationship. It might have promised some accumulation of political capital, and yet, despite her well-connected background, she did not gain many political kudos or much career benefit from her informing—not even for her aggressive interventions in the operation that culminated in the arrest of Rudolf Kunze in 1978. What did secret capital matter to her if she could never use any of its interest or use it to travel to the West and publish her works? Any gains became a phantom form of symbolic capital, an illusory source of prestige that she soon ceased to believe in.

For Anderson, keeping secrets posed no moral dilemma, and belonging to a privileged group of insiders was probably not a real attraction. Instead, working for the Stasi promised to raise him up in cultural and political terms; it represented a boost of sociocultural capital that held the possibility of elevating him to the hallowed company of figures such as Heiner Müller and Wolf Biermann. Anderson's role models were certainly not the party-loyal, rank-and-file members of the Stasi, with whom he never identified. Nevertheless, to his officers' credit they managed to create in Anderson a sense of belonging to something that was larger than himself—even if this something was a political underground culture that he could spearhead.

The Stasi's obsession with the underground seems to have inadvertently influenced Anderson. He also started to think of the underground as having a historical mission, which he could lead, provided he could carve out a niche for himself there. Like Maja Wiens at the start of her informing career, Anderson delighted in the sense of adventure and risk involved in his undercover assignations. As Barbara Miller writes, secrecy and intrigue were important for some.[9] Others had more trouble accepting that lies were an integral part of their work. According to Georg Simmel, lies are necessary for a secret society to function—especially one under threat from outside. It appears that lies were tolerated by Paul Wiens and Maja Wiens, relished or rationalized by Anderson as part of postmodern existence, but became intolerable for Gratzik.

Of all the cases explored in this book, Anderson stood the greatest chance of coping with the dissembling and simulation, the split loyalties, the double betrayal, and the contradictions of needing to police his own activities. For a brief period in the early 1980s he maniacally managed to pursue his own agendas and continue to keep his Stasi handlers happy. Nonetheless, from the Stasi's perspective, the experiment with simulation within an entire literary group or even across multiple groups came unstuck, although the hyperactive Anderson was in many respects the perfect candidate for the job. Anderson had the confidence and self-conviction to wish to be the center of attention, but as his officers were to discover, he was too independent, anarchic, and unreliable. Thus, the plan to turn the authentic underground into a Stasi simulation did not bear fruit—there were too many underground networks with too much momentum behind them. So despite Anderson's presence on the inside, the alternative public spaces continued to expand well beyond what a few IMs might imagine they could control. Eventually, most of the GDR's underground writers found an audience, either through *tamizdat* in the West or in tolerated *samizdat*—in magazines such as *Entwerter/Oder*. Other writers were eventually published by Aufbau in Gerhard Wolf's series *Außer der Reihe*, which was produced during 1988-91.[10]

In the last decade of the GDR's existence a fundamental problem with the MfS became apparent in its paranoid and obsessive persecution of dissidence and internal opposition. German historian Lutz Niethammer sees this problem encapsulated in the "decomposition measures" (*Zersetzungsmaßnahmen*), which effectively helped to erode the Stasi's legitimacy when the rest of the communist world was relaxing its practices.[11] The fossilization of the Stasi into an inert parallel society, its defensiveness and isolation in the face of demands for *glasnost* and *perestroika*, are responses characteristic of a secret society in the process of dissolution. The Stasi became a victim of its own decomposition—and the informants who abandoned the Stasi ship during the regime's final decade, namely Paul Gratzik, Maja Wiens, and eventually Sascha Anderson, were telling indications of its failings. The fact that the Stasi lost prized recruits, some of whom were extremely valuable in its battle to crush dissidence, reveals the extent of the bankruptcy of the regime and of the MfS as its loyal servant. The ministry lost once ardent acolytes and committed initiates to the inimical forces of renewal and change that it had fought so determinedly to control. In all, at a time when the ministry was contracting rather than expanding, it lost vital informants to the enemy. This enemy, it transpired, had more to offer than a fossilized secret police service and an illegitimate political instrument of the law. In 1989 informers such as Maja Wiens and

Paul Gratzik joined the masses of demonstrators for change—whether they advocated remaining in the GDR or leaving is immaterial. In the final phase of the fall of the republic the Stasi ceased being the SED's "keeper of order" (*Ordnungshüter*), becoming, rather, "the most absurd fractal of its social demise."[12]

The Stasi's alienation from the party occurred despite four decades of close cooperation.[13] Notwithstanding its unchecked expansion, the Stasi remained until the end a handmaiden of power. As a consequence, when the politburo began to lose its grip on power during the 1980s, so did the Stasi. Without clear direction from the party, the state of secrets began to collapse like a house of cards. Ultimately, the secret surveillance society upheld by the Stasi became one of the reasons why the MfS, along with the party leadership, failed to liberalize like the Soviet Union under the impact of glasnost. It is also one of the reasons why it continued, instead, with its self-segregation. Having developed into a "ruling parallel society," the Ministry for State Security not only contributed to the collapse of the East German regime, it also actively aided the destruction of the communist experiment through its blind and aggressive isolationism, which it maintained until the bitter end.[14]

NOTES

INTRODUCTION

1. Abram M. Shulsky and Gary J. Schmitt, *Silent Warfare: Understanding the World of Intelligence*, 3rd ed. (Washington DC: Potomac, 2002), 18.
2. See Mike Dennis, *The Stasi: Myth and Reality* (London: Routledge, 2003), 44.
3. For background to the use of the term "octopus" for the Stasi, see David Bathrick, *The Powers of Speech: The Politics of Culture in the GDR* (Lincoln: University of Nebraska Press, 1995), 220.
4. Ilko-Sascha Kowalczuk, *Stasi konkret: Überwachung und Repression in der DDR* (München, Germany: C. H. Beck, 2013), 136–37.
5. William Glenn Gray, *Germany's Cold War: The Global Campaign to Isolate East Germany 1949-1969* (Chapel Hill: University of North Carolina Press, 2003), 10.
6. Dennis, *The Stasi*, 4.
7. Jefferson Adams, "The Stasi and the Party: From Coordination to Alienation," *GHI Bulletin Supplement* 9 (2014): 99.
8. Kowalczuk, *Stasi konkret*, 190.
9. Jens Gieseke, *The History of the Stasi: East Germany's Secret Police 1945-1990* (New York: Berghahn, 2014), 82–83.
10. See Christian Booß and Helmut Müller-Enbergs, *Die indiskrete Gesellschaft: Studien zum Denunziationskomplex und zu inoffiziellen Mitarbeitern* (Frankfurt am Main, Germany: Verlag für Polizeiwissenschaft, 2014), 18; Joachim Walther, *Sicherungsbereich Literatur: Schriftsteller und Staatssicherheit in der Deutschen Demokratischen Republik* (Berlin: Ch. Links, 1996), 554. Other research has questioned the alleged growth in numbers of informants from 1973 to 1975 and put the overall figure of domestic IMs slightly lower; see Kowalczuk, *Stasi konkret*, 218.
11. Jefferson Adams, *Historical Dictionary of German Intelligence* (Lanham MD: Scarecrow, 2009), 205.

12. Dennis, *The Stasi*, 41.
13. Gary Bruce, *The Firm: The Inside Story of the Stasi* (Oxford: Oxford University Press, 2010), 14.
14. David Lyon, *Surveillance Studies: An Overview* (Cambridge: Polity, 2007), 23.
15. See Lyon, *Surveillance Studies*, 204.
16. Michel Foucault, *Discipline and Punish: The Birth of the Prison*, trans. Alan Sheridan (Harmondsworth, UK: Penguin, 1982), 200.
17. Dennis, *The Stasi*, xi.
18. Foucault, *Discipline and Punish*, 183.
19. Graham Sewell and James R. Barker, "Neither Good, Nor Bad, but Dangerous: Surveillance as an Ethical Paradox," in *Surveillance Studies Reader*, ed. Sean P. Hier and Joshua Greenberg (Maidenhead, UK: Open University Press, 2007), 358.
20. For insights into the spytech world of the Stasi see Kristie Macrakis, *Seduced by Secrets: Inside the Stasi's Spy-Tech World* (Cambridge: Cambridge University Press, 2008).
21. Kowalczuk makes a similar point that informants were "particularly close to the target" (*an der Zielperson besonders nah dran*). Kowalczuk, *Stasi konkret*, 212.
22. Helmut Müller-Enbergs, ed., *Inoffizielle Mitarbeiter des Ministeriums für Staatssicherheit, Teil 1: Richtlinien und Durchführungsbestimmungen* (Berlin: Ch. Links, 1996), 51.
23. Gieseke, *The History of the Stasi*, 81.
24. Gieseke, *The History of the Stasi*, 81.
25. Kowalczuk, *Stasi konkret*, 92.
26. Theo Buck, "Verhinderte Innovation: Die in der DDR ungedruckt gebliebenen Bücher von Uwe Johnson und Hans Joachim Schädlich," in *Rückblicke auf die Literatur der DDR*, ed. Hans-Christian Stillmark (Amsterdam: Rodopi, 2002), 11-12.
27. Stephen Brockmann, *The Writers' State: Constructing East German Literature 1945-1959* (Rochester NY: Camden House, 2015), 9.
28. Brockmann, *The Writers' State*, 18.
29. Brockmann, *The Writers' State*, 15.
30. Dennis, *The Stasi*, 116.
31. Walther, *Sicherungsbereich Literatur*, 15.
32. Walther, *Sicherungsbereich Literatur*, 140-41.
33. Dennis, *The Stasi*, 116; Walther, *Sicherungsbereich Literatur*, 557.
34. Walther, *Sicherungsbereich Literatur*, 739.
35. Walther, *Sicherungsbereich Literatur*, 739-40.
36. Walther, *Sicherungsbereich Literatur*, 557.
37. Bruce, *The Firm*, 82.
38. John C. Schmeidel, *Stasi: Shield and Sword of the Party* (London: Routledge, 2008), 34.

39. Schmeidel, *Stasi*, 35.
40. Dennis, *The Stasi*, 116.
41. Barbara Miller, *The Stasi Files Unveiled: Guilt and Compliance in a Unified Germany* (New Brunswick NJ: Transaction, 2004), 139.
42. Walther, *Sicherungsbereich Literatur*, 670–71.
43. Annekatrin Hendel, dir., *Vaterlandsverräter* (Berlin: IT WORKS! 2011), DVD.
44. Kowalczuk, *Stasi konkret*, 212.
45. See Hans-Joachim Maaz, *Die Entrüstung: Deutschland, Deutschland, Stasi, Schuld und Sündenbock* (Berlin: Argon, 1992), 7.
46. Lavinia Stan, *Transitional Justice in Post-Communist Romania: The Politics of Memory* (Cambridge: Cambridge University Press, 2013), 60.
47. Klaus Stoltenberg, *Stasi-Unterlagen-Gesetz* (Berlin: Nomos, 1992), 68.
48. Annette Weinke, "Der Umgang mit der Stasi und ihren Mitarbeitern," in *Vergangenheitsbewältigung am Ende des zwanzigsten Jahrhunderts*, ed. Helmut König, Michael Kohlstruck, and Andreas Wöll (Wiesbaden, Germany: Springer, 1998), 180.
49. Kowalczuk, *Stasi konkret*, 235.
50. Dennis, *The Stasi*, 97.
51. Helmut Müller-Enbergs, ed., *Inoffizielle Mitarbeiter des Ministeriums für Staatssicherheit, Teil 3: Statistiken* (Berlin: Ch. Links, 2008), 107.
52. Gieseke, *The History of the Stasi*, 90–91.
53. Schmeidel, *Stasi*, 43.
54. Walther, *Sicherungsbereich Literatur*, 517–18.
55. See Walther, *Sicherungsbereich Literatur*, 517.
56. See Ian Hodder, "The Entanglement of Humans and Things: A Long-Term View," *New Literary History* 45, no. 1 (2014): 20.
57. Choi Chatterjee and Karen Petrone, "Models of Selfhood and Subjectivity: The Soviet Case in Historical Perspective," in *Mass Dictatorship and Modernity*, ed. Michael Kim, Michael Schoenhals, and Yong-Woo Kim (Basingstoke, UK: Palgrave Macmillan, 2013), 206.
58. Sheila Fitzpatrick, *Tear Off the Masks! Identity and Imposture in Twentieth-Century Russia* (Princeton NJ: Princeton University Press, 2005), 152.
59. Fitzpatrick, *Tear Off the Masks*, 152.
60. Joshua Feinstein, *The Triumph of the Ordinary: Depictions of Daily Life in the East German Cinema 1949–1989* (Chapel Hill: University of North Carolina Press, 2002), 221–22.
61. Bathrick, *The Powers of Speech*, 34.
62. Steven Pfaff, *Exit-Voice Dynamics and the Collapse of East Germany: The Crisis of Leninism and the Revolution of 1989* (Durham NC: Duke University Press, 2006), 73.

63. Helmut Irmen, *Stasi und DDR-Militärjustiz: Der Einfluss des Ministeriums für Staatssicherheit auf Strafverfahren und Strafvollzug in der Militärjustiz der DDR* (Berlin: De Gruyter, 2014), 137.
64. Secrecy is generally regarded as "essential to intelligence operations." See Shulsky and Schmitt, *Silent Warfare*, xiii.
65. Müller-Enbergs, *Inoffizielle Mitarbeiter, Teil 1*, 553.
66. For a discussion of the use of the terms "late-totalitarian" and "post-totalitarian," particularly for the middle years of the regime, see Mary Fulbrook, "The Concept of 'Normalisation' and the GDR in Comparative Perspective," in *Power and Society in the GDR, 1961–1979: The "Normalization of Rule"?*, ed. Mary Fulbrook (New York: Berghahn, 2009), 12. For a discussion of the GDR as a "late-totalitarian welfare and surveillance state" see Klaus Schroeder, *Der SED-Staat: Geschichte und Strukturen der DDR 1949–1990* (Köln, Germany: Böhlau, 2013).
67. See the first study to use the concept of habitus in GDR studies: Stephen Parker and Matthew Philpotts, *"Sinn und Form": The Anatomy of a Literary Journal* (Berlin: De Gruyter, 2009), 168–76.
68. Pierre Bourdieu, *Outline of a Theory of Practice* (Cambridge: Cambridge University Press, 1977), 261.
69. Hannah Arendt, *The Origins of Totalitarianism* (Orlando FL: Harvest, 1968), 218.
70. Rachel Weil, *A Plague of Informers: Conspiracy and Political Trust in William III's England* (New Haven CT: Yale University Press, 2013), 140.
71. See Gieseke, *The History of the Stasi*, 84.
72. See Gieseke, *The History of the Stasi*, 85.
73. Booß and Müller-Enbergs, *Die indiskrete Gesellschaft*, 18.
74. See Booß and Müller-Enbergs, *Die indiskrete Gesellschaft*, 19, 22; Anita Krätzner, "Zur Anwendbarkeit des Denunziationsbegriffs für die DDR-Forschung," in *Hinter vorgehaltener Hand: Studien zur historischen Denunziationsforschung*, ed. Anita Krätzner (Göttingen, Germany: Vandenhoeck & Ruprecht, 2015), 153–64, at 160.
75. Booß and Müller-Enbergs, *Die indiskrete Gesellschaft*, 19.
76. Gieseke, *The History of the Stasi*, 86; Booß and Müller-Enbergs, *Die indiskrete Gesellschaft*, 88.
77. Booß and Müller-Enbergs assert that the SED had no mass support and that its rule was also "fragile" due to the division of Germany. See Booß and Müller-Enbergs, *Die indiskrete Gesellschaft*, 17.
78. Booß and Müller-Enbergs, *Die indiskrete Gesellschaft*, 23.
79. Booß and Müller-Enbergs, *Die indiskrete Gesellschaft*, 88.
80. See Georg Simmel, *The Sociology of Georg Simmel*, ed. and trans. Kurt H. Wolff (Glencoe IL: Free Press, 1950), 332.
81. See Simmel, *The Sociology of Georg Simmel*, 334.

82. See Simmel, *The Sociology of Georg Simmel*, 334.
83. See Simmel, *The Sociology of Georg Simmel*, 346.
84. See Simmel, *The Sociology of Georg Simmel*, 347.
85. See Simmel, *The Sociology of Georg Simmel*, 358.
86. See Simmel, *The Sociology of Georg Simmel*, 359.
87. Andreas Glaeser, *Divided in Unity: Identity, Germany, and the Berlin Police* (Chicago: University of Chicago Press, 1999), 195.
88. Uwe Spiekermann, "The Stasi and the HV A: Contemporary Research and Contemporary Resonance," *GHI Bulletin Supplement* 9 (2014): 12.
89. Mario Del Pero, "The Role of Covert Operations in US Cold War Foreign Policy," in *Secret Intelligence in the Twentieth Century*, ed. Heike Bungert, Jan G. Heitmann, and Michael Wala (London: Frank Cass, 2003), 68.
90. See Alison Lewis, Valentina Glajar, and Corina L. Petrescu, "Introduction," in *Cold War Spy Stories From Eastern Europe*, ed. Valentina Glajar, Alison Lewis, and Corina L. Petrescu (Lincoln NE: Potomac, 2019), 3-6.
91. Fiona Capp, *Writers Defiled: Security Surveillance of Australian Authors and Intellectuals 1920-1960* (South Yarra, Australia: McPhee Gribble, 1993), 31-35.
92. Simmel, *The Sociology of Georg Simmel*, 316.
93. Simmel, *The Sociology of Georg Simmel*, 345.
94. Krätzner argues that the research on the MfS had led to a heightened awareness of the breaches of trust in the GDR. See Anita Krätzner, "Einleitung," in *Hinter vorgehaltener Hand: Studien zur historischen Denunziationsforschung*, ed. Anita Krätzner (Göttingen, Germany: Vandenhoeck & Ruprecht, 2015), 11.
95. Jens Gieseke, *Die hauptamtlichen Mitarbeiter der Staatssicherheit: Personalstruktur und Lebenswelt 1950-1989/90* (Berlin: Ch. Links, 2000), 127.
96. Gieseke, *Die hauptamtlichen Mitarbeiter der Staatssicherheit*, 128.
97. In the early years, in particular, superior material conditions such as better remuneration and access to privileges caused the politburo to complain about the arrogant behavior of Stasi officers. See Gieseke, *Die Hauptamtlichen Mitarbeiter der Staatssicherheit*, 144.
98. Arendt, *The Origins of Totalitarianism*, 219.
99. See Simmel, *The Sociology of Georg Simmel*, 345.
100. Walther, *Sicherungsbereich Literatur*, 517.
101. Walther, *Sicherungsbereich Literatur*, 517.
102. Lutz Niethammer, "Die SED und 'ihre' Menschen: Versuch über das Verhältnis zwischen Partei und Bevölkerung als bestimmendem Moment innerer Staatssicherheit," in *Staatspartei und Staatssicherheit: Zum Verhältnis von SED und MfS*, ed. Siegfried Suckut and Walter Süß (Berlin: Ch. Links, 1997), 339.
103. Hannah Arendt, *Eichmann in Jerusalem: A Report on the Banality of Evil* (London: Penguin, 2006), 288.

104. Capp, *Writers Defiled*, 10.
105. Bruce, *The Firm*, 70.
106. Kathryn Waddington, *Gossip and Organizations* (London: Routledge, 2012), 7.
107. Bruce, *The Firm*, 70.
108. Pierre Bourdieu, *Distinction: A Social Critique of the Judgment of Taste* (Abingdon, UK: Routledge, 1984), 116.
109. Pierre Bourdieu, *The Logic of Practice*, trans. Richard Nice (Stanford CA: Stanford University Press, 1990), 118.
110. David Swartz, *Culture and Power: The Sociology of Pierre Bourdieu* (Chicago: Chicago University Press, 1997), 92.
111. See Gieseke, *The History of the Stasi*, 80.
112. Müller-Enbergs, *Inoffizielle Mitarbeiter, Teil 1*, 221.
113. Klaus-Dietmar Henke and Roger Engelmann, "Einleitung," in *Aktenlage: Die Bedeutung der Unterlagen des Staatssicherheitsdienstes für die Zeitgeschichtsforschung*, ed. Klaus-Dietmar Henke and Roger Engelmann (Berlin: Ch. Links, 1995), 9.
114. Spiekermann, "The Stasi and the HV A," 17.
115. Valentina Glajar, "'You'll Never Make a Spy Out of Me': The File Story of 'Fink Susanne,'" in *Secret Police Files from the Eastern Bloc: Between Surveillance and Life Writing*, ed. Valentina Glajar, Alison Lewis, and Corina L. Petrescu (Rochester NY: Camden House, 2016), 57.
116. See Capp, *Writers Defiled*, 10.
117. Booß and Müller-Enbergs, *Die indiskrete Gesellschaft*, 106.
118. Ingrid Kerz-Rühling and Tomas Plänkers, *Verräter oder Verführte: Eine psychoanalytische Untersuchung Inoffizieller Mitarbeiter der Stasi* (Berlin: Ch. Links, 2004).
119. See Booß and Müller-Enbergs, *Die indiskrete Gesellschaft*, 110–11.
120. See Cristina Vatulescu on the Soviet files as "arresting biographies." Cristina Vatulescu, *Police Aesthetics: Literature, Film, and the Secret Police in Soviet Times* (Stanford CA: Stanford University Press, 2010), 37–43. See also my work on the files as "hostile unauthorized biography": Alison Lewis, "Reading and Writing the Stasi File: On the Uses and Abuses of the File as (Auto)biography," *German Life & Letters* 56, no. 4 (2003): 383; and Capp, *Writers Defiled*, 5.
121. Clifford Geertz, *The Interpretation of Cultures* (New York: Basic Books, 1973), 7.
122. Geertz, *The Interpretation of Cultures*, 9.
123. Geertz, *The Interpretation of Cultures*, 6.
124. Mary Fulbrook, *The Anatomy of a Dictatorship: Inside the GDR 1949–1989* (Oxford: Oxford University Press, 1995).
125. Mary Fulbrook, *The People's State: East German Society from Hitler to Honecker* (New Haven CT: Yale University Press, 2005), viii.
126. Booß and Müller-Enbergs, *Die indiskrete Gesellschaft*, 22.

127. Georg Simmel, "The Sociology of Secrecy and of Secret Societies," *American Journal of Sociology* 11, no. 4 (1906): 446.
128. Simmel, "The Sociology of Secrecy and of Secret Societies," 448.
129. Jürgen Kocka, "The GDR: A Special Kind of Modern Dictatorship," in *Dictatorship as Experience: Towards a Socio-Cultural History of the GDR*, ed. Konrad H. Jarausch, trans. Eve Duffy (New York: Berghahn, 1999), 47–69. For an overview of the ways in which the GDR has been classified see Thorsten Diedrich and Hans Ehlert, "'Moderne Diktatur'—'Erziehungsdiktatur'—'Fürsorgediktatur' oder was sonst? Das Herrschaftssystem der DDR und der Versuch seiner Definition," *Potsdamer Bulletin für Zeithistorische Studien* 12 (1998): 17–25.
130. Benedict Anderson, *Imagined Communities: Reflections on the Origins and Spread of Nationalism* (London: Verso, 1991), 25.
131. The Firm was a common name used by Stasi employees prior to the fall of the Berlin Wall. See Bruce, *The Firm*, 47.
132. Gieseke, *Die Hauptamtlichen Mitarbeiter der Staatssicherheit*, 118.
133. Gieseke, *Die Hauptamtlichen Mitarbeiter der Staatssicherheit*, 118.
134. Helmut Müller-Enbergs suggests that the percentage of IMs in Gera who were women, 16.7 percent, is most likely to be representative for the whole of the GDR. See Müller-Enbergs, *Inoffizielle Mitarbeiter, Teil 3*, 89f.
135. See Müller-Enbergs, *Inoffizielle Mitarbeiter, Teil 3*, 94.
136. See Siegfried Prokop, "Zur politischen und sozialen Entwicklung der Intelligenz der DDR (1955–1961)," *Jahrbuch für Geschichte* 31 (1984): 153–86.
137. Sara Ahmed, *Cultural Politics of Emotion* (New York: Routledge, 2004), 90.
138. Ahmed, *Cultural Politics of Emotion*, 90.
139. David Lyon, "The Search for Surveillance Theories," in *Theorizing Surveillance: The Panopticon and Beyond*, ed. David Lyon (Abingdon, UK: Routledge, 2011), 8.

1. RECRUITING WRITERS FOR THE STASI

1. Joachim Walther, *Sicherungsbereich Literatur: Schriftsteller und Staatssicherheit in der Deutschen Demokratischen Republik* (Berlin: Ch. Links, 1996), 486.
2. Mike Dennis, *The Stasi: Myth and Reality* (London: Routledge, 2003), 98.
3. Ilko-Sascha Kowalczuk, *Stasi konkret: Überwachung und Repression in der DDR* (München, Germany: C. H. Beck, 2013), 186.
4. Helmut Müller-Enbergs, ed., *Inoffizielle Mitarbeiter des Ministeriums für Staatssicherheit, Teil 3: Statistiken* (Berlin: Ch. Links, 2008), 101.
5. Walther, *Sicherungsbereich Literatur*, 486.
6. Müller-Enbergs, *Inoffizielle Mitarbeiter, Teil 3*, 101.
7. Müller-Enbergs, *Inoffizielle Mitarbeiter, Teil 3*, 103.
8. Kowalczuk points out that there was a huge range in the types of individuals recruited as informants, depending on the classification of informant. Most

were only recruited in the category of IMS ("unofficial collaborator for the politically operative penetration and securing of an area of responsibility") to collect information and report security breaches or dangers; 20 percent were enlisted in the category of GMS, a much more harmless category of observing occurrences in their workplace, which is not addressed in this book. See Kowalczuk, *Stasi konkret*, 220–21.

9. Cited in Müller-Enbergs, *Inoffizielle Mitarbeiter, Teil 3*, 107.
10. Müller-Enbergs, *Inoffizielle Mitarbeiter, Teil 3*, 107.
11. Guideline 21 from 1952 mentions these two groups explicitly and suggests engaging with their mentality to ensure their cooperation. See Müller-Enbergs, *Inoffizielle Mitarbeiter, Teil 3*, 171.
12. Guideline 21 from 1952 expressly mentions "*Druck*" (force) as a means of recruitment. See Müller-Enbergs, *Inoffizielle Mitarbeiter, Teil 3*, 172.
13. Müller-Enbergs, *Inoffizielle Mitarbeiter, Teil 3*, 107.
14. E. Tory Higgins, *Beyond Pleasure and Pain: How Motivation Works* (Oxford: Oxford University Press, 2012), 233.
15. Higgins, *Beyond Pleasure and Pain*, 233.
16. See Richard van Eck, *Gaming and Cognition: Theories and Practices from the Learning Sciences* (Hershey NY: Information Science Reference, 2010), 261.
17. Müller-Enbergs, *Inoffizielle Mitarbeiter, Teil 3*, 107.
18. See E. Tory Higgins et al., "Achievement Orientations from Subjective Histories of Success: Promotion Pride versus Prevention Pride," *European Journal of Social Psychology* 31, no. 1 (2001): 3–23.
19. Charles S. Carver, Yael E. Avivi, and Jean-Philippe Laurenceau, "Approach, Avoidance, and Emotional Experiences," in *Handbook of Approach and Avoidance Motivation*, ed. Andrew J. Elliot (New York: Psychology Press, 2008), 386.
20. Carver, Avivi, and Laurenceau, "Approach, Avoidance, and Emotional Experiences," 386.
21. Müller-Enbergs, *Inoffizielle Mitarbeiter, Teil 3*, 92.
22. Georg Simmel, *The Sociology of Georg Simmel*, ed. and trans. Kurt H. Wolff (Glencoe IL: Free Press, 1950), 331.
23. Simmel, *The Sociology of Georg Simmel*, 313.
24. Simmel, *The Sociology of Georg Simmel*, 313.
25. Helmut Müller-Enbergs, ed., *Inoffizielle Mitarbeiter des Ministeriums für Staatssicherheit, Teil 1: Richtlinien und Durchführungsbestimmungen* (Berlin: Ch. Links, 1996), 62.
26. Jens Gieseke, *The History of the Stasi: East Germany's Secret Police 1945–1990* (New York: Berghahn, 2014), 79.
27. Müller-Enbergs, *Inoffizielle Mitarbeiter, Teil 1*, 62–63.
28. Müller-Enbergs, *Inoffizielle Mitarbeiter, Teil 3*, 18.

29. Müller-Enbergs, *Inoffizielle Mitarbeiter, Teil 3*, 273.
30. Mathilde Dau, "... und vergeßt das Gelächter nicht," *Weimarer Beiträge* 25, no. 7 (1979): 94.
31. See Sara Jones, *Complicity, Censorship and Criticism: Negotiating Space in the GDR Literary Sphere* (Berlin: De Gruyter, 2011).
32. BStU, MfS, AIM, file 771/68, vol. I, fol. 18.
33. Mike Dennis and Norman LaPorte, *State and Minorities in Communist East Germany* (New York: Berghahn, 2011), 31.
34. Dennis and LaPorte, *State and Minorities*, 31.
35. See Annegret von Wietersheim, *"Aber—ist mein liebster laut": Ambivalenzen in Biographie und lyrischem Werk von Paul Wiens* (Heidelberg, Germany: Universitätsverlag Winter, 2014), 60.
36. See Wietersheim, *"Aber—ist mein liebster laut,"* 60.
37. Paul Wiens, "Erinnerung an Heine: Zum 100. Todestag," in Paul Wiens, *Einmischungen: Publizistik 1949-1981* (Berlin: Aufbau, 1982), 38-39.
38. Dau, "... und vergeßt das Gelächter nicht," 94.
39. Wietersheim, *"Aber—ist mein liebster laut,"* 62.
40. See Wietersheim, *"Aber—ist mein liebster laut,"* 62.
41. Irmtraud Morgner, *Amanda: Ein Hexenroman* (Berlin: Aufbau, 1983), 144.
42. Wietersheim, *"Aber—ist mein liebster laut,"* 64.
43. Paul Wiens, "Für Johannes R. Becher," *Neue Deutsche Literatur* 6, no. 12 (1958): 26.
44. Wietersheim, *"Aber—ist mein liebster laut,"* 23.
45. See Wietersheim, *"Aber—ist mein liebster laut,"* 65.
46. Dau, "... und vergeßt das Gelächter nicht," 94.
47. Paul Wiens, "Drei Bemerkungen," in Wiens, *Einmischungen*, 112.
48. Quoted in Wietersheim, *"Aber—ist mein liebster laut,"* 66.
49. Günther Rücker, "Paul Wiens zum Gedenken," *Sinn und Form* 3 (1982): 478.
50. See Stephen Brockmann, *Literature and German Reunification* (Cambridge: Cambridge University Press, 1999), 80.
51. Wolf Biermann, "Der Lichtblick im gräßlichen Fatalismus der Geschichte: Büchner-Preis-Rede," in *Der Sturz des Dädalus* (Köln, Germany: Kiepenheuer & Witsch, 1992), 54.
52. Biermann, "Der Lichtblick im gräßlichen Fatalismus," 54.
53. Biermann, "Der Lichtblick im gräßlichen Fatalismus," 55.
54. Biermann, "Der Lichtblick im gräßlichen Fatalismus," 56.
55. Biermann, "Der Lichtblick im gräßlichen Fatalismus," 56.
56. See Sascha Anderson, "Ein hoffentlich schöner und lang anhaltender Amoklauf," *Frankfurter Allgemeine Zeitung*, October 30, 1991.
57. Helga M. Novak, "Offener Brief an Wolf Biermann, Sarah Kirsch und Jürgen Fuchs," *Der Spiegel*, October 28, 1991, 329.

58. Hermann Vinke, ed., *Akteneinsicht Christa Wolf: Zerrspiegel und Dialog; Eine Dokumentation* (Darmstadt, Germany: Luchterhand, 1993).
59. Others who outed themselves were Heinz Kahlau, Leonhard Lorek, and Andreas Sinakowski. See Ian Wallace, "Writers and the *Stasi*," in *Re-assessing the GDR: Papers from a Nottingham Conference*, ed. J. H. Reid (Amsterdam: Rodopi, 1994), 116.
60. Novak, "Offener Brief," 329.
61. Novak, "Offener Brief," 329.
62. Novak, "Offener Brief," 329.
63. Novak, "Melancholy Is Mandatory: Interview with Uta Beiküfner," *Signandsight.com*, January 26, 2006, http://www.signandsight.com/features/555.html.
64. Helga M. Novak, *Vogel Federlos* (Darmstadt, Germany: Luchterhand, 1982), 9.
65. Novak, "Melancholy Is Mandatory."
66. Novak, *Vogel Federlos*, 7.
67. Novak, *Vogel Federlos*, 12.
68. Novak, "Melancholy Is Mandatory."
69. See her records in her personal file in BStU, MfS, file 916/61, fol. 52.
70. Novak, "Melancholy Is Mandatory."
71. John Connelly, *Captive University: The Sovietization of East German, Czech, and Polish Higher Education 1945–1956* (Chapel Hill: University of North Carolina Press, 2000), 2.
72. Helga M. Novak, *Im Schwanenhals* (Frankfurt am Main, Germany: Schöffling, 2013), 12.
73. Novak, *Im Schwanenhals*, 12.
74. Brigitte Klump, *Das rote Kloster: Als Zögling in der Kaderschmiede der Stasi* (München, Germany: Herbig, 1991), 131.
75. Müller-Enbergs, *Inoffizielle Mitarbeiter, Teil 1*, 37.
76. Müller-Enbergs, *Inoffizielle Mitarbeiter, Teil 1*, 99–100.
77. Müller-Enbergs, *Inoffizielle Mitarbeiter, Teil 1*, 107.
78. Müller-Enbergs, *Inoffizielle Mitarbeiter, Teil 1*, 107.
79. Müller-Enbergs, *Inoffizielle Mitarbeiter, Teil 1*, 213.
80. Müller-Enbergs, *Inoffizielle Mitarbeiter, Teil 1*, 213.
81. Klump, *Das rote Kloster*, 132–33.
82. Klump, *Das rote Kloster*, 134.
83. Novak, *Im Schwanenhals*, 66.
84. Novak, *Im Schwanenhals*, 43.
85. Novak, *Im Schwanenhals*, 43.
86. Novak, *Im Schwanenhals*, 11.
87. Novak, *Im Schwanenhals*, 30.
88. Novak, *Im Schwanenhals*, 85.

89. Novak, *Im Schwanenhals*, 89.
90. Novak, *Im Schwanenhals*, 90.
91. Novak, *Im Schwanenhals*, 93.
92. Novak, *Im Schwanenhals*, 94.
93. Renate Ellmenreich, "Frauenbild im Ministerium für Staatssicherheit der DDR—Mein Einblick," *Weibblick* 16 (1994): 14-16. *Weibblick* was the quarterly journal of the Unabhängiger Frauenverband (UFV, Independent Women's Association).
94. See, for instance, Uta Falck, *VEB Bordell: Geschichte der Prostitution in der DDR* (Berlin: Ch. Links, 1998); Angela Schmole, "Frauen im Ministerium für Staatssicherheit," *Horch und Guck* 10, no. 34 (2001): 15-19; Müller-Enbergs, *Inoffizielle Mitarbeiter, Teil 3*, 95.
95. Novak, *Im Schwanenhals*, 92.
96. Novak, *Im Schwanenhals*, 95.
97. Novak, *Im Schwanenhals*, 99.
98. Markus Wolf mostly refers to Juliets as those secretaries or lovers whom his Romeo agents used to gather intelligence in the West. However, he also outlines the case of Gabriele Gast, who became a type of Juliet for the HV A. See Markus Wolf, with Anne McElvoy, *Man without a Face: The Autobiography of Communism's Greatest Spymaster* (New York: Public Affairs, 1997), 157.
99. Novak, *Im Schwanenhals*, 94.
100. Novak, *Im Schwanenhals*, 95.
101. Novak, *Im Schwanenhals*, 96.
102. Novak, *Im Schwanenhals*, 96.
103. Novak, *Im Schwanenhals*, 102.
104. Novak, *Im Schwanenhals*, 95.
105. Novak, *Im Schwanenhals*, 102.
106. Novak, *Im Schwanenhals*, 103.
107. Novak, *Im Schwanenhals*, 104.
108. Novak, *Im Schwanenhals*, 109.
109. Novak, *Im Schwanenhals*, 109.
110. Novak, *Im Schwanenhals*, 112.
111. Novak, *Im Schwanenhals*, 111.
112. Novak, *Im Schwanenhals*, 111-12.
113. Novak, *Im Schwanenhals*, 111.
114. Novak, *Im Schwanenhals*, 116.
115. Novak, *Im Schwanenhals*, 122.
116. Novak, *Im Schwanenhals*, 159.
117. Novak, *Im Schwanenhals*, 152.
118. See Paul Wiens, "Das Kombinat," *Aufbau* 7 (1951): 30-38.
119. See Wietersheim, *"Aber—ist mein liebster laut,"* 137.

120. BStU, MfS, AIM, file 771/68, vol. I, fol. 13.
121. See Wietersheim, *"Aber—ist mein liebster laut,"* 150-53.
122. Unless otherwise indicated all translations of literary works are mine.
123. Rosemary Rehahn, "Drei in einer großen Stadt," *Wochenpost*, March 17, 1962.
124. See his remark to his officer in 1971 that he was bourgeois and sympathized with Marxism, but wasn't a Marxist. BStU, MfS, AIM, file 7781/83, vol. I/3, fol. 51.
125. See Wietersheim, *"Aber—ist mein liebster laut,"* 90.
126. BStU, MfS, AIM, file 771/68, vol. I, fol. 11.
127. See Walther, *Sicherungsbereich Literatur*, 804; and Therese Hörnigk, "PEN im Visier der Staatssicherheit," in *Schriftsteller als Intellektuelle: Politik und Literatur im Kalten Krieg*, ed. Sven Hanuschek et al. (Tübingen, Germany: Niemeyer, 2000), 258.
128. In the obituaries published after his death there are numerous references to his ubiquitous smoking; see Siegfried Pitschmann, "Unzeitiger Verlust," *Neue Deutsche Literatur*, no. 6 (1982): 17.
129. BStU, MfS, AIM, file 771/68, vol. I, fol. 13.
130. BStU, MfS, AIM, file 771/68, vol. I, fols. 1-10.
131. Wietersheim, *"Aber—ist mein liebster laut,"* 92.
132. BStU, MfS, AIM, file 771/68, vol. I, fol. 13.
133. BStU, MfS, AIM, file 771/68, vol. I, fol. 13.
134. See his speech in Deutscher Schriftstellerverband, ed., *V. Deutscher Schriftstellerkongress vom 25. bis 27. Mai 1961* (Berlin: Aufbau, 1962), 185-86.
135. See Wietersheim, *"Aber—ist mein liebster laut,"* 77.
136. See Wietersheim, *"Aber—ist mein liebster laut,"* 92.
137. Morgner, *Amanda*, 144-45.
138. Morgner, *Amanda*, 145.
139. Morgner, *Amanda*, 144.
140. See Ingrid Kerz-Rühling and Tomas Plänkers, *Verräter oder Verführte: Eine psychoanalytische Untersuchung Inoffizieller Mitarbeiter der Stasi* (Berlin: Ch. Links, 2004), 139.
141. Müller-Enbergs, *Inoffizielle Mitarbeiter, Teil 1*, 44.
142. Müller-Enbergs, *Inoffizielle Mitarbeiter, Teil 1*, 44.
143. BStU, MfS, AIM, file 771/68, vol. I, fol. 15.
144. BStU, MfS, AIM, file 771/68, vol. I, fol. 15.
145. The Stasi waived the need for a signature, particularly from intellectuals, when recruiting from within church communities. Dennis, *The Stasi*, 97.
146. According to Barbara Miller, the first step usually involved having recruits sign an oath of secrecy. The Stasi would later obtain their signature on a more formal pledge to work for the ministry. Christa Wolf balked at the first step of swearing herself to secrecy, and thus the Stasi never really managed to enlist her for the

long term. See Barbara Miller, *The Stasi Files Unveiled: Guilt and Compliance in a Unified Germany* (New Brunswick NJ: Transaction, 2004), 39.
147. BStU, MfS, AIM, file 771/68, vol. I, fol. 16.
148. Ralph Jessen, "Mobility and Blockage during the 70s," in *Dictatorship as Experience: Towards a Socio-Cultural History of the GDR*, ed. Konrad H. Jarausch, trans. Eve Duffy (New York: Berghahn, 1999), 342.
149. Jessen, "Mobility and Blockage," 343.
150. Siegfried Prokop, "Zur politischen und sozialen Entwicklung der Intelligenz der DDR (1955-1961)," *Jahrbuch für Geschichte* 31 (1984): 153-86.
151. Gieseke, *The History of the Stasi*, 88.
152. Annette Schumann, *Kulturarbeit im sozialistischen Betrieb: Gewerkschaftliche Erziehungspraxis in der SBZ/DDR 1946 bis 1970* (Köln, Germany: Böhlau, 2006), 93-94.
153. See Matthias Braun, "Das Jahr 1959—Erwin Strittmatter und der 'Bitterfelder Weg,'" in *Es geht um Erwin Strittmatter oder Vom Streit um die Erinnerung*, ed. Matthias Braun and Carsten Gansel (Göttingen, Germany: V & R unipress, 2012), 111-32, esp. 117-24.
154. See John Griffith Urang, *Legal Tender: Love and Legitimacy in the East German Cultural Imagination* (Ithaca NY: Cornell University Press, 2010), 85.
155. See Uta G. Poiger, *Jazz, Rock, and Rebels: Cold War Politics and American Culture in a Divided Germany* (Berkeley: University of California Press, 2000), 212.
156. Jonathan Sperber, "17 June 1963: Revisiting a German Revolution," *German History* 22 (2004): 631.
157. See Poiger, *Jazz, Rock, and Rebels*, 208.
158. BStU, MfS, BV Dresden, AIM, file 2736/81, vol. I/I, fol. 32.
159. BStU, MfS, BV Dresden, AIM, file 2736/81, vol. I/I, fol. 17.
160. BStU, MfS, BV Dresden, AIM, file 2736/81, vol. I/I, fol. 28.
161. BStU, MfS, BV Dresden, AIM, file 2736/81, vol. I/I, fol. 32.
162. BStU, MfS, BV Dresden, AIM, file 2736/81, vol. I/I, fol. 13.
163. Urang, *Legal Tender*, 86.
164. BStU, MfS, BV Dresden, AIM, file 2736/81, vol. I, fol. 18.
165. BStU, MfS, BV Dresden, AIM, file 2736/81, vol. I, fol. 19.
166. BStU, MfS, BV Dresden, AIM, file 2736/81, vol. I/A, fol. 7.
167. BStU, MfS, BV Dresden, AIM, file 2736/81, vol. I/A, fols. 8-9.
168. The same applies to Dieter Noll, Walter Flegel, Günter Görlich, Gerhard Holtz-Baumert, and Jan Koplowitz. Walther argues that all of these writers were enlisted on a voluntary basis and that they all gave their services "consciously, voluntarily and willingly." See Walther, *Sicherungsbereich Literatur*, 486. My reading of Gratzik's file is that his attitude to the regime fluctuated considerably over the course of his informing, as did his willingness to inform.

169. BStU, MfS, BV Dresden, AIM, file 2736/81, vol. I/A, fol. 75.
170. BStU, MfS, BV Dresden, AIM, file 2736/81, vol. I/A, fol. 75.
171. BStU, MfS, BV Dresden, AIM, file 2736/81, vol. I/A, fol. 79.
172. BStU, MfS, BV Dresden, AIM, file 2736/81, vol. I/A, fol. 82.

2. INFORMANTS AND MOTIVATION

1. Helmut Müller-Enbergs, ed., *Inoffizielle Mitarbeiter des Ministeriums für Staatssicherheit, Teil 3: Statistiken* (Berlin: Ch. Links, 2008), 273.
2. See Gary Bruce, *The Firm: The Inside Story of the Stasi* (Oxford: Oxford University Press, 2010), 54.
3. Jens Gieseke, *The History of the Stasi: East Germany's Secret Police 1945-1990* (New York: Berghahn, 2014), 87.
4. Joachim Walther, *Sicherungsbereich Literatur: Schriftsteller und Staatssicherheit in der Deutschen Demokratischen Republik* (Berlin: Ch. Links, 1996), 670.
5. Walther, *Sicherungsbereich Literatur*, 682.
6. Walther, *Sicherungsbereich Literatur*, 673.
7. See Walther, *Sicherungsbereich Literatur*, 673.
8. Charles S. Carver, Yael E. Avivi, and Jean-Philippe Laurenceau, "Approach, Avoidance, and Emotional Experiences," in *Handbook of Approach and Avoidance Motivation*, ed. Andrew J. Elliot (New York: Psychology Press, 2008), 386.
9. BStU, MfS, BV Dresden, AIM, file 2736/81, vol. I/A, fol. 131.
10. BStU, MfS, BV Dresden, AIM, file 2736/81, vol. I/A, fol. 142.
11. BStU, MfS, BV Dresden, AIM, file 2736/81, vol. I/A, fol. 143.
12. BStU, MfS, BV Dresden, AIM, file 2736/81, vol. I/A, fol. 145.
13. BStU, MfS, BV Dresden, AIM, file 2736/81, vol. I/A, fol. 147.
14. BStU, MfS, BV Dresden, AIM, file 2736/81, vol. I/A, fol. 147.
15. BStU, MfS, BV Dresden, AIM, file 2736/81, vol. I/A, fol. 148.
16. BStU, MfS, BV Dresden, AIM, file 2736/81, vol. I/A, fol. 148.
17. BStU, MfS, BV Dresden, AIM, file 2736/81, vol. I/A, fol. 148.
18. BStU, MfS, BV Dresden, AIM, file 2736/81, vol. I/A, fol. 148.
19. BStU, MfS, BV Dresden, AIM, file 2736/81, vol. I/A, fol. 164.
20. BStU, MfS, BV Dresden, AIM, file 2736/81, vol. I/A, fol. 164.
21. BStU, MfS, BV Dresden, AIM, file 2736/81, vol. I/A, fol. 152.
22. BStU, MfS, BV Dresden, AIM, file 2736/81, vol. I/A, fol. 152.
23. BStU, MfS, BV Dresden, AIM, file 2736/81, vol. I/A, fol. 152.
24. BStU, MfS, BV Dresden, AIM, file 2736/81, vol. I/A, fol. 143.
25. BStU, MfS, BV Dresden, AIM, file 2736/81, vol. I/A, fol. 179.
26. BStU, MfS, BV Dresden, AIM, file 2736/81, vol. I/A, fol. 154.
27. Marc Silbermann and Henning Wrage, "Introduction: DEFA at the Crossroads; Remapping the Terrain," in *DEFA at the Crossroads of East German Cinema and*

International Film Culture, ed. Marc Silbermann and Henning Wrage (Berlin: De Gruyter, 2014), 8.
28. BStU, MfS, BV Dresden, AIM, file 2736/81, vol. I/I, fol. 81.
29. BStU, MfS, BV Dresden, AIM, file 2736/81, vol. I/II, fol. 34.
30. BStU, MfS, BV Dresden, AIM, file 2736/81, vol. II/II, fol. 37.
31. BStU, MfS, BV Dresden, AIM, file 2736/81, vol. I/I, fol. 90.
32. BStU, MfS, BV Dresden, AIM, file 2736/81, vol. I/I, fol. 90.
33. BStU, MfS, BV Dresden, AIM, file 2736/81, vol. II/II, fol. 38.
34. BStU, MfS, BV Dresden, AIM, file 2736/81, vol. I/I, fol. 90.
35. See, for instance, Werner Bräunig's novel *Der Rummelplatz*, which fell victim to harsh criticism at the time of the Eleventh Plenary and was never finished. It appeared posthumously over forty years later in 2011. Heiner Müller is another example of an author who suffered, particularly after 1965. See Stephen Parker and Matthew Philpotts, *"Sinn und Form": The Anatomy of a Literary Journal* (Berlin: De Gruyter, 2009), 86–88.
36. Gert Loschütz, "Kaum je ein Zugehörigkeitsglück," *Frankfurter Allgemeine Zeitung*, February 26, 2013.
37. Helga M. Novak, *Im Schwanenhals* (Frankfurt am Main, Germany: Schöffling, 2013), 174.
38. Novak, *Im Schwanenhals*, 192.
39. Novak, *Im Schwanenhals*, 193.
40. BStU, MfS, file 916/61, fol. 48.
41. BStU, MfS, file 916/61, fol. 52.
42. See BStU, MfS, file 916/61, fols. 49, 53.
43. BStU, MfS, file 916/61, fol. 49.
44. BStU, MfS, file 916/61, fol. 49.
45. Novak, *Im Schwanenhals*, 193.
46. Novak, *Im Schwanenhals*, 193.
47. Novak, *Im Schwanenhals*, 281.
48. Novak, *Im Schwanenhals*, 282.
49. Novak, *Im Schwanenhals*, 285.
50. Novak, *Im Schwanenhals*, 285.
51. Novak, *Im Schwanenhals*, 287.
52. Novak, *Im Schwanenhals*, 296.
53. BStU, MfS, AP, file 13823/92, fol. 26.
54. BStU, MfS, AP, file 13823/92, fol. 13.
55. Novak, *Im Schwanenhals*, 296.
56. Novak, *Im Schwanenhals*, 294.
57. Novak, *Im Schwanenhals*, 310.
58. See Walther, *Sicherungsbereich Literatur*, 670.

59. Arno Polzin, "Robert Havemanns Zusammenarbeit mit Geheimdiensten," in *Annäherungen an Robert Havemann: Biographische Studien und Dokumente*, ed. Bernd Florath (Göttingen, Germany: Vandenhoeck & Ruprecht, 2016), 104.
60. Novak, *Im Schwanenhals*, 300.
61. Novak, *Im Schwanenhals*, 303.
62. Novak, *Im Schwanenhals*, 303.
63. Novak, *Im Schwanenhals*, 306.
64. Novak, *Im Schwanenhals*, 307.
65. BStU, MfS, AP, file 13823/92, fol. 14.
66. BStU, MfS, AP, file 13823/92, fol. 14.
67. Novak, *Im Schwanenhals*, 308.
68. BStU, MfS, AP, file 13823/92, fol. 10.
69. BStU, MfS, AP, file 13823/92, fol. 32.
70. Novak, *Im Schwanenhals*, 313.
71. Ian Wallace offers a neat typology of six categories of writers in relation to the Stasi. His third category comprises those writers whom the Stasi tried but failed to recruit, such as Klaus Schlesinger, Wolf Biermann, Günter de Bruyn, Karl-Heinz Jakobs, Bernd Wagner, Uwe Kolbe, Johannes Jansen, and Siegmar Faust. See Ian Wallace, "Writers and the *Stasi*," in *Re-assessing the GDR: Papers from a Nottingham Conference*, ed. J. H. Reid (Amsterdam: Rodopi, 1994), 116. Novak's case is most comparable to those of Schlesinger and Biermann.
72. To register an informant with their superiors, officers had to first set up an IM-*Vorlauf* and then create an IM-*Vorgang*. During the phase of setting up an IM-*Vorlauf*, candidates were vetted without their knowledge "thoroughly and from all sides" (*gründlich und allseitig*) with respect to "suitability, reliability, and preparedness" (*Eignung, Zuverlässigkeit und Bereitschaft*). Until 1960 there were no regulations governing how the person was to be registered, and in 1968 the form of the parts of the file was prescribed. IM-*Vorgang* was the term used once a formal file was set up and maintained. It usually consisted of three separate parts in which different documents were filed. See Roland Lucht, ed., *Das Archiv der Stasi: Begriffe* (Göttingen, Germany: Vandenhoeck & Ruprecht, 2015), 126–27.
73. BStU, MfS, AIM, file 771/68, vol. I, fol. 141.
74. BStU, MfS, AIM, file 771/68, vol. I, fol. 142.
75. According to Müller, unpaid dues was the official justification; Müller maintained that this was, ironically, true, since he had not bothered to pay his membership fees. It goes without saying that Müller was a thorn in the side of the Writers' Guild, and, as such, he was more likely expelled for ideological reasons. See Heiner Müller, *Krieg ohne Schlacht: Leben in zwei Diktaturen* (Köln, Germany: Kiepenheuer & Witsch, 1992), 188.
76. BStU, MfS, AIM, file 771/68, vol. I, fol. 106.

77. See Annegret von Wietersheim, *"Aber—ist mein liebster laut": Ambivalenzen in Biographie und lyrischem Werk von Paul Wiens* (Heidelberg, Germany: Universitätsverlag Winter, 2014), 96.
78. BStU, MfS, AIM, file 7781/83, vol. I/3, fol. 84.
79. BStU, MfS, AIM, file 771/68, vol. II, fol. 178.
80. See Wietersheim, *"Aber—ist mein liebster laut,"* 170.
81. See Wietersheim, *"Aber—ist mein liebster laut,"* 171.
82. See Wietersheim, *"Aber—ist mein liebster laut,"* 170.
83. Quoted in Wietersheim, *"Aber—ist mein liebster laut,"* 184.
84. Uwe Berger, "Im Dienst," *Neue Deutsche Literatur* (1982): 27.
85. See Wietersheim, *"Aber—ist mein liebster laut,"* 185.
86. Berger, "Im Dienst," 27.
87. See Wietersheim, *"Aber—ist mein liebster laut,"* 184.
88. Wiens, "Gespräch mit Christian Löser," in Paul Wiens, *Einmischungen: Publizistik 1949-1981* (Berlin: Aufbau, 1982), 244.
89. Wiens, "Gespräch mit Christian Löser," 240.
90. Quoted in Wietersheim, *"Aber—ist mein liebster laut,"* 189.
91. BStU, MfS, AIM, file 771/68, vol. I, fol. 138.
92. BStU, MfS, AIM, file 771/68, vol. I, fol. 138.
93. Wietersheim, *"Aber—ist mein liebster laut,"* 92.
94. Walther details a case in November 1966 when one of Schiller's sources, the popular author Rudi Strahl, refused outright to collaborate because he had discovered that the Stasi had been instrumental in having his latest film banned. He did not see why he should support the Stasi when the Stasi did not support him. Walther, *Sicherungsbereich Literatur*, 703.
95. BStU, MfS, AIM, file 771/68, vol. II, fol. 248.
96. BStU, MfS, AIM, file 771/68, vol. II, fol. 248.
97. Walther, *Sicherungsbereich Literatur*, 165.
98. Jens Gieseke, *Die hauptamtlichen Mitarbeiter der Staatssicherheit: Personalstruktur und Lebenswelt 1950-1989/90* (Berlin: Ch. Links, 2000), 345.
99. Wiens was the object of Measure A of Department 26; this meant that his telephone was tapped early in the 1960s and again later during the same decade, in connection with the Prague Spring, when his loyalty to the Stasi vacillated. See Walther, *Sicherungsbereich Literatur*, 335, 597.
100. Walther, *Sicherungsbereich Literatur*, 597.
101. Wietersheim, *"Aber—ist mein liebster laut,"* 80.
102. Wietersheim, *"Aber—ist mein liebster laut,"* 197.
103. Helmut Müller-Enbergs, ed., *Inoffizielle Mitarbeiter des Ministeriums für Staatssicherheit, Teil 1: Richtlinien und Durchführungsbestimmungen* (Berlin: Ch. Links, 1996), 236.

104. BStU, MfS, BV Dresden, AIM, file 2736/81, vol. II/II, fol. 41.
105. BStU, MfS, BV Dresden, AIM, file 2736/81, vol. II/II, fol. 40.
106. BStU, MfS, BV Dresden, AIM, file 2736/81, vol. II/II, fol. 43.
107. BStU, MfS, BV Dresden, AIM, file 2736/81, vol. II/II, fol. 43.
108. BStU, MfS, BV Dresden, AIM, file 2736/81, vol. II/II, fol. 105.
109. BStU, MfS, BV Dresden, AIM, file 2736/81, vol. II/II, fol. 138. See Gratzik's incriminating reports on Brigitte Hering, in which he passes on an argument with her about the need for liberalization after 1968. Ernst-Georg Hering and his son both give testimony in the documentary film about Gratzik and speak about a falling out between Gratzik and the Hering family without specifying its relation to suspicions that Gratzik was working for the Stasi. See BStU, MfS, BV Dresden, AIM, file 2736/81, vol. II/II, fol. 177.
110. BStU, MfS, BV Dresden, AIM, file 2736/81, vol. II/II, fol. 158.
111. BStU, MfS, BV Dresden, AIM, file 2736/81, vol. II/II, fol. 159.
112. See BStU, MfS, BV Dresden, AIM, file 2736/81, vol. II/II, fol. 299.
113. BStU, MfS, BV Dresden, AIM, file 2736/81, vol. II/II, fol. 238.
114. Roger Engelmann et al., eds., *Das MfS-Lexikon: Begriffe, Personen und Strukturen der Staatssicherheit der DDR* (Berlin: Ch. Links, 2012), 173.
115. Walther, *Sicherungsbereich Literatur*, 595.
116. BStU, MfS, BV Dresden, AIM, file 2736/81, vol. I/I, fol. 132.
117. BStU, MfS, BV Dresden, AIM, file 2736/81, vol. I/I, fol. 132.
118. BStU, MfS, BV Dresden, AIM, file 2736/81, vol. I/I, fol. 167.
119. BStU, MfS, ANS, AOPK, file 16402/89, fol. 12.
120. BStU, MfS, ANS, AOPK, file 16402/89, fol. 9.
121. BStU, MfS, BV Dresden, AIM, file 2736/81, vol. I/I, fol. 134.
122. BStU, MfS, BV Dresden, AIM, file 2736/81, vol. I/I, fol. 134.
123. BStU, MfS, BV Dresden, AIM, file 2736/81, vol. I/I, fol. 134.
124. BStU, MfS, BV Dresden, AIM, file 2736/81, vol. I/I, fol. 152.

3. POLICING AND LIVING

1. See David Childs, *The GDR: Moscow's German Ally* (Abingdon, UK: Routledge, 2015), 80–81.
2. See Childs, *The GDR*, 80–81.
3. See M. E. Sarotte, "Spying Not Only on Strangers: Documenting Stasi Involvement in German-German Negotiations," in *The Cold War: Cold War Espionage and Spying*, ed. Lori Lyn Bogle (New York: Routledge, 2001), 72.
4. Angela Stent, *From Embargo to Ostpolitik: The Political Economy of West German–Soviet Relations 1955–1980* (Cambridge: Cambridge University Press, 1981), 154.
5. Stefan Wolle, *Die heile Welt der Diktatur: Alltag und Herrschaft in der DDR 1971–1989* (Berlin: Ch. Links, 1998), 35–39.

6. Andreas Malycha, *Die SED in der Ära Honecker: Machtstrukturen, Entscheidungsmechanismen und Konfliktfelder in der Staatspartei 1971 bis 1989* (Berlin: De Gruyter Oldenbourg, 2014), 177.
7. Wolle, *Die heile Welt der Diktatur*, 239.
8. Roger Woods, *Opposition in the GDR under Honecker 1971-85: An Introduction and Documentation* (New York: Palgrave Macmillan, 1986), 55.
9. Carol Anne Costabile-Heming, "GDR Literature during the 1970s," in *Beyond 1989: Re-Reading German Literary History since 1945*, ed. Keith Bullivant (New York: Berghahn, 1997), 39.
10. See Stephen Parker and Matthew Philpotts, *"Sinn und Form": The Anatomy of a Literary Journal* (Berlin: De Gruyter, 2009), 168f.
11. Dennis Tate, "'. . . vielleicht nur für Franz geschrieben': Volker Braun's Intertextual Tributes to His Special Relationship with Franz Fühmann," in *Volker Braun in Perspective*, ed. Rolf Jucker (Amsterdam: Rodopi, 2004), 80; see also Parker and Philpotts, *"Sinn und Form,"* 354.
12. Costabile-Heming, "GDR Literature during the 1970s," 37.
13. Tate, "'. . . vielleicht nur für Franz geschrieben,'" 82.
14. Wolle, *Die heile Welt der Diktatur*, 239.
15. See Dennis Tate, "Autobiographical Writing in the GDR Era," in *Rereading East Germany: The Literature and Film of the GDR*, ed. Karen Leeder (Cambridge: Cambridge University Press, 2016), 96.
16. See Joachim Walther, *Sicherungsbereich Literatur: Schriftsteller und Staatssicherheit in der Deutschen Demokratischen Republik* (Berlin: Ch. Links, 1996), 743.
17. Manfred Hempel's study found that motives for collaborating could alter. See Helmut Müller-Enbergs, ed., *Inoffizielle Mitarbeiter des Ministeriums für Staatssicherheit, Teil 3: Statistiken* (Berlin: Ch. Links, 2008), 108.
18. Müller-Enbergs, *Inoffizielle Mitarbeiter, Teil 3*, 109.
19. Walther, *Sicherungsbereich Literatur*, 253.
20. Walther, *Sicherungsbereich Literatur*, 254-55.
21. Walther, *Sicherungsbereich Literatur*, 259.
22. Walther, *Sicherungsbereich Literatur*, 260.
23. Walther, *Sicherungsbereich Literatur*, 256.
24. See Annegret von Wietersheim, *"Aber—ist mein liebster laut": Ambivalenzen in Biographie und lyrischem Werk von Paul Wiens* (Heidelberg, Germany: Universitätsverlag Winter, 2014), 197-98.
25. Quoted in Wietersheim, *"Aber—ist mein liebster laut,"* 198.
26. Quoted in Wietersheim, *"Aber—ist mein liebster laut,"* 198.
27. BStU, MfS, AIM, file 7781/83, vol. I/3, fol. 130ff.
28. BStU, MfS, AIM, file 771/68, vol. II, fol. 276.

29. See Geoffrey Westgate, *Strategies under Surveillance: Reading Irmtraud Morgner as a GDR Writer* (Amsterdam: Rodopi, 2002), 177.
30. See Walther, *Sicherungsbereich Literatur*, 606. See also the first fifty pages of the third volume of Wiens's personnel file, BStU, MfS, AIM, file 7781/83, vol. I/3, fols. 1-50.
31. BStU, MfS, AIM, file 7781/83, vol. I/3, fol. 51.
32. BStU, MfS, AIM, file 7781/83, vol. I/3, fol. 128.
33. BStU, MfS, AIM, file 7781/83, vol. I/3, fol. 129.
34. This is reported in Wietersheim, *"Aber—ist mein liebster laut,"* 101.
35. BStU, MfS, AIM, file 7781/83, vol. I/3, fol. 106.
36. BStU, MfS, file A 131/76, vol. I, fol. 29.
37. Wietersheim, *"Aber—ist mein liebster laut,"* 100.
38. Wietersheim, *"Aber—ist mein liebster laut,"* 101.
39. Uwe Berger amassed a thick Stasi file of six volumes and 2,255 leaves: BStU, MfS, file A 131/76; and BStU, MfS, AIM, file 8382/91. For a detailed analysis of Berger's recruitment as an informant see Alison Lewis, "The Stasi's Secret War on Books: Uwe Berger and the Cold War Spy as Informant and Book Reviewer," in *Cold War Spy Stories from Eastern Europe*, ed. Valentina Glajar, Alison Lewis, and Corina L. Petrescu (Lincoln NE: Potomac, 2019), 105-6.
40. BStU, MfS, file A 131/76, vol. II/1, fol. 12.
41. BStU, MfS, file A 131/76, vol. II/1 fol. 12.
42. BStU, MfS, file A 131/76, vol. II/6, fol. 325.
43. BStU, MfS, file A 131/76, vol. II/1, fol. 13.
44. BStU, MfS, file A 131/76, vol. II/1, fol. 43.
45. BStU, MfS, file A 131/76, vol. II/1, fol. 44.
46. BStU, MfS, file A 131/76, vol. II/1, fol. 44.
47. BStU, MfS, file A 131/76, vol. II/1, fol. 15.
48. See notes on his file about travel in July 1978 to Moscow and two large cities in Siberia, Irkutsk and Bratsk: BStU, MfS, file A 131/76, vol. II/5, fol. 107. For a more comprehensive examination of Berger's motives and his relationship to Wiens, see Lewis, "The Stasi's Secret War on Books," 107-11.
49. BStU, MfS, file A 131/76, vol. II/1, fol. 69.
50. BStU, MfS, file A 131/76, vol. II/1, fol. 69.
51. BStU, MfS, file A 131/76, vol. II/1, fol. 69.
52. BStU, MfS, file A 131/76, vol. II/1, fol. 80.
53. BStU, MfS, file A 131/76, vol. II/1, fol. 80.
54. Susan Sontag, *"Illness as Metaphor" and "AIDS and Its Metaphors"* (London: Penguin, 2009), 5.
55. BStU, MfS, file A 131/76, vol. II/1, fol. 80.

56. BStU, MfS, file A 131/76, vol. II/1, fol. 82.
57. BStU, MfS, file A 131/76, vol. II/1, fol. 89.
58. BStU, MfS, file A 131/76, vol. II/1, fol. 89.
59. BStU, MfS, file A 131/76, vol. II/1, fol. 89.
60. BStU, MfS, file A 131/76, vol. II/1, fol. 89.
61. BStU, MfS, file A 131/76, vol. II/1, fol. 98.
62. BStU, MfS, file A 131/76, vol. II/1, fol. 98.
63. BStU, MfS, file A 131/76, vol. II/1, fol. 100.
64. BStU, MfS, file A 131/76, vol. II/1, fol. 100.
65. BStU, MfS, file A 131/76, vol. II/1, fol. 101.
66. BStU, MfS, file A 131/76, vol. II/1, fol. 101.
67. BStU, MfS, file A 131/76, vol. II/1, fol. 102.
68. BStU, MfS, file A 131/76, vol. II/1, fol. 109.
69. BStU, MfS, file A 131/76, vol. II/1, fol. 110.
70. BStU, MfS, file A 131/76, vol. II/1, fol. 110.
71. BStU, MfS, file A 131/76, vol. II/1, fol. 110.
72. Stephen Brockmann, *The Writers' State: Constructing East German Literature 1945-1959* (Rochester NY: Camden House, 2015), 20.
73. Paul Wiens, "Metabolism," in *German Poetry in Transition 1945-1990*, ed. and trans. Charlotte Melin (Hanover NH: University Press of New England, 1999), 235.
74. Wiens, "Metabolism," 235.
75. Wiens, "Metabolism," 235.
76. BStU, MfS, AIM, file 7781/83, vol. II/2, fols. 1-2.
77. BStU, MfS, AIM, file 7781/83, vol. II/3, fols. 1-2.
78. BStU, MfS, AIM, file 7781/83, vol. II/4, fols. 1-2; and BStU, MfS, AIM, file 7781/83, vol. II/5, fols. 1-2.
79. See Walther, *Sicherungsbereich Literatur*, 613n978.
80. Walther, *Sicherungsbereich Literatur*, 655.
81. For a detailed account of Wiens's involvement in arresting Matthies see Walther, *Sicherungsbereich Literatur*, 606-9.
82. See Walther, *Sicherungsbereich Literatur*, 604-5.
83. See Walther, *Sicherungsbereich Literatur*, 606.
84. Walther, *Sicherungsbereich Literatur*, 601.
85. Walther, *Sicherungsbereich Literatur*, 602.
86. BStU, MfS, AIM, file 7781/83, vol. I/3, fol. 276.
87. Wietersheim, *"Aber—ist mein liebster laut,"* 102.
88. This is reported in Wietersheim, *"Aber—ist mein liebster laut,"* 102.
89. Walther, *Sicherungsbereich Literatur*, 345.
90. Günter Kunert, *Erwachsenenspiele* (München, Germany: DTV, 2001), 290.

91. Therese Hörnigk, "PEN im Visier der Staatssicherheit," in *Schriftsteller als Intellektuelle: Politik und Literatur im Kalten Krieg*, ed. Sven Hanuschek et al. (Tübingen, Germany: Niemeyer, 2000), 258.
92. BStU, MfS, AIM, file 771/68, vol. II, fol. 205.
93. BStU, MfS, AIM, file 7781/83, vol. I/3, fols. 430-31.
94. See Walther, *Sicherungsbereich Literatur*, 807.
95. BStU, MfS, AIM, file 7781/83, vol. II/3, fol. 140.
96. One example is handing over a sketch of Sarah Kirsch's apartment to the Stasi. See Wietersheim, *"Aber—ist mein liebster laut,"* 102.
97. Walther, *Sicherungsbereich Literatur*, 615.
98. Wiens's fourth wife also confirmed this view in an interview. See Wietersheim, *"Aber—ist mein liebster laut,"* 102.
99. BStU, MfS, BV Dresden, AIM, file 2736/81, vol. I/I, fol. 134.
100. BStU, MfS, BV Dresden, AIM, file 2736/81, vol. II/II, fol. 303.
101. BStU, MfS, BV Dresden, AIM, file 2736/81, vol. I/I, fol. 134.
102. BStU, MfS, BV Dresden, AIM, file 2736/81, vol. I/I, fol. 134.
103. BStU, MfS, BV Dresden, AIM, file 2736/81, vol. I/I, fol. 134.
104. BStU, MfS, BV Dresden, AIM, file 2736/81, vol. I/I, fols. 132-33.
105. BStU, MfS, BV Dresden, AIM, file 2736/81, vol. II/II, fol. 304.
106. BStU, MfS, BV Dresden, AIM, file 2736/81, vol. II/II, fol. 304.
107. BStU, MfS, BV Dresden, AIM, file 2736/81, vol. II/II, fol. 304.
108. BStU, MfS, BV Dresden, AIM, file 2736/81, vol. II/II, fol. 304.
109. BStU, MfS, BV Dresden, AIM, file 2736/81, vol. II/II, fol. 304.
110. Crystal Parikh, *An Ethics of Betrayal: The Politics of Otherness in Emergent U.S. Literatures and Culture* (New York: Fordham University Press, 2009), 2.
111. BStU, MfS, BV Dresden, AIM, file 2736/81, vol. I/I, fol. 164.
112. In the first report Wenzel wrote for his superior on his initial encounter with "Peter" in 1969, he observed that Gratzik suffered from a "political-ideological lack of clarity," which was reflected in his plays (BStU, MfS, BV Dresden, AIM, file 2736/81, vol. II/II, fol. 40).
113. BStU, MfS, BV Dresden, AIM, file 2736/81, vol. II/II, fol. 40.
114. BStU, MfS, BV Dresden, AIM, file 2736/81, vol. II/II, fol. 40.
115. BStU, MfS, BV Dresden, AIM, file 2736/81, vol. I/I, fol. 172.
116. BStU, MfS, BV Dresden, AIM, file 2736/81, vol. I/I, fol. 135.
117. BStU, MfS, BV Dresden, AIM, file 2736/81, vol. I/I, fol. 135.
118. BStU, MfS, BV Dresden, AIM, file 2736/81, vol. II/III, fol. 37.
119. BStU, MfS, BV Dresden, AIM, file 2736/81, vol. I/I, fol. 136.
120. BStU, MfS, BV Dresden, AIM, file 2736/81, vol. II/III, fol. 56.
121. BStU, MfS, BV Dresden, AIM, file 2736/81, vol. II/III, fol. 56.
122. BStU, MfS, BV Dresden, AIM, file 2736/81, vol. II/III, fol. 56.

123. BStU, MfS, BV Dresden, AIM, file 2736/81, vol. II/III, fol. 56.
124. BStU, MfS, BV Dresden, AIM, file 2736/81, vol. II/III, fol. 56.
125. BStU, MfS, BV Dresden, AIM, file 2736/81, vol. II/III, fol. 57.
126. BStU, MfS, BV Dresden, AIM, file 2736/81, vol. II/III, fol. 58.
127. BStU, MfS, BV Dresden, AIM, file 2736/81, vol. II/III, fol. 70.
128. BStU, MfS, BV Dresden, AIM, file 2736/81, vol. II/III, fol. 73.
129. BStU, MfS, BV Dresden, AIM, file 2736/81, vol. II/III, fol. 73.
130. BStU, MfS, BV Dresden, AIM, file 2736/81, vol. II/III, fol. 73.
131. BStU, MfS, BV Dresden, AIM, file 2736/81, vol. II/III, fol. 73.
132. BStU, MfS, BV Dresden, AIM, file 2736/81, vol. II/III, fols. 76-77.
133. Walther implies that a few of the authors, such as Gratzik, Günter Kunert, and Fritz Rudolf Fries, may not have been initiated into the full intentions of the three organizers; see Walther, *Sicherungsbereich Literatur*, 342.
134. Walther, *Sicherungsbereich Literatur*, 407.
135. Walther, *Sicherungsbereich Literatur*, 403.
136. BStU, MfS, BV Dresden, AIM, file 2736/81, vol. II/III, fol. 75.
137. According to Walther, IMS "Johannes" obtained the manuscript from the Härtls and also wrote a review of the couple's work: see Walther, *Sicherungsbereich Literatur*, 406.
138. Walther, *Sicherungsbereich Literatur*, 404.
139. Walther, *Sicherungsbereich Literatur*, 404-5.
140. Walther, *Sicherungsbereich Literatur*, 405.
141. BStU, MfS, BV Dresden, AIM, file 2736/81, vol. II/III, fol. 82.
142. Gratzik suggests this as a solution to his officer; see BStU, MfS, BV Dresden, AIM, file 2736/81, vol. II/III, fol. 81.
143. See BStU, MfS, BV Dresden, AIM, file 2736/81, vol. II/III, fol. 95.
144. See Walther, *Sicherungsbereich Literatur*, 339-41.
145. See Walther, *Sicherungsbereich Literatur*, 342.
146. See Walther, *Sicherungsbereich Literatur*, 340.
147. BStU, MfS, BV Dresden, AIM, file 2736/81, vol. II/III, fol. 101.
148. See Walther, *Sicherungsbereich Literatur*, 342.
149. See Walther, *Sicherungsbereich Literatur*, 342.
150. See Walther, *Sicherungsbereich Literatur*, 413.
151. Walther, *Sicherungsbereich Literatur*, 182.

4. THE SECRET WAR ON DIVERSION

1. Carole K. Fink, *Cold War: An International History* (Boulder CO: Westview, 2013), 174.
2. Rusanna Gaber, *Politische Gemeinschaft in Deutschland und Polen: Zum Einfluss der Geschichte auf die politische Kultur* (Wiesbaden, Germany: VS Verlag für Sozialwissenschaften), 103.

3. Gaber, *Politische Gemeinschaft in Deutschland und Polen*, 103.
4. See Joachim Walther, *Sicherungsbereich Literatur: Schriftsteller und Staatssicherheit in der Deutschen Demokratischen Republik* (Berlin: Ch. Links, 1996), 168; and John C. Schmeidel, *The Stasi: Shield and Sword of the Party* (London: Routledge, 2008), 27.
5. Jens Gieseke, *The History of the Stasi: East Germany's Secret Police 1945-1990* (New York: Berghahn, 2014), 98.
6. Walther, *Sicherungsbereich Literatur*, 167.
7. Walther, *Sicherungsbereich Literatur*, 165.
8. Walther, *Sicherungsbereich Literatur*, 168.
9. Walther, *Sicherungsbereich Literatur*, 169.
10. Walther, *Sicherungsbereich Literatur*, 185.
11. Walther, *Sicherungsbereich Literatur*, 187.
12. Walther, *Sicherungsbereich Literatur*, 173.
13. Walther, *Sicherungsbereich Literatur*, 188.
14. See Walther, *Sicherungsbereich Literatur*, 188.
15. Schmeidel, *The Stasi*, 31.
16. Schmeidel, *The Stasi*, 30.
17. See Helmut Müller-Enbergs, ed., *Inoffizielle Mitarbeiter des Ministeriums für Staatssicherheit, Teil 1: Richtlinien und Durchführungsbestimmungen* (Berlin: Ch. Links, 1996), 51.
18. Müller-Enbergs, *Inoffizielle Mitarbeiter, Teil 1*, 53.
19. See Gary Bruce, *The Firm: The Inside Story of the Stasi* (Oxford: Oxford University Press, 2010), 53.
20. Quoted in Matthias Braun, "Staatssicherheit und Literatur," in *DDR-Literatur: Eine Archivexpedition*, ed. Ulrich von Bülow and Sabine Wolf (Berlin: Ch. Links, 2014), 56.
21. Gilles Deleuze and Félix Guattari, *A Thousand Plateaus: Capitalism and Schizophrenia*, trans. Brian Massumi (London: Continuum, 1987), 10.
22. Walther, *Sicherungsbereich Literatur*, 677.
23. Roger Engelmann et al., eds., *Das MfS-Lexikon: Begriffe, Personen und Strukturen der Staatssicherheit der DDR* (Berlin: Ch. Links, 2012), 174-75. See BStU, MfS, AIM, file 9457/86, 6 vols.
24. There is a note on file in 1974 to the effect that Maja Wiens was forced to sign an oath of secrecy about her mother's Stasi connections. See BStU, MfS, AIM, file 9457/86, vol. I/1, fol. 164. Maja Wiens appears to have thought that her mother only carried out missions in the West and in connection with uncovering people smugglers. After her mother's death Wiens was distraught to find evidence that her mother spied on her and her family. See BStU, MfS, BVfS Berlin, AOP, file 1224/91, vol. 8, fol. 111.

25. Walther, *Sicherungsbereich Literatur*, 185.
26. For instance, new surveillance operations were launched to deal with Ulrich Plenzdorf, Franz Fühmann, Rolf Schneider, Stephan Hermlin, Sarah Kirsch, and Günter Kunert, and in the district offices separate departments were created to cope with the new threat from literary circles. See Walther, *Sicherungsbereich Literatur*, 169.
27. See Guideline 1/68 in Müller-Enbergs, *Inoffizielle Mitarbeiter, Teil 1*, 265.
28. Müller-Enbergs writes of the risks of "deconspiring" occurring even at the recruitment phase. Müller-Enbergs, *Inoffizielle Mitarbeiter, Teil 1*, 106.
29. BStU, MfS, BVfS Berlin, AOP, file 1224/91, vol. 1, fol. 105.
30. BStU, MfS, BVfS Berlin, AOP, file 1224/91, vol. 1, fol. 106.
31. BStU, MfS, BVfS Berlin, AOP, file 1224/91, vol. 1, fol. 107.
32. BStU, MfS, BVfS Berlin, AOP, file 1224/91, vol. 1, fol. 108.
33. BStU, MfS, BVfS Berlin, AOP, file 1224/91, vol. 1, fol. 108.
34. BStU, MfS, BVfS Berlin, AOP, file 1224/91, vol. 1, fol. 109.
35. BStU, MfS, BVfS Berlin, AOP, file 1224/91, vol. 1, fol. 112.
36. BStU, MfS, BVfS Berlin, AOP, file 1224/91, vol. 1, fol. 112.
37. BStU, MfS, BVfS Berlin, AOP, file 1224/91, vol. 1, fol. 106.
38. BStU, MfS, BVfS Berlin, AOP, file 1224/91, vol. 1, fol. 113.
39. BStU, MfS, BVfS Berlin, AOP, file 1224/91, vol. 1, fol. 115.
40. BStU, MfS, BVfS Berlin, AOP, file 1224/91, vol. 1, fol. 115.
41. BStU, MfS, BVfS Berlin, AOP, file 1224/91, vol. 1, fol. 116.
42. Walther, *Sicherungsbereich Literatur*, 860.
43. Müller-Enbergs, *Inoffizielle Mitarbeiter, Teil 1*, 348.
44. For Biermann's own recollection of how these events unfolded, see Wolf Biermann, *Warte nicht auf bessre Zeiten! Die Autobiographie* (Berlin: Propyläen, 2016), 333-40.
45. BStU, MfS, BV Dresden, AIM, file 2736/81, vol. II/III, fol. 81.
46. BStU, MfS, BV Dresden, AIM, file 2736/81, vol. II/III, fol. 128.
47. Biermann, *Warte nicht auf bessre Zeiten!*, 329-32.
48. BStU, MfS, BV Dresden, AIM, file 2736/81, vol. II/III, fol. 128.
49. BStU, MfS, BV Dresden, AIM, file 2736/81, vol. II/III, fol. 128.
50. BStU, MfS, BV Dresden, AIM, file 2736/81, vol. II/III, fol. 125.
51. See BStU, MfS, BV Dresden, AIM, file 2736/81, vol. II/III, fol. 143.
52. See BStU, MfS, BV Dresden, AIM, file 2736/81, vol. II/III, fol. 143.
53. Ilko-Sascha Kowalczuk, *Stasi konkret: Überwachung und Repression in der DDR* (München, Germany: C. H. Beck, 2013), 246.
54. See BStU, MfS, BV Dresden, AIM, file 2736/81, vol. II/III, fol. 144.
55. BStU, MfS, BV Dresden, AIM, file 2736/81, vol. II/III, fol. 144.
56. BStU, MfS, BV Dresden, AIM, file 2736/81, vol. II/III, fol. 144.
57. BStU, MfS, BV Dresden, AIM, file 2736/81, vol. II/III, fol. 157.

58. BStU, MfS, BV Dresden, AIM, file 2736/81, vol. II/III, fol. 165.
59. BStU, MfS, BV Dresden, AIM, file 2736/81, vol. II/III, fol. 162.
60. BStU, MfS, BV Dresden, AIM, file 2736/81, vol. II/III, fol. 162.
61. BStU, MfS, BV Dresden, AIM, file 2736/81, vol. II/III, fol. 168.
62. BStU, MfS, BV Dresden, AIM, file 2736/81, vol. II/III, fol. 174.
63. BStU, MfS, BV Dresden, AIM, file 2736/81, vol. II/III, fol. 174.
64. BStU, MfS, BV Dresden, AIM, file 2736/81, vol. II/III, fol. 178.
65. BStU, MfS, BV Dresden, AIM, file 2736/81, vol. II/III, fol. 178.
66. BStU, MfS, BV Dresden, AIM, file 2736/81, vol. I/I, fol. 33.
67. BStU, MfS, BV Berlin, Abt. XX/4314, vol. 2/2, fol. 272.
68. BStU, MfS, BV Berlin, Abt. XX/4314, vol. 2/2, fol. 272.
69. BStU, MfS, AIM, file 7781/83, vol. II/3, fol. 121.
70. BStU, MfS, AIM, file 771/68, vol. I, fol. 106.
71. BStU, MfS, AIM, file 771/68, vol. I, fol. 106.
72. Morgner is a peripheral figure in Wiens's Stasi file, as Geoffrey Westgate correctly notes. In the 1,723 pages of reports in part 2 of the file, there are thirteen mentions of Morgner. See Geoffrey Westgate, *Strategies under Surveillance: Reading Irmtraud Morgner as a GDR Writer* (Amsterdam: Rodopi, 2002), 180.
73. Westgate, *Strategies under Surveillance*, 177.
74. Westgate, *Strategies under Surveillance*, 177.
75. BStU, MfS, AIM, file 7781/83, vol. II/3, fol. 40.
76. Westgate, *Strategies under Surveillance*, 180.
77. See Westgate, *Strategies under Surveillance*, 244.
78. Westgate, *Strategies under Surveillance*, 244.
79. Westgate, *Strategies under Surveillance*, 244.
80. "Seine Augen, die viele Länder und Tode gesehen hatten, umlegten sich mit Lachfältchen, wenn er urteilen mußte. Er urteilte entschieden, aber sein Blick entzog sich dabei. Laura bewunderte diese Urteilsweise, die nicht imitierbar war. Sie liebte das menschliche Unikat. Daß es männlichen Geschlechts war, hatte zweitrangige Bedeutung." Irmtraud Morgner, *Amanda: Ein Hexenroman* (Berlin: Aufbau, 1983), 145.
81. See Walther, *Sicherungsbereich Literatur*, 350n226.
82. Annegret von Wietersheim, *"Aber—ist mein liebster laut": Ambivalenzen in Biographie und lyrischem Werk von Paul Wiens* (Heidelberg, Germany: Universitätsverlag Winter, 2014), 102.
83. BStU, MfS, BVfS Berlin, AOP, file 1224/91, vol. 1, fol. 117.
84. Rudolf Kunze, email to Alison Lewis, January 31, 2014.
85. Birgit Dahlenburg, "Manfred Kastners Stadtlandschaften als 'Nature morte,'" in *Ausstellungskatalog zu dem Surrealist Manfred Kastner (1943-1988)* (Greifswald, Germany: Ernst Moritz Arndt Universität Greifswald, 2008), 9.

86. Dahlenburg, "Manfred Kastners Stadtlandschaften," 11.
87. Dahlenburg, "Manfred Kastners Stadtlandschaften," 9.
88. Rudolf Kunze, email to Alison Lewis, January 31, 2014.
89. Rudolf Kunze, email to Alison Lewis, January 31, 2014.
90. Rudolf Kunze, email to Alison Lewis, January 31, 2014.
91. Rudolf Kunze, email to Alison Lewis, January 31, 2014.
92. Guntolf Herzberg and Kurt Seifert, *Rudolf Bahro—Glaube an das Veränderbare: Eine Biographie* (Berlin: Ch. Links, 2002), 214.
93. Katrin Passens, *MfS-Untersuchungshaft: Funktionen und Entwicklung von 1971 bis 1989* (Berlin: Lukas, 2012), 164.
94. Passens, *MfS-Untersuchungshaft*, 169.
95. Passens, *MfS-Untersuchungshaft*, 168.
96. Rudolf Kunze, email to Alison Lewis, February 13, 2014.
97. BStU, MfS, BVfS Berlin, AOP, file 1224/91, vol. 3, fol. 41.
98. BStU, MfS, BVfS Berlin, AOP, file 1224/91, vol. 3, fol. 43.
99. Cristina Vatulescu, "Arresting Biographies: The Secret Police File in the Soviet Union and Romania," *Comparative Literature* 56, no. 3 (2004): 243–61.
100. Helmut Irmen, *Stasi und DDR-Militärjustiz: Der Einfluss des Ministeriums für Staatssicherheit auf Strafverfahren und Strafvollzug in der Militärjustiz der DDR* (Berlin: De Gruyter, 2014), 22.
101. Clemens Vollnhals, "Der Schein der Normalität: Staatssicherheit und Justiz in der Ära Honecker," in *Staatspartei und Staatssicherheit: Zum Verhältnis von SED und MfS*, ed. Siegfried Suckut and Walter Süß (Berlin: Ch. Links, 1997), 215.
102. Vollnhals, "Der Schein der Normalität," 220.
103. This statistic is provided by Vollnhals, "Der Schein der Normalität," 219.
104. Sigrid Averesch, "Anwalt Brennecke und das Offiziersehrenwort," *Berliner Zeitung*, January 22, 1996.
105. BStU, MfS, BVfS Berlin, AOP, file 1224/91, vol. 3, fol. 47.
106. BStU, MfS, BVfS Berlin, AOP, file 1224/91, vol. 3, fol. 47.
107. BStU, MfS, BVfS Berlin, AOP, file 1224/91, vol. 3, fol. 47.
108. BStU, MfS, BVfS Berlin, AOP, file 1224/91, vol. 3, fol. 48.
109. BStU, MfS, BVfS Berlin, AOP, file 1224/91, vol. 3, fol. 84.
110. BStU, MfS, BVfS Berlin, AOP, file 1224/91, vol. 3, fol. 85.
111. BStU, MfS, BVfS Berlin, AOP, file 1224/91, vol. 3, fol. 85.
112. BStU, MfS, BVfS Berlin, AOP, file 1224/91, vol. 3, fol. 86.
113. BStU, MfS, BVfS Berlin, AOP, file 1224/91, vol. 3, fol. 87.
114. BStU, MfS, BVfS Berlin, AOP, file 1224/91, vol. 3, fol. 90.
115. BStU, MfS, BVfS Berlin, AOP, file 1224/91, vol. 3, fol. 91.
116. BStU, MfS, BVfS Berlin, AOP, file 1224/91, vol. 3, fols. 84–103.
117. BStU, MfS, BVfS Berlin, AOP, file 1224/91, vol. 3, fol. 93.

118. BStU, MfS, BVfS Berlin, AOP, file 1224/91, vol. 3, fol. 96.
119. BStU, MfS, BVfS Berlin, AOP, file 1224/91, vol. 3, fol. 97.
120. These paragraphs had been revised and tightened up by the politburo on February 15, 1977. Passens, *MfS-Untersuchungshaft*, 108-10.
121. BStU, MfS, BVfS Berlin, AOP, file 1224/91, vol. 3, fol. 97.
122. BStU, MfS, BVfS Berlin, AOP, file 1224/91, vol. 3, fol. 97.
123. A flurry of arrests followed in the first months after the Biermann fiasco, and a steady stream of them occurred over subsequent years. Katrin Passens reports on sixty-eight arrests from November 16 to December 31, 1976. Passens, *MfS-Untersuchungshaft*, 156. The Stasi used arrests for the least prominent suspects; see Schmeidel, *The Stasi*, 84.
124. Rudolf Kunze, email to Alison Lewis, February 13, 2014.
125. BStU, MfS, BVfS Berlin, AOP, file 1224/91, vol. 3, fol. 106.
126. Rudolf Kunze, email to Alison Lewis, February 13, 2014.
127. BStU, MfS, BVfS Berlin, AOP, file 1224/91, vol. 3, fol. 115.
128. BStU, MfS, BVfS Berlin, AOP, file 1224/91, vol. 3, fol. 118.
129. BStU, MfS, BVfS Berlin, AOP, file 1224/91, vol. 3, fol. 122.
130. Averesch, "Anwalt Brennecke und das Offiziersehrenwort."
131. See Averesch, "Anwalt Brennecke und das Offiziersehrenwort."
132. BStU, MfS, BVfS Berlin, AOP, file 1224/91, vol. 3, fol. 136.
133. BStU, MfS, BVfS Berlin, AOP, file 1224/91, vol. 1, fol. 123.
134. BStU, MfS, BVfS Berlin, AOP, file 1224/91, vol. 1, fol. 123.
135. BStU, MfS, BVfS Berlin, AOP, file 1224/91, vol. 1, fol. 123.
136. BStU, MfS, BVfS Berlin, AOP, file 1224/91, vol. 3, fol. 164.
137. BStU, MfS, BVfS Berlin, AOP, file 1224/91, vol. 1, fol. 125.
138. See Roland Berbig and Holger Jens Karlson, "'Leute haben sich als Gruppe erwiesen': Zur Gruppenbildung bei Wolf Biermanns Ausbürgerung," in *In Sachen Biermann: Protokolle, Berichte und Briefe zu den Folgen einer Ausbürgerung*, ed. Roland Berbig et al. (Berlin: Ch. Links, 1994), 26-27.
139. BStU, MfS, AIM, file 7781/83, vol. II/3, fol. 65.
140. BStU, MfS, AIM, file 7781/83, vol. II/3, fol. 65.
141. See BStU, MfS, AIM, file 7781/83, vol. I/3, fol. 50.
142. BStU, MfS, AIM, file 7781/83, vol. II/3, fol. 120.
143. Becker received the Heinrich Mann Prize of the Academy of the Arts for *Jakob der Lügner* (*Jakob the Liar*, 1969) in 1971. See Sander L. Gilman, *Jurek Becker: A Life in Five Worlds* (Chicago: University of Chicago Press, 2003), 78.
144. BStU, MfS, AOP, file 15087/84, vol. 4, fol. 9.
145. BStU, MfS, AIM, file 7781/83, vol. II/3, fol. 158.
146. BStU, MfS, AIM, file 7781/83, vol. II/3, fol. 158.
147. BStU, MfS, AIM, file 7781/83, vol. II/3, fol. 159.

148. BStU, MfS, AIM, file 7781/83, vol. II/3, fol. 159.
149. See, for instance, the memoirs written by some of the children, such as Susanne Schädlich, *Immer wieder Dezember: Der Westen, die Stasi, der Onkel und ich* (München, Germany: Droemer, 2009); and the edited collection of essays about exile in the West as experienced by the children: Susanne Schädlich and Anna Schädlich, eds., *Ein Spaziergang war es nicht: Kindheiten zwischen Ost und West* (München, Germany: Heyne, 2012).
150. BStU, MfS, AOP, file 15087/84, vol. 3, fol. 119.
151. BStU, MfS, AOP, file 15087/84, vol. 4, fol. 8.
152. BStU, MfS, AIM, file 7781/83, vol. II/3, fol. 164.
153. BStU, MfS, AOP, file 15087/84, vol. 4, fol. 9.
154. BStU, MfS, AOP, file 15087/84, vol. 4, fol. 10.
155. BStU, MfS, AOP, file 15087/84, vol. 4, fol. 10.
156. See the account by Schädlich's daughter in Susanne Schädlich, *Immer wieder Dezember*, 13–15.
157. The others were Bettina Hindemith, Ingo Haas, and Jutta Bartus. BStU, MfS, AOP, file 15087/84, vol. 4, fol. 14.

5. SIMULATION AND SECRET POLICING

1. Jens Gieseke, *The History of the Stasi: East Germany's Secret Police 1945–1990* (New York: Berghahn, 2014), 99.
2. Joachim Walther, *Sicherungsbereich Literatur: Schriftsteller und Staatssicherheit in der Deutschen Demokratischen Republik* (Berlin: Ch. Links, 1996), 188.
3. Walther, *Sicherungsbereich Literatur*, 189.
4. Walther, *Sicherungsbereich Literatur*, 186.
5. See Klaus Michael, "Unabhängige Literatur in der DDR," *Bundeszentrale für politische Bildung*, September 6, 2012, http://www.bpb.de/geschichte/deutsche-geschichte/autonome-kunst-in-der-ddr/55789/unabhaengige-literatur-in-der-ddr.
6. See Birgit Dahlke, "Underground Literature? The Unofficial Culture of the GDR and Its Development after the *Wende*," in *Rereading East Germany: The Literature and Film of the GDR*, ed. Karen Leeder (Cambridge: Cambridge University Press, 2016), 161f.
7. These included Franz Fühmann, Rainer Kirsch, Heiner Müller, Volker Braun, and Elke Erb. See Dahlke, "Underground Literature?," 166. Gerhard Wolf was another such mentor; he sought to give new writers a voice in the GDR. See Gerrit-Jan Berendse, *Grenz-Fallstudien: Essays zum Topos Prenzlauer Berg in der DDR-Literatur* (Berlin: Erich Schmidt, 1999), 36.
8. See Matthias Peter, *Die Bundesrepublik im KSZE-Prozess 1975–1983: Die Umkehrung der Diplomatie* (Berlin: De Gruyter Oldenbourg, 2015), 11–12; also Matthias Peter and Hermann Wentker, "'Helsinki-Mythos' oder 'Helsinki-Effekt'? Der

KSZE-Prozess zwischen internationaler Politik und gesellschaftlicher Transformation. Zur Einleitung," in *Die KSZE im Ost-West-Konflikt: Internationale Politik und gesellschaftliche Transformation 1975-1990*, ed. Matthias Peter and Hermann Wentker (Berlin: De Gruyter Oldenbourg, 2012), 4.

9. See Anja Mihr, "Amnesty International, die Menschenrechte und der KSZE-Prozess: Der Fall der DDR," in Peter and Wentker, *Die KSZE im Ost-West-Konflikt*, 234; and Walther, *Sicherungsbereich Literatur*, 83.
10. Peter, *Die Bundesrepublik im KSZE-Prozess*, 6.
11. Mihr, "Amnesty International," 238.
12. Quoted in Walther, *Sicherungsbereich Literatur*, 101.
13. Walther, *Sicherungsbereich Literatur*, 83.
14. Craig Hayden, *The Rhetoric of Soft Power: Public Diplomacy in Global Contexts* (Lanham MD: Lexington, 2012), 39.
15. Helmut Müller-Enbergs, ed., *Inoffizielle Mitarbeiter des Ministeriums für Staatssicherheit, Teil 1: Richtlinien und Durchführungsbestimmungen* (Berlin: Ch. Links, 1996), 51.
16. Müller-Enbergs, *Inoffizielle Mitarbeiter, Teil 1*, 53.
17. Müller-Enbergs, *Inoffizielle Mitarbeiter, Teil 1*, 53.
18. Müller-Enbergs, *Inoffizielle Mitarbeiter, Teil 1*, 57.
19. Müller-Enbergs, *Inoffizielle Mitarbeiter, Teil 1*, 103.
20. Müller-Enbergs, *Inoffizielle Mitarbeiter, Teil 1*, 58f.
21. Müller-Enbergs, *Inoffizielle Mitarbeiter, Teil 1*, 104.
22. Walther, *Sicherungsbereich Literatur*, 638.
23. Walther, *Sicherungsbereich Literatur*, 638.
24. Walther, *Sicherungsbereich Literatur*, 638.
25. Walther, *Sicherungsbereich Literatur*, 638.
26. Walther, *Sicherungsbereich Literatur*, 638.
27. Walther, *Sicherungsbereich Literatur*, 639.
28. Walther, *Sicherungsbereich Literatur*, 639.
29. Rainer Schedlinski was a much more simulated member of the underground than Anderson and needed encouragement to publish in the West, for example. See chapter 3 in Alison Lewis, *Die Kunst des Verrats: Der Prenzlauer Berg und die Staatssicherheit* (Würzburg, Germany: Königshausen & Neumann, 2003), 71-88, 123ff.
30. Matthias Braun, *Kulturinsel und Machtinstrument: Die Akademie der Künste, die Partei und die Staatssicherheit* (Göttingen, Germany: Vandenhoeck & Ruprecht, 2007), 12.
31. Stephen Parker and Matthew Philpotts, *"Sinn und Form": The Anatomy of a Literary Journal* (Berlin: De Gruyter, 2009), 188.
32. Jean Baudrillard, *Simulacra and Simulation*, trans. Sheila Faria Glaser (Ann Arbor: University of Michigan Press, 1994), 2.

33. Frank Schirrmacher, "Verdacht und Verrat: Die Stasi-Vergangenheit verändert die literarische Szene," *Frankfurter Allgemeine Zeitung*, November 5, 1991; and Frank Schirrmacher, "Ein grausames Spiel," *Frankfurter Allgemeine Zeitung*, October 25, 1991.
34. Wolf Biermann, "Laß, o Welt, o laß mich sein! Rede zum Eduard-Mörike-Preis," *Die Zeit*, November 15, 1991.
35. See Walter Pape, *1870/1871-1989/1990: German Unifications and the Change of Literary Discourse* (Berlin: De Gruyter, 1993), 279.
36. Over 2,500 metal workers in Weimar had joined in the national protests, among other demands calling for lower quotas and the resignation of the regime. The ringleaders of the demonstration were arrested and sentenced, and one was shot during the skirmishes in nearby Jena. In Berlin, Soviet tanks rolled down the main streets of the divided city and crushed the uprising almost as quickly as it had sprung into life.
37. Dorothee Wierling, "Wie (er)findet man eine Generation? Das Beispiel des Geburtsjahrganges 1949 in der DDR," in *Generationalität und Lebensgeschichte im 20. Jahrhundert*, ed. Jürgen Reulecke and Elisabeth Müller-Luckner (Berlin: De Gruyter Oldenbourg, 2003), 225.
38. Mary Fulbrook, *Dissonant Lives: Generations and Violence through the German Dictatorships* (Oxford: Oxford University Press, 2011), 255.
39. Sascha Anderson, *Sascha Anderson* (Köln, Germany: DuMont, 2002), 13.
40. Sascha Anderson, *Jeder Satellit hat einen Killersatelliten* (Berlin: Rotbuch, 1982), 15.
41. Anderson, *Sascha Anderson*, 13.
42. BStU, MfS, HA XX/9, file 1119, fol. 101.
43. BStU, MfS, HA XX/9, file 1119, fol. 231.
44. See Walther, *Sicherungsbereich Literatur*, 639.
45. Anderson, *Sascha Anderson*, 108.
46. Anderson, *Sascha Anderson*, 113.
47. Anderson, *Sascha Anderson*, 118.
48. Anderson, *Sascha Anderson*, 79.
49. Anderson, *Sascha Anderson*, 78.
50. BStU, MfS, HA XX/9, file 1119, fol. 176.
51. Anderson, *Sascha Anderson*, 124.
52. BStU, MfS, HA XX/9, file 1119, fol. 176.
53. BStU, MfS, HA XX/9, file 1119, fol. 178.
54. BStU, MfS, HA XX/9, file 1119, fol. 180.
55. BStU, MfS, HA XX/9, file 1119, fol. 181.
56. BStU, MfS, ZA, AIM, file 7423/91, 11th addendum, fol. 3.
57. BStU, MfS, ZA, AIM, file 7423/91, 1st addendum, fol. 2.
58. BStU, MfS, ZA, AIM, file 7423/91, 1st addendum, fols. 2-3.

59. See BStU, MfS, ZA, AIM, file 7423/91, 1st addendum, fol. 6.
60. See BStU, MfS, ZA, AIM, file 7423/91, 1st addendum, fol. 33; and Anderson, *Sascha Anderson*, 135.
61. See BStU, MfS, ZA, AIM, file 7423/91, 1st addendum, fol. 50.
62. BStU, MfS, ZA, AIM, file 7423/91, 1st addendum, fol. 52.
63. See BStU, MfS, ZA, AIM, file 7423/91, 1st addendum, fol. 47.
64. For an analysis of the difference between file and memory, see Alison Lewis, "Zu einer Topologie des Bösen: Die Kollaboration mit der Stasi und das postkommunistische Sündenregister von Lüge und Verrat, " in *Die Sieben Todsünden: Festschrift für Günter Blamberger*, ed. Martin Roussel (München, Germany: Wilhelm Fink, 2015), 151-77.
65. See Walther, *Sicherungsbereich Literatur*, 483-84.
66. See BStU, MfS, ZA, AIM, file 7423/91, 1st addendum, fol. 53.
67. BStU, MfS, ZA, AIM, file 7423/91, 1st addendum, fol. 53.
68. BStU, MfS, ZA, AIM, file 7423/91, 1st addendum, fol. 54.
69. BStU, MfS, ZA, AIM, file 7423/91, 1st addendum, fol. 59.
70. BStU, MfS, ZA, AIM, file 7423/91, 1st addendum, fol. 61.
71. BStU, MfS, ZA, AIM, file 7423/91, 1st addendum, fol. 62.
72. BStU, MfS, ZA, AIM, file 7423/91, 1st addendum, fol. 63.
73. Walther, *Sicherungsbereich Literatur*, 640.
74. Walther, *Sicherungsbereich Literatur*, 640.
75. BStU, MfS, ZA, AIM, file 7423/91, 1st addendum, fol. 64.
76. Anderson, *Sascha Anderson*, 174.
77. Anderson, *Sascha Anderson*, 184.
78. Anderson, *Sascha Anderson*, 186.
79. BStU, MfS, ZA, AIM, file 7423/91, 1st addendum, fol. 67.
80. BStU, MfS, ZA, AIM, file 7423/91, 1st addendum, fol. 68.
81. See BStU, MfS, ZA, AIM, file 7423/91, 1st addendum, fol. 69.
82. BStU, MfS, ZA, AIM, file 7423/91, 1st addendum, fol. 70.
83. BStU, MfS, ZA, AIM, file 7423/91, 1st addendum, fol. 70.
84. BStU, MfS, ZA, AIM, file 7423/91, 1st addendum, fol. 70.
85. Annegret von Wietersheim, *"Aber—ist mein liebster laut": Ambivalenzen in Biographie und lyrischem Werk von Paul Wiens* (Heidelberg, Germany: Universitätsverlag Winter, 2014), 83.
86. The poem was also printed with small alterations in his first volume of poetry: Anderson, *Jeder Satellit hat einen Killersatelliten*, 63.
87. Wiens was notorious for solving crossword puzzles during meetings. See a communication from Rainer Kirsch to Annegret von Wietersheim in Wietersheim, *"Aber—ist mein liebster laut,"* 110.
88. Anderson, *Jeder Satellit hat einen Killersatelliten*, 49.

89. Karen J. Leeder, *Breaking Boundaries: A New Generation of Poets in the GDR* (Oxford: Clarendon, 1996), 76.
90. Gérard Genette, *Narrative Discourse: An Essay in Method*, trans. Jane E. Lewin (Ithaca NY: Cornell University Press 1980), 114.
91. Wietersheim comes to this conclusion, and to help explain Wiens's loyalty as an informant she includes Wiens's problematic childhood and the loss of his mother. Wietersheim, *"Aber—ist mein liebster laut,"* 93. See also Ingrid Kerz-Rühling and Tomas Plänkers, *Verräter oder Verführte: Eine psychoanalytische Untersuchung Inoffizieller Mitarbeiter der Stasi* (Berlin: Ch. Links, 2004), 139.
92. See, for instance, BStU, MfS, AIM, file 7781/83, vol. II/5, fol. 301.
93. BStU, MfS, AIM, file 7781/83, vol. II/5, fol. 347.
94. BStU, MfS, AIM, file 7781/83, vol. II/5, fol. 348.
95. See the reference to flowers in the meeting report. BStU, MfS, AIM, file 7781/83, vol. II/5, fol. 348.
96. See BStU, MfS, AIM, file 7781/83, vol. II/5, fol. 354.
97. Walther, *Sicherungsbereich Literatur*, 253-54.
98. Walther, *Sicherungsbereich Literatur*, 259-60.
99. BStU, MfS, BVfS Berlin, AOP, file 1224/91, vol. 3, fol. 176.
100. BStU, MfS, BVfS Berlin, AOP, file 1224/91, vol. 1, fol. 377.
101. BStU, MfS, BVfS Berlin, AOP, file 1224/91 vol. 1, fol. 376.
102. BStU, MfS, BVfS Berlin, AOP, file 1224/91, vol. 1, fol. 136.
103. BStU, MfS, BVfS Berlin, AOP, file 1224/91, vol. 1, fol. 137.
104. Joachim Walter, "Der fünfte Zensor: Das MfS als die letzte Instanz," in *Zensur im modernen deutschen Kulturraum*, ed. Beate Müller (Tübingen, Germany: Niemeyer, 2003), 131-48.
105. BStU, MfS, BVfS Berlin, AOP, file 1224/91, vol. 1, fol. 138.
106. BStU, MfS, BVfS Berlin, AOP, file 1224/91, vol. 1, fol. 138.
107. BStU, MfS, BVfS Berlin, AOP, file 1224/91, vol. 1, fol. 138.
108. BStU, MfS, BVfS Berlin, AOP, file 1224/91, vol. 1, fols. 141-42.
109. BStU, MfS, BVfS Berlin, AOP, file 1224/91, vol. 1, fol. 142.
110. BStU, MfS, BVfS Berlin, AOP, file 1224/91, vol. 1, fol. 145.
111. BStU, MfS, BVfS Berlin, AOP, file 1224/91, vol. 1, fol. 152.
112. BStU, MfS, BVfS Berlin, AOP, file 1224/91, vol. 1, fol. 152.
113. BStU, MfS, BVfS Berlin, AOP, file 1224/91, vol. 1, fol. 168.
114. BStU, MfS, BVfS Berlin, AOP, file 1224/91, vol. 1, fol. 168.
115. BStU, MfS, BVfS Berlin, AOP, file 1224/91, vol. 1, fol. 170.
116. BStU, MfS, BVfS Berlin, AOP, file 1224/91, vol. 1, fol. 170.
117. BStU, MfS, BVfS Berlin, AOP, file 1224/91, vol. 1, fol. 171.
118. BStU, MfS, BVfS Berlin, AOP, file 1224/91, vol. 1, fol. 171.
119. BStU, MfS, BVfS Berlin, AOP, file 1224/91, vol. 1, fol. 172.

120. BStU, MfS, BVfS Berlin, AOP, file 1224/91, vol. 1, fol. 172.
121. BStU, MfS, BVfS Berlin, AOP, file 1224/91, vol. 1, fol. 173.
122. BStU, MfS, BVfS Berlin, AOP, file 1224/91, vol. 1, fol. 174.
123. BStU, MfS, BVfS Berlin, AOP, file 1224/91, vol. 1, fol. 174.
124. Walther mentions another, similar case in connection with Wiens, namely that of Gabriele Eckart, who also succeeded in breaking off her ties to the Stasi. Walther, *Sicherungsbereich Literatur*, 707–15.
125. BStU, MfS, BVfS Berlin, AOP, file 1224/91, vol. 1, fol. 164.
126. BStU, MfS, BVfS Berlin, AOP, file 1224/91, vol. 1, fol. 165.
127. BStU, MfS, BVfS Berlin, AOP, file 1224/91, vol. 1, fol. 166.
128. BStU, MfS, BVfS Berlin, AOP, file 1224/91, vol. 1, fol. 165.
129. BStU, MfS, BV Berlin, Abt. XX, file 4314, vol. 2/2, fol. 274.
130. BStU, MfS, BV Berlin, Abt. XX, file 4314, vol. 2/2, fol. 274.
131. BStU, MfS, ANS, AOPK, file 16402/89, fol. 45.
132. BStU, MfS, ANS, AOPK, file 16402/89, fol. 45.
133. BStU, MfS, ANS, AOPK, file 16402/89, fol. 46.
134. Gratzik complained in 1976 that his application to join the guild had been rejected. BStU, MfS, ANS, AOPK, file 16402/89, fol. 23.
135. Anderson, *Sascha Anderson*, 191.
136. See Michael, "Unabhängige Literatur in der DDR."
137. See Petra Boden, "Strukturen der Lenkung von Literatur," in *MachtSpiele: Literatur und Staatssicherheit im Fokus Prenzlauer Berg*, ed. Peter Böthig and Klaus Michael (Leipzig, Germany: Reclam, 1993), 220.
138. Sascha Anderson and Elke Erb, ed. *Berührung ist nur eine Randerscheinung: Neue Literatur aus der DDR* (Köln, Germany: Kiepenheuer & Witsch, 1985).
139. BStU, MfS, HA XX/AKG, file 1493, fol. 20.
140. BStU, MfS, HA XX/AKG, file 1493, fol. 20.
141. BStU, MfS, HA XX/AKG, file 1493, fol. 20.
142. BStU, MfS, HA XX/AKG, file 1493, fol. 23.
143. Anderson, *Sascha Anderson*, 79.
144. Anderson, *Sascha Anderson*, 175.
145. BStU, MfS, ZA, AIM, file 7423/91, 1st addendum, fol. 87; and BStU, MfS, ZA, AIM, file 7423/91, 4th addendum, fol. 51.
146. BStU, MfS, ZA, AIM, file 7423/91, 1st addendum, fol. 129.
147. BStU, MfS, ZA, AIM, file 7423/91, 1st addendum, fol. 129.
148. BStU, MfS, ZA, AIM, file 7423/91, 1st addendum, fol. 87.
149. One exception is the characterization of Gabi Kachold, who appears in his reports as "very ambitious." See BStU, MfS, ZA, AIM, file 7423/91, 4th addendum, fol. 95.
150. See Jan Faktor, "Zehn Punkte zur Prenzlauer Berg-Szene," in Böthig and Michael, *MachtSpiele*, 100.

151. Wilfriede Maaß, "Ich habe immer nur gearbeitet," in *Durchgangszimmer Prenzlauer Berg: Eine Berliner Künstlersozialgeschichte der 1970er und 1980er Jahre in Selbstauskünften*, ed. Barbara Felsman and Annett Gröschner (Berlin: Lukas, 1999), 218.
152. Christoph Tannert, "Man brennt wofür man glüht: Die Keramikwerkstaat von Wilfriede Maaß," in *brennzeiten: Die Keramikwerkstaat Wilfriede Maaß: 1980-1989-1998*, ed. Ingeborg Quaas and Henryk Gericke (Berlin: Lukas, 2014), 48.
153. Anderson, *Sascha Anderson*, 205.
154. See "Quelle: IMB 'David Menzer,'" in Böthig and Michael, *MachtSpiele*, 263.
155. Anderson, *Sascha Anderson*, 205.
156. See Klaus Michael, "Eine verschollene Anthologie," in Böthig and Michael, *MachtSpiele*, 203.
157. Anderson, *Sascha Anderson*, 202.
158. Carol Anne Costabile-Heming, "Surveillance and the GDR's Cultural Sphere: Franz Fühmann, the State, and the Stasi," *German Life & Letters* 73, no. 3 (July 2019): 347.
159. Michael, "Eine verschollene Anthologie," 204.
160. Anderson, *Sascha Anderson*, 213; and BStU, MfS, HA XX/9, file 601, fols. 84-85.
161. Michael, "Eine verschollene Anthologie," 208.
162. Michael, "Eine verschollene Anthologie," 212.
163. Anderson, *Sascha Anderson*, 205.
164. Anderson, *Sascha Anderson*, 206.
165. BStU, MfS, ZA, AIM, file 7423/91, 5th addendum, fol. 101.
166. Walther, *Sicherungsbereich Literatur*, 289.
167. He calls Jochen Berg "quiet" ("Quelle: IMB 'David Menzer,'" 253), Stefan Döring and Thomas Günther "quiet" ("Quelle: IMB 'David Menzer,'" 254), Detlef Opitz "quiet" ("Quelle: IMB 'David Menzer,'" 257), Thomas Günther "constructive" ("Quelle: IMB 'David Menzer,'" 254), and Uwe Kolbe "active and objective" ("Quelle: IMB 'David Menzer,'" 256).
168. Anderson, *Sascha Anderson*, 226.
169. "Quelle: IMB 'David Menzer,'" 255.
170. "Quelle: IMB 'David Menzer,'" 255.
171. "Quelle: IMB 'David Menzer,'" 261.
172. "Quelle: IMB 'David Menzer,'" 261.
173. "Quelle: IMB 'David Menzer,'" 261.
174. Michael, "Eine verschollene Anthologie," 214. Also see Anderson's argument that most should be allowed into the Writers' Guild in "Quelle: IMB 'David Menzer,'" 272.
175. See Lewis, *Die Kunst des Verrats*, 188; and Anderson's suggestion in 1984 to integrate writers in BStU, MfS, ZA, AIM, file 7423/91, 9th addendum, fol. 99.

176. BStU, MfS, ZA, AIM, file 7423/91, 4th addendum, fol. 54.
177. See Klaus Michael's use of the term for Anderson in Klaus Michael, "Samisdat-Literatur in der DDR und der Einfluß der Staatssicherheit," *Deutschland-Archiv* 26, no. 11 (1993): 1259.
178. BStU, MfS, ZA, AIM, file 7423/91, 4th addendum, fol. 59.
179. Anderson, *Jeder Satellit hat einen Killersatelliten*, 32–33.
180. Leeder, *Breaking Boundaries*, 234.
181. Leeder, *Breaking Boundaries*, 235.
182. Leeder, *Breaking Boundaries*, 49.
183. See "Stefan Döring: heutmorgestern," in *planet lyrik*, March 12, 2010, http://www.planetlyrik.de/stefan-doring-heutmorgestern/2010/03/.
184. "Aber ich bin—außer in der Literatur—nie einem Menschen so nahe gekommen, daß ich ihn hätte denken hören." Anderson, *Sascha Anderson*, 254.
185. Anderson also seems to have rationalized his Stasi connections by not writing incriminating reports about his closest friends, or by writing none at all in the case of Bert Papenfuß, and reporting more extensively on colleagues whom he disliked, such as Lutz Rathenow. See Lewis, *Die Kunst des Verrats*, chaps. 7–8.
186. See Klaus Michael's account of how, on behalf of the Stasi, in 1984 Anderson stifled the initiative to form an independent association of writers and artists. Michael, "Unabhängige Literatur in der DDR."
187. See Lewis, *Die Kunst des Verrats*, chap. 8.
188. See Berendse, *Grenz-Fallstudien*, 59–60. According to Klaus Michael there were around three informants who were active in the underground; Anderson, Rainer Schedlinski, and Sören Naumann, who was IM "Michael Müller." The latter was responsible for organizing exhibitions and readings in Dresden in the Förstereistrasse 2, where meetings of the producers of the journal *Und* took place. See Michael, "Unabhängige Literatur in der DDR."
189. This was more pronounced in regions other than in the capital city. See Matthias Braun, "Dramaturgie der Repression—Der ZOV 'Bühne,'" in *Bühne der Dissidenz und Dramaturgie der Repression: Ein Kulturkonflikt in der späten DDR*, ed. Lutz Niethammer and Roger Engelmann (Göttingen, Germany: Vandenhoeck & Ruprecht, 2014), 124–25.
190. See Braun, "Dramaturgie der Repression," 190.

6. THE CULTURE WARS

1. Joachim Walther, *Sicherungsbereich Literatur: Schriftsteller und Staatssicherheit in der Deutschen Demokratischen Republik* (Berlin: Ch. Links, 1996), 179.
2. Walther, *Sicherungsbereich Literatur*, 189.
3. See Friedericke Kind-Kovács and Jessie Labov, "Introduction," in *Samizdat, Tamizdat, and Beyond: Transnational Media during and after Socialism*, ed. Friedericke

Kind-Kovács and Jessie Labov (New York: Berghahn, 2013), 3-4. According to the editors of this collection, *samizdat* refers to texts that have not been endorsed by official organs of the state, ranging from "clandestine underground operations" to "independent publishing." The lesser known term *tamizdat* refers to texts published abroad, either as reprinted samizdat texts or appearing for the first time in the West.

4. The concept aboveground is used in a recent study of samizdat and tamizdat with the intention of blurring the boundaries between official and nonofficial cultures. In reality such boundaries were rather more complex than commonly thought. See Kind-Kovács and Labov, "Introduction," 5.
5. Gary Bruce, *The Firm: The Inside Story of the Stasi* (Oxford: Oxford University Press, 2010), 67-68.
6. Kevin D. Haggerty, "Tearing Down the Walls: On Demolishing the Panopticon," in *Theorizing Surveillance: The Panopticon and Beyond*, ed. David Lyon (Abingdon, UK: Routledge, 2006), 28.
7. David Lyon, "The Search for Surveillance Theories," in Lyon, *Theorizing Surveillance*, 8.
8. See Walther, *Sicherungsbereich Literatur*, 673.
9. BStU, MfS, BVfS Berlin, AOP, file 1224/91, vol. 9, fol. 1.
10. BStU, MfS, BVfS Berlin, AOP, file 1224/91, vol. 9, fol. 1.
11. BStU, MfS, BVfS Berlin, AOP, file 1224/91, vol. 9, fol. 1.
12. BStU, MfS, BVfS Berlin, AOP, file 1224/91, vol. 9, fols. 1-3.
13. BStU, MfS, BVfS Berlin, AOP, file 1224/91, vol. 2, fol. 167.
14. BStU, MfS, BVfS Berlin, AOP, file 1224/91, vol. 2, fol. 166.
15. BStU, MfS, BVfS Berlin, AOP, file 1224/91, vol. 2, fol. 175.
16. BStU, MfS, BVfS Berlin, AOP, file 1224/91, vol. 2, fol. 198.
17. BStU, MfS, BVfS Berlin, AOP, file 1224/91, vol. 2, fol. 206.
18. BStU, MfS, BVfS Berlin, AOP, file 1224/91, vol. 2, fol. 235.
19. BStU, MfS, BVfS Berlin, AOP, file 1224/91, vol. 2, fol. 236.
20. BStU, MfS, BVfS Berlin, AOP, file 1224/91, vol. 2, fol. 240.
21. BStU, MfS, BVfS Berlin, AOP, file 1224/91, vol. 2, fol. 241.
22. BStU, MfS, BVfS Berlin, AOP, file 1224/91, vol. 2, fol. 254.
23. BStU, MfS, BVfS Berlin, AOP, file 1224/91, vol. 9, fol. 5.
24. BStU, MfS, BVfS Berlin, AOP, file 1224/91, vol. 9, fol. 6.
25. BStU, MfS, BVfS Berlin, AOP, file 1224/91, vol. 9, fol. 3.
26. BStU, MfS, BVfS Berlin, AOP, file 1224/91, vol. 2, fol. 263.
27. Walther, *Sicherungsbereich Literatur*, 680-81.
28. Walther, *Sicherungsbereich Literatur*, 680.
29. Walther, *Sicherungsbereich Literatur*, 680.
30. BStU, MfS, BVfS Berlin, AOP, file 1224/91, vol. 2, fol. 278.

31. BStU, MfS, BVfS Berlin, AOP, file 1224/91, vol. 4, fol. 252.
32. BStU, MfS, BV Berlin, Abt. XX, file 4314, vol. 2/2, fol. 43.
33. BStU, MfS, BV Berlin, Abt. XX, file 4314, vol. 2/2, fol. 44.
34. BStU, MfS, BV Berlin, Abt. XX, file 4314, vol. 2/2, fol. 44.
35. BStU, MfS, ZA, AIM, file 7423/91, 10th addendum, fol. 118.
36. BStU, MfS, ZA, AIM, file 7423/91, 10th addendum, fol. 118.
37. The main agent trailing Gratzik at this time was Horst Simon, IME "Schönberg." Walther, *Sicherungsbereich Literatur*, 295.
38. BStU, MfS, ZA, AIM, file 7423/91, 10th addendum, fol. 119.
39. BStU, MfS, ZA, AIM, file 7423/91, 10th addendum, fol. 119.
40. BStU, MfS, ZA, AIM, file 7423/91, 10th addendum, fol. 119.
41. BStU, MfS, ZA, AIM, file 7423/91, 4th addendum, fol. 105.
42. BStU, MfS, ZA, AIM, file 7423/91, 2nd addendum, fol. 52.
43. Anderson, *Sascha Anderson*, 197.
44. See Jan Faktor, "Zehn Punkte zur Prenzlauer Berg-Szene," in *MachtSpiele: Literatur und Staatssicherheit im Fokus Prenzlauer Berg*, ed. Peter Böthig and Klaus Michael (Leipzig, Germany: Reclam, 1993), 95.
45. See Karen J. Leeder, *Breaking Boundaries: A New Generation of Poets in the GDR* (Oxford: Clarendon, 1996), 81.
46. Anderson and his friends devoured the works of postmodern theorists, such as Michel Foucault, as Anderson testified in an interview. See Paul Cooke, *Speaking the Taboo: A Study of the Work of Wolfgang Hilbig* (Amsterdam: Rodopi, 2000), 40. See also Robert von Hallberg, "Introduction," in *Literary Intellectuals and the Dissolution of the State: Professionalism and Conformity in the GDR*, ed. Robert von Hallberg (Chicago: University of Chicago Press, 1996), 32; and David Bathrick, *The Powers of Speech: The Politics of Culture in the GDR* (Lincoln: University of Nebraska Press, 1995), 239-40.
47. Bathrick, *The Powers of Speech*, 239.
48. Anderson, *Sascha Anderson*, 192.
49. Anderson, *Sascha Anderson*, 294.
50. BStU, MfS, ZA, AIM, file 7423/91, 4th addendum, fols. 109-10; and Anderson, *Sascha Anderson*, 224.
51. See Anderson's report from November 19, 1982, on Schleime and her resolve to "try everything" to leave "all within the law." BStU, MfS, HA XX/9, file 644, fol. 260.
52. BStU, MfS, HA XX/9, file 644, fol. 260.
53. Herlinde Koelbl, "Ich sagte, ich trete in den Hungerstreik," *Zeit Online*, August 25, 2011.
54. Anderson, *Sascha Anderson*, 214.
55. Anderson, *Sascha Anderson*, 221.

56. See BStU, MfS, ZA, AIM, file 7423/91, 4th addendum, fol. 98.
57. Anderson, *Sascha Anderson*, 221.
58. Anderson, *Sascha Anderson*, 226.
59. Anderson, *Sascha Anderson*, 240-41.
60. Anderson, *Sascha Anderson*, 246.
61. Anderson, *Sascha Anderson*, 246.
62. Anderson, *Sascha Anderson*, 203.
63. See BStU, MfS, ZA, AIM, file 7423/91, 9th addendum, fol. 98.
64. See BStU, MfS, ZA, AIM, file 7423/91, 9th addendum, fol. 94.
65. BStU, MfS, ZA, AIM, file 1054/91, vol. II/1, fol. 439.
66. BStU, MfS, ZA, AIM, file 1054/91, vol. II/1, fol. 443.
67. BStU, MfS, HA XX/AKG, file 1424, fol. 101.
68. BStU, MfS, HA XX/AKG, file 1424, fol. 102.
69. BStU, MfS, HA XX/AKG, file 1424, fol. 104.
70. BStU, MfS, HA XX/AKG, file 1424, fol. 105.
71. BStU, MfS, HA XX/AKG, file 1424, fol. 108.
72. BStU, MfS, HA XX/AKG, file 1424, fol. 111.
73. BStU, MfS, HA XX/AKG, file 1424, fol. 119.
74. BStU, MfS, HA XX/AKG, file 1424, fol. 119.
75. BStU, MfS, HA XX/AKG, file 1424, fol. 119.
76. Quoted in Cooke, *Speaking the Taboo*, 219.
77. BStU, MfS, HA XX/AKG, file 1424, fol. 183.
78. Faktor, "Zehn Punkte zur Prenzlauer Berg-Szene," 96, 106.
79. For example, in February 1983 the Poppes received a fine of 200 marks for breaching regulations about public events, no doubt partly because Anderson reported on the monthly readings at their home. See BStU, MfS, ZA, AIM, file 7423/91, 7th addendum, fol. 44.
80. An instance of his reports making an arrest more likely was his reporting on Katja Havemann's video camera. See BStU, MfS, ZA, AIM, file 7423/91, 8th addendum, fol. 89. An example of his reports jeopardizing the safety of his associates relates to Rüdiger Rosenthal, who was arrested and beaten because of a petition against the militarization of the GDR. See "Der Verräter seiner Freunde," *Der Spiegel*, December 9, 1991.
81. "Untergrund in Aspik," BStU, MfS, ZA, AIM, file 1054/91, vol. II/3, fol. 139.
82. Heiner Sylvester, "Kuchenkrümel Kommunismus," *Der Spiegel*, September 23, 1985, 236.
83. Sylvester, "Kuchenkrümel Kommunismus," 236.
84. BStU, MfS, ZA, AIM, file 7423/91, 11th addendum, fol. 3.
85. BStU, MfS, ZA, AIM, file 7423/91, 11th addendum, fol. 3.
86. BStU, MfS, ZA, AIM, file 7423/91, 11th addendum, fol. 3.

87. Anderson, *Sascha Anderson*, 281.
88. BStU, MfS, HA XX/9, file 1119, fol. 176.
89. BStU, MfS, ANS, AOPK, file 16402/89, fol. 1.
90. BStU, MfS, ANS, AOPK, file 16402/89, fol. 1.
91. BStU, MfS, ANS, AOPK, file 16402/89, fol. 1.
92. Wiens's informant dossier was included at the start of her victim dossier, and thus constitutes the first four volumes of her entire Stasi dossier, which is now archived as BStU, MfS, BVfS Berlin, AOP, file 1224/91. See Walther, *Sicherungsbereich Literatur*, 686.
93. BStU, MfS, BVfS Berlin, AOP, file 1224/91, vol. 8, fol. 26.
94. BStU, MfS, BVfS Berlin, AOP, file 1224/91, vol. 8, fol. 32.
95. BStU, MfS, BVfS Berlin, AOP, file 1224/91, vol. 8, fol. 108.
96. BStU, MfS, BVfS Berlin, AOP, file 1224/91, vol. 8, fol. 123.
97. BStU, MfS, BVfS Berlin, AOP, file 1224/91, vol. 8, fol. 124.
98. BStU, MfS, BVfS Berlin, AOP, file 1224/91, vol. 9, fol. 73.
99. BStU, MfS, BVfS Berlin, AOP, file 1224/91, vol. 8, fol. 125.
100. BStU, MfS, BVfS Berlin, AOP, file 1224/91, vol. 8, fol. 125.
101. BStU, MfS, BVfS Berlin, AOP, file 1224/91, vol. 3, fol. 184.
102. BStU, MfS, BVfS Berlin, AOP, file 1224/91, vol. 1, fol. 172.
103. BStU, MfS, BVfS Berlin, AOP, file 1224/91, vol. 3, fol. 223.
104. BStU, MfS, BVfS Berlin, AOP, file 1224/91, vol. 3, fol. 251.
105. BStU, MfS, BVfS Berlin, AOP, file 1224/91, vol. 4, fol. 10.
106. BStU, MfS, BVfS Berlin, AOP, file 1224/91, vol. 3, fol. 361–62.
107. BStU, MfS, BVfS Berlin, AOP, file 1224/91, vol. 4, fol. 110.
108. Rudolf Kunze, email to Alison Lewis, January 31, 2014.
109. Wiens's first novel was initially rejected for publication within the GDR but was eventually allowed to be published by Neues Leben in 1983 under the title *Traumgrenzen*. This was her last attempt to use a state-run publisher; in the late 1980s she resorted to self-publishing.
110. Helga M. Novak, "Monolog eines Buchhändlers," in Helga M. Novak, *Aufenthalt in einem Irrenhaus: Gesammelte Prosa* (Frankfurt am Main, Germany: Schöffling, 1995), 256. See Izabela Surynt, "Leben als Exil: Zum Schaffen von Helga M. Novak," in *Deutsch-deutsches Literaturexil: Schriftstellerinnen und Schriftsteller aus der DDR in der Bundesrepublik*, ed. Walter Schmitz and Jörg Bernig (Dresden, Germany: Thelem, 2009), 172.
111. Helga M. Novak, *Im Schwanenhals* (Frankfurt am Main, Germany: Schöffling, 2013), 334.
112. Novak, *Im Schwanenhals*, 334.
113. Novak, *Im Schwanenhals*, 334.
114. Novak, *Im Schwanenhals*, 335.

115. Novak, *Im Schwanenhals*, 313.
116. Novak's poetry has been read, however, as performing an "unsparing" critique of socialism in the GDR; the political systems of her various travel destinations have found their way into her work. See Surynt, "Leben als Exil," 174.
117. Novak, *Im Schwanenhals*, 316.
118. Novak, *Im Schwanenhals*, 58.
119. Novak, *Im Schwanenhals*, 58.
120. Novak, *Im Schwanenhals*, 321.
121. Cited in Surynt, "Leben als Exil," 176.
122. Novak, *Im Schwanenhals*, 311.
123. Jürgen Fuchs, "Vorwort," in Helga M. Novak, *Grünheide Grünheide: Gedichte, 1955-1980* (Darmstadt, Germany: Luchterhand, 1983), 6.
124. Fuchs, "Vorwort," 6.
125. Fuchs, "Vorwort," 7.
126. Fuchs, "Vorwort," 7.
127. Novak, *Im Schwanenhals*, 322.
128. Novak, *Im Schwanenhals*, 316.
129. Novak, *Im Schwanenhals*, 331.
130. Novak, *Im Schwanenhals*, 331.
131. Novak, *Im Schwanenhals*, 334.
132. Novak, *Im Schwanenhals*, 328.
133. Novak, *Im Schwanenhals*, 326.
134. Novak, *Im Schwanenhals*, 324-25.
135. Novak, *Im Schwanenhals*, 328.
136. Novak, *Im Schwanenhals*, 328.
137. Novak, *Im Schwanenhals*, 342.
138. Novak, *Im Schwanenhals*, 329.
139. Novak, *Im Schwanenhals*, 328.
140. Uwe Spiekermann, "The Stasi and the HV A: Contemporary Research and Contemporary Resonance," *GHI Bulletin Supplement* 9 (2014): 15.
141. Spiekermann, "The Stasi and the HV A," 16.
142. Spiekermann, "The Stasi and the HV A," 16.

CONCLUSION

1. David Lyon, "The Search for Surveillance Theories," in *Theorizing Surveillance: The Panopticon and Beyond*, ed. David Lyon (Abingdon, UK: Routledge, 2011), 8.
2. See Helmut Müller-Enbergs, ed., *Inoffizielle Mitarbeiter des Ministeriums für Staatssicherheit, Teil 1: Richtlinien und Durchführungsbestimmungen* (Berlin: Ch. Links, 1996), 49.
3. Lyon, "The Search for Surveillance Theories," 8.

4. Jefferson Adams, *Historical Dictionary of German Intelligence* (Lanham MD: Scarecrow, 2009), 100.
5. Barbara Miller, *The Stasi Files Unveiled: Guilt and Compliance in a Unified Germany* (New Brunswick NJ: Transaction, 2004), 102.
6. Miller, *The Stasi Files Unveiled*, 62.
7. See Jens Gieseke, *The History of the Stasi: East Germany's Secret Police 1945–1990* (New York: Berghahn, 2014), 114.
8. See Gieseke, *The History of the Stasi*, 114.
9. Miller, *The Stasi Files Unveiled*, 46.
10. Those writers include Stefan Döring, Rainer Schedlinski, Jan Faktor, Andreas Koziol, Reinhard Jirgl, Gabriele Kachold, Bert Papenfuß-Gorek, and Peter Brasch.
11. Lutz Niethammer, "Einleitung," in *Bühne der Dissidenz und Dramaturgie der Repression: Ein Kulturkonflikt in der späten DDR*, ed. Lutz Niethammer and Roger Engelmann (Göttingen, Germany: Vandenhoeck & Ruprecht, 2014), 52.
12. Niethammer, "Einleitung," 51.
13. See Adams, *Historical Dictionary of German Intelligence*, 100.
14. Niethammer, "Einleitung," 51.

SELECTED BIBLIOGRAPHY

Archives

BStU. Der Bundesbeauftragte für die Unterlagen des Staatssicherheitsdienstes der ehemaligen Deutschen Demokratischen Republik (The Federal Commissioner for the Records of the State Security Service of the former German Democratic Republic). Berlin, Germany.
> MfS, AIM, file 771/68, 2 vols.
> MfS, AIM, file 1054/91, 5 vols.
> MfS, AIM, file 7781/83, 6 vols.
> MfS, AIM, file 9457/86, 6 vols.
> MfS, ANS, AOPK, file 16402/89, 1 vol.
> MfS, AOP, file 15087/84, 4 vols.
> MfS, AP, file 13823/92, 1 vol.
> MfS, BV Dresden, AIM, file 2736/81, 6 vols.
> MfS, BVfS Berlin, AOP, file 1224/91, 10 vols.
> MfS, file A 131/76, 6 vols.
> MfS, file 916/61, 1 vol.
> MfS, HA XX/AKG, file 1493, 1 vol.
> MfS, HA XX/9, file 1119, 1 vol.
> MfS, ZA, AIM, file 7423/91, 11 vols.

Published Works

Adams, Jefferson. *Historical Dictionary of German Intelligence*. Lanham MD: Scarecrow, 2009.
——. "The Stasi and the Party: From Coordination to Alienation." *GHI Bulletin Supplement* 9 (2014): 99–112.

Ahmed, Sara. *Cultural Politics of Emotion*. New York: Routledge, 2004.
Anderson, Benedict. *Imagined Communities: Reflections on the Origins and Spread of Nationalism*. London: Verso, 1991.
Anderson, Sascha. *Jeder Satellit hat einen Killersatelliten*. Berlin: Rotbuch, 1982.
———. *Sascha Anderson*. Köln, Germany: DuMont, 2002.
Anderson, Sascha, and Elke Erb, eds. *Berührung ist nur eine Randerscheinung: Neue Literatur aus der DDR*. Köln, Germany: Kiepenheuer & Witsch, 1985.
Arendt, Hannah. *Eichmann in Jerusalem: A Report on the Banality of Evil*. London: Penguin, 2006.
———. *The Origins of Totalitarianism*. Orlando FL: Harvest, 1968.
Bathrick, David. *The Powers of Speech: The Politics of Culture in the GDR*. Lincoln: University of Nebraska Press, 1995.
Baudrillard, Jean. *Simulacra and Simulation*. Translated by Sheila Faria Glaser. Ann Arbor: University of Michigan Press, 1994.
Berbig, Roland, and Holger Jens Karlson. "'Leute haben sich als Gruppe erwiesen': Zur Gruppenbildung bei Wolf Biermanns Ausbürgerung." In *In Sachen Biermann: Protokolle, Berichte und Briefe zu den Folgen einer Ausbürgerung*, edited by Roland Berbig, Arne Born, Jörg Judersleben, Holger J. Karlson, Dorit Krusche, Christoph Martinkat, and Peter Wruck, 11-28. Berlin: Ch. Links, 1994.
Berendse, Gerrit-Jan. *Grenz-Fallstudien: Essays zum Topos Prenzlauer Berg in der DDR-Literatur*. Berlin: Erich Schmidt, 1999.
Berger, Uwe. "Im Dienst." *Neue Deutsche Literatur* (1982): 27-28.
Biermann, Wolf. "Der Lichtblick im gräßlichen Fatalismus der Geschichte: Büchner-Preis-Rede." In *Der Sturz des Dädalus: Oder, Eizes für die Eingeborenen der Fidschi-Inseln über den IM Judas Ischariot und den Kuddelmuddel in Deutschland seit dem Golfkrieg*, 48-63. Köln, Germany: Kiepenheuer & Witsch, 1992.
———. *Warte nicht auf bessre Zeiten! Die Autobiographie*. Berlin: Propyläen, 2016.
Boden, Petra. "Strukturen der Lenkung von Literatur." In *MachtSpiele: Literatur und Staatssicherheit*, edited by Klaus Michael and Peter Böthig, 217-27. Leipzig, Germany: Reclam, 1993.
Booß, Christian, and Helmut Müller-Enbergs. *Die indiskrete Gesellschaft: Studien zum Denunziationskomplex und zu inoffiziellen Mitarbeitern*. Frankfurt am Main, Germany: Verlag für Polizeiwissenschaft, 2014.
Bourdieu, Pierre. *Distinction: A Social Critique of the Judgment of Taste*. Abingdon, UK: Routledge, 1984.
———. *The Logic of Practice*. Translated by Richard Nice. Stanford CA: Stanford University Press, 1990.
———. *Outline of a Theory of Practice*. Cambridge: Cambridge University Press, 1977.
Braun, Matthias. "Dramaturgie der Repression—Der ZOV 'Bühne.'" In *Bühne der Dissidenz und Dramaturgie der Repression: Ein Kulturkonflikt in der späten DDR*,

edited by Lutz Niethammer and Roger Engelmann, 121-235. Göttingen, Germany: Vandenhoeck & Ruprecht, 2014.

———. "Das Jahr 1959—Erwin Strittmatter und der 'Bitterfelder Weg.'" In *Es geht um Erwin Strittmatter oder Vom Streit um die Erinnerung*, edited by Matthias Braun and Carsten Gansel, 111-32. Göttingen, Germany: V & R unipress, 2012.

———. *Kulturinsel und Machtinstrument: Die Akademie der Künste, die Partei und die Staatssicherheit*. Göttingen, Germany: Vandenhoeck & Ruprecht, 2007.

———. "Staatssicherheit und Literatur." In *DDR-Literatur: Eine Archivexpedition*, edited by Ulrich von Bülow and Sabine Wolf, 53-61. Berlin: Ch. Links, 2014.

Brockmann, Stephen. *Literature and German Reunification*. Cambridge: Cambridge University Press, 1999.

———. *The Writers' State: Constructing East German Literature 1945-1959*. Rochester NY: Camden House, 2015.

Bruce, Gary. *The Firm: The Inside Story of the Stasi*. Oxford: Oxford University Press, 2010.

Buck, Theo. "Verhinderte Innovation: Die in der DDR ungedruckt gebliebenen Bücher von Uwe Johnson und Hans Joachim Schädlich." In *Rückblicke auf die Literatur der DDR*, edited by Hans-Christian Stillmark, 11-44. Amsterdam: Rodopi, 2002.

Capp, Fiona. *Writers Defiled: Security Surveillance of Australian Authors and Intellectuals 1920-1960*. South Yarra, Australia: McPhee Gribble, 1993.

Carver, Charles S., Yael E. Avivi, and Jean-Philippe Laurenceau. "Approach, Avoidance, and Emotional Experiences." In *Handbook of Approach and Avoidance Motivation*, edited by Andrew J. Elliot, 385-97. New York: Psychology Press, 2008.

Chatterjee, Choi, and Karen Petrone. "Models of Selfhood and Subjectivity: The Soviet Case in Historical Perspective." In *Mass Dictatorship and Modernity*, edited by Michael Kim, Michael Schoenhals, and Yong-Woo Kim, 205-29. Basingstoke, UK: Palgrave Macmillan, 2013.

Childs, David. *The GDR: Moscow's German Ally*. Abingdon, UK: Routledge, 2015.

Cooke, Paul. *Speaking the Taboo: A Study of the Work of Wolfgang Hilbig*. Amsterdam: Rodopi, 2000.

Costabile-Heming, Carol Anne. "GDR Literature during the 1970s." In *Beyond 1989: Re-Reading German Literary History since 1945*, edited by Keith Bullivant, 35-48. New York: Berghahn, 1997.

———. "Surveillance and the GDR's Cultural Sphere: Franz Fühmann, the State, and the Stasi." *German Life & Letters* 73, no. 3 (July 2019): 335-56.

Dahlke, Birgit. "Underground Literature? The Unofficial Culture of the GDR and Its Development after the *Wende*." In *Rereading East Germany: The Literature and Film of the GDR*, edited by Karen Leeder, 160-79. Cambridge: Cambridge University Press, 2016.

Dau, Mathilde. ". . . und vergeßt das Gelächter nicht." *Weimarer Beiträge* 25, no. 7 (1979): 93-112.

Del Pero, Mario. "The Role of Covert Operations in US Cold War Foreign Policy." In *Secret Intelligence in the Twentieth Century*, edited by Heike Bungert, Jan G. Heitmann, and Michael Wala, 68-82. London: Frank Cass, 2003.

Dennis, Mike. *The Stasi: Myth and Reality*. London: Routledge, 2003.

Dennis, Mike, and Norman LaPorte. *State and Minorities in Communist East Germany*. New York: Berghahn, 2011.

Deutscher Schriftstellerverband, ed., *V. Deutscher Schriftstellerkongress vom 25. bis 27. Mai 1961*. Berlin: Aufbau, 1962.

Diedrich, Thorsten, and Hans Ehlert. "'Moderne Diktatur'—'Erziehungsdiktatur'—'Fürsorgediktatur' oder was sonst? Das Herrschaftssystem der DDR und der Versuch seiner Definition." *Potsdamer Bulletin für Zeithistorische Studien* 12 (1998): 17-25.

Ellmenreich, Renate. "Frauenbild im Ministerium für Staatssicherheit der DDR—Mein Einblick." *Weibblick* 16 (1994): 14-16.

Engelmann, Roger, Bernd Florath, Helge Heidemeyer, Daniela Münkel, Arno Polzin, and Walter Süß, eds. *Das MfS-Lexikon: Begriffe, Personen und Strukturen der Staatssicherheit der DDR*. Berlin: Ch. Links, 2012.

Faktor, Jan. "Zehn Punkte zur Prenzlauer Berg-Szene." In *MachtSpiele: Literatur und Staatssicherheit im Fokus Prenzlauer Berg*, edited by Peter Böthig and Klaus Michael, 91-111. Leipzig, Germany: Reclam, 1993.

Falck, Uta. *VEB Bordell: Geschichte der Prostitution in der DDR*. Berlin: Ch. Links, 1998.

Feinstein, Joshua. *The Triumph of the Ordinary: Depictions of Daily Life in the East German Cinema 1949-1989*. Chapel Hill: University of North Carolina Press, 2002.

Fink, Carole K. *Cold War: An International History*. Boulder CO: Westview, 2013.

Fitzpatrick, Sheila. *Tear Off the Masks! Identity and Imposture in Twentieth-Century Russia*. Princeton NJ: Princeton University Press, 2005.

Foucault, Michel. *Discipline and Punish: The Birth of the Prison*. Translated by Alan Sheridan. Harmondsworth, UK: Penguin, 1982.

Fulbrook, Mary. *The Anatomy of a Dictatorship: Inside the GDR 1949-1989*. Oxford: Oxford University Press, 1995.

———. "The Concept of 'Normalisation' and the GDR in Comparative Perspective." In *Power and Society in the GDR, 1961-1979: The "Normalization of Rule"?*, edited by Mary Fulbrook, 1-30. New York: Berghahn, 2009.

———. *Dissonant Lives: Generations and Violence through the German Dictatorships*. Oxford: Oxford University Press, 2011.

———. *The People's State: East German Society from Hitler to Honecker*. New Haven CT: Yale University Press, 2005.

Gaber, Rusanna. *Politische Gemeinschaft in Deutschland und Polen: Zum Einfluss der Geschichte auf die politische Kultur*. Wiesbaden, Germany: VS Verlag für Sozialwissenschaften.

Geertz, Clifford. *The Interpretation of Cultures*. New York: Basic Books, 1973.

Gieseke, Jens. *Die hauptamtlichen Mitarbeiter der Staatssicherheit: Personalstruktur und Lebenswelt 1950-1989/90*. Berlin: Ch. Links, 2000.

——. *The History of the Stasi: East Germany's Secret Police 1945-1990*. New York: Berghahn, 2014.

Gilman, Sander L. *Jurek Becker: A Life in Five Worlds*. Chicago: University of Chicago Press, 2003.

Glajar, Valentina. "'You'll Never Make a Spy Out of Me': The File Story of 'Fink Susanne.'" In *Secret Police Files from the Eastern Bloc: Between Surveillance and Life Writing*, edited by Valentina Glajar, Alison Lewis, and Corina L. Petrescu, 56-83. Rochester NY: Camden House, 2016.

Glajar, Valentina, Alison Lewis, and Corina L. Petrescu, eds. *Secret Police Files from the Eastern Bloc: Between Surveillance and Life Writing*. Rochester NY: Camden House, 2016.

Glajar, Valentina, Alison Lewis, and Corina L. Petrescu, eds. *Cold War Spy Stories from Eastern Europe*. Lincoln NE: Potomac, 2019.

Gray, William Glenn. *Germany's Cold War: The Global Campaign to Isolate East Germany 1949-1969*. Chapel Hill: University of North Carolina Press, 2003.

Haggerty, Kevin D. "Tearing Down the Walls: On Demolishing the Panopticon." In *Theorizing Surveillance: The Panopticon and Beyond*, edited by David Lyon, 23-45. London: Routledge, 2006.

Hallberg, Robert von, ed. *Literary Intellectuals and the Dissolution of the State: Professionalism and Conformity in the GDR*. Chicago: University of Chicago Press, 1996.

Hayden, Craig. *The Rhetoric of Soft Power: Public Diplomacy in Global Contexts*. Lanham MD: Lexington, 2012.

Hendel, Annekatrin, dir. *Anderson*. Berlin: IT WORKS!, 2014, DVD.

——. *Vaterlandsverräter*. Berlin: IT WORKS!, 2011, DVD.

Henke, Klaus-Dietmar, and Roger Engelmann, eds. *Aktenlage: Die Bedeutung der Unterlagen des Staatssicherheitsdienstes für die Zeitgeschichtsforschung*. Berlin: Ch. Links, 1995.

Herzberg, Guntolf, and Kurt Seifert. *Rudolf Bahro—Glaube an das Veränderbare: Eine Biographie*. Berlin: Ch. Links, 2002.

Higgins, E. Tory, Ronald S. Friedman, Robert E. Harlow, Lorraine Chen Idson, Ozlem N. Ayduk, and Amy Taylor. "Achievement Orientations from Subjective Histories of Success: Promotion Pride versus Prevention Pride." *European Journal of Social Psychology* 31, no. 1 (2001): 3-23.

Hodder, Ian. "The Entanglement of Humans and Things: A Long-Term View." *New Literary History* 45, no. 1 (2014): 19-36.

Hörnigk, Therese. "PEN im Visier der Staatssicherheit." In *Schriftsteller als Intellektuelle: Politik und Literatur im Kalten Krieg*, edited by Sven Hanuschek, Therese Hörnigk, and Christine Malende, 249-68. Tübingen, Germany: Niemeyer, 2000.

Irmen, Helmut. *Stasi und DDR-Militärjustiz: Der Einfluss des Ministeriums für Staatssicherheit auf Strafverfahren und Strafvollzug in der Militärjustiz der DDR.* Berlin: De Gruyter, 2014.
Jessen, Ralph. "Mobility and Blockage during the 70s." In *Dictatorship as Experience: Towards a Socio-Cultural History of the GDR*, edited by Konrad H. Jarausch, translated by Eve Duffy, 341–60. New York: Berghahn, 1999.
Jones, Sara. *Complicity, Censorship and Criticism: Negotiating Space in the GDR Literary Sphere.* Berlin: De Gruyter, 2011.
Kerz-Rühling, Ingrid, and Tomas Plänkers. *Verräter oder Verführte: Eine psychoanalytische Untersuchung Inoffizieller Mitarbeiter der Stasi.* Berlin: Ch. Links, 2004.
Kind-Kovács, Friedericke, and Jessie Labov, eds. *Samizdat, Tamizdat, and Beyond: Transnational Media during and after Socialism.* New York: Berghahn, 2013.
Klump, Brigitte. *Das rote Kloster: Als Zögling in der Kaderschmiede der Stasi.* München, Germany: Herbig, 1991.
Kocka, Jürgen. "The GDR: A Special Kind of Modern Dictatorship." In *Dictatorship as Experience: Towards a Socio-Cultural History of the GDR*, edited by Konrad H. Jarausch, translated Eve Duffy, 47–69. New York: Berghahn, 1999.
Kowalczuk, Ilko-Sascha. *Stasi konkret: Überwachung und Repression in der DDR.* München, Germany: C. H. Beck, 2013.
Krätzner, Anita. "Zur Anwendbarkeit des Denunziationsbegriffs für die DDR-Forschung." In *Hinter vorgehaltener Hand: Studien zur historischen Denunziationsforschung*, edited by Anita Krätzner, 153–64. Göttingen, Germany: Vandenhoeck & Ruprecht, 2015.
Leeder, Karen J. *Breaking Boundaries: A New Generation of Poets in the GDR.* Oxford: Clarendon, 1996.
Lewis, Alison. *Die Kunst des Verrats: Der Prenzlauer Berg und die Staatssicherheit.* Würzburg, Germany: Königshausen & Neumann, 2003.
———. "Reading and Writing the Stasi File: On the Uses and Abuses of the File as (Auto)biography." *German Life & Letters* 56, no. 4 (2003): 377–97.
———. "Zu einer Topologie des Bösen: Die Kollaboration mit der Stasi und das postkommunistische Sündenregister von Lüge und Verrat." In *Die Sieben Todsünden: Festschrift für Günter Blamberger*, edited by Martin Roussel, 151–77. München, Germany: Wilhelm Fink, 2015.
———. "The Stasi's Secret War on Books: Uwe Berger and the Cold War Spy as Informant and Book Reviewer." In *Cold War Spy Stories from Eastern Europe*, edited by Valentina Glajar, Alison Lewis, and Corina L. Petrescu, 99–134. Lincoln NE: Potomac, 2019.
Lucht, Roland, ed. *Das Archiv der Stasi: Begriffe.* Göttingen, Germany: Vandenhoeck & Ruprecht, 2015.

Lyon, David. "The Search for Surveillance Theories." In *Theorizing Surveillance: The Panopticon and Beyond*, edited by David Lyon, 3–20. Abingdon, UK: Routledge, 2011.
———. *Surveillance Studies: An Overview*. Cambridge: Polity, 2007.
Maaß, Wilfriede. "Ich habe immer nur gearbeitet." In *Durchgangszimmer Prenzlauer Berg: Eine Berliner Künstlersozialgeschichte der 1970er und 1980er Jahre in Selbstauskünften*, edited by Barbara Felsman and Annett Gröschner, 259–64. Berlin: Lukas, 1999.
Maaz, Hans-Joachim. *Die Entrüstung: Deutschland, Deutschland, Stasi, Schuld und Sündenbock*. Berlin: Argon, 1992.
Macrakis, Kristie. *Seduced by Secrets: Inside the Stasi's Spy-Tech World*. Cambridge: Cambridge University Press, 2008.
Michael, Klaus. "Samisdat-Literatur in der DDR und der Einfluß der Staatssicherheit." *Deutschland-Archiv* 26, no. 11 (1993): 1255–66.
———. "Unabhängige Literatur in der DDR." *Bundeszentrale für politische Bildung*, September 6, 2012, http://www.bpb.de/geschichte/deutsche-geschichte/autonome-kunst-in-der-ddr/55789/unabhaengige-literatur-in-der-ddr.
———. "Eine verschollene Anthologie." In *MachtSpiele: Literatur und Staatssicherheit*, edited by Klaus Michael and Peter Böthig, 202–16. Leipzig, Germany: Reclam, 1993.
Michael, Klaus, and Peter Böthig, eds. *MachtSpiele: Literatur und Staatssicherheit*. Leipzig, Germany: Reclam, 1993.
Mihr, Anja. "Amnesty International, die Menschenrechte und der KSZE-Prozess: Der Fall der DDR." In *Die KSZE im Ost-West-Konflikt: Internationale Politik und gesellschaftliche Transformation 1975–1990*, edited by Matthias Peter and Hermann Wentker, 233–48. Berlin: De Gruyter Oldenbourg, 2012.
Miller, Barbara. *The Stasi Files Unveiled: Guilt and Compliance in a Unified Germany*. New Brunswick NJ: Transaction, 2004.
Morgner, Irmtraud. *Amanda: Ein Hexenroman*. Berlin: Aufbau, 1983.
Müller, Heiner. *Krieg ohne Schlacht: Leben in zwei Diktaturen*. Köln, Germany: Kiepenheuer & Witsch, 1992.
Müller-Enbergs, Helmut, ed. *Inoffizielle Mitarbeiter des Ministeriums für Staatssicherheit, Teil 1: Richtlinien und Durchführungsbestimmungen*. Berlin: Ch. Links, 1996.
———. *Inoffizielle Mitarbeiter des Ministeriums für Staatssicherheit, Teil 3: Statistiken*. Berlin: Ch. Links, 2008.
Niethammer, Lutz. "Die SED und 'ihre' Menschen: Versuch über das Verhältnis zwischen Partei und Bevölkerung als bestimmendem Moment innerer Staatssicherheit." In *Staatspartei und Staatssicherheit: Zum Verhältnis von SED und MfS*, edited by Siegfried Suckut and Walter Süß, 307–40. Berlin: Ch. Links, 1997.

Niethammer, Lutz, and Roger Engelmann, eds. *Bühne der Dissidenz und Dramaturgie der Repression: Ein Kulturkonflikt in der späten DDR*. Göttingen, Germany: Vandenhoeck & Ruprecht, 2014.

Novak, Helga M. *Aufenthalt in einem Irrenhaus: Gesammelte Prosa*. Frankfurt am Main, Germany: Schöffling, 1995.

———. *Grünheide Grünheide: Gedichte, 1955-1980*. Darmstadt, Germany: Luchterhand, 1983.

———. *Im Schwanenhals*. Frankfurt am Main, Germany: Schöffling, 2013.

———. "Melancholy Is Mandatory: Interview with Uta Beiküfner." *Signandsight.com*, January 26, 2006, http://www.signandsight.com/features/555.html.

———. *Vogel Federlos*. Darmstadt, Germany: Luchterhand, 1982.

Pape, Walter. *1870/1871-1989/1990: German Unifications and the Change of Literary Discourse*. Berlin: De Gruyter, 1993.

Parker, Stephen, and Matthew Philpotts. *"Sinn und Form": The Anatomy of a Literary Journal*. Berlin: De Gruyter, 2009.

Passens, Katrin. *MfS-Untersuchungshaft: Funktionen und Entwicklung von 1971 bis 1989*. Berlin: Lukas, 2012.

Peter, Matthias. *Die Bundesrepublik im KSZE-Prozess 1975-1983: Die Umkehrung der Diplomatie*. Berlin: De Gruyter Oldenbourg, 2015.

Peter, Matthias, and Hermann Wentker. "'Helsinki-Mythos' oder 'Helsinki-Effekt'? Der KSZE-Prozess zwischen internationaler Politik und gesellschaftlicher Transformation. Zur Einleitung." In *Die KSZE im Ost-West-Konflikt: Internationale Politik und gesellschaftliche Transformation 1975-1990*, edited by Matthias Peter and Hermann Wentker, 1-14. Berlin: De Gruyter Oldenbourg, 2012.

Pfaff, Steven. *Exit-Voice Dynamics and the Collapse of East Germany: The Crisis of Leninism and the Revolution of 1989*. Durham NC: Duke University Press, 2006.

Pitschmann, Siegfried. "Unzeitiger Verlust." *Neue Deutsche Literatur* no. 6 (1982): 17-19.

Polzin, Arno. "Robert Havemanns Zusammenarbeit mit Geheimdiensten." In *Annäherungen an Robert Havemann: Biographische Studien und Dokumente*, edited by Bernd Florath, 101-14. Göttingen, Germany: Vandenhoeck & Ruprecht, 2016.

Prokop, Siegfried. "Zur politischen und sozialen Entwicklung der Intelligenz der DDR (1955-1961)." *Jahrbuch für Geschichte* 31 (1984): 153-86.

Quaas, Ingeborg, and Henryk Gericke, eds. *brennzeiten: Die Keramikwerkstaat Wilfriede Maaß 1980-1989-1998*. Berlin: Lukas, 2014.

"Quelle: IMB 'David Menzer.'" In *MachtSpiele: Literatur und Staatssicherheit*, edited by Klaus Michael and Peter Böthig, 250-73. Leipzig, Germany: Reclam, 1993.

Rabinow, Paul, ed. *The Foucault Reader*. Harmondsworth, UK: Penguin, 1984.

Rücker, Günther. "Paul Wiens zum Gedenken." *Sinn und Form* 3 (1982): 478-80.

Sarotte, M. E. "Spying Not Only on Strangers: Documenting Stasi Involvement in German-German Negotiations." In *The Cold War: Cold War Espionage and Spying*, vol. 4, edited by Lori Lyn Bogle, 71–86. New York: Routledge, 2001.

Schädlich, Susanne. *Immer wieder Dezember: Der Westen, die Stasi, der Onkel und ich.* München, Germany: Droemer, 2009.

Schädlich, Susanne, and Anna Schädlich, eds. *Ein Spaziergang war es nicht: Kindheiten zwischen Ost und West.* München, Germany: Heyne, 2012.

Schmeidel, John C. *Stasi: Shield and Sword of the Party.* London: Routledge, 2008.

Schmole, Angela. "Frauen im Ministerium für Staatssicherheit." *Horch und Guck* 10, no. 34 (2001): 15–19.

Schroeder, Klaus. *Der SED-Staat: Geschichte und Strukturen der DDR 1949–1990.* Köln, Germany: Böhlau, 2013.

Schumann, Annette. *Kulturarbeit im sozialistischen Betrieb: Gewerkschaftliche Erziehungspraxis in der SBZ/DDR 1946 bis 1970.* Köln, Germany: Böhlau, 2006.

Sewell, Graham, and James R. Barker. "Neither Good, Nor Bad, but Dangerous: Surveillance as an Ethical Paradox." In *Surveillance Studies Reader*, edited by Sean P. Hier and Joshua Greenberg, 181–94. Maidenhead, UK: Open University Press, 2007.

Shulsky, Abram M., and Gary J. Schmitt. *Silent Warfare: Understanding the World of Intelligence*, 3rd ed. Washington DC: Potomac, 2002.

Simmel, Georg. *The Sociology of Georg Simmel.* Edited and translated by Kurt H. Wolff. Glencoe IL: Free Press, 1950.

———. "The Sociology of Secrecy and of Secret Societies." *American Journal of Sociology* 11, no. 4 (1906): 441–98.

Sperber, Jonathan. "17 June 1963: Revisiting a German Revolution." *German History* 22 (2004): 619–43.

Spiekermann, Uwe. "The Stasi and the HV A: Contemporary Research and Contemporary Resonance." *GHI Bulletin Supplement* 9 (2014): 11–31.

Stan, Lavinia. *Transitional Justice in Post-Communist Romania: The Politics of Memory.* Cambridge: Cambridge University Press, 2013.

Stent, Angela. *From Embargo to Ostpolitik: The Political Economy of West German–Soviet Relations 1955–1980.* Cambridge: Cambridge University Press, 1981.

Stoltenberg, Klaus. *Stasi-Unterlagen-Gesetz.* Berlin: Nomos, 1992.

Surynt, Izabela. "Leben als Exil: Zum Schaffen von Helga M. Novak." In *Deutschdeutsches Literaturexil: Schriftstellerinnen und Schriftsteller aus der DDR in der Bundesrepublik*, edited by Walter Schmitz and Jörg Bernig, 173–87. Dresden, Germany: Thelem, 2009.

Tate, Dennis. "Autobiographical Writing in the GDR Era." In *Rereading East Germany: The Literature and Film of the GDR*, edited by Karen Leeder, 88–105. Cambridge: Cambridge University Press, 2016.

——. "'. . . vielleicht nur für Franz geschrieben': Volker Braun's Intertextual Tributes to His Special Relationship with Franz Fühmann." In *Volker Braun in Perspective*, edited by Rolf Jucker, 71-90. Amsterdam: Rodopi, 2004.

Urang, John Griffith. *Legal Tender: Love and Legitimacy in the East German Cultural Imagination*. Ithaca NY: Cornell University Press, 2010.

van Eck, Richard. *Gaming and Cognition: Theories and Practices from the Learning Sciences*. Hershey NY: Information Science Reference, 2010.

Vatulescu, Cristina. "Arresting Biographies: The Secret Police File in the Soviet Union and Romania." *Comparative Literature* 56, no. 3 (2004): 243-61.

——. *Police Aesthetics: Literature, Film, and the Secret Police in Soviet Times*. Stanford CA: Stanford University Press, 2010.

Vinke, Hermann, ed. *Akteneinsicht Christa Wolf: Zerrspiegel und Dialog; Eine Dokumentation*. Darmstadt, Germany: Luchterhand, 1993.

Vollnhals, Clemens. "Der Schein der Normalität: Staatssicherheit und Justiz in der Ära Honecker." In *Staatspartei und Staatssicherheit: Zum Verhältnis von SED und MfS*, edited by Siegfried Suckut and Walter Süß, 213-48. Berlin: Ch. Links, 1997.

Wallace, Ian. "Writers and the *Stasi*." In *Re-assessing the GDR: Papers from a Nottingham Conference*, edited by J. H. Reid, 115-28. Amsterdam: Rodopi, 1994.

Walther, Joachim. "Der fünfte Zensor: Das MfS als die letzte Instanz." In *Zensur im modernen deutschen Kulturraum*, edited by Beate Müller, 131-48. Tübingen, Germany: Niemeyer, 2003.

——. *Sicherungsbereich Literatur: Schriftsteller und Staatssicherheit in der Deutschen Demokratischen Republik*. Berlin: Ch. Links, 1996.

Weinke, Annette. "Der Umgang mit der Stasi und ihren Mitarbeitern." In *Vergangenheitsbewältigung am Ende des zwanzigsten Jahrhunderts*, edited by Helmut König, Michael Kohlstruck, and Andreas Wöll, 167-91. Wiesbaden, Germany: Springer, 1998.

Westgate, Geoffrey. *Strategies under Surveillance: Reading Irmtraud Morgner as a GDR Writer*. Amsterdam: Rodopi, 2002.

Wiens, Paul. *Einmischungen: Publizistik 1949-1981*. Berlin: Aufbau, 1982.

——. "Für Johannes R. Becher." *Neue Deutsche Literatur* 6, no. 12 (1958): 25-31.

——. "Das Kombinat." *Aufbau* 7 (1951): 30-38.

Wierling, Dorothee. "Wie (er)findet man eine Generation? Das Beispiel des Geburtsjahrganges 1949 in der DDR." In *Generationalität und Lebensgeschichte im 20. Jahrhundert*, edited by Jürgen Reulecke and Elisabeth Müller-Luckner, 217-28. Berlin: De Gruyter Oldenbourg, 2003.

Wietersheim, Annegret von. *"Aber—ist mein liebster laut": Ambivalenzen in Biographie und lyrischem Werk von Paul Wiens*. Heidelberg, Germany: Universitätsverlag Winter, 2014.

Wolf, Markus, with Anne McElvoy. *Man without a Face: The Autobiography of Communism's Greatest Spymaster*. New York: Public Affairs, 1997.

Wolle, Stefan. *Die heile Welt der Diktatur: Alltag und Herrschaft in der DDR 1971–1989*. Berlin: Ch. Links, 1998.

Woods, Roger. *Opposition in the GDR under Honecker 1971–85: An Introduction and Documentation*. New York: Palgrave Macmillan, 1986.

INDEX

Ahmed, Sara, xxxvi
Die Alternative: Zur Kritik des real existierenden Sozialismus (Bahro), 118, 119, 123
Amanda (Morgner), 8-9, 23-24, 80-81, 116
Der andere Weg (Gratzik), 41
Anderson (documentary film), 175, 183
Anderson, Benedict, xxxiii
Anderson, Edith, 139
Anderson, Sascha: ambivalence and disillusionment, 140-42, 159-61, 175, 177-78, 181-82; background, 138-39; denial of Stasi collaboration, 11; emigration from GDR, 181-83; intelligence and reports, 157-58, 160, 163, 173-74, 247n167, 248n185, 251nn79-80; *Jeder Satellit hat einen Killersatelliten*, 143; and Maja Wiens, 169; mentioned, xviii, 10, 136; and Paul Gratzik, 155, 173-74; *Poesiealbum*, 159; poetic style and themes, 52, 161-62, 163; recruitment, 139-40; *Sascha Anderson*, 163, 175, 176; sense of self, 175-77, 210; writing career and underground influence, 139, 142-43, 156-57, 158-60, 178-81, 209-10
Apitz, Bruno, xviii, 39
Arendt, Hannah, xxiii, xxvi, xxvii
Außer der Reihe (Wolf), 210
Australian Security Intelligence Organisation, xxvi, xxvii

Bahro, Rudolf: *Die Alternative: Zur Kritik des real existierenden Sozialismus*, 118, 119, 123
Bartsch, Kurt, xviii
Basic Treaty (1972), 135
Bathrick, David, xxi, 176
Baudrillard, Jean, 137
Becher, Johannes R., 55, 56
Becker, Jurek, 128; *Jakob der Lügner*, 240n143
Beckett, Samuel, 76
Bentham, Jeremy, xiv
Beredte Welt (Wiens), 20
Berg, Jochen, 247n167
Berger, Uwe, 52, 73-78
Berührung ist eine Randerscheinung, 157, 163, 181

Besson, Benno, 60
Biermann, Wolf: expulsion of, 103, 107, 113; on informants, 10–11; mentioned, 41, 91, 202, 228n71; as Stasi target, 100, 103–4; supporters of, 113–14, 126–27, 129; on underground simulation, 137–38
Biskup, Renate, 59–60, 62, 110
Bitterfeld Way, 26
blackmail, xix, 2, 14, 16–18, 31, 33
Böhm, Horst, 110
Böhme, Ibrahim, 204
Booß, Christian, xxiii, xxiv, 216n77
Brandt, Willy, 65
Brasch, Peter, 254n10
Braun, Volker, 85, 241n7
Bräunig, Werner: *Der Rummelplatz*, 227n35
Brennecke, Burkhardt, 125
Brockmann, Stephen, xvi, 79
Brosche, Karl, 56
Bruce, Gary, 35, 166
Bruyn, Günter de, 228n71
Büchner, Georg, 10

Capp, Fiona, xxvii–xxviii
censorship, 67, 77, 93–96, 150–51, 159
Chirico, Giorgio de, 117
coercion: and blackmail, xix, 2, 14, 16–18, 31, 33; and psychological manipulation, 87–92, 108–9, 184, 205–6; as Stasi recruitment method, xix, 2–3, 156
Criminal Code, 123
Criminal Code Amendment Acts (1977; 1979), 119
cultural surveillance: and censorship, 67, 77, 93–96, 150–51, 159; as concept, xvi–xvii; and Eleventh Plenary, 41, 48, 50–51, 54, 227n35; expansion of, 99–100; of youth, 26, 28. *See also* underground culture; Writers' Guild
Czechoslovakia, Prague Spring in, 56–57

Dau, Mathilde, 8
DEFA (Deutsche Film-Aktiengesellschaft), 41
Deleuze, Gilles, 102
Dennis, Mike, xv, xvi, xix, 7
denunciation culture, xxiii–xxiv
dependencies, system of, xx
détente, 65, 99
Dienstgeheimnis: Ein Nächtebuch (Wiens), 52
Dietze, Gabriele, xviii, 173
Djačenko, Boris, 16
Döring, Stefan, 163, 247n167, 254n10
Dost, Hans Jörg, 59
double agents, 81, 207–8

East Germany. *See* GDR
Eckart, Gabriele, 246n124
Edel, Peter, 21
Eleventh Plenary, 41, 48, 50–51, 54, 227n35
Endler, Adolf, xviii
Erb, Elke, 181, 241n7
Etkind, Efim, 82

Faktor, Jan, 254n10
Faust, Siegmar, 228n71
FDGB (Free German Trade Union Federation), 21
FDJ (Society for German-Soviet Friendship), 21
Federal Republic of Germany. *See* West Germany
Feinstein, Joshua, xxi

Fitzpatrick, Sheila, xx–xxi
Flegel, Walter, 225n168
Foucault, Michel, xiv–xv, 250n46
Franke, Conrad, 71–72, 115
Fries, Fritz Rudolf, 21, 235n133
Fuchs, Jürgen, 194, 202
Fühmann, Franz, xviii, 159, 178, 237n26, 241n7
Fulbrook, Mary, xxxii

Gagarin, Yuri, 70
Gast, Gabriele, 223n98
GDR (German Democratic Republic): classes and social mobility in, 25–26; détente, 65, 99; and Soviet-West German Renunciation of Force Treaty, 65–66; uprising (1953), 138, 243n36. *See also* SED
Geertz, Clifford, xxxi, 83, 144
Genette, Gérard, 144
German People's Police, xxiii
German Writers' Guild. *See* Writers' Guild
Gestapo, xiv
Gieseke, Jens, xix, xxiii
Glaeser, Andreas, xxv
Gorbachev, Mikhail, 186
Görlich, Günter, 57, 225n168
Grass, Günter, 22, 85
Gratzik, Paul: ambivalence and disillusionment, 37–38, 39, 41–42, 60–61, 62–63, 87, 108; *Der andere Weg*, 41; background, 27; and "Berlin Stories" project, 93–95, 113, 235n133; incentives for continued Stasi collaboration, 42–43, 62, 107, 109; intelligence and reports, 28–29, 38–40, 59–60, 108, 230n109; *Kohlenkutte*, 154–55, 172, 173; *Malwa*, 58; mentioned, xviii; political views and affiliations, 27–28, 29, 61–62, 89, 172, 183, 184–85, 234n112; psychological manipulation of, 87–92, 108–9, 184, 205–6; reassigned to Günter Wenzel, 58–59; recruitment and motivations, 27, 28, 30–31, 183–84; and severed ties with Stasi, 110–13, 153–54; "Staatsgammler," 110; surveillance of, 61, 62, 113, 172–74; *Transportpaule: Monolog*, 107, 109, 154; in underground, 155, 171–72; writing career, 41, 42–43, 57–58, 62, 107, 154–55
Grünheide Grünheide (Novak), 194
Guattari, Félix, 102
Günther, Thomas, 247n167

Haeger, Monika, 204
Haggerty, Kevin, 167
Hamlet (Shakespeare), 161–62
Die Hamletmaschine (Müller), 161–62
handlers. *See* officers
Härtl, Heide, 93
Havemann, Katja, 251n80
Havemann, Robert: and Helga Novak, 47–48, 49, 195; mentioned, 41, 115; political views, 46
HA XX: overview, xvii; surveillance and treatment of writers, 99–100, 134–35
HA XX/7: growth, 165; informant numbers, 69; overview, xvii, 66; surveillance of Maja Wiens, 169–70, 185
HA XX/9: growth, 165; overview, xvii, 133
HA XX/OG: and Biermann affair, 103–4; overview, 100; restructuring, 133
Heine, Henrich, 7, 8
Helsinki Accords (1975), 130, 134, 175
Hempel, Manfred, 2–3, 4, 68

INDEX 269

Hendel, Annekatrin, 29, 40, 58, 111–12, 154, 175, 183–84. See also *Anderson*; *Vaterlandsverräter*
Hering, Brigitte, 60, 230n109
Hering, Ernst-Georg, 60, 230n109
Hermlin, Stephan, 7, 85–86, 113, 126, 237n26
Heym, Stefan, 7, 41, 67, 84, 189
Higgins, E. Tory, 3
Hoffmann, Hans-Joachim, 134
Holtz-Baumert, Gerhard, 225n168
Honecker, Erich, 67, 99, 172
Höpcke, Klaus, 13, 14, 109
human rights violations, 130

identity: dynamics in GDR, xx–xxi; in Helga Novak's works, 191–92; and management of double life, xxi, xxii, 82–83, 114, 115, 152, 175–77, 181–82, 208; in Paul Wiens's works, 51–52, 53–54, 70, 79–80; in Sascha Anderson's works, 161–62
Das Impressum (Kant), 67
Im Schwanenhals (Novak), 12, 15, 191
informants (*Inoffizielle Mitarbeiter*, IM): categories of, xvii–xviii, 219–20n8; commitment benefits and challenges, 34–35, 68; genders, xxxiv, 100, 219n134; IMB rank, xviii, 2, 61, 126, 140; IME rank, 85; IMS rank, xvii, 220n8; IMV rank, 2, 61, 106; lapsed, 166–67; leading positions, 136; *Mitarbeiter* term, xxiv, 5; motivations and incentives, xix–xxi, xxiii, xxvi–xxvii, 2–4, 203–6; numbers, xiv, xv, xvii, xviii; registration procedure, 228n72; SED membership, 2; simulation concept, 137–38; sources on, xviii–xix, xxix–xxxi; Stasi guidelines on separation from, 35–36; Stasi methods and guidelines on officer-informant relationships, 33, 58, 79, 206–7; Stasi methods and guidelines on recruitment of, 2–4, 14, 17, 24, 104, 135, 220nn11–12, 224nn145–46; Stasi methods and guidelines on retention of, 34–35, 57, 107; sticky surveillance concept, xxxvi, 101–2, 114; and victim-perpetrator distinction, xviii–xix; writers as, xvi–xvii, xviii. See also Anderson, Sascha; Gratzik, Paul; Novak, Helga M.; Wiens, Maja; Wiens, Paul
Institute for Teacher Education (Weimar), 29, 38
international travel, 50–51, 70–71, 85–86, 109–10, 130

Jakob der Lügner (Becker), 240n143
Jakobs, Karl-Heinz, 228n71
Jansen, Johannes, 228n71
Jeder Satellit hat einen Killersatelliten (Anderson), 143
Jentsch, Bernd, 85
Jewish communists, 7. See also Wiens, Paul
Jirgl, Reinhard, 254n10
Juliet agents, 17–18, 223n98

Kachold, Gabi, 246n149, 254n10
Kahlau, Heinz, 140, 142
Der Kaiser ist nackt (journal), 159
Kant, Hermann, 21, 95; *Das Impressum*, 67
Kant, Uwe, 95
Karlsdottir, Maria. See Novak, Helga M.
Kastner, Manfred, 117–18
Kerbach, Ralf, 177, 178
Khrushchev, Nikita, 22
Kindheitsmuster (Wolf), 67
Kirsch, Rainer, 241n7
Kirsch, Sarah, 85, 114, 115–16, 129, 234n96, 237n26
Klump, Brigitte, 18–19; *Das rote Kloster*, 13–15
Kocka, Jürgen, xxxii

Kohlenkutte (Gratzik), 154–55, 172, 173
Kolbe, Uwe, 159, 178–79, 228n71, 247n167
Kopelew, Lew, 83
Koplowitz, Jan, 225n168
Kowalczuk, Ilko-Sascha, xix, 214n21, 219–20n8
Koziol, Andreas, 254n10
Krätzner, Anita, 217n94
Krauße-Anderson, Monika, 138
Kunert, Günter, 50, 85, 114, 127, 129, 235n133, 237n26
Kunze, Reiner, 50–51, 67, 85, 129
Kunze, Rudolf: application to leave GDR, 118–19; arrest and trial, 123–24, 125; on Maja Wiens, 190; Stasi's interest in, 117–18; surveillance of, 119–20, 121–23

Lange, Erika, 22
LaPorte, Norman, 7
Lautenschlager, Erika, 22, 103, 236n24
Lawrence, T. E., xxvi
Leeder, Karen, 162
Leskien, Jürgen, 95
Lorek, Leonhard, 181
Lyon, David, xiv

Maaß, Ekkehard, 172
Maaß, Wilfriede, 158, 172
Malwa (Gratzik), 58
Matthies, Frank-Wolf, 83
Maurer, Georg, 46
MfS. *See* Stasi
Michael, Klaus, 160, 180, 248n188
Mielke, Erich, xiii, 66, 94, 99, 135
Mikado (journal), 159
Miller, Barbara, xviii, 209, 224n146
Ministerium für Staatssicherheit. *See* Stasi
Mitscherlich, Alexander and Margarete: *Die Unfähigkeit zu trauern*, 24

Mittig, Rudi, 66, 130
moral concerns, xxv, 4
Morgner, Irmtraud: *Amanda*, 8–9, 23–24, 80–81, 116; marriage to Paul Wiens, 71, 85; Paul Wiens's surveillance of, 71, 114, 115–16, 127–28, 238n72
Mucke, Dieter, 48
Müller, Heiner: *Die Hamletmaschine*, 161–62; mentioned, 227n35; and Paul Gratzik, 59, 60, 111; and Paul Wiens, 114; in underground, 241n7; and Writers' Guild, 50, 228n75
Müller-Enbergs, Helmut, xxiii, xxiv, 216n77, 219n134

Nachrichten aus der dritten Welt (Wiens), 20–21, 51
Naumann, Sören, 248n188
Neubert, Werner, 95–96
Neue Deutsche Literatur (journal), 143
Neumann, Gert, 93, 96
New Manner of Speaking (Die neue Sagart), 163
Niethammer, Lutz, xxvii, 210
Noll, Dieter, 225n168
Novak, Charlotte and Karl, 12
Novak, Helga M.: background, 12; confession of Stasi collaboration, 11–12, 195–97; exile from GDR, 19–20, 45–46, 49, 191–95; expulsions from university, 16, 18–19, 48; *Grünheide Grünheide*, 194; *Im Schwanenhals*, 12, 15, 191; mentioned, xviii; political views and affiliations, 12–13, 19; recruitment and motivations, 13–14, 15–18, 30, 204; return to GDR, 20, 44–45, 46–47, 195; and Robert Havemann, 46, 47–48; surveillance of, 16, 48; and victim-perpetrator distinction, 43–44; *Vogel federlos*, 12; writing career, 43, 46, 194, 253n116

INDEX   271

officers (*Hauptamtliche Mitarbeiter*): assigned to Maja Wiens, 104–5, 117, 123, 124, 149, 151–53; assigned to Paul Gratzik, 38, 40, 41–42, 58–59, 87–92, 108–12; assigned to Paul Wiens, 22, 50, 54–56, 57, 69, 71–75, 77, 84, 115, 145–46; assigned to Sascha Anderson, 140; numbers, xiv
operational case (*Operativer Vorgang*, OV), xvii
operational person check (*Operative Personenkontrolle*, OPK), xvii, 73
Opitz, Detlef, 163, 247n167

panopticon, xiv–xv
Papenfuß-Gorek, Bert, 163, 248n185, 254n10
Parikh, Crystal, 88
Passens, Katrin, 240n123
PEN Club, 21, 85
Pfaff, Steven, xxi
Pinkus, Theodor, 127
Pinter, Harold, 76
Plaumann, Eberhard, 149, 151–53
Plenzdorf, Ulrich, xviii, 85, 93, 237n26
Poesiealbum (Anderson), 159
political underground activity. *See* underground culture
Pönig, Rolf: espionage psychology expertise, 69, 147; and Paul Wiens, 69, 71–75, 77, 84, 115, 145–46; and Uwe Berger, 73–75, 77; Writers' Guild assignment, 66
Poppe, Sabine, 59
Poppe, Ulrike and Gerd, 158, 180, 251n79
Prague Spring, 56–57
progressive classes, 25–26
prostitutes, 17–18
PUT (*politische Untergrundtätigkeit*). *See* underground culture

Rathenow, Lutz, 172, 180, 248n185
Reimann, Brigitte, xviii
Reinhardt, Peter, 66
Reise, Peter, 104–5, 117, 123, 124, 149
Reuter, Wolfgang, 133
Rosenthal, Rüdiger, 180, 251n80
Das rote Kloster (Klump), 13–15
Rücker, Günther, 9
Der Rummelplatz (Bräunig), 227n35

samizdat, 133–34, 163, 165, 249n3. *See also* underground culture
Sascha Anderson (Anderson), 163, 175, 176
Schädlich, Hans Joachim, 129–30; *Versuchte Nähe*, 128, 129
Schedlinski, Rainer, 136, 163, 242n29, 248n188, 254n10
Schiller, Hans, 22, 49–50, 54–56, 66, 69
Schindler, Johannes, 22
Schirrmacher, Frank, 137
Schleime, Cornelia, 177
Schlesinger, Klaus, 85, 93, 106, 189, 228n71
Schmeidel, John C., xvii
Schneider, Rolf, 85, 237n26
Schulz, Max Walter, 48
secrecy: capital earned through, xxviii; as concept, xxiv; and denunciation, xxiii–xxiv; as fundamental principle of Stasi, xxii; and gossip, xxvii–xxviii; justification of, xxv, xxvii, 4–5
secret societies: forms of, xxiv–xxvi; and reciprocity, xxvi, xxix; sense of belonging, xxvi–xxvii, xxxiii
SED (Socialist Unity Party): Central Committee, 13, 41, 159; Eleventh Plenary, 41, 48, 50–51, 54, 227n35; under Erich Honecker, 67; fragile claim to power, xxiv, 216n77; Helga Novak's

membership, 13, 19; membership among Stasi officers and informers, 1–2; Stasi as organ of, xiv
Seghers, Anna, 7, 39, 58
Shakespeare, William: *Hamlet*, 161–62
Simmel, Georg, xxiv–xxv, xxvi, xxxii, 4–5, 27, 209
Simon, Hedwig ("Luschka") and Bernhardt, 121, 124–25
Simon, Horst, 250n37
simulation: as concept, 137–38
Sinn und Form (journal), 67
Socialist Unity Party. *See* SED
Sonnensucher (film), 21, 23
Sontag, Susan, 76
Spiekermann, Uwe, 199
Spira, Steffie, 58, 59, 111
"Staatsgammler" (Gratzik), 110
Stade, Martin, 63, 93, 95, 108
Stalin, Joseph, 20, 22
Stan, Lavinia, xviii
Stasi (Ministerium für Staatssicherheit, MfS): archives, xviii–xix, xxix–xxxi; criminal investigation authority, 120–21; growth, xiii–xiv, xv; informant recruitment methods and guidelines, 2–4, 14, 17, 24, 104, 135, 220nn11–12, 224nn145–46; informant retention methods and guidelines, 34–35, 57, 107; informant separation guidelines, 35–36; narrative features in files, 144; officer-informant relationship methods and guidelines, 33, 58, 79, 206–7; secrecy as fundamental principle, xxii, 5; as secret society, xxvi–xxix; SED membership, 1–2. *See also* HA XX; informants; officers
sticky surveillance, xxxvi, 101–2, 114
Stoph, Willi, 65
Strahl, Rudi, 115, 229n94

Strittmatter, Erwin, xviii, 145
surveillance power: as concept, xiv–xv. *See also* cultural surveillance

tamizdat, 165, 249n3. *See also* underground culture
Templin, Wolfgang, 170
Transit Agreement (1971), 135
Transportpaule: Monolog (Gratzik), 107, 109, 154
Traumgrenzen (Wiens), 149–51, 252n109
travel visas, 50–51, 70–71, 109–10, 130
Troike, Helmut, 22

Ulbricht, Walter, 67
… und deine Liebe auch (film), 21
underground culture: informant numbers, 180; and older generation of writers, 134, 241n7; Paul Gratzik as member of, 155, 171–72; publications and political initiatives, 133–34, 157, 158–60, 163, 165, 178–81; simulation of, 137–38; as Stasi target, 133, 134, 156–58, 163–64, 165–66. *See also* Anderson, Sascha
Die Unfähigkeit zu trauern (Mitscherlich), 24

Vaterlandsverräter (documentary film): Gabriele Dietze in, xviii; Günter Wenzel in, 62, 110, 154; Paul Gratzik in, 29, 40, 58, 59, 88, 111–12, 183–85; Renate Biskup in, 59–60; Sascha Anderson in, 173, 174
Vatulescu, Cristina, 120
Versuchte Nähe (Schädlich), 128, 129
Vier Linien aus meiner Hand (Wiens), 51–52
Vogel, Frank, 21
Vogel federlos (Novak), 12

Wagner, Bernd, 228n71
Wallace, Ian, 228n71
Walther, Joachim, xix, xxvii, 36, 61, 83, 141, 225n168, 229n94, 235n133, 235n137, 246n124
Wander, Fred, xviii
Wegner, Bettina, 126, 149, 152, 189, 190
Wenzel, Günter: assigned to Paul Gratzik, 42, 57; handling of Paul Gratzik, 58–59, 60, 61–62, 87–92, 108–12; on Paul Gratzik's character, 59, 91, 108, 110, 154, 234n112
Western youth culture, 26, 28
Westgate, Geoffrey, 115, 238n72
West Germany: and GDR peaceful coexistence rhetoric, 65, 100; GDR's fear of exposure to, 78, 135; Greens, 151, 168, 169, 189; publishers in, 46, 129, 154, 165, 172, 175, 179; Soviet-West German Renunciation of Force Treaty (1970), 65–66
Wiens, Maja: ambivalence and disillusionment, 148–49, 151–53, 188–89; contradictory file history, 207–8; intelligence and reports, 116–17, 119–20, 121–26, 149, 152, 188; parents' Stasi connections, 103, 187, 236n24; and Paul Gratzik, 172; political views and affiliations, 151, 152, 169, 189–91; recruitment, 100, 103, 104–6; as security risk, 168–69, 170, 187; surveillance and intimidation of, 168, 169–71, 185–87; *Traumgrenzen*, 149–51, 252n109
Wiens, Paul: ambivalence and disillusionment, 50, 53–57, 80–81; appeal to Stasi, 21–22; *Beredte Welt*, 20; and Biermann affair, 126–27; childhood and youth, 7–9, 23–24, 245n91; *Dienstgeheimnis: Ein Nächtebuch*, 52;
illness and death, 145–47; incentives for continued Stasi collaboration, 70–71, 72–73, 84–85, 86, 147–48; informant file reopened, 68–70, 72; intelligence and reports, 81–84, 85–86, 114–16, 127–28, 144–45; Jewish identity, 7–8; as mentor to Sascha Anderson, 142–43; *Nachrichten aus der dritten Welt*, 20–21, 51; poetic style and themes, 20–21, 51–54, 70, 73, 74; political views and affiliations, 6–7, 21, 22, 50–51, 73, 147–48; recruitment and motivations, 22–23, 24–25, 30; and Schädlich affair, 128–30; *Sonnensucher*, 21, 23; special arrangement as informant, 24–25, 49–50, 71, 72; surveillance of, 56, 73–78, 114–15, 229n99; *...und deine Liebe auch*, 21; *Vier Linien aus meiner Hand*, 51–52; writing career, 10, 20, 21, 73
Wietersheim, Annegret von, 51, 245n91
Wogatzki, Benito, xviii
Wolf, Christa, xviii, 11, 25, 40, 85; *Kindheitsmuster*, 67
Wolf, Gerhard, 85, 241n7; *Außer der Reihe*, 210
Wolf, Konrad, 21
Wolf, Markus, 17
Wollenberger, Vera, 171
Wollweber, Ernst, xiv
women: informant numbers, xxxiv, 100, 219n134; Juliet agents, 17–18, 223n98; and misogyny in Stasi, 103. See also Novak, Helga M.; Wiens, Maja
Wood, Roger, 67
working classes, 25–26
writers: as informants, xvi–xvii, xviii; and international travel, 50–51, 70–71, 85–86, 109–10, 130;

working-class, 26. *See also* underground culture
Writers' Guild: "Berlin Stories" project, 92–96; and Biermann affair, 113–14, 126–27, 129, 165; and Heiner Müller, 50, 228n75; informant numbers, xvii; and Maja Wiens, 169; *Neue Deutsche Literatur*, 143; Paul Wiens's membership and presidency, 10, 20, 57, 73; Paul Wiens's surveillance of, 81, 84–85, 128–30; pledges, 52–53; and Prague Spring, 56–57; and Sascha Anderson, 159; Stasi surveillance strategy, 66, 68

youth culture, 26, 28

CPSIA information can be obtained
at www.ICGtesting.com
Printed in the USA
LVHW091301250821
696077LV00001B/16